SIDNEY SUSSEX

A History

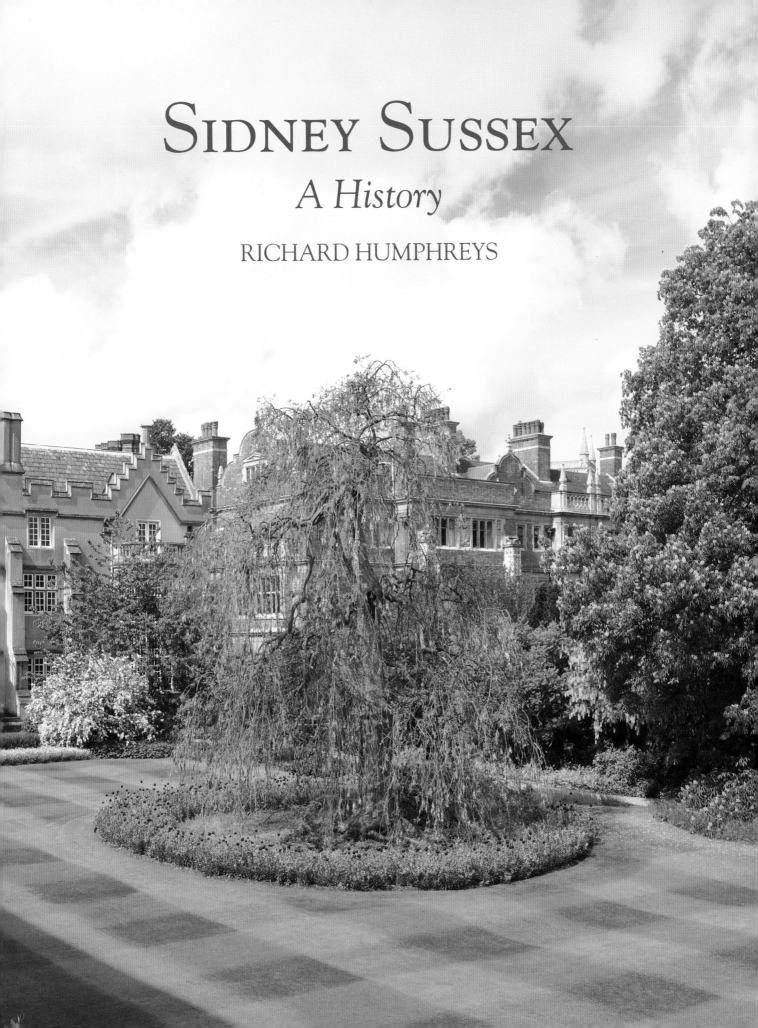

SIDNEY SUSSEX

A History

RICHARD HUMPHREYS

A catalogue record for this book is available from the British Library.

ISBN 978-0-9563594-0-7

Project management: Cambridge Editorial Partnership Ltd, www.camedit.com
Design and layout: Paul Barrett Book Production, www.pbbp.co.uk
Picture research: Gill Metcalfe
Index: Mark Kerr
Print production in association with Book Production Consultants Ltd
25–27 High Street, Chesterton, Cambridge, CB4 1ND, United Kingdom
Printed and bound in Great Britain by Butler Tanner & Dennis

Author's Note
The capitalisation used when referring to the U/university and C/colleges, their M/masters and F/fellows, not to mention the T/tripos and many other S/subjects, is a particularly awkward matter in a book of this length and divides opinion. In the interests of readability, and after consulting other publications and canvassing a wide variety of opinions, it has been decided to keep capitalisation in these areas to a minimum.

Subscribers

The Master and Fellows of Sidney Sussex would like to thank all those members and friends of the College whose support and generosity has made the publication of this history possible.

In memory of Jeremy Allen (1961)
  1942–2009
Ian Peter Allnutt (1935)
Nigel Andrew
In memory of Richard Ankerson
  1913–2001
Penny Atkinson (1986)
Mr R H Bainbridge (1946)
Howard Baker (1982)
Claire Banham
David Batt (1995)
Dr P M J Bennett (1952)
Andrew Bershadski (2005)
Mrs Glyn Biggs
Dr John Biggs (1994)
Lord Karan Bilimoria (1986)
H John B Birks (1963)
David Blake (1961) and James Blake
  (1992)
Julian Blake (2000)
Tim Blanning (1960)
Catherine Bond (1979)
Kingsmill Bond (1986)
Don Brech (1961)
John Brock (1948)
Dr Alison Brown (1976)
Sir Neil Butterfield (1961)
Christina Forbes Cameron (2004)
Donald James Forbes Cameron
  (1967)
In memory of Hugh Forbes Cameron
  (1937) 1917–2002
Kenneth Carpenter (1941)
Dr Allan T Casey (1954)
Gordon Chilton (1945)
In memory of Iain C K Clarke (1950)
  1927–2006
Murray Clayson (1979)

J H Clement (Lent 1948)
Sophie Condon (1987)
Robert Cooper (1977)
David Coulson (1971)
Rachel Cox, née Walker (1991)
Professor T M Cox, Fellow 1990–
In memory of Kenneth A Coyte
  (1951)
Rebecca L Coyte (1979)
In memory of Stanley E Coyte
  (1912)
Richard Anthony Crabb (1957)
In memory of Joy Denyer 1915–2009,
  mother of Sandra Dawson, Master,
  1999–2009
Richard Dingle (1974)
John Donnelly (1988)
Dr A P Draycott (1961)
Dr K G Eickhoff (1943)
Professor Craig Elliffe (1985)
Andreas Fahrmeir (1995)
Randal Faulkner (1967)
Roger France (Reader-at-Chapel,
  2003–2008)
Dr Heinz Fuchs (1997)
Mr Kevin F Gangar (1974)
Sir Patrick Garland (1948)
James M Gibert (1980)
In memory of Andy Gibson (1992)
  1973–2003
Paul Gilbert (1977)
Claire M Goodeve (2000)
Alex M Graham (1992)
The Reverend Tony Graham
  (1953)
D H Gray (1958)
Nick Gray (1982)
Philip C Green (1947)

Professor Norman N Greenwood
  (1948)
Greville R Gunson (1948)
J S Hall (1973)
J A F Harvey (1935)
Jim and Gail Herder
Dr K Herrmanns (1991)
R J Hill (1953)
In memory of Talbot Hill (1939)
  1921–1996
Joshua Ho How Hoang (1986)
Dr D W Holliday (1960)
Gerry Hollington (1972)
Bryan Hopkisson (1960)
In memory of Harold Payne Hudd
  1916–1977
Dr N P Hudd (1964)
Adrian Huggins (1970)
R H F Hunter (1961)
Kenneth Huxley-Robinson (1991)
Geoffrey C Illing (1970)
Leslie V Illing (1939)
Michael F Illing (1974)
In memory of Vincent C Illing (1909)
  1890–1969
In memory of D R P (Tim) Jolly
  (1953) 1931–2008
Mark E P Jolly (1975)
I A Kellett (1967)
Peter Kennerley (1975)
A Khazen (1993)
Andrew Kinnier (1991)
A W J Knight (1952)
Alan Lancashire (1945)
Stewart Lang (1970)
Dr Ray Lee (1963)
In memory of Chris Lees
  1946–2006

Iris Steren Leslie, born 4th April
  2009
Guy Lester (1981)
In memory of Charles Harold Wilfrid
  Lewis 1905–1986
Christopher David Henry Lewis
  (1958)
In memory of Henry Thomas Lewis
  1861–1936
Sir John Lindsay (1956)
Peter Lipscomb (1959)
Dr Peter G Llewellyn (1957)
Christopher C K Lucas (1959)
Keith Luck (1978)
George Luckraft (1977)
Dr Paul G N Main (1966)
Sir Ravinder Nath Maini (1956)
Andrew P J Major (1990)
Alison Marriott (1986)
James Mayall (1957)
Simone Mayer (2006)
W Kenneth McCarter (1979)
Professor Alan Mercer (1950)
Professor Jack M Miller (1964)
Nicholas Morrell (1961)
Brian Newman (1966)
In memory of Professor Donald H
  Northcote, Master, 1976–1992
I R Oldcorn (1961)
John Osborn (1962)
Lois May Overvoorde (2009)
Christopher Parish (1954)
Robert Henry Parkinson (1954)
Norman Peacock (1943)
Denis Petkovic (1986)
Claire Preston and Kevin Jackson
In memory of Professor Charalambos
  Proukakis (1934–2009)

David Purchase (1961)
Dr Michael Purshouse (1970)
Dr Roger Pyrah (1955)
Alan Redfern (1952)
Philip Courtney Redfern (1956)
Colin Reeves (1949)
Jolyon C P Ridgwell (1999)
Gwilym Roberts (1943)
P M B Roberts (1948)
Gilbert Rodway (1957)
Lt John Charles Rutter RN (2000)
Peter Salway (1951)
Christina Sanderson (2006)
Hagen Schulze
Frank Sear (1963)
John Sennett (1953)
Charles Sherwood (1978)
Simon Sherwood (1979)
Derek Shorthouse (1951)
David J Smith (1958)
Max Stechman (2007)
In memory of Bruce Stephen (1938)
  1920–2004
Ian Stephen (1962)
Isobel Stephen (1991)
In memory of Stuart Stephen (1937)
  1918–1999
Lord Stevens of Ludgate (1956)
C L Stevenson (1952)
The Revd Dr Keith Straughan,
  Fellow 2000–2008
In memory of Dr J M J Supramaniam
Paul A J Supramaniam (1982)
In memory of Kenneth Sutcliffe
  1935–2006
Jamal J Sutton (2005)
Mr G V Taylor (1943)
Ian C Taylor (1982)

Susan E F Taylor (1988)
Steven Thomas (1977)
Richard Wojciech Tobiasiewicz
  (1980)
In memory of Sara Treglia (1986)
  1968–1994
In memory of Mike Tyrrell (1966)
  1948–2002
Zygmunt Tyszkiewicz (1952)
Mrs Mahdi Van Dijk in memory of
  Hil Van Dijk
Gib van Ert (1996)
In memory of Mark Wainwright
  (1977) 1957–1992
Mark Waldron (1987)
In memory of John Michael
  Wallace-Hadrill (1916–1985)
Ian and Liz Wallis
Anthony Robert Watts (1963)
Peter George Watts (1981)
In memory of Eric S Willbourn
  (1908) 1889–1977
Roger S Willbourn (1972)
Tony Willenbruch (1970)
Rachel Mary Williams (2006)
David Woods (1970)
J A Wood (1954)
Gordon Wright (1972)
Martin Young (1987)
Paul Zatz (1958)

The Master and Fellows are very
grateful to those members of College
who have chosen to support the
publication of this book through
anonymous contributions.

Contents

Foreword

Whatever first comes to mind when we think of a Cambridge college – beautiful gardens, academic excellence, heritage buildings, domestic controversy, media criticism, cobbled courtyards, antediluvian plumbing, gatherings in black gowns, complicated governance, sport, art, political action and drama led by students – the full meaning of what it is to be a college will be largely lost unless the account is set in a context of time, place and people. This is what Richard Humphreys has done for Sidney. He tells a story spanning some 400 years of our history, largely through the eyes and pens of those who inhabited or overlooked these walls, and in doing so he enriches our understanding of the period as well as of the College. Sidney has always been a community of scholars dedicated to 'the mainteynance of good learninge', as the words of the Foundress's will require; but the manner of that 'mainteynance', and the focus of that 'good learninge', have followed curious and diverse paths through religious and political turmoil, through fundamentally different and contested philosophies about the place of education in society, and through the interpretation of rights and obligations of the masters, fellows and scholars who hold the governance of the College in their hands.

Change, even in a Cambridge college, is constant: sometimes quiet and barely perceptible, yet always in some way reflecting an interplay between the idiosyncrasies, interests and wisdom of both individual action and collective governance, together with wider social, economic, political and religious forces. Through a dedicated mining of the College archives, an appreciation of the timely publication of the *Dictionary of National Biography*, an empathy with many of our forebears and a profound sense of time and place, Richard Humphreys has written a College history on a different plane from many. It will tickle the historical imagination through its quiet revelations and scholarship, as well as its candour and humour.

I am delighted to introduce this volume, on completing my 10-year term as Master, to celebrate the importance of Sidney's past and the vitality of its present, and to note a profound belief that, as with all living communities dedicated to learning and the advancement of knowledge, the best is always yet to come as Sidney is recreated with each generation of students, fellows, staff and masters.

Professor Dame Sandra Dawson, Master, 1999–2009

CHAPTER I

'Our Design'

My last is Sydney College, that great Name,
That's flown so far upon the wings of Fame.
That now and ever will
All full-swoln mouths, and all wide places fill.

—Anon., 'Upon the Rarities of the Most
Renowned University of Cambridge', 1673

SIDNEY SUSSEX COLLEGE was founded on St Valentine's Day, 1596 at the exact centre of an extraordinary period in British history, bounded by Henry VIII's divorce in 1532 and the restoration of the monarchy in 1660. For the foundress, Lady Frances Sidney, Countess of Sussex, as for her contemporaries, all events, private and public, were providential and indissolubly linked. The moment of Sidney's foundation was both a deeply personal statement and a significant historical event during a period that shaped the nation's religious and political destiny.

Frances Sidney was an infant at the time of Henry VIII's Reformation in the 1530s, when the Franciscan friary on whose land her college was to be built was dissolved. The rapid destruction of the ancient Catholic church in England and the unsteady, violent rise of its modern Protestant successor determined both her intentions and the college's original character.

In her teens Frances' brother Henry was an intimate friend of Edward VI and her family became closely identified with the boy-king's severe Protestantism. Following the unsettling and bloody interlude of Mary's Catholic revival in the 1550s, Frances became a loyal member of Elizabeth's court as a lady-in-waiting, and travelled to Ireland with her husband, Thomas Radcliffe, third Earl of Sussex, during his demanding spell as Lord Lieutenant. In the 1560s she identified her religious views with those of Elizabeth's church settlement, as expressed in the Acts of Uniformity and Supremacy and in the Thirty-Nine Articles. Thomas Radcliffe was responsible for the suppression of the pro-Catholic northern earls' uprising in 1569 and, following the excommunication of the Queen by the Pope in 1570, Lady Frances drew ever closer to the royal circle around the chief minister, William Cecil, and the Archbishop of Canterbury, John Whitgift.

OPPOSITE: *Lady Frances Sidney, Countess of Sussex (detail), by an Anglo-Netherlandish artist, c1570–75*

By the time of her death in 1589, the Countess of Sussex had witnessed or been affected by some exceptional events: the launch of the Catholic Counter-Reformation in the 1540s; the St Bartholomew's Day massacre of French Protestants in Paris in 1572; wars with Spain – in the Netherlands, where her nephew Sir Philip Sidney died in 1586, and at sea, most memorably in the defeat of the Armada in 1588; Drake's and Frobisher's voyages (Lady Frances pledged £140 to the latter's futile attempts to mine gold from Arctic rock); the alarmingly successful infiltration of England by Catholic priests trained in Douai and Rouen, leading to extreme measures taken against all recusants; the rise of radical Puritanism throughout England and notably at Cambridge, as well as the start of its suppression by Whitgift; and the Babington plot against Elizabeth in 1586, which ensured the execution of Mary, Queen of Scots the following year. The Countess's own personal life was marred by accusations of disloyalty and by further scandal after her husband's death in 1583, making her all the more determined to leave a permanent memorial attesting to her godly virtue.

Following Lady Frances' death, an extraordinary half century and more saw Essex's rebellion; the accession of James 1; the Gunpowder Plot; the publication of the Authorised Version of the Bible; the Thirty Years' War; the accession of Charles 1 and his fatal period of personal rule; the outbreak of Civil War, which led to the execution of Charles I in 1649; and the establishment of Cromwell's Protectorate in the 1650s.

'Malicious Speeches': the Honour of Lady Frances Sidney

Late-16th-century stained glass panel with Lady Frances' arms from Cassiobury House, Hertfordshire, purchased in 1923, now in the Senior Combination Room, Cloister Court

Born in or about 1531, Frances Sidney was the fourth daughter of Sir William Sidney, who was descended from a family of Sussex and Surrey landowners. A prominent courtier and soldier, Sir William was a veteran both of the Battle of Flodden and of sea battles against the French. His frequent rewards from Henry VIII and his son Edward VI included being made a Knight of the Garter in 1542 and, in 1552, the grant of lands at Penshurst, Kent, where the Sidney family still lives.

Sir William Sidney's only son, Henry, was a close companion of Edward VI, whose rigorously Protestant education he had shared and who had died in his arms in 1553. Henry, by now married to Mary Dudley, daughter of the strongly Protestant Duke of Northumberland, seems to have found it easy enough to accommodate himself to his friend's successor, the Catholic Queen Mary. He accompanied the Earl of Bedford's mission to secure Philip II of Spain's signature to a marriage treaty with Mary and, indeed, the Spanish king became godson to Henry's son and Lady Frances' nephew, the great courtier and poet Philip Sidney.

In April 1555 Frances Sidney, by now a well-educated young woman, married the recently widowed Thomas Radcliffe, Lord Fitzwalter, at Hampton Court. Radcliffe, who became the third Earl of Sussex in 1557, had been on the marriage treaty trip to Spain in 1552 with Henry Sidney, following which he was appointed Gentleman of the Privy Chamber to Philip II. Philip, King of England from 1554 to 1558, attended Radcliffe's and Frances' wedding, taking part in the celebratory jousting tournament.

When Radcliffe was sent to Ireland in 1556 as Lord Deputy, Frances' brother accompanied him as Under-Treasurer and *de facto* second-in-command.

Penshurst Place, Kent, today

Sussex became Lord Lieutenant in 1557, and was in Ireland, with frequent returns to court, until 1564. During his period of service he developed an intense rivalry with his brother-in-law's master, Robert Dudley, Earl of Leicester. This bitter political conflict, made famous in Sir Walter Scott's novel *Kenilworth* (1821), in which Sussex was characterised by his 'high blood and frank bearing', had major repercussions for Lady Frances and contributed to her eventual decision to found a Cambridge college.

Following his arduous career and mixed fortunes in Ireland, often made almost impossible by the machinations of Leicester and Henry Sidney, Sussex returned to England and was party to the efforts to marry Queen Elizabeth to the Catholic Austrian Archduke Charles. Of course, this was guaranteed to infuriate his enemy, the emphatically Protestant Leicester, who wished to marry Elizabeth himself. The tension between these positions grew to the point where the supporters of Sussex, and his ally the Duke of Norfolk, sported purple badges against Leicester's men in yellow, all of them going about court armed.

In 1568 Sussex was appointed to the office of President of the North, having failed to take over from his brother-in-law Henry in Wales. He immediately found himself embroiled in the flight of Mary Stuart from Scotland following the murder of her husband Henry Stewart, Lord Darnley. He survived the plot to marry his ally

Norfolk to Mary and to displace Elizabeth's Secretary of State William Cecil; he was
then responsible for defeating the northern earls' uprising in 1569, and the decisive
action against the Scots that followed in 1570.

Lady Frances was by Sussex's side throughout this tumultuous period of his career.
In 1571, while in Berwick, she contracted smallpox, which probably disfigured her
face. Sussex wrote that when he visited her 'she took greater comfort … than all
they [the doctors] did besides'. In 1572 the Countess was at court when her husband
was made chamberlain of the household and in 1573 they were granted New Hall in
Boreham, Essex, a former home of Mary Tudor, to which they made extensive and
grandiose alterations. A porcupine crest, the Sidney beast, is still prominent in one
of the corridors. New Hall remained the property of the Radcliffes until its sale to
George Villiers, soon to be Duke of Buckingham, in 1622.

Lady Frances and Sussex were now important and secure members of the court.
Sussex was favoured by Cecil and Lady Frances by Elizabeth, although he was still
plagued by enduring animosity from 'the Gypsy' Leicester and Henry Sidney. Sussex,
along with Cecil, Leicester, Sir Christopher Hatton and Sir Francis Walsingham,
were at the heart of Elizabeth's Council and Lady Frances, by now a lady of the bedchamber, exchanged New Year gifts with the Queen.

Sussex had supported the 'French Match' of Elizabeth to the Duke of Anjou in
the 1570s and opposed Leicester's bid to intervene in the war in the Low Countries in

*New Hall, Boreham,
Essex. The Earl of Sussex
built the spectacular
south façade of the north
range with its canted bay
windows in the 1570s.
The building now houses a
convent school*

Bermondsey House, south view, by J C Buckler, 1827. Guildhall Library, London

the early 1580s. By the time he became ill in September 1582, these positions were fast becoming unfashionable, and he died at his house in Bermondsey in June 1583, aware that Leicester's plans were likely to be favoured. Radcliffe's bowels were buried at Bermondsey and his body at Boreham church, where his effigy on the splendid tomb, designed by the Netherlandish mason Richard Stevens of Southwark, can still be seen next to those of his grandfather and father. He left his wife the house in Bermondsey, land in Essex and Norfolk, over £3,000 worth of jewels and 4,000 ounces of plate.

By the time Lady Frances died at Bermondsey in March 1589, her fortunes had changed dramatically for the worse. Against the background of frequent Catholic plots, the death of her nephew Sir Philip Sidney after the Battle of Zutphen in 1586, the execution of Mary Queen of Scots in 1587 and the resulting Armada scare of 1588, her final years were ones of desperate personal and political intrigue and accusations about her loyalty.

During Sussex's illness in 1583 unnamed enemies poisoned his attitude towards his wife, leading the Countess to seek help through the couple's friend, Sir Christopher Hatton, in recovering her husband's and the Queen's good opinion of her. She was assailed, she

Radcliffe Tomb, Boreham church, Essex, by Richard Stevens. Detail showing the figure of Thomas Radcliffe, 3rd Earl of Sussex

wrote, by 'malicious speeches and unconscionable extremities of those who took advantage of my Lord's painful weakness to work my disgrace'.

Lady Frances was undoubtedly a loyal and devoted wife and subject, but she lived in a vicious world of courtly intrigue and political ambition. She was well aware of the 'vigilant malice' of those who had 'long complotted' her ruin, but could not endure the pain brought about by those who 'espied their time, when my Lord through anguish and torments was brought to his utmost weakness, to break the perfect bond and love of twenty-eight years continuance…'.

As if such smears against her good name were not enough, in 1586 a further scandal broke out around the Countess. The maverick Lincolnshire MP and classical translator Arthur Hall, a ward of William Cecil and former servant of the Earl of Sussex, tried unsuccessfully to woo her. Hall, by his own admission 'overweenyng of himself' and considered by many to be rash if not mad, responded to her implacable resistance by writing the 'Hungaryous Hystory'. This account of their relationship, begun at some point after both had been widowed in 1582–3, was so libellous that the Queen, encouraged by the Countess and the Lord Chamberlain, supported Hall's imprisonment in the Marshalsea and Fleet prisons in 1588–9. The Countess's relations, the Haringtons, had all but a few copies of the book burned. As she lay on her deathbed in her house in Bermondsey in December 1588, her most recent accuser in jail, her treacherous brother dead as a political failure in 1586, and her husband's worst enemy, Leicester, very recently dead in September, the Countess of Sussex wrote her last will and testament.

Fool's Gold

In 1578 Lady Frances invested heavily in Martin Frobisher's futile voyage to the Arctic to seek gold. The largest mine he excavated, on the coast of Baffin Island, was named after her. Like many, she lost her money for 450 tons of worthless black ore.

Lady Frances' position at court as a patron of learning is underlined by the dedication to her of books such as a translation in 1581 by Thomas Rogers of the Danish theologian Niels Hemmingsen's *The Faith of the Church Militant*. In his dedication Rogers advocated education as a primary bulwark against popery and heresy, the two evils Sidney Sussex College was founded to fight against.

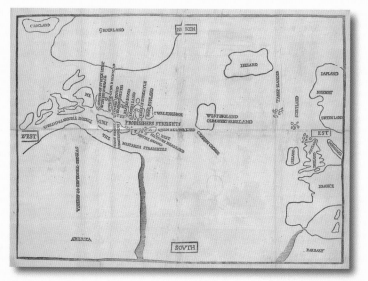

Baffin Island, woodcut attributed to James Beare, principal surveyor with Martin Frobisher's 1578 voyage, showing the countess's mine. Collection James Ford Bell Library, University of Minnesota

In Defence of Her Loyalty

'Albeit I am now beaten down with many afflictions and calamities hardly to be borne of flesh and blood, yet is there no grief that pierceth me so deeply as that by sinister suggestion I should be defamed to be undutiful to your most excellent majesty, and injurious to the honour of my dear Lord lately deceased. For the first, I appeal to God himself, the searcher of hearts and revenger of all disloyalties; for the second, I appeal to none but unto my most gracious Queen, whether I have not … been more careful of his health, honour, and well doing than of mine own soul and safety; refusing all friends and friendships in this world for so dear a Lord, whom I followed in health and sickness … were it not for the fear of God's revenge, I could with all my heart redeem them with the sacrifice of my life.'
—Lady Frances Sidney to Queen Elizabeth after Sussex's death, 'from the poor careful close of Bermondsey', 18 September 1583

'Dieu me Garde de Calomnie': Lady Frances' Will

Aged 58, the loyal, learned, devout and much maligned Lady Frances Sidney still had a great deal to achieve in the few months remaining to her. That her personal motto had become 'Dieu me Garde de Calomnie' ('God protect me from calumny') says much about her motives. Left a good fortune by her husband, the Countess set about ensuring posterity was kinder to her reputation than her contemporaries had been to her in her final years.

Her will, which was contested unsuccessfully by some members of the Sidney family, made wide-ranging provision. She left most of her worldly possessions and much of her wealth to her family, friends and servants, and to the poor of 'Barmonzey', Barking and Boreham. Twenty-eight pages of minutely detailed description show the social range of her world and the extent of her belongings. To her 'welbeloued nephewe Sir Robert Scidney knight' she left all manner of luxury items, includ-ing 'a standinge testorne of Crymson velvet', 'a greate Fetherbedd and a boulster a paire of Pillowes a wooll quilt', 'eight peaces of hangings of Immagrie of the story of Nathan the Asserian', 'a close stole of Crymeson velvet imbrothered with my name with goulde and silver', 'six glasse bottles garnished with silver', 'a ship of Cristall garnished with silver' and 'a faire Chayne of Martynes makinge of divers fashioned linckes'.

Robert Sidney's wife received 'a gowne of black satten with a garde Cutt upon gold' as well as various items of jewellery such as a 'Frenche Chaine with Ones of pearle with a hooke at it Containing iiij and vj linckes besides the little golde linckes and a crosse of dyamondes with thre faire pearle at it'. Other named beneficiaries, such as her nephew 'Thomas Scydney', who was left 'Fower hundred poundes' and a chain with 'a porpintyne of silver', received velvet kirtles, furniture, hangings with good Protestant subjects such as 'the storie of Hester', quilts, 'quishions', gold cups and suites of precious 'buttons'. Over 100 people, from ladies of the court to kitchen staff, received everything from elaborate jewel pendants to small sums of cash.

Yet the childless Lady Frances had higher ambitions than simply to spread her considerable wealth among those closest to her. She bequeathed an annuity of £20 for two lectures in divinity at Westminster Abbey each year, in perpetuity, and £100 for poor preachers in London and the suburbs, and for debtors in Ludgate and the King's Bench prisons. There was also money for the magnificent tomb in her memory that

The Foundress's Bequest

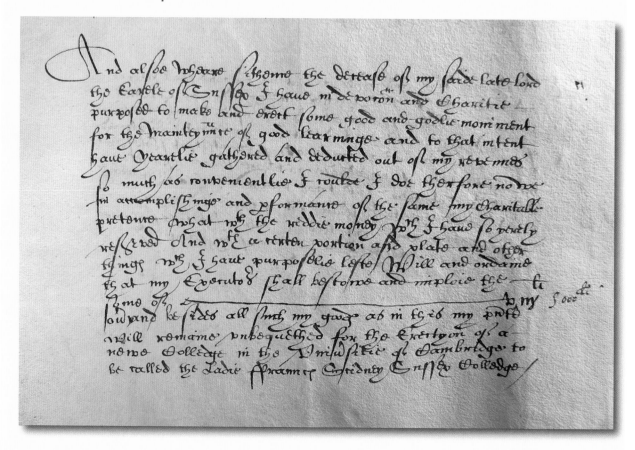

And alsoe wheare sithence the decease of my saide late lord the Earele of Sussex I have in devocion and Charitie purposed to make and erect some good and godlie monument for the mainteynance of good learninge and to that intent haue yearelie gathered and deducted out of my revenues so much as convenientlie I coulde I doe therfore nowe in accomplishinge and performance of the same my Charitable pretence what with the reddie money which I haue so yerely reserved And with a certen portion and plate and other thinges which I haue purposelie lefte Will and ordaine that my executors shall bestowe and imploie the some of v m li souerand besides all such my goodes as in this presente Will remaine vnbequethed for the Erectyon of a newe Colledge in the Vniuersitie of Cambridge to be called the Ladie Fraunces Scidney Sussex Colledge.

Tomb of Lady Frances Sidney, Countess of Sussex, probably by Richard Stevens, Chapel of St Paul, Westminster Abbey

still dominates the Chapel of St Paul, Westminster Abbey, where her funeral took place on 15 April 1589. This large 'table tomb' was probably also made by Richard Stevens, the creator of the Sussex tombs at Boreham. Her funeral sermon was delivered by the venerable Dean of St Paul's, Alexander Nowell. Aged 72, Nowell was an exile and hero of the early Reformation, the author of the church's prescribed longer and shorter catechisms, and a great educational philanthropist.

Above all, however, there was Lady Frances' true and lasting monument, Sidney Sussex College. Her will made provision for the building of a new college in Cambridge and the purchase of an estate to maintain a master, 10 fellows and 20 scholars; if the bequest was found insufficient to achieve her aim of a new college, it was to be diverted to the enlargement of Clare Hall.

'Godly and Virtuous': the Founding Executors

The truth is that Lady Frances' bequest was barely enough to achieve her ambition of founding a Cambridge college. As Thomas Fuller wrote of the founding of his much-loved 'Sidney College' in his 1655 history of Cambridge: 'Alas! What is five thousand pounds to buy the site, build and endow a college therewith?' Sir Walter Mildmay had given over six times as much towards the recent founding of Emmanuel in 1584. Royal foundations such as Trinity had immeasurably more. After various payments, indeed, the sum available was only £3,327, 8s and 10d – by today's values in terms of average earnings, about £7 million. By 1601 £2,614, 4s had been spent on building, the equivalent of about £5.5 million.

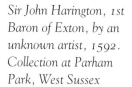

Sir John Harington, 1st Baron of Exton, by an unknown artist, 1592. Collection at Parham Park, West Sussex

Exton Old Hall after the fire of 1810, photograph c1860. The Old Hall was built by Sir John Harington's father and added to by Sir John and Sir Baptist Hicks. The frontage was 150 feet. A further fire in 1915 reduced it to a bare ruin

Lady Frances chose her executors for their friendship, family connections, religious sympathies, political clout and, in one instance, wealth: her nephew Sir John Harington and her cousin Henry Bosvil; the Oxford academic and conservative churchman Nicholas Bond; the close friend of Burghley, Gabriel Goodman, Dean of Westminster; the lawyer Robert Forth; and, as principal executor, for his 'great honour, wisdom, zeal in religion and virtue', the lawyer and politician Henry Grey, sixth Earl of Kent. Supervising these six men was the Countess's friend and mentor, John Whitgift, Archbishop of Canterbury. All of them received gifts in her will.

The Countess of Sussex founded Sidney Sussex in part as a personal memorial in praise of her sullied name, and in part as an institution to support the new national polity and religion of which she considered herself to have been a loyal member. However, Sidney only came into being because of the loyalty, determination and generosity of Harington and Kent, a fact inscribed on the College fabric in the form of their coats of arms still visible today. From Lady Frances' death on 9 March 1589 until Foundation Day on 14 February 1596, they worked tirelessly to make her vision a reality.

'The Glory of Thy Worth': Sir John Harington

Sir John Harington was born around 1539–40, the eldest son of Sir James Harington of Exton, the dominant landowner in Rutland, and his wife Lucy Sidney, Lady Frances' older sister. Trained at the Inner Temple, John Harington was an MP for Rutland and a Justice of the Peace. In 1571 he married Anne Keilway, from whose father the couple inherited Combe Abbey, Warwickshire, in 1581. This great house and the magnificent Tudor mansions at Exton and Burley-on-the-Hill were his main residences throughout his life. He acknowledged his aunt's importance by christening one of his daughters Frances.

The Harington coat of arms over the doorway into the Old Parlour and Hall, originally set into one of the oriel windows facing on to Sidney Street

Knighted in 1584, Harington served under Sussex's greatest rival, Robert Dudley, Earl of Leicester, in the Netherlands in 1585, and was a chief mourner at his funeral. An ardent Protestant with a powerful sense of social and national duty, he was an MP for Warwickshire in 1586, and in that year accompanied Mary Queen of Scots through the county on her way to Fotheringay Castle in Northamptonshire. In the 1590s Harington was made deputy lieutenant of Rutland and Warwickshire. In 1592 he succeeded his father and inherited one of the greatest landed fortunes in England. He was estimated to have an income of around £7,000 a year in 1600.

In 1595–96, the year of Sidney's foundation, Harington arranged for Shakespeare's bloody dynastic tragedy *Titus Andronicus* to be performed at Burley-on-the-Hill as part of sumptuous New Year's celebrations involving all his family, kinsmen and estate. The 12 days of feasting, entertainment, hunting and worship, initiated by the Lord of Misrule after Christmas, involved over 1,000 revellers and must have cost an enormous sum of money. Witnessed by the Huguenot informer Jacques Petit, who was acting as a tutor to Harington's three-year-old heir John, the New Year's Day play was probably performed by the Lord Chamberlain's Men. It was followed by a masque written by Harington's brother-in-law Sir Edward Wingfield, whose three sons attended Sidney in the early years. It is likely that William Shakespeare was among the actors that evening.

Thus, by the time he became an executor of his aunt's will, Harington was a very powerful figure in the East Midlands, connected by family and politics to other great dynasties in the region, such as the Noels of Brooke and the Montagus of Boughton. The marriage of his daughter Lucy to the third Earl of Bedford was a sign of his great ambition, the dowry probably helping eventually to bankrupt him. His great wealth and power led to his elevation as first Baron Harington of Exton shortly after the accession of James I in 1603. Harington was a distant relation of the King, whom he entertained at Burley-on-the-Hill on the grand coronation progress from Scotland to London. Harington commissioned a panegyric poem from Samuel Daniel to celebrate the auspicious event at 'Burley-Harington in Rutlandshire':

> The pulse of England never more did beat
> So strong as now – Nor ever were our hearts
> Let out to hopes so spacious and so great,
> As now they are – Nor ever in all parts
> The whole complexion of the Commonwealth,
> Did we thus feel so comfortable heat,
> As now the glory of thy worth imparts:
> So weak before, hop'd never more for health.

Harington was also highly devout. His famous cousin John Harington, the writer, recalled seeing him and Thomas Cecil taking a cure for gout at the spa at Bath and noted their great piety in the face of pain: 'each did despise his own malady and hold death in derision, because both did not despair of eternal life'.

Contemporary drawing of the execution of Mary, Queen of Scots in the Great Hall at Fotheringay, 8 February 1587, Scottish school. Henry Grey, 6th Earl of Kent, is the figure marked '2' on the stage. Private collection

The popularity of Sidney Sussex among the sons of the nobility and upper gentry during the Jacobean age was in no small part due to Harington's influence and royal favour. His appointment as guardian of James's daughter, Princess Elizabeth; his daughter Lucy's marriage to Edward Russell, third Earl of Bedford; his friendship with James's queen, Anne of Denmark; and his son John's close friendship with Henry, Prince of Wales, all added to his reputation as one of the leading peers of the realm and his family's position as among the greatest of the day. The family's sudden collapse a decade later had major repercussions for Sidney Sussex.

'Great Honour, Wisdom, Zeal...': Sir Henry Grey

Henry Grey of Wrest in Bedfordshire was born in 1541 and succeeded his brother Reginald as sixth Earl of Kent in 1573. A Gray's Inn lawyer and member of the Queen's household, he was politically and personally close to the Countess of Sussex at court and this connection recommended him to her as a principal executor. A major figure in Bedfordshire politics, in 1586 he was one of the commissioners appointed to try Mary, Queen of Scots and, with George Talbot, Earl of Shrewsbury, was a Joint Commissioner for her execution at Fotheringay on 3 February 1587. He can be seen sitting next to Talbot on the execution stage in a contemporary drawing of one of the most dramatic domestic events of Elizabeth's reign. Grey's account of the execution is one of the great eyewitness testimonies of British history, attentive to every detail, moving in its sense of Mary's humanity and tinged with a sense of guilt that not even a die-hard Protestant could overcome. Grey objected to Mary's using a

Licence granted by Queen Elizabeth I to Henry, Earl of Kent and Sir John Harington to found the 'College of the Lady Frances Sidney Sussex', Westminster, 25 July 1594

An image of the Sacred Heart from one of the manuscripts in the Sidney Muniment Room that underlines the early founders' and fellows' fascination with the Catholic culture they opposed and that Mary, Queen of Scots embodied in her martyrdom.

Sacred Heart with eye weeping tears, illustrating an English translation of the 'Fifteen Os' prayers on the Passion attributed to St Bridget of Sweden, from Sarum Book of Hours, *c1470s*

Catholic Bible to swear her oath of innocence and records her reply: 'If I swear on the book which I believe to be the true version, will your lordship not believe my oath more than if I were to swear on a translation in which I do not believe?' Grey asked forgiveness just before the execution, to which Mary replied, 'I forgive you with all my heart'.

Others in the background of the drawing include various Haringtons and Montagus, the East Midlands grandees who did so much to shape the early years of Sidney Sussex. All of them would have witnessed the botched execution, which took three nervous strokes by the axeman, supposedly leaving Mary's lips quivering in silent prayer for 15 minutes after her decapitation.

Grey continued in royal favour under King James. Like Harington, he laboured diligently to found Sidney, and until his death in 1615, shortly after Harington's, he was intimately involved in College business and was deferred to by the first three masters, James Montagu, Francis Aldrich and Samuel Ward.

Detail of alabaster tomb of Henry Grey, Earl of Kent, De Grey Mausoleum, Flitton church, Bedfordshire. Grey built the famous mausoleum and is shown with his wife, Mary Cotton

'A Heart Unto a Crown': How to Found a College

These two noble executors in pursuance of the will of this testatrix, according to her desire and direction therein, presented Queen Elizabeth a jewel, being like a star, of rubies and diamonds, with a ruby in the midst thereof, worth an hundred and forty pounds, having on the back side a hand delivering up a heart unto a crown. At the delivery hereof they humbly requested of her Highness a Mortmain to found a College, which she graciously granted unto them… —Thomas Fuller, *History of the University of Cambridge*, 1655

Coat of arms of Henry Grey, Earl of Kent, on the east wall of the Chapel, an elaborate painted stone survival from the early buildings

Harington and Kent, no doubt encouraged by Archbishop Whitgift – who had been master of Trinity and was keen to encourage the education of learned ministers for the Church of England at Cambridge – decided early on that the task before them was worth the trouble and set about gaining the Queen's all-important support for the new college. Lady Frances' will had included generous provision for achieving this aim, in particular the jewel to be given to Elizabeth. The Queen's consent eventually resulted in a charter with a wax impression of the Royal Great Seal drawn up in 1594 and still owned by the College.

Such gifts of jewellery were part and parcel of transactions with the Queen at the time, helping to persuade her in some matter or acting as tokens of regard for favours received. The Sidney jewel, now lost, was made by a major goldsmith of the period, John Stockbridge of Cripplegate, and its imagery of a star is frequently found in Tudor jewellery, as is the device of the 'hande deliv'inge upp a hart unto a Crowne', the sort of image that was part of the symbolic courtly language of the age. It was a language in which Lady Frances was clearly fluent. When the celebrated Bess of Hardwick had wanted advice on what New Year's gift to offer Elizabeth in 1576, the Countess of Sussex and Lady Cobham suggested that, rather than the usual mundane gold cup or suchlike, she present an embroidered satin cloak with flower patterns, gold spangles and silk embroidery. The foundress's nephew, Sir Philip Sidney, indeed, had given his aunt a jewel as a token of his love. Such know-how about the royal sensibility helped, in its own small way, to ease Sidney's foundation.

A Counter-Counter-Reformation: 16th-Century Cambridge

Our design in founding the College is that it may be made a seminarium of learned men from which the largest number may be made available to instruct the people in the Christian faith. —College Statutes, 1596

If there was one overriding reason for founding Sidney Sussex, it was to assist in the fight against a resurgent Roman Catholic church and the foreign invasion it threatened. With hindsight it is easy to see Elizabethan England as a supremely confident society bearing the origins of the British Empire; during Lady Frances Sidney's lifetime, however, things seemed far more insecure. From the 1540s the Counter-Reformation intended to defeat Protestantism by every means possible. Whether by Armada or Jesuit priest, England was to be brought back into the fold, and Elizabeth and her ministers were determined to overcome this threat. Universities were a central part of their strategy.

Sidney was the 16th college to be founded at Cambridge and, until Downing opened in 1800, was its youngest. The 16th century had seen the foundation of Christ's (1505), St John's (1511), Magdalene (1542), Trinity (1546) and Emmanuel (1584). Like the world around it, the university changed significantly during the century, embracing humanism when Erasmus was at Queens' in 1509–14, fighting off Henry VIII's attacks on its privileges and very existence in the 1530s and, by the 1540s, becoming a leading centre of Protestant thought. It produced three great Protestant martyrs under Queen Mary in the 1550s – Nicholas Ridley, Hugh Latimer and Thomas Cranmer – and by the time Elizabeth visited Cambridge in 1564, the university was seen by many as a hotbed of the 'forward Protestantism' favoured by the returning Marian academic exiles.

William Cecil, the university's Chancellor until 1598, and John Whitgift, a great friend to Sidney's founders, sought with great difficulty to impose the moderate Elizabethan religious settlement right up until the College's foundation. Catholics were barred, of course, and had to travel abroad for higher education, but Puritans were in many ways trickier to control, resistant to the conformity the Church of England sought to impose on them. Whitgift's great adversary, Thomas Cartwright of Trinity, was the leader of the Puritan faction, 'these rash young heads that are so soon ripe to climb into pulpits', as Cecil called them. Puritanism was seen not only as a potential heresy but also as a threat to political and social stability. Its emphasis was on personal interpretation of the Bible and rejection of the church hierarchy and liturgical traditions and vestments, as expressed in Cartwright's controversial lectures; and it was regarded by conservatives as a source of dangerous innovation in a country facing severe economic and social strains as well as the distinct threat of foreign invasion sanctioned by Rome. Order was to be maintained by bishops in dioceses and ministers in parishes, all under the control of the monarchy through archbishops.

Whitgift, against stiff opposition, forced through new statutes for Cambridge in 1570, which in effect moved power away from the university's central institutions and towards an oligarchy of the Vice-Chancellor and masters of the colleges. Royal authority over the university was also considerably

William Perkins (1558–1602), by an unknown artist

enhanced. These new powers allowed Whitgift to eject Cartwright from his professorship and fellowship and to pursue a draconian policy against the Puritans for nearly three decades.

The disputes between radicals and conservatives in matters of doctrine as well as constitution continued, and the colleges began to acquire distinct theological characters, with St John's, Christ's and Emmanuel identified in particular with Calvinist Puritanism. Their fellowships produced the most influential theologians, teachers and preachers of the time, such as William Whitaker, William Perkins and Samuel Ward of Ipswich, who became one of the first Sidney fellows.

Stained glass windows in the Old Library, created from medieval Franciscan glass excavated in Cloister Court in 1958

Sidney's foundation met an immediate need for new colleges in Cambridge as the student population grew markedly in the late-16th century, tracking a similar growth in the nation's overall population. In 1564 there were 1,200 students; in 1600 there were 2,000, with many more staying to take degrees than previously. The demand for new student accommodation and teaching, however, came from the pressure of enormous historical forces affecting Elizabethan England. Whether from a radical or conservative point of view, it was widely felt that more educated men were needed for the Church of England, just as new justices of the peace, doctors and teachers were required. A fast-growing population, many of whom were living in abject poverty, subject to sudden and incurable outbreaks of plague and disease, increasingly hard to control and even threatening the order of things, required the firmest and most widespread pastoral and spiritual care possible. Sidney's priestly undergraduates were trained to go out into the parishes of England and wage an urgent holy war from the pulpit against a multitude of threats: Catholicism, atheism, Anabaptism and other heresies, witchcraft, astrology, superstition, gambling, drink, sexual excess and perversion, treason and republicanism.

'Dead Men's Bones': Grey Friars

The area of this church is easily visible in Sidney College garden, where the depression and subsidency of the bowling green east and west, present the dimensions thereof, and I have oft found dead men's bones thereabouts.
—Thomas Fuller, *The History of the University of Cambridge*, 1655

Map of Cambridge (detail), 1592, by John Hamond, showing the derelict Grey Friars site shortly before the executors took possession. Bodleian Library, Oxford

The next step for the executors was to find and secure a plot of land on which to build a college. Cambridge had been heavily built up along the river, 'Heighe Warde' (now King's Parade) and Trumpington Street in the Middle Ages, and more recent collegiate building had tended to occur further east where there was more land: Jesus in 1498, Christ's in 1505 and Emmanuel in 1584 are typical examples of this trend.

Like Jesus and Emmanuel, Sidney was built on a former religious site. It seems likely the land had already been identified as a possible location for the College during Lady Frances' lifetime. The large site remaining near the centre was that of the old Grey Friars. This was the great Franciscan foundation built in the second half of the 13th century with its huge church, cloisters, refectory, dormitory, schoolhouse, library, infirmary, orchard and gardens. The last of these lay to the east of the King's Ditch, a defensive feature that ran through the College grounds in the early-17th century as virtually an open sewer.

Until it was dissolved by Henry VIII, Grey Friars was an important institution for town and university alike: its church was open to the public, as were the school and graveyard, and the church was used for university ceremonies of 'commencement' in the early-16th century. Local businessmen left legacies to ensure the friars prayed for them. The Franciscans were also important in the development of Cambridge as a university through their teaching, attracting internationally renowned scholars. Today Sidney commemorates the presence of the great Catholic philosopher John Duns Scotus with a plaque in Cloister Court near where he would have lectured in about 1300.

The Franciscans continued to build on the site throughout the 14th century. In 1327 the order constructed a drinking-water supply using a source in Madingley, a

Plaque commemorating the presence of Duns Scotus at the Grey Friars c1300, installed in Cloister Court in 1966

Saeculo exeunte XIII
IOANNES DUNS SCOTUS
Ordinis Fratrum Minorum
Subtilis ingenii mentisque acutae
Testimonia hic proferens conspicua
Speciosa doctrinae forma
Hanc illustravit Studiorum Universitatem

Anno vero a nativitate septingentesimo,
Fratres Minores, qui in loco Conventum Ordinis
habuere insignem, unde lux manavit fulgida,
hoc erexere monumentum.

A·D·XIII·KAL·OCT·MCMLXVI

new mile-long conduit to replace an earlier one that passed through the land now occupied by Trinity College and came into what is now Cloister Court. This conduit still supplies the fountain in Trinity's Great Court.

When Grey Friars was visited by Thomas Cromwell's commissioners in about September 1538 they found fewer than 30 demoralised friars, a site in disrepair and a library with few books. Most movable assets were taken and, forced to acknowledge that their practices were superstitious and meaningless, the majority of the friars left to become Anglican parish priests.

The church continued to be used for university ceremonies for a while. With the founding of Trinity College in 1545, however, the King found a new use for the empty Grey Friars – as a building yard full of good stone for his new college. Ironically, until the intervention of Katherine Parr, Henry VIII had considered closing the whole university down, so rich had the pickings been from the monasteries. By the mid-1550s little was left of the friary except some outbuildings and the refectory. The land, conveyed to Trinity in 1546, was mainly leased to local builders and yeomen for cultivation and other purposes, and although the town of Cambridge sought to buy it as the site of a new hospital for the poor, it remained Trinity's property until Harington and Kent approached the college armed with the Queen's blessing in the early 1590s.

The antiquary and loyal Anglican Henry Spelman's *The History and Fate of Sacrilege*, written in the early-17th century, detailed the 'strange misfortunes and grievous accidents', through childlessness, violent death and other curses of those, including the Earl of Sussex, who had acquired 'consecrated places' in the Reformation. Sidney Sussex, however, was a foundation with religion at its heart and was doubtless considered by Spelman to be exempt from such divine punishment.

'Excuses and Delayes': Negotiating with Trinity, 1589–1595

'AND WHEREAS in the last parliament of our said Soueraigne Ladie the Queenes Matie holden at Westminster in ye five and thirtithe yere of her highnes said Raigne amongst other thinges it was enacted That the late Scite of the dissolved howse of the Graye Fryers in or nere Cambridge might be sould or lett in fee farme or otherwyse for the erecting of a newe Colledge in the Vniuersitie of Cambridge…

'ALL THAT PARCELL OF LAND conteyning by estimacion Three Acres….nowe enclosed with a stone wall, togeather with the said wall and walles; And all howses and buildinges, in or uppon ye said parcel of lande with thappurtenaunces; And all draynes watercourses wayes passages profittes commodities advantages and hereditamentes whatsoeuer, to the said parcelll of land nowe belonging, or in anywyse appertayning…And all priviliges, fraunchises, and liberties to be had vsed and enioyed in and uppon ye premises or any of them or by any Inhabitantes…To have and to hold ye said parcel of land…for euer…yelding and paying therefore yerelie to the said Mr Fellowes and Scholers…The yerelie rent of Thirtene powndes six shillings eight pennce…' —Formal conveyance of the Grey Friars site to Sidney, 10 September 1595

Trinity College, understandably, was not keen to lose its valuable 'parcell of land', and this led to protracted negotiations in which the Queen and Whitgift intervened on the executors' behalf. Harington and Kent also had in their favour an act of parliament dating from Queen Mary's reign that allowed for the site to be sold or let for the creation of a new college. However, against this, Trinity's statutes forbade any alienation of property and so a new act would be required to allow it. An act was duly passed in 1593, following representations by Harington and Kent, empowering Trinity to sell or let the land. The Queen then wrote to the master and fellows of Trinity:

'Wee, considering that their suite tendeth to a common benefite of our Realme, to the amplifying of our Universitie, and the beautifying of our towne of Cambridge, have been moved…to require you, as we doe by these presents, that you would presently sell or graunt the said site of the Friars, for some reasonable price, to the said Executors…

'Whereunto wee doubt not, but that of your owne disposition you will shew yourselves soe ready, considering that the same tendeth to the advancement of learning, whereof you are professors, That wee shall not neede to vse any arguments, other then to move you to the speedie doeing thereof.'

This nearly settled the matter, yet Trinity had further misgivings. It was concerned about the compensation it would receive and in July 1595 wrote to Whitgift:

'At first at your Graces motion and for the foundacion of a Colledge, we have not bene vnwillinge to parte with the Scite of the late dissoluted Gray Fryers in Cambridge, to no smale damage and prejudice of our Colledge inheritance, so consideringe the delaies and slender recompence to be expected for so large and beneficiall a graunte as we haue entred into, we are bold eftsonnes to recommend the serious consideracion thereof to your Graces wisdome, and wonted care of our poore Colledge; well hopinge that as we haue referred our demaunds in this behalf to your Graces determinacion, so your Grace wilbe well pleased to award vs aboue the fee farme of twenty markes, some proporcion of monie answerable to the buildinges, and

Aquamanile (a vessel for pouring water over the hands) in the form of a cow, Grimston ware, Norfolk, early 14th century, found during the building of South Court in the 1930s

The Foundress's seal
(enlarged)

Silver seal-die almost
certainly used by the
Foundress as her
personal seal during her
widowhood. The motto –
DIEV ME GARDE DE
CALVMNIEZ – is that
adopted by Lady Frances
when she was in ill-favour
with Queen Elizabeth I
after the death of the Earl
of Sussex in 1583

other comodities of stone and stuffe, as well within as aboue the ground, which by estimacion of workemen beinge of great valew, we are content to leaue behinde us…'

Whitgift's reply was quick and pointed. Referring to the 'olde building standing within the wall of the Grey-Fryers now used for a malting-howsse', he told his 'loving frendes' at Trinity that while they must wait for him to come to Cambridge to inspect the site before making a judgement on the value of any compensation, 'I verye hartelye pray you for the avoiding of further excuses and delays in so good a purpose, that you would in the mean tyme with as much expedicion as may bee, finisshe and make perfect the assurance betwixt the College and Sir John Harrington for the said Grey-Friers…'.

The lengthy negotiations were drawn to a close with a formal conveyance of the site to the executors on 10 September 1595. The conveyance made one proviso to ensure the executors acted fairly swiftly to erect the new college: 'yf the said Colledge…be not erected and builded within seaven yeres next eme-diatly ensuing the date of these presentes That then these present Indentures and all and euery thing and matter therein conteyned And euery other acte and actes, thing and thinges, hereafter to be made for the further assurance of the premises to be vtterlie voyde frustrate and of none effecte…'.

A week later Whitgift decided Sidney should pay Trinity 100 marks before the conveyance was sealed. On 10 October Kent sent Nevile the money with a letter from his seat at Wrest, reminding Trinity of the great efforts the executors had so far put into getting to this point: 'The tyme asked hathe bynne longe, the charges and trobles very great to the executors to bring to passe that hath bynne done, the money remaininge but very smale to finnyshe that which is begunne…'. A week ear-lier Harington had written to Nevile from Burley-on-the-Hill asking that Trinity be generous to the fledgling institution: 'I suppose his Lordship hathe awarded you a farr greater somme than you either expected or would your selfe haue demaunded, and I have appointed this bearer to deliuer you so much of the same somme as you will take, prayinge you to haue consideration that how much you shall abate of this somme, so much shall Sydney Colledge be furthered and bettered by your good meanes and fauour.' Trinity's accounts for this period show no receipt for a sum of money from Sidney's executors and we may therefore assume that Kent and Harington's pleas were heard sympathetically.

'Her Owne Kindred': James Montagu, MA

Sidney was already under construction and a master had been chosen. James Montagu was the fifth son of Sir Edward Montagu of Boughton and Elizabeth Harington. Elizabeth Harington, Sir John's sister, was daughter of Sir James Harington of Exton

James Montagu, Bishop of Winchester, by an unknown artist

Edward Montagu, 1st Baron Montagu of Boughton, by an unknown artist, 1621–39

and Lucy Sidney, the Countess of Sussex's sister. James Montagu was therefore Lady Frances' great-nephew. His brother, another Edward, was a major benefactor to Sidney and his portrait still hangs in the Hall, near those of James and their great-aunt. James had been a fellow commoner at Christ's College and was clearly a very talented, capable and ambitious young man. His uncle, Sir John Harington, approached the Vice-Chancellor and nine heads of colleges to ask their opinion about appointing such a young man; Montagu was 24 in 1592 and had not attained his DD degree. Harington told them that in the matter of this important position, 'it was in the minde of the honourable foundresse to have an especiall regarde to those of her owne kindred'. With some caution the university authorities approved the appointment.

It was an inspired move. Montagu took charge of the building of the College and acted as an energetic and shrewd master until April 1608, when he became Bishop of Bath and Wells. Before moving on to Winchester in 1616 he had spent large sums of his own money on the abbey at Bath and the chapel at the Bishop's Palace at Wells. At his death in 1618 he left money to James I, a gold cup to the Marquess, later Duke, of Buckingham, and rents and books to Sidney. His bowels were buried at Greenwich and his body in a lavish canopied tomb at Bath.

Montagu's career as a college master and a prominent figure in the Jacobean Church of England casts much light on the founding impulses and early history of Sidney Sussex. The Montagus and Haringtons had made an immediate and favourable impression on King James before and at the moment of his accession and their families became closely identified with the new monarch's court and patronage. James Montagu was made a royal chaplain in 1603. As a careful and moderate Calvinist who was also committed to episcopacy, he was very soon held to be an ideal candidate for the revived post of Dean of the Chapel Royal. Montagu was a significant literary figure too, one of the elite group who translated the great 1611 Authorised Version of the Bible, as well as the editor and translator of King James's literary works. Great diplomacy was required in handling the King's often unrealistic intellectual ambitions, whether at his famous literary feasts or in the royal lodgings at Newmarket and Royston where he composed his works, drawing on the libraries at nearby Cambridge. Montagu was frequently holed up for weeks at a time with the King at Newmarket from late 1607 while he wrote his various responses to Catholic critics such as Cardinal Bellarmine. Montagu claimed in his introduction to the King's works that James's efforts were clearly guided by God; that the Sidney master's input was equally important is certain.

The great statesman and scientific philosopher Francis Bacon considered Montagu to be one of the three most influential members of the royal household. Sir John Harington's appointment as guardian to Princess Elizabeth and the favouritism given to his daughter Lucy and son John add to the sense of how powerfully placed Sidney's founding families were during James's reign. When 'Bertie' Montagu preached at the wedding of Princess Elizabeth to the Elector Palatine in 1613, Sidney could reasonably be considered to have been at the height of its worldly consequence.

'The New College – or Palace Rather – of Sidney'

Haec inter media aspicies mox surgere tecta
Culminibus niveis roseisque nitentia muris:
Nobilis haec doctis sacrabit femina musis,
Conjugio felix, magno felicior ortu,
Insita Sussexo proles Sidneia trunco

Soon you will behold these dewellings rising in the midst,
Shining with their snow-white pinnacles and rosy walls:
A noble lady consecrated these to the learned muses,
A fortunate marriage, more fortunate in its great origin
The grafted offspring of the Sidney stem.
—Giles Fletcher, *De Literis Antiquae Britanniae*, 1633

The Moravian Count Waldstein's description of Sidney as a 'palace' while on his tour of England in the summer of 1600 suggests that Montagu had by that year built an impressive-looking college. He had been given power of attorney by Sir John

Elizabethan brickwork on the north side of Hall Court, in the cloister facing Jesus Lane

Nobilissima D.D. Francisca Sidney Sussexiae comitissa, D. Henrici Sidney equ: Aur: Hiberniae Proregis, et Walliae Praesidis, soror, viri celeberrimi Philippi Sidney equ: aur: Amita. Mou
ex sincero erga Religionem reformatam affectu, huic Collegio fundando reliquit. Testamenti ejus executores primarij erant D. Henricus Grey Cantij Comes, et D. Iohannes Harrington
Scholares viginti alendos Curarunt ut dotaretur, Anno 1598, haec, ejusq imaginem intueris structura collegiorum numerum adauxit. Inceptis hisce, aliij Pietatis et bonarum litera
ibus extructum, Collegio adjunxerit, quam Socijs et Scholaribus alijs inquirendis haud contemnenda proposuerit emolumenta, non uno nomine seipsum posteritati celebrandum co
nardus Smith civis Londinensis, mr. Petrus Blundel Tivertoniensis, Ioh. Freeston, Francis Combes Armig, et Mr. Downham Joemans. Inter Benefactores, praeter praedictos viros
ni. Bathon. et Wellen, postea Winton Episcopus, Regiae Majestati a secretioribus consilijs, et D. Iohn Brereton equ aur, qui non tam propriae famae quam communi nostrum utilit
literariae decus et Adjumentum attulere, enumerantur Reverendis, in Christo pater Iohn Bramhal Archieps, Armachanus, Sethus Ward Sarisburiensis, Exoniensis primum Antist

Sidney Sussex College, from Cantabrigia Illustrata, 1690, by David Loggan

The right-hand coat-of-arms surmounts a dedication to William Brownlow (1680), one of a number of members of the Lincolnshire family who attended the College in the later 17th century. Their home at Belton House is one the great houses of this period. The Sidney arms in the top left corner were first granted to the College in 1675 by the Garter King of Arms. They impale the arms of Radcliffe and Sidney on a shield, appropriate to a corporate body. The familiar impalement on a lozenge was the form appropriate to a widow. The small building just behind the wall at the end of the Fellows' Garden is a privy, one of only two in the College. The other was for the sole use of the master

Ralph Symons

The architect chosen to build Sidney was Ralph Symons, a freemason of Westminster, who had built Emmanuel College a few years earlier, and was soon to be at work on Trinity's Great Court under the supervision of Dr Thomas Nevile. Symons received an initial payment of £20 on 23 March 1595. Symons, the local builder George Wigges of Histon, and James Montagu worked closely together on the building of Sidney for the next three-and-a-half years. Montagu's accounts for the period include various signatures by Symons, usually spelt phonetically as 'RAFE SIMONS', the 'N' reversed and accompanied by a monogram.

Ralph Symons, by an unknown artist. Emmanuel College, Cambridge

Harington in February 1595 to pay out the sums of money, channelled to him in instalments, necessary to have the College ready for habitation by Michaelmas term 1598. A first load of stone was bought from nearby Barrington on 23 March 1595, and in his day-book Montagu records a momentous occasion that took place in the presence of the masters of Peterhouse, Christ's and Trinity Hall, and other university dignitaries: 'The first stone of this College was laid by myselfe on the 20th day of May 1595, in the presence of Dr. Soame Dep. Vice. Chan., Dr. Barwell, Dr. Cowell, and others'. The first stone was laid 'at ye corner towards ye fellowes orchard' – that is, near the northeast corner of the Hall where the great bay window still is.

This occasion preceded the formal conclusion of negotiations with Trinity in September by four months; a letter from Montagu to the Earl of Kent describes Harington entering the site to inaugurate the digging of the foundations with his next concern being to 'conclud with Trinity Colledg for albeit the bargan be agreed on yet the bookes are not sealed'.

The old accounts also give a vivid picture of the day-to-day business of building a college in the late-16th century. Simple initials of the illiterate show that money was paid out to the contractor John Atkinson for timber; the joiner Andrew Chapman for the wainscot, screen and furniture in the Hall; Richard Thorpe, a stonemason, who carved the shields of arms on the exterior of the Hall and the intricate designs on the main gate; the plasterer Edward Meeres; and the smith Richard Brasher. A nameless labourer is recorded 'fauling from the scaffold', a reminder of how dangerous such sites could be.

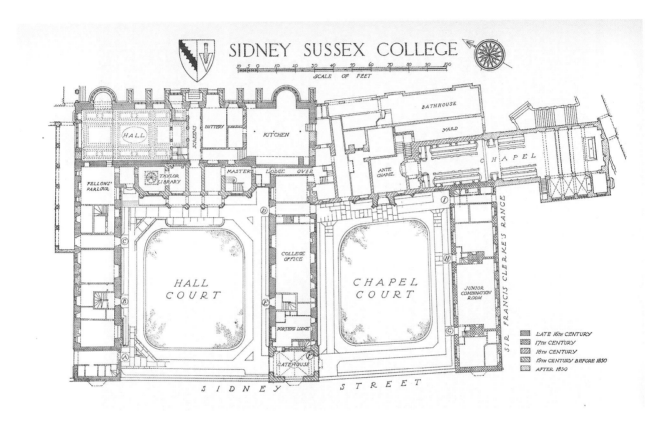

ABOVE: *Plan of Sidney's front courts, from* An Inventory of the Historical Monuments in the City of Cambridge, *1959 (HMSO), part II*

LEFT: *A detail from David Loggan's 1690 print of Sidney, showing the ornate part of the Fellows' Garden with a summer house and a mound surmounted by a sundial*

The exterior of the new building was to be made of red brick with stone facings, its interior of timber and plaster. The site itself provided ample stone, gravel and sand to lay the foundations and to raise the walls above water level. Huge quantities of bricks were purchased, in batches of between 10,000 and 40,000 on occasion, arriving from locations such as Ely and Burrough Green. Lime came up the Cam from nearby Reach and was unloaded at the quay by Magdalene Bridge, where a man was paid to guard it overnight. Soft white clunch stone came from Haslingfield and, down the river Ouse and fenland waterways from Castor, near Peterborough, came freestone, paving stones and slate. From the royal forest at Rockingham in Northamptonshire came timber. George Write of Yaxley delivered large amounts of stone from a nearby abbey (probably Ramsey), a further instance of new Protestant foundations plundering the remains of pre-Reformation religious sites. For smaller items, Stourbridge Fair on the outskirts of Cambridge was the source for slats and nails.

By August 1597, the last of Trinity's tenants had vacated the site and a year later, in August 1598, a well was dug and two pumps constructed, to make good the loss of the old Grey Friars conduit to Trinity. One pump was for College needs and one, on the Sidney Street side of the College wall, was accessible to the townspeople of Cambridge. A wooden 'house of office' supplied the College's sanitary needs.

The extent of the College at its opening in 1598 was simply a three-sided court, (now Hall Court) entered through an unfinished gate in the centre of the screen wall on the western Conduit Street (now Sidney Street) side, with a Master's Lodge over the Hall, kitchen and buttery on the east side, and two three-storey accommodation wings, with attics, projecting east-west. A pathway from the front gate through the screens passage to the Hall and on to the gardens and then the orchards beyond the King's Ditch, gave the layout a dynamic quality, drawing the site together around a strong axis.

To the south of the Hall and Lodge lay a Chapel, which was crudely created from the remains of the Grey Friars' old refectory by clearing rubble and erecting a thatched roof. Unconsecrated, and facing northwest-southwest in typical Protestant style, the Chapel was improved a few years later.

Sidney was modelled loosely on the form of Elizabethan country houses such as those at Burton Agnes and Burton Constable in Yorkshire, with a further architectural debt to the three-sided courts fashionable in France a few decades earlier. The two ranges of chambers had a top storey with small attics and symmetrically arranged dormer windows capped with stone ornaments. The windows were in a modern rectangular style, rather than arched. On the street end of these wings were oriel windows decorated with the Harington arms.

Waldstein noted on 12 July 1600 that Sidney was 'very fine with a particularly splendid hall'. From the outside of this main building, seven gables were visible, with two small staircase towers in the corners of the court balancing the grand central tower, and the porch to the Hall decorated with Kent's arms and classical columns.

OPPOSITE: *A view into the 1590s tie-and-collar-beam roof of the Hall, now obscured by the rococo ceiling installed in the mid-18th century*

These smaller towers led, on the left, to the Fellows' Parlour and, to the right, up to the Master's Lodge. On the eastern side of the Hall and Lodge range, overlooking the gardens, two large bay windows made a strong visual statement, with a fine lantern over the roof containing the College bell.

The interior of the Hall was tall and dominated by a plain tie-and-collar-beam roof, which still exists above the present 18th-century ceiling. The moulded and painted wainscotting was made of deal, rather than the more expensive oak, and the seating originally attached to this can be seen in early-19th-century prints. With more windows than survive today, particularly on the Hall Court side, the Hall was well lit. A large open fire in the centre of the room was one of the few sources of heat available in the College at this time, another being in the Fellows' Parlour, and another upstairs in the Master's Lodge.

Life in the chambers would have been very cramped. Sidney quickly became a popular college and large numbers of undergraduates needed accommodation. The original statutes stipulated that scholars were to sleep four to a chamber and a tutor was obliged to have two or more of his students sleeping in his room. Each student had a small study area partitioned off in a corner of the room. Early records show that even fellows had to share rooms or sleep in the Parlour or Master's Lodge.

Other structures were built, mainly to the south of the site, such as a rush house, a bake house, stables and brewery. Four sundials helped to define the scholarly and religious day. One was 'over ye arch which leades towards the fellows orchard and garden' and one 'was over ye Hall dore and which is now in ye Library'. These last two were given by the College porter Christopher Meeres.

One of the most important spaces, naturally, was the kitchen, 'which began the 28th day of Auguste' 1598. A contemporary inventory lists among its contents brass pots, pans, skillets, a ladle, gridiron, pewter, frying pan, 'water tubbe' and 'salt box'. Excavations in the 1930s preparatory to the building of South Court revealed fragments of plates and drinking vessels as well as pottery candlesticks.

After the last Trinity tenants had left in 1597 it was possible to develop the gardens, and in spring 1599 the new gardener, John Simon, was levelling the ground and planting. Soil, sand and compost were delivered for the beds, and walls were built. The gardens were divided between the master's area to the south and the fellows' area to the north. Each had an orchard and pleasure garden, and the fellows had a long lawn that was used as a bowling green. Loggan's print gives a fair idea of how the gardens would have looked (see the detail on page 31) and shows a remarkably attractive arrangement of features from the period of more formal design before the romantic look we are familiar with today.

Beyond the gardens, towards the east, the King's Ditch flowed malodorously until 1607, when James Montagu, at his own cost, had a clear running stream diverted into it. At the same time a pensioner's father, Stephen Peck of Leicestershire, had a number of sycamore trees brought from London by the famous carrier Thomas Hobson and planted along the bank of the improved water course. The last of these survived until a gale in 1935. The area beyond the water would have been where Cromwell played the football he was notoriously fonder of than academic study.

'Divine Duties': Sidney's First Chapel

Others have complained that it was never ceremoniously consecrated, which they conceive essential thereunto, whilst there want not their equals in learning and religion who dare defend that the continued series of divine duties (praying, preaching, administering the sacrament) publicly practised for more than thirty years, without the least check or control of those in authority, in a place set apart to that purpose, doth sufficiently consecrate the same.

—Thomas Fuller, *The History of the University of Cambridge*, 1655

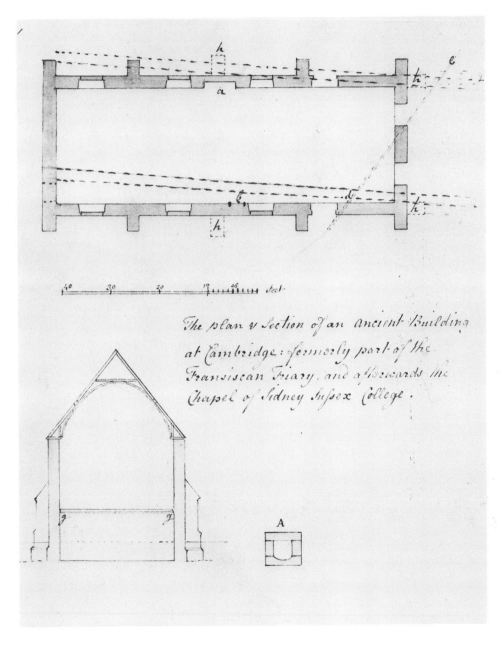

A plan and section of the old Sidney Chapel made by the architect James Essex before his major alterations in the 1770s, showing the adjustment of the alignment he made to the new Chapel

Sidney, though fashionable among the well-to-do hoping to give their sons a year or two acquiring some learning and social contacts, was at its heart a Protestant seminary and so the central feature of the site was its chapel. The surviving Franciscan refectory where the friars had eaten, as the later discovery of animal bones and eating utensils showed, was used as its basis. Although it is often claimed that this unfussy use of a north-south oriented old staff canteen, as at Emmanuel, was a distinctly Puritan move, Christ's, a pre-Reformation college, had a chapel with a northeast-southwest orientation. Nevertheless, the High Church visitors to Cambridge in the 1630s did report back to Archbishop Laud unfavourably about the Sidney chapel's most offensive feature – it was unconsecrated. The Sidney fellow Thomas Fuller, no Puritan himself, saw little problem with this.

In 1595 the old refectory building was a derelict malting house with a cellar, no ceiling, and a rubbish-strewn floor of plaster and clay. It lay south of the Hall, and not quite in line with it. Montagu had it cleared, thatched, and roughly fitted up with the necessities for holding services from the opening of the College in August 1598. In 1601, according to an early chronology of Sidney's first 20 years, the Chapel was 'begun', which suggests that funds had been raised to improve the original crude structure. Ralph Symons was paid £10 for his designs and a further £112 was spent on materials and labour. The walls were strengthened and buttressed, an ante-chapel separated from the main room, and a first floor put in, which acted as a 'chapel chamber' and a library. All the walls and ceilings were plastered by Matthews and Meeres, the main chapel having decorative plaster pendants.

Though Sidney was a Protestant seminary, it was also in effect an organ of the Elizabethan state and thus the royal arms were prominently displayed, painted on the large window at the south end of the Chapel. Beneath this, instead of an overly Catholic-style altar with crucifix, candlesticks and steps, was a communion table. A 1639 inventory of College goods itemises the sparse furniture as a movable pulpit and three desks, one for a Bible and the others 'for the use of them that read common places'. There was no organ and choir, but rather a lot of psalm-singing, in keeping with the austere liturgy of the times.

The Earl of Kent's Steeple Cup, silver gilt, London, maker WR, 1610–11, total height 19 7/8 inches (50 cm)

The Chapel seems to have become more elaborately equipped and fitted out in the following decade or so. The Earl of Kent made a gift of magnificent parcel-gilt communion plate, along with napery and table cloths, in 1611, and in 1612 Montagu, by now the Bishop of Bath and Wells, paid for the south ('east') end to be wainscotted. In the same year Sir John Harington provided stone for paving the floor. There are early records of two iron wall-hung candlesticks and 36 brass ones were purchased in 1638. Three carpets for the communion table are listed in 1639, one of green French cloth and one of velvet fringed with gold with the College arms embroidered on it. The donor was Robert Hudson of London, who also gave Sidney a velvet hanging and a pulpit cushion.

Flagon and communion cup with paten cover, from the Earl of Kent's chapel plate, silver, parcel gilt, London, maker WR, 1610–11

The original College statutes dwell in some detail on the master's duties with respect to the chapel services. He was to take part in public prayers every day, with all the fellows, scholars, pensioners and others living in College, including servants. Each term he was to preach at least one sermon to the fellows and scholars.

'This Benjamin College': Securing the Finances

This is the least foundation in the University, and before Downing College, the last.
—George Dyer, *A History of the University of Cambridge*, 1814

Sidney's finances were precarious from the start and, with a few exceptions along the way, not until the 20th century did they improve significantly beyond the merely manageable. The College's initial relative poverty focused the minds of its founders and gave the College a legacy of a thrifty yet proudly inventive approach to its money matters. Dyer's quotation above was adapted from Thomas Fuller, who likened Cambridge's youngest college to Benjamin, youngest son of Jacob in the Book of Genesis:

'We usually observe infants born in the seventh month, though poor and pitiful creatures, are vital; and with great care and good attendance, in time prove proper persons. To such a *partus septimestris* may Sidney College well be resembled, so low, so lean, and little at the birth thereof…Yet such was the worthy care of her honourable executors, that this Benjamin College – the least, and last in time, and born after (as he at) the death of the mother – thrived in a short time to a competent strength and stature'. Benjamin, Jacob's most beloved 'son of my right hand', bravely led the weakest of the 12 tribes of Israel, an appropriate image perhaps of Sidney's modest means yet zealous purpose.

A Harington farthing (type 1b), 1613–14, enlarged to show the Harington fret at about the 1 o'clock position on the reverse; the actual sized image shows the obverse. Private collection

From 1596 Sidney slowly built up an income to support its master, fellows and scholars, though it rarely found enough to extend or improve its buildings. At its inception Sidney's annual income was a paltry £30, the rent from the manor of Baginton near Coventry in Warwickshire, bought for £400 from Harington's brother James out of Lady Frances' legacy. This was supplemented by £30 a year from Harington for the first four years and, for the following four years, £110 per annum. In 1608 Harington, in completion of his trust as an executor, and after having given generously from his own funds towards the building, endowed the College with his manor of Saleby near Louth in Lincolnshire. The Sidney master was lord of the manor of Saleby until it was sold in 1920.

In total Harington's benefactions to Sidney exceeded those of the foundress, a fact gratefully

acknowledged by the College, and his release from further obligation was undoubt-edly a blessing as he had been incurring heavy expenses as the guardian of the prof-ligate Princess Elizabeth. When he died in 1613 he left his children debts totalling millions of pounds in today's money. The King's grant in 1613 of the sole right for three years to coin tin-surfaced copper farthings, known as 'Haringtons', did him little good. The coins were so tiny and their value so dubious that the saying 'not worth a brass farthing' is said to derive from the 'Harington'.

In 1599 James Montagu's brother Edward, later first Baron Montagu of Boughton, granted the College a thousand-year lease of 45 acres of land in Burwash near Hastings in East Sussex, the income from which established three exhibitions (later changed to scholarships), two for boys from Oundle School in Northamptonshire and one from Sussex.

Further endowments followed over the next decade, mostly from businessmen who felt they had social responsibilities and who sought some personal commemora-tion. The most important was the devout and childless Peter Blundell, who died in 1601. Blundell was an enormously wealthy wool-trader and entrepreneur of Tiverton in Devon, whose most famous memorial is the school named after him in his home town. The chief executor of his fascinating will was his friend Sir John Popham, the Lord Chief Justice of the Common Pleas, architect of the 1597 Poor Laws, fen

Clee church, Lincolnshire, 1844, by Robert Phelps, Master, 1843–90; a fine watercolour made by Phelps 'on the spot in the summer'. Sidney bought the manor of Clee in 1616 with money bequeathed by Peter Blundell

drainer, and a founder of the Virginia Company. Popham may have been behind the benefaction of four of the six scholarships Blundell wanted established for 'the increase of good and godly preachers of the Gospel'. The two others in this £2,000 package went to Popham's old Oxford college, Balliol.

Two of the Sidney scholarships became fellowships for students in divinity, and all the appointments were to be paid for out of the income from the manor of Itterby, near Clee in Lincolnshire, which was purchased for £1,400 in 1616. This was a sparsely populated area of farming land, whose 20 or so tenants throughout the 17th century paid Sidney about £80 per annum on 21-year leases, around 10 per cent of College income from 1640.

Blundell's fellows were to act as tutors to Blundell's scholars and it was expected that some scholars would become fellows. After seven years both fellows and scholars had to apply themselves to the study of divinity and go into orders as soon as 'by law they may'. Blundell, after bequeathing money to his nephews, left cash disbursements of £32,000 plus a further £8,000 to various individuals and institutions, a sum that dwarfs that bequeathed by Lady Frances. He was commemorated each year on St Peter's Day with a sermon in the Sidney chapel for which the fellow delivering it was to be paid 10 shillings. On the same day 40 shillings was to be allowed for 'exceeding through the Hall'.

Interior of Blundell's School, Tiverton, c1840, lithograph by B Rudge of Bedford

A view from the lower school showing the partition and the upper school beyond. Up to 200 boys were taught at a time in these two rooms

Some Early Benefactors

In 1602, Leonard Smith, a citizen of London and member of the Fishmongers' Company, left £120 for a 'Mr Smith's Fellowship', and in 1604 a scholarship was endowed out of his will with a preference for a pupil of Holt School in North Norfolk. The fellow, to be elected by the Fishmongers, was to be priested within three years or face expulsion.

In 1603 Sir John Hart, a former Mayor of London, left £30 to the College library; £600 to purchase an estate of £42 per annum; £20 for maintaining the master, a Greek lecturer and two fellows; and £4 each for four poor scholars, preferably from Coxwold School in North Yorkshire. This was enhanced in 1618 by a gift of £200 from his son-in-law, Sir George Bolles (1599).

In 1607, John Freestone of Altofts in West Yorkshire, who had founded a grammar school in nearby Normanton in 1592, left an 80-acre estate of £25 per annum at Stamford in Lincolnshire to Emmanuel to provide for fellowships, scholarships and general funds. Emmanuel, a wealthy College, refused the legacy on the grounds that it was insufficient; and Sidney, still short of funds and therefore its full complement of fellows, applied for it successfully.

OPPOSITE: The Master's Lodge and Cloister Court today

CHAPTER 2

'May Heaven Guard This Realm' 1596–1609

…And I have also read somewhere…that the statutes are many of them bad, and must be altered, but where there is no knowledge, there should be no opinion.

—George Dyer, *A History of the University of Cambridge*, 1814

COLLEGES ARE A form of legal corporation and require both the sanction of the monarch and law, and appropriate restrictions on their activities. Sidney's original statutes, in force with little change until 1860, were lengthy, exhaustive and officious. Framed by the executors, they were based mainly on Emmanuel's statutes of a decade earlier. In spite of their often tedious academic Latin prose, they give us wonderful insights into the early years of Sidney's collegiate life.

Sidney's primary mission was to train godly ministers in word and sacrament for the Church of England. In the evocative imagery of the statutes' opening paragraphs, the best seeds are watered with the streams of learning and transplanted to the church, which is nourished by such fruit. Continuing the horticultural metaphor, the statutes demand that the College be not too narrow or enclosed a plot but a spacious meadow where young men, like bees, can gather pollen from many kinds of flower. From their Sidney hive these bees will fly to the church and feed it with their honey. Those drones who fail to conform to the rules of the hive will be bitten and stung and driven forth.

The head of the College was the master. In 1598, when the statutes were given to the College, this was the 30-year-old James Montagu. The master was to be an Englishman, at least a Master of Arts, in holy orders, and must abhor and detest

OPPOSITE: *A view of the north side of Hall Court from the Cloister Court lawn, showing an expanse of the original Elizabethan brickwork*

'popery and all heresies, superstitions and errors'. His role is described as disciplinary and financial. Though strict and possessed of considerable power, the master was to encourage good behaviour and diligent work by rewards and kindness. He was to be given a handsome set of chambers in the Lodge, an annual stipend of £20, two shillings a week for his 'commons' (meals), and 26 shillings and eight pence per annum to pay his domestic staff. In addition he was to have a large garden, a pigeon house, and the produce of all the College grounds, excluding that of the Fellows' Garden. The rules for the election of a new master were intricate in defining eligibility and process, and include the stipulation that the fellows, scholars and pensioners should meet at 5 a.m. in the chapel on the day of election.

Of course, Sidney's first fellows were from other colleges, especially Emmanuel, Christ's, Trinity, and St John's. Subsequent fellows were to be Englishmen, with a Bachelor or Master of Arts degree, and chosen from the College scholars, with a preference given to poorer students and those from the counties of Rutland and Kent. This reflected the foundress's and Harington's local affiliations. In the case of Rutland men, further preference was to be given to pupils of Robert Johnson's great Protestant grammar school foundations at Uppingham and Oakham. If no such men could be found, others might be considered, but if the master or any fellow proposed a wealthy man they were to be fined half a year's dividend of the College income.

Fellows had to have studied for six years in the University of Cambridge, be well versed in Hebrew, Greek and Latin, and understand the scholastic principles of rhetoric, dialectic and physics. Importantly, they should profess pure religion without any taint of popery or other heresy. The election process was conducted by two fellows over three days of examination, including a theological examination by the dean on the last day. The successful candidates were to study philosophy and to take part in weekly theological disputations, taking it in turns to act as a respondent to two opponents. They were to be in holy orders within three years, on pain of expulsion from the 'hive'. All fellows had to proceed to the Bachelor of Divinity degree and to vacate their positions seven years after becoming eligible for the DD degree.

Fellows were expected to set an example to the students and so were forbidden from frequenting taverns, bearing arms, or staying out after 9 or 10 p.m., depending on the time of year. They were to give way to their seniors both in and out of College. They were not permitted to keep dogs, hawks, or play at dice or cards. The annual stipend was 20 shillings, with two extra shillings for commons and 20 shillings for clothing. Upon the acquisition of a property or

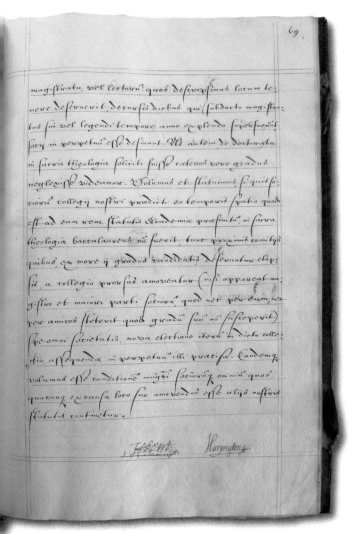

A page from the College Statutes, with the signatures of Henry Grey, Earl of Kent and Sir John Harington

benefice above £20, a fellow had to vacate his position. Fellows were allowed 30 *dies lusorios* or 'play days' each year, with the master's permission.

Each year a dean, or catechist, was elected to support the master in his disciplinary duties. His work, for which he received 43 shillings and four pence, included reading the statutes aloud each year, approving absences, and punishing unpunctuality. Fines for fellows ranged from one halfpenny for 'tardiness' at chapel, to six shillings and eight pence for neglect of his course of College 'disputations'. Students might also incur fines for lateness and neglect of work, and the youngest could be punished in the Hall like schoolboys, *virga corrigatur*, that is, with the rod. More importantly, during term the dean was to preside at a theological disputation in the Chapel each Friday between 4 p.m. and 6 p.m. On Sunday at 3 p.m., he was to expound for one hour on some article of the Christian faith. He was also required to examine the progress of undergraduates and oversee the work of College servants.

The master's financial duties were supported by a keeper of the chest. The main chest carried all the College's money and was kept in the treasury in the Lodge, along with other chests containing College belongings. Each chest had three keys with copies kept by the master, senior fellow and the keeper. The College seal was kept separately in a little chest for which only the master had keys. Audits were held in the Michaelmas and Easter terms, when the master gave the fellows a full account of all expenditure and income as well as displaying the College treasure and other muniments.

Nearer to the life of the Hall and kitchen, the steward was to take monthly payments for commons at a price to be set by the master. After each Saturday supper in Hall the steward, or manciple, gave a weekly account of the victuals at an audit to be attended by all fellows on pain of a two pence fine.

The College tutors, who were not necessarily fellows, were to take responsibility for the conduct and work of a number of pupils determined by the master. Two or more pupils were to sleep in a tutor's room, probably in low-wheeled truckle beds in the corners, while small areas were created as studies. The tutors were the most important figures in an undergraduate's life. As well as teaching them, they had to ensure students did not go into town for anything other than lectures without permission and that they returned within permitted hours. They were thus intimate moral as well as spiritual and intellectual mentors, acting *in loco parentis*.

The head lector's duty was to listen to at least one of the daily lectures given in the Hall after morning chapel by the sub-lectors, who had to be fellows or otherwise suitably qualified; he was paid 13 shillings and four pence a quarter. He lectured occasionally on Aristotle, Plato or Cicero, and also supervised all disputations and exercises. The head lector also examined the students as necessary in subjects and by methods chosen by the master, and administered punishments for tardiness in the form of fines or beatings. If these measures did not work, the lector was to bring the offender before the master and fellows for further admonishment and possible expulsion.

There was a hierarchy of students dominated by two distinct social and educational types – on the one hand were the scholars, and on the other fellow-commoners.

Scholars were to be elected from among applicants defined as '*pauperiores, probiores, aptiores*' (the poorer, more virtuous, more suitable) who intended to study theology and to take holy orders. As with fellows, preference would be given to boys from Rutland and Kent, chosen by the master and his colleagues; they were awarded a weekly food allowance of 12 pence and an annual clothes allowance of 14 shillings and 8 pence. The successful candidates, as well as working extremely hard for many hours each day, had to read the scriptures during meals in Hall. In groups of about six, they would take an oath of obedience and wait at high table. Their own plain meals consisted of a pewter mug of beer and a piece of bread, after chapel at about 6 a.m., at lunch at 10 a.m. and at supper at 5 p.m.

The other 'top' students were the sons of nobles and the upper gentry, known as fellow-commoners (Cromwell was one). They were most likely to spend only a year or two at Sidney, gaining some general education and the correct religious beliefs. They were allowed to sit with the fellows in the Hall and share their 'commons', hence their title. The statutes express the greatest concern that such young men, who were often older than most of their contemporaries, should be of unblemished character and sworn to behaviour compatible with that of the sober and studious fellows and scholars, both in and out of College. Typically, however, their behaviour, dress and attitudes left much to be desired, though they were important in helping

Elizabethan panelling from the old Hall, now in the Sidney accountant's office

the College balance its books; like pensioners, who ranked lower socially, fellow-commoners paid for their time at Sidney. Two shillings per quarter was the fee during the first decade following the College's foundation. Sidney's institutional attitude to its wealthy members probably matched that expressed in the university statutes of 1595, which prohibited the wearing of 'any long or curled locks, great Ruffes, velvet Pantables, velvet Breeches, coloured nether Stockes, or any other coloured apparell'.

At the bottom of the social pile came the sizars (probably from 'sizings' or portions of food), boys from humble or impoverished backgrounds who could pay their way through university by acting as servants to fellows and fellow-commoners. They were often from very similar backgrounds to scholars but had not won the financial support of a scholarship. Many of Sidney's most distinguished early members came to the College as sizars.

All students had to attend public prayers in the Chapel and as many university sermons as possible. Failure to do either resulted in admonishment by the master in the presence of the dean. This could mean being 'put out of commons', which for a poor student would mean considerable deprivation and even starvation. Repeated tardiness could lead to fines, birching or expulsion. Other punishable offences included gossiping, assembling in chambers to play, gamble or waste time, and playing football in the courts. The fellows were to keep a constant eye out for misdemeanours and report malfeasance to the dean or master.

In short, life for most undergraduates was harsh, strict and under constant surveillance. The university statutes of 1595 prohibited the 'hurtfull and unscolerlike exercise of Football and meetings tending to that end', except in colleges and among students of the same college. Some of the stricter colleges, such as Sidney seems to have been, did not even allow that. Naturally there was to be no 'Bull-bayting, Bear-baytings, Common bowling places, Nine-hoals, or such like unlawfull games'.

'Woe to Drunkards': the First Fellows

> In Barnwell, near to Cambridge, one at the sign of the plough, a lusty young man, with two of his neighbours, and one woman in their company, agreed to drink a barrel of strong beer. They drunk up the vessel. Three of them died within four and twenty hours, the fourth hardly escaped after great sickness. This I have under a justice of peace's hand, near dwelling, besides the common fame.
> —Samuel Ward of Ipswich, *Woe to Drunkards: A Sermon*, 1622

In 1596 Montagu, Harington and Kent nominated a number of foundation fellows. All of them had to wait two years before they could come into residence in 1598, when the building was sufficiently complete to offer them accommodation and students to instruct. Many of them were men of outstanding intellectual ability and went on to achieve major reputations as theologians, scholars and churchmen. While Sidney's fellowship changed in size and character over the first 50 years, these early fellows gave the College its enduring reputation as a 'nursery of Puritanism'.

'The Rigidest Sort': William Bradshaw

William Bradshaw, from the Puritan heartlands of Leicestershire, was a 25-year-old former scholar of Emmanuel who had been supported as a student by Sir Edward Hastings, a relation and rival of the Haringtons in Midlands politics. Through the influence of the master of Emmanuel, Laurence Chaderton, a friend of James Montagu, Bradshaw was appointed to a fellowship at Sidney in 1596. While he waited for his chambers to become ready he acted as a tutor to the Governor of Guernsey's children. This was significant: Guernsey had established a Presbyterian system and was thus one of the most Puritan parts of the kingdom. 'Perchard a Garnseyman' arrived as a pensioner in 1600, testifying to the importance of this connection for the College. Jean Perchard was later a major figure in Guernsey Calvinism, notoriously having three women burnt for what he believed was the witchcraft behind his wife's death.

Bradshaw shared his chambers at Sidney with another major Puritan figure, his friend Thomas Gataker, and was soon ordained in the Church of England. At the request of various local gentlemen, Bradshaw became a popular itinerant preacher and lecturer at nearby villages such as Steeple Morden and Abington, thus adhering to the spirit of the statutes. As a fellow, Bradshaw published the radical essay *A Trial of Subscription* in 1599, which urged ministers to conform only to the strictures of their own consciences. Later the same year, the Bishop of London, Richard Bancroft, wrote to Montagu and the Vice-Chancellor to complain that Bradshaw had distributed a

'He Yet Speaketh'

Daniel Evance, son of a London mercer, entered Sidney as a pensioner in 1629. He was a celebrated and published preacher and became the rector of Calbourne on the Isle of Wight where he died in 1652, aged 39. His unusual brass memorial there, erected by his wife Hanna, has images of Time and Death, a quote from Hebrews 11: 4 blessing 'the just man's memory', and a two-stanza verse that ends with an anagram of his name, 'I CAN DEAL EVEN'.

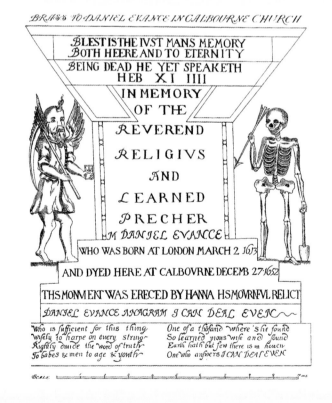

book by the controversial Nottinghamshire farmer, preacher and exorcist John Darrell. Darrell, who had first met Bradshaw in Leicestershire, had attacked Bancroft's chaplain following the latter's accusation that his immensely popular exorcisms were fraudulent. Darrell was imprisoned and Bradshaw left Cambridge for a few months to exercise his ministry in the countryside.

Bradshaw left Sidney in July 1601 and became a tutor to a godly Leicestershire family. He was also a preacher and writer, and his polemical works were published in secret by the Puritan publisher William Jones. The most famous work was the internationally influential *English Puritanisme: Containeing the Maine Opinions of the Rigidest Sort of those that are Called Puritanes* (1605). This attacked episcopacy and proposed the individual congregation as the basis for church government, though Bradshaw claimed, significantly, that this would strengthen the King's authority rather than diminish it. James Montagu, his former master, would hardly have agreed. Bradshaw, though loyal to the social hierarchy, led a furtive underground life until he married and settled as a preacher in Derbyshire, where he was highly regarded for his pastoral skills. The influence of his writings on New England congregationalism in particular was considerable.

William Bradshaw, English Puritanisme, 1605, title page. York Minster Library

'Lovely Gravity': Thomas Gataker

Thomas Gataker preached his friend Bradshaw's funeral sermon at Chelsea, where he had died while travelling in 1618. Before a packed congregation, he praised Bradshaw's 'studious, humble, and affectionate, liberal, upright' nature. Gataker himself was the son of a London vicar and joined Sidney's fellowship from St John's in 1596 at the age of 22. He was noted by his funeral orator Simeon Ashe for his 'lovely gravity'. While he waited for the building work to finish, he worked as a tutor for William Ayloffe of Essex, teaching him Hebrew and preparing his son for entry to Cambridge. After coming into residence at Sidney, Gataker, like his roommate Bradshaw, was part of the scheme initiated by former tutors at St John's to preach in neglected Cambridgeshire parishes.

It seems that soon after Bradshaw's departure following the Darrell episode, Gataker decided to leave Cambridge, again in the true spirit of the founding statutes. He returned to London where he developed a complex network of godly churchmen, lawyers and merchants and refused many offers of church and academic appointment. Montagu tried to entice him back to Sidney to take up a position as a Hebrew lecturer funded by Lord Harington; when he refused this, Montagu got him a lectureship at Lincoln's Inn instead. During the Interregnum, Gataker refused the mastership of Trinity offered to him by the then Chancellor, Sidney man Edward Montagu, 2nd Earl of Manchester. Gataker eventually became rector at Rotherhithe in Surrey.

His many religious works included an edition of *Balme from Gilead*, whose author was another Sidney fellow, Samuel Ward of Ipswich, as well as sermons and tracts of his own, satirical attacks on astrology, and the funeral sermon in 1626 of the Sidney fellow Richard Stock. His most famous theological work was *Of the Nature and Use of Lots* (1619), which defended gambling when not used for divination. Card-playing and dice were activities Sidney undergraduates were strictly forbidden to enjoy. The death of three wives, two children, imprisonment in the 1620s, and the rise of the High Church party sent Gataker into obscurity for 10 years. However, he continued to write and study, and his enduring legacy after his death in 1654 was his remarkable edition of the works of the Roman Emperor and stoic philosopher Marcus Aurelius. Stoicism was an important aspect of the intellectual climate of the times, not least for Sidney men on either side of the growing political and religious divide, as we shall see. Gataker was a member of the Westminster Assembly during the 1640s, along with a number of other Sidney men. His son Charles went up to Sidney as a pensioner in 1629 and became a tutor to Viscount Falkland, and later a conforming priest in London after the Restoration.

'This Giddiness': Samuel Ward of Ipswich

Samuel Ward, not to be confused with his namesake, the third Sidney master, was born in Haverhill, Suffolk, near the Essex border and close to Cambridge, the son of a local Puritan preacher whose tomb inscription refers to him as 'full of hot zeal, full of true love…a burning lampe, a shining light'. His widow married the great Puritan lecturer of nearby Wethersfield, Richard Rogers, whose *Seven Treatises* (1603) became the outstanding Puritan manual of practical divinity and the godly life for generations of devout men and women.

Ward entered St John's as a scholar in 1594 and joined the Sidney fellowship in 1599, staying until his marriage in 1604. Like Bradshaw and Gataker, he wasted little time in becoming ordained, and was a popular and inspirational preacher in the nearby countryside, particularly in his home town of Haverhill and along the Stour valley. Like Rogers, he ministered mainly to the poor, who were increasingly affected by the decline of the local cloth industry. His impact on his audiences was enormous and his sermon on the conversion of Zaccheus led to the conversion of the young Samuel Fairclough, later a famous East Anglian preacher. Ward heard his confession with 'great affection and tenderness' and his words to the boy on the gospel ensured a life-long convert. Ward was presumably equally influential on the consciences of many Sidney undergraduates.

In 1605 Ward became town preacher, on a salary far greater than he could receive at Sidney, in the exceptionally godly Ipswich, where he was enormously influential, both spiritually and politically. This was exactly what the founders had been after. Thomas Fuller later described his fellow Sidneian as 'having a care over and a love

from all the parishes in that populous place'. Ward took control of the local grammar school and was given funds to open a library for local preachers, and local knights, businessmen and preachers gave books and money to it. Ward's zealous Puritan attitudes can still be seen in the effacing of crosses and references to saints in the books.

Ward was a brilliant public performer and prose stylist, and an original visual artist and emblematist. All three talents got him into trouble with the authorities – particularly his celebrated patriotic 1621 engraving *The Double Deliverance*, published in Amsterdam. This so angered the Spanish ambassador in London, Count Gondomar, that Ward was imprisoned in the Fleet for a year. Probably drawn five years earlier, it is a remarkable image, popular enough to be used for commercially produced linen hangings. It shows the two great providential events in England's history: the defeat of the Armada in 1588, on the left, and the discovery of the Gunpowder Plot in 1605, on the right. Its offence to Gondomar resided in its depiction of the Catholic King of Spain in the tent in the centre conferring with the Pope (who was the anti-Christ to Ward and his audience) and his council, and being looked upon favourably by gargoyle-like devils. Guy Fawkes, shown on the right, accompanied by another devil carrying a papal bull, moves towards parliament in his fatal attempt to destroy Protestant England.

Ward was probably the most brilliant exemplar of the Sidney statutes' aim to get learned churchmen into the towns and countryside to produce good Protestants and patriotic Englishmen through preaching. He was loyal to church and crown, but also principled and brave, and a constant thorn in the side of the High Church reformers in the 1630s. His enemies included Archbishop Laud, who was told that Ward was behind the large numbers leaving England for America: 'Of the breeders of these persons Mr Ward is chief of those parts (who) has caused this giddiness'. A town in Massachusetts was named Samuel Ward during his lifetime, and attempts to remove him from office led to riots in Ipswich. His epitaph in St Mary-le-Tower, Ipswich, reads:

Watch Ward! Yet a little while
And He that shall come, will come.

Ward died a wealthy man, and two of his sons went to Sidney, Samuel in 1621 and Nathaniel in 1628. The former was a schizophrenic who murdered his brother-in-law in 1661; the latter a Cambridgeshire rector. Predestination conferred no favours even on the godliest families.

Samuel Ward of Ipswich (1577–1640), by an unknown artist, 1620. Ipswich Museums

*Ward's Sermons (1636) included a verse set between woodcuts of lighted beacons:
'Watch, WARD, and keepe thy Garments tight,
    For I come Thiefe-like at Midnight.
    All-seeing, never slumb'ring Lord;
Be thou my Watch, Ile be thy WARD'*

The Double Deliverance, 1621, engraving by Samuel Ward of Ipswich. British Museum

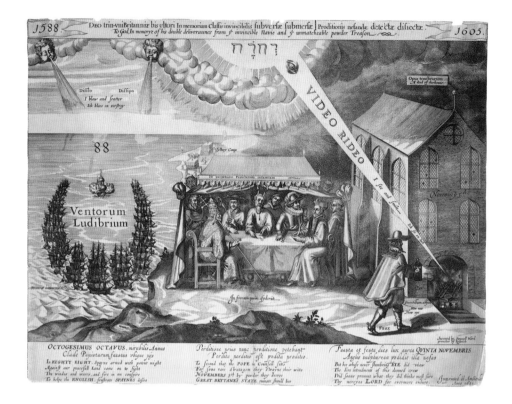

The Double Deliverance, 1621, engraving by Samuel Ward of Ipswich. British Museum

'Devilish Conspiracy': Gunpowder, Treason and Sidney

I am not yet recovered from the fever occasioned by these disturbances… was out five days in peril of death, in fear for the great charge I left at home…This poor lady hath not yet recovered the surprise, and is very ill and troubled… May Heaven guard this realm from all such future designs and keep us in peace and safety. —Lord Harington to his cousin, Sir John Harington of Kelston, 1605

Ward's engraving reminds us that Sidney was closely connected with the drama of the Gunpowder Plot in 1605. A central, if confused, aim of the plotters was to replace James I with his nine-year-old daughter Princess Elizabeth; this plan was thwarted when they failed to blow up the King and his parliament. Elizabeth was living at Combe Abbey under the care of her guardian, Lord Harington of Exton, the Sidney founder. On 7 November, Harington was forewarned of a bid to snatch the princess from his house, and with only two hours to spare he took her to Coventry, where she was placed under armed guard. He then set off to Holbeach, Warwickshire, in the company of Sir Fulke Greville, to besiege the mastermind behind the plot, Robert Catesby. In the ensuing fighting on 8 November, Catesby was killed. Harington wrote to his cousin, the writer Sir John Harington of Kelston, about the 'late devilish conspiracy' and asked for his vigilance against the designs of 'evil-minded Catholics' in his own county.

One of those in the Combe Abbey household removed to Coventry for safety along with the princess was Daniel Dyke, a Sidney MA and chaplain to the Haringtons and their royal ward. The following year he was made a fellow of Sidney and dedicated his sermon of thanksgiving on deliverance from the plot to Princess Elizabeth, of whose virtues he said he had been 'a daily eye-witness'.

James Montagu's brother, the Sidney benefactor Sir Edward Montagu of Boughton, then a Northamptonshire MP, was a staunch Puritan who supported many godly ministers and preachers in his county and their fight against drunkenness, clerical pluralism and avoidance of the sabbath. He is best known, however, for initiating the bill, passed in 1606, for a public thanksgiving on 5 November for the deliverance of the King and nation from the Gunpowder Plot. Sidney can thus claim to have played a part in the establishment of one of England's greatest annual festivals: Bonfire Night.

Sidney's archives carry other evidence of the College's close connection to this most providential of historical events: a book on logic belonging to one of the plotters, Everard Digby, and one from the library of the prominent Northamptonshire Catholic, Sir Thomas Tresham of Rushton, whose son Francis was almost certainly the conspirator who forewarned the authorities of the plot. The Treshams were no doubt among those Midlands Catholics Harington believed were jealous of his royal favour and behind an attempt to incite rebellion in the area and his own murder. Francis Tresham was personally investigated by the Attorney-General, Sir Edward Coke, a copy of whose work *La Sept Part des Reports* of 1608 is inscribed to James Montagu and also sits in the Muniment Room at Sidney.

The Sidney collection also includes a copy of the official account of the trial of Guy Fawkes and his co-conspirators and, drawn heavily from this source, the only known manuscript of a long Latin poem by the composer, lawyer and physician Thomas Campion, *De Pulverea Coniuratione* (On the Gunpowder Plot) (c1615), dedicated to King James. James Montagu, who was much involved in the discussions about the oath of allegiance and post-plot propaganda exercises, was probably the donor of the manuscript and perhaps even an inspiration or advisor to its production. The highly providential poem deals with all aspects of the plot, beginning in the underworld and ending at Combe Abbey with the plotters on their knees begging for pardon. It eulogises Lord Harington, under whose safe protection, in spite of 'brigands' wishes', Princess Elizabeth will blossom, and places the whole plot against an elaborate background of cosmic significance and divine intervention. The poem warns of a sad destiny for Harington:

Sed reducem sua tecta senem (sic astra minantur)
Haud vnquam excipient, nec cernet patria tellus,
Mors iter obsidio premet, affectusque seniles
(But his roof will never see this old man back again (this the stars do threaten), nor will his country see him again; death with slow siege and old age's decay will check his journey.)

John Milton, whose much-loved tutor at Christ's, Nathaniel Tovey, was a former Sidney sizar, is thought to have been influenced by Campion's poem when writing *Paradise Lost*. To add to the interest, Tovey's father John, a Coventry priest and schoolmaster, was a tutor to Sir John Harington's son, John, a Sidney undergraduate and the great friend of Prince Henry, at Combe Abbey. Nathaniel lived in the Harington household from 1602, and was therefore quite likely one of those who were rescued from the plotters on 7 November 1605. Nathaniel's education, after his father and the younger Sir John died following their trip to Europe, was entrusted to Lucy Harington, a major benefactress of the Sidney library.

'The Right Eye of the Prince of Wales': Sir John Harington the Younger

Ever since King James had been entertained by Sir John on his progress to London in 1603, the Haringtons had become favourites of the royal family. The younger John Harington became one of the aristocratic companions of Henry, Prince of Wales when he was 11 and Henry was nine. They quickly became inseparable friends, and something of this is evident in the remarkable portrait of the pair by Robert Peake, now in the Metropolitan Museum of Art in New York. The setting is probably Harington's father's estate at Burley-on-the-Hill in Rutland, and the prince is shown sheathing his sword after giving the *coup de grâce* to a stag following a hunt. Harington obediently holds the stag's antlers, while the prince's horse, groom and dog are shown in the background. Both boys are dressed in fashionable hunting costumes resembling contemporary suits of armour, and Henry wears the jewel of the Order of the Garter. Harington's coat of arms hangs above his head on the tree, while that of England hangs above Henry.

While Henry was an obsessive sportsman and horse-fancier, as this image suggests, he was also a great patron of arts and learning, and a militant Protestant with a passion for all military matters. Concerns about his mother's crypto-Catholicism and the general uncertainty about religious matters at the time meant that those close to King James were keen to make Henry a distinctly Protestant prince. John Harington was thus groomed to be not only a loyal companion but also a learned advisor in all spiritual and intellectual matters.

With this role as a royal mentor in mind, he was sent to Sidney Sussex in 1607 as a fellow-commoner, where he spent a year learning orthodox Anglican doctrine and enhancing his already considerable general knowledge and cultural range. There his immediate or close contemporaries included Henry, Earl of Huntingdon's brother Edward Hastings, who died on Raleigh's fateful last voyage to Guiana in 1617; Richard Dugard, later a famous tutor at Sidney; and a number of great future Puritan churchmen and sermonisers, such as Daniel Cawdrey, Henry Root, John Denne and Samuel Buggs. There were about 20 students admitted in Harington's year, two-thirds of whom were reasonably wealthy fee-paying pensioners, with a few scholars and sizars, such as Denne, and one other fellow-commoner, the obscure William Westlid from Lincolnshire. The fellows responsible for Harington's education

Henry, Prince of Wales and Sir John Harington the Younger, by Robert Peake the Elder, 1603.
Metropolitan Museum of Art, New York

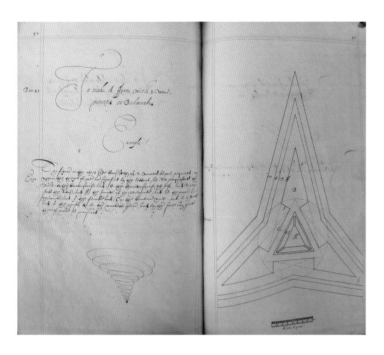

Instructions on making a fort with three bulwarks, from A Mathematicall Discourse *by John Waymouth, presented to Sir John Harington the Younger c1610*

included, on the one hand, the family tutor and Puritan preacher Daniel Dyke and, on the other, John Pocklington, who became a chaplain to Charles 1 and a well-known anti-Puritan controversialist.

Throughout his short life, Harington's highly devout day began at 4 or 5 a.m. with meditation, prayer, reading from the Bible, and a theological work such as Calvin's *Institutes*. He then spent about four hours studying, followed by conversation with friends, and riding. After lunch he retired to meditate on a sermon he had recently heard, and then continued his studies in history, warfare, mathematics and navigation. The many Harington books bequeathed to Sidney and now in the Muniment Room include Harington's manuscript copy of *A Mathematicall Discourse*, specially written for him by the shadowy scholar John Waymouth. After supper, he prayed with his servants and then withdrew to write his diary, confessing his sins and temptations. His worst failings were written in a code only he and God could decipher. Just before sleep, to guard against evil dreams and fantasies, a servant read to him from the Bible.

In the summer of 1608, Harington and his tutor John Tovey, the former Coventry schoolmaster, left England with a 10-strong entourage on an 18-month grand tour of Europe. Instructed by Henry to send back reports on all matters, especially political and military ones, he visited Brussels, where he met Archduke Albert, and attended lectures at the Protestant University of Heidelberg. He arrived in Florence just after Grand Duke Cosimo de' Medici's wedding, and then headed towards Rome on the invitation of the Catholic exile Sir Anthony Standen. Fearing the Inquisition would arrest the Puritan Tovey, however, the party went instead to Venice. The English ambassador Sir Henry Wotton recommended him to the anti-papal Doge, claiming that he 'will one day govern the kingdom'. Harington stayed for six months, studying the republican form of government, and claiming the local religion to be pure and without popish 'intermixture'.

Harington returned home via Vienna and Prague, sending regular reports to Henry, Prince of Wales about the increasingly tense European political scene and the varieties of modern fortification to be seen. On his return, at the age of only 17, he became the MP for Coventry and spent much time and money in charitable work in the local community. The early Sidney foundation fellow Richard Stock, a severe anti-Catholic preacher and friend of Thomas Gataker, wrote in his funeral sermon for Harington that immediately after the youth returned to England, 'by way of thankfulness to God, he gave yearly, by the hand of a private friend, twenty pounds to the poor. And the second sabbath after his landing in England, (having spent the day before with his tutor Mr Tovey in prayer, fasting and thanksgiving) he heard the Word, received the sacrament, and gave to the poor of that parish five pounds…Yea, such were his bowels of tender mercy, that he gave a tenth part of his yearly allowance, which was a thousand pounds, to pious and charitable uses.'

'The Pattern of Virtue': Bertie's Boys

Aside from the socially elevated Harington junior, what became of the others who went to Sidney in the College's first decade? Sidney attracted the sons of the nobility and gentry, particularly those from the approved families, regions and religious persuasion. In many cases there were tight patterns of inter-relations between such families, which carried over through a number of generations. Their paths continued to cross long after they left Sidney.

Fellow-commoners, we have seen, were given dining rights alongside the fellows, and were likely to stay about a year before going on the grand tour, to the law courts, the court, or back to their family estates. The first name in the Sidney register in September 1598 was 'Mr Edward Harrington', a fellow-commoner and eldest son of Sir James Harington, first Baronet of Ridlington, Rutland, the elder Sir John's brother. His grandfather had married Lady Frances Sidney's sister Lucy, and his brother Henry went up to Sidney in autumn 1599. Another early student was the Londoner Daniel Tuvill who went on to become an influential preacher and moral essayist.

Other prominent East Midlands families of the time who saw Sidney as the right choice for their sons included the Bodendines (or Bodenhams) of Ryhall, Rutland; the Bolles of Scampton, Lincolnshire; the Hastings of Ashby de-la-Zouch, Leicestershire; the Noels of Brooke, Rutland; the Wilmers of Sywell, Northamptonshire; the Wingfields of Kimbolton, Huntingdonshire; and the Wrays of Glentworth, Lincolnshire. The Gorings of Sussex were an exception to this strong regional bias. Many of these young men became prominent political figures and were involved in the Civil War of the 1640s, often on opposite sides. Typically, their fathers were major landowners and local MPs, JPs, sheriffs and lieutenants, with a pronounced Puritan inclination.

These Sidney families were often linked to the Haringtons or Montagus as well as to one another, though on occasion we also find them political rivals. The Noels, for instance, were in bitter dispute with the Haringtons for many years from 1601 over their respective powers in Rutland. Edward Noel 2nd Viscount Campden, from Ridlington, died in Oxford while supporting the King in 1643, went up in 1598 with his cousin Edward Harington. The Noels bought Exton from the Haringtons after their financial collapse. William Wilmer, like Noel, suffered as a loyal royalist in the Civil War; yet the fiercely parliamentarian Sir Edward Wingfield fought Catholics in Ireland and witches in Huntingdonshire in the early 1640s. His three brothers went to Sidney in the first few years after the foundation, and most sent their sons to Sidney; one of these was Bodenham Wingfield (1632), whose name demonstrates the continuing connections between the families.

The Wrays, a considerable dynasty with Presbyterian sympathies, were closely tied to the Montagus of Boughton through marriage. The grandfather of Sidney's earliest Wrays was Sir Christopher, Speaker of the House of Commons, who sentenced many traitors in the 1570s and 1580s and who was one of the judges who passed sentence on Mary, Queen of Scots. His son's eldest boy, Sir John Wray (1600), was a major patron of Puritan ministers in Lincolnshire and hoped to 'unloose the long and deep

The Harington basin and ewer, silver-gilt, London, maker Sir Ralph Warren, 1606–07

This basin and ewer were given to Sidney when Sir John Harington, later 2nd Baron Harington of Exton, was admitted as a fellow-commoner in 1607. Both ewer and basin are decorated with rocaille ornament and sea creatures, which are based on engravings by Adrian Collaert. The only comparable surviving items of this quality are among the gifts of James I and Charles I to Tsar Mikhail Romanov, now in the Moscow Kremlin Armoury Museum.

Titulum ne horresce novantis,
Non rapit Imperium vis tua, sed recipit.
Ausonius de Severo.   will Marshall sculp

fangs of superstition and popery' in the county. During the Civil War he was a major figure in the Eastern Association. Wray's brother William (1602) 'died a lunatic' in 1630, according to the register, while another brother, Edward (also 1602), became a court favourite of James I and the Duke of Buckingham. Groom of the Bedchamber by 1619, Edward was honoured in 1620 by the dedication to him, as 'the pattern of virtue', of *Fantasies in Three Parts* by his Cambridge friend, the great court musician Orlando Gibbons.

Many early Sidney men were later loyal to the monarchy, even if their religion was Puritan in origin. The great courtier and diplomat George Goring, later Lord Goring, Earl of Norwich, arrived at Sidney as a fellow-commoner in Easter 1600, the son of a bankrupt Sussex squire, with great social ambitions. Like John Harington the younger, the young Goring became close to Prince Henry and Princess Elizabeth, driven in his case by family debt to ascend the courtly ladder. A cavalier by nature, he was loved by King James and his son Charles as 'chiefe and Master Fool', and went on to accompany Charles on the disastrous trip to Madrid to secure the Spanish Match in 1623. We shall see later that Sidney alumni were involved on either side of this episode. Goring survived the Civil War, and exile after it, to be buried at Westminster Abbey in 1663. This was shortly after a number of Sidney men, famously Cromwell, had been disinterred from their tombs there.

ABOVE LEFT: *Tomb of Edward Noel, 2nd Viscount Campden and his wife Juliana Hicks, by Joshua Marshall, Chipping Campden Church, Gloucestershire*

ABOVE RIGHT: *Charles Aleyn, The Historie of that Wise Prince, Henrie the Seventh 1638, frontispiece by William Marshall. Bodleian Library, Oxford*

Aleyn was tutor to the poet and translator Sir Edmund Sherburne (1616–1702), who wrote a prefatory poem for this work

One of these unfortunate corpses was that of Thomas May, who went to Sidney as a fellow-commoner in 1609, aged 13. Like Goring, he was from Sussex, from an iron-founding family of Mayfield who had powerful social pretensions and insecure finances. Rather than entering the church, he became a well-known playwright, poet and classical scholar and translator in London, his first comedies of the 1620s, such as *The Heir*, reflecting the widespread contemporary obsession with inheritance, found also in the works of Ben Jonson. It seems this may have been performed in Cambridge in 1622: it would have appealed greatly to undergraduates of the time. By contrast, May's Roman tragedies, such as *Cleopatra* (1626), show his deep involvement in the political culture of his times, and his translation of Lucan's great epic *The Pharsalia* (1627) was produced at a time when loyal Protestants were becoming concerned about King Charles I's political and religious affiliations. May, however, was a strong contender for Poet Laureate, a position he coveted, and throughout the 1630s his writing showed none of Lucan's republican sympathies. His verse narratives of that decade, such as *Henry II* and *Edward III*, were written at the King's command. They are close in style and emphasis to his friend Charles Aleyn's poetry of the period; Aleyn went to Sidney in 1617, the year after Cromwell. There is a certain nostalgia for Elizabethan heroic chivalry in the mould of Sir Philip Sidney in Aleyn's work, which makes it ambiguously both of its time and yet deeply old-fashioned.

May failed to become Laureate, that honour going to Sir William Davenant in 1637, though he dedicated his 'completion' of Lucan to the King in 1640. Like many Sidney men, May, after much heart-searching, sided with parliament in the Civil War; he was falsely suspected of having done so out of pique about the laureateship. He worked as a much-satirised propagandist for parliament and in 1647 published the first-ever account of the Civil Wars, *The History of the Parliament of England which began November the Third 1640*, following it in 1650 with a Latin version that continued the story up to the King's execution. Clarendon's more famous royalist *History of the Rebellion* (1702–04) was a direct response to May's book; Lord Chatham is not alone among historians in claiming that May's book was 'honester and more instructive than Clarendon's'. May's state funeral at Westminster in 1650 showed the great esteem in which he was held by the triumphant forces of his fellow Sidneians, Oliver Cromwell and Edward Montagu, Earl of Manchester. Marvell's satire, *Tom May's Death*, was strangely prescient in imagining that his body would one day be disinterred and thrown out of the Abbey.

In 1608, a year before May arrived at Sidney, the 14-year-old John Bramhall of Pontefract, Yorkshire, matriculated as a grammar school-educated scholar. His career makes a fascinating

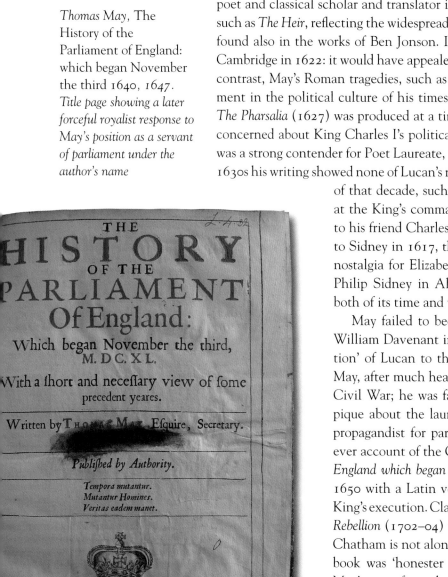

Thomas May, The History of the Parliament of England: which began November the third 1640, *1647. Title page showing a later forceful royalist response to May's position as a servant of parliament under the author's name*

THE
HISTORY
OF THE
PARLIAMENT
Of England:
Which began November the third,
M. DC. XL.
With a ſhort and neceſſary view of ſome
precedent yeares.

Written by THOMAS MAY, Eſquire, Secretary.

Publiſhed by Authority.

Tempora mutantur.
Mutantur Homines.
Veritas eadem manet.

Imprinted at *London* by *Moſes Bell,* for *George Thomaſon,*
at the Signe of the Roſe and Crown in St. *Pauls* Church Yard,
M. DC. XL. VII.

and poignant contrast with that of May. His Sidney contemporaries included a Wingfield and a Bodendine, George Goring's younger brothers Edward and Henry, as well as the future politician and anti-astrology writer John Melton and the city businessman, politician and creator of Cambridge's first Arabic lectureship, Sir Thomas Adams. His first biographer, Bishop Vesey of Limerick, assures his readers that, while at Sidney, Bramhall was a paragon, 'all his acts and exercises… performed with the easiness and smoothness that argues clean strength and sufficiency'. His great intellectual mentor was Samuel Ward, who became master in 1609, and Bramhall recalled: 'When I was a young student in theology, Dr Ward declared his mind unto me to this purpose, that it was impossible that the present controversies of the Church should be rightly determined or reconciled, without a deep insight into the doctrine of the Primitive Fathers, and a competent skill in school theology. The former affordeth a right pattern, and the second smootheth it over and planeth away the knots.'

John Bramhall, Archbishop of Armagh, by an unknown artist

Bramhall spent eight years at Sidney, overlapping with his future enemy Cromwell, before going on to a glittering, if tricky, career in the Church of England. He quickly established his reputation as a brilliant debater on behalf of the church against Catholicism at the time of the Spanish Match in 1623. Because of this, and because he was also a formidable administrator and politician, Bramhall was appointed to high position in Ireland in the 1630s, where he was plunged into that country's deep dangers and complexities with a brief to impose order. He was as great an enemy of Scottish Presbyterians as he was of native Catholics, and fought vigorously for the episcopalian position. An unrepentant loyalist, like his mentor Samuel Ward, Bramhall fled to Europe in 1644 with his new patron, the Marquess of Newcastle. He stayed abroad until the Restoration, when he was consecrated Archbishop of Armagh in great pomp at St Patrick's Cathedral, Dublin.

Bramhall, like May, was an intellectual engaged with the great political, philosophical and religious questions of his time, admired down to the 20th century by writers such as T S Eliot. He is best known today for his long-running argument with the philosopher Thomas Hobbes, also an exile, over the relationship between liberty and necessity. They had met at Newcastle's residence in Paris in 1645, and their initial discussion continued in pamphlet form for a decade. Bramhall was a libertarian Christian while Hobbes was a determinist, and the essentials of their disagreements established a debate that continues to this day. Starting on the wrong side politically, Bramhall ended up, unlike May, on the right side, his reputation underlined by Cromwell's remark about his fellow alumnus, that he 'would have given a good sum of money for the Irish Canterbury'.

CHAPTER 3

'Learning and Piety' 1609–1643

None thy quick sight, grave judgment can beguile,
So skilled in tongues, so sinewy in style;
Add to all these that peaceful soul of thine,
Meek, modest, which all brawlings doth decline.

—Thomas Goad, dedicatory verse in
Samuel Ward, *Gratia Discriminans*, 1626

JAMES MONTAGU'S NICKNAME, 'Bertie', as he was called by his friends and by King James, suggests something of the worldly ease of the man. He was the intimate friend and spiritual mentor of the great Bess of Hardwick in her old age, who left him £20 in her will; the shrewd flatterer of King James; and later Bishop of Winchester. Bertie's successor, after the brief mastership of the short-lived Francis Aldrich, was a very different man with an altogether different destiny.

Samuel Ward's career as master of Sidney from 1610 to 1643 witnessed an even more extraordinary epoch in English history than that experienced by Lady Frances. This was especially true of the final decade, which ended in the outbreak of the English Civil War. Ward was intimately involved in the intellectual, academic and religious controversies of his time, from his work as a translator of the 1611 Bible, and his attendance as a representative at the Synod of Dort in 1618, to the Cambridge resistance to the Laudian High Church reforms of the 1630s. But, as his voluminous correspondence demonstrates, he was deeply affected by the increasingly tense political situation and was finally to suffer from it at the hands of former students. The Spanish Match, the Palatinate Wars, the disputes over ship money, and the outbreak of war in 1642 were all events and episodes that had a direct bearing on the life of the College.

OPPOSITE: *Samuel Ward, by Valentine Ritz, 1721 (copy of a lost original, last recorded 1813)*

'Novelties both in Rites and Doctrines': Conflict in Stuart Cambridge

When Ward complained in 1634 of 'novelties both in Rites and Doctrines' he was referring to the new master of Corpus but hinting at the growing religious disputes in Cambridge. Indeed, Cambridge during Ward's mastership was no less turbulent than it had been in the late-16th century. The university's powers were increased and from 1604 it had the right to return members to parliament, which exacerbated its already difficult relations with the town over matters of precedence. Both King James and later his son Charles had a real interest in learning and theology, but their generosity to the university in some areas came at a cost. Legislation required conformity to the Prayer Book, the compulsory wearing of surplices and an oath of allegiance to the monarchy through the so-called 'Three Articles'. While Bertie Montagu encouraged conformity, Samuel Ward found such acquiescence far more difficult. In 1604 Ward, still an Emmanuel fellow, noted that 'Dr Montagu hath also appointed' the surplice 'to be worn in Sidn. College. Now what remaineth but that we (unless we will be singular) should take it up.' A few months later, Ward, following the great Puritan disappointment when the Hampton Court Conference failed to settle religious matters in their favour, was still unhappy about the surplice and wrote: 'Alas! We little expected that King James would have been the first permitter of it, to be brought into our College...' Yet Cambridge was politically loyal to the crown throughout the period, even though it might offer sulky liturgical disobedience; as the House of Commons became less convinced of the divine right of kings, so the university was in its eyes an object of great suspicion.

King James's official visits to Cambridge in 1615 and 1624 were the occasion of great feasting and entertainment, and were a high point in relations between royalty and the university. The fawning sentiments of verses written by members of all colleges on such occasions (and also at royal marriages and funerals) are often almost painful to read today. Some events had special meaning for Sidney, home of loyal Protestantism. At the early death of Henry, Prince of Wales in 1612, Samuel Ward and the Scotsman John Young, Cromwell's tutor Richard Howlett, and Richard Danford, wrote Latin verses expressing their genuine distress. Students also wrote such verses; ironically, Tom May, coming to the end of his undergraduate career at 'Sid. Coll.', offered the following in conclusion to a three-stanza poem:

> Thy shining vertues made the earth admire thee,
> And rare perfections made the heavens desire thee;
> Else could we not have seene so sad an houre,
> The hopes of England cropt in fairest floure.
> Nor had too early mourning, reav'd our Rest,
> But thou thy kingdoms, we had thee possest.

With the accession of Charles I in 1625, the poetry continued but the rumblings began, and the divisions widened. As we shall see, Archbishop Laud's Arminianism and ritualism invoked fears of popery and the weakening of the strict Calvinist theology to which Ward and his colleagues held fast. Laudian opponents, such as William Beale of Jesus, Richard Montague of King's, and John Cosin of Peterhouse, began to assert royally sanctioned influence in the university. Two antagonistic parties began to form. The royal favourite Buckingham's election as Chancellor in 1626 incensed the Commons and the Cambridge Puritans. When Charles dissolved parliament in 1629, it was the last time for a decade that MPs were able to engage directly with university affairs; the next occasion, however, would be explosive.

During the 1630s the assaults on those religious traditions dear to Samuel Ward led many Cambridge men to leave the university to go underground as rural preachers, or even to settle in America. Against this background of exile and collegiate tension, the university suffered from an unprecedented level of royal interference

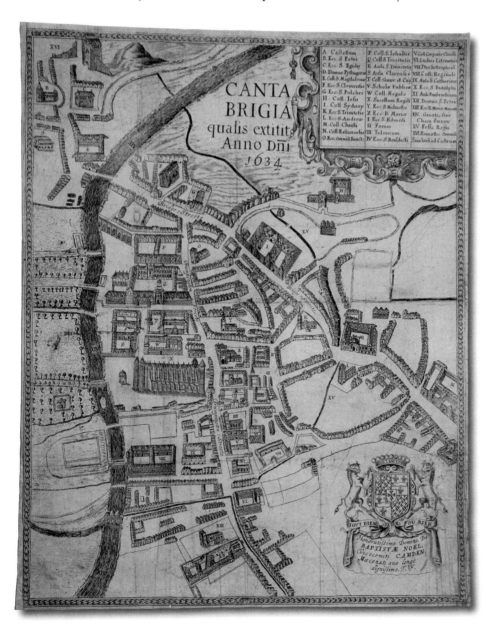

Map of Cambridge, 1634.
Private collection

This map was dedicated to Baptist Noel, later 3rd Viscount Campden, by the Sidney fellow Thomas Fuller, who used it in his History of the University of Cambridge (1655). It is based on a 1574 map by Richard Lyne and inserts a larger-than-life image of Sidney in the space originally occupied by the empty Grey Friars site. The fiercely royalist Baptist, who succeeded his father Edward (1600) as Viscount in 1643, took his MA at Sidney in 1628, the year before his friend Fuller entered the College as a fellow-commoner. Fuller was elected fellow in 1631 during the chancellorship of Henry Rich, Earl of Holland. Critics of the ecclesiastical changes were harassed and arrested, and in 1634 Ward complained to his great friend Archbishop James Ussher, that 'new heads are brought in, and they are backed in maintaining novelties, and them which broach new opinions…'

William Laud became Archbishop of Canterbury in 1633. By 1636 he had royal approval to make a formal visitation to Cambridge, and although this never happened, his intentions were clear to Ward and his allies. Laud wished to reform what he saw as Puritan abuses in respect of public prayers, the disuse of clerical habits, and the neglect of fast days. Sidney's unconsecrated Chapel had for some time been a source of displeasure, with its wrongly placed communion table and individual liturgy. By 1640 the atmosphere in Cambridge was highly volatile and Archbishop Ussher was advising his now fast-ageing friend Ward to put his papers in order.

'Thus Sin I Daily': the Young Samuel Ward

14 June 1595 My negligence in not calling God before I went to the chapel, and the little desire I had there to call on God, and my drowsiness in God's service. My sins even through the whole day, being Sunday: (1) my negligence aforesaid, (2) my hearing of the sermon without that sense which I should have had, (2) [*sic*] in not praying God to bless it to me afterward, (3) in not talking of good things at dinner being the posteriorums day, (4) in the immoderate use of God's creatures, (5) in sleeping immediately after dinner, (6) in not preparing me to sermon til it tolled, (7) in sluggish hearing of God's word, and that for my great dinner, (8) in hearing another sermon sluggishly, (9) in returning home and omitting our repetition of sermons, by reason that my countryman Eubank was with me, (11) [*sic*] in not exhorting him to any good thing, (12) in not going to evening prayers, (13) in supplying liberally, never remembering our poor brethren, (14) in not taking order to give the poor women somewhat at 7 o'clock, (15) my dullness in stirring of my brother to Christian meditations, (16) my want of affections in hearing the sermons repeated, (17) my sluggishness in prayer, and thus sin I daily against thee, O Lord. —Samuel Ward's diary

Samuel Ward wrote to Archbishop Laud in 1640: 'My life and all that know me, can testify for me, that I have studied peace, and have withstood any disturbance in the Church, to my most ability.' Half a century earlier, in the 1590s, as a young pensioner at Christ's, and then as a fellow at Emmanuel, Ward was a zealous Puritan who might have been expected to relish disturbing the church. His diary of 1592–1601, the years during which his future College came into being, offers us a unique insight into the mind of a 'forward Protestant' of the late-Elizabethan period. One of the most famous entries, quoted above, has helped to define modern ideas of the earnest Puritan conscience.

As if such dreadful sins were not enough, Ward elsewhere cites 'adulterous thoughts', his 'wandering mynd on herbals at prayer time', and his 'glutony the night before' as instances of his utterly fallen nature. In particular his greediness appalled him: he ate too much cheese and too many pears and raisins, and above all was disgraceful with plums: 'My longing after damsens. When I made the vow

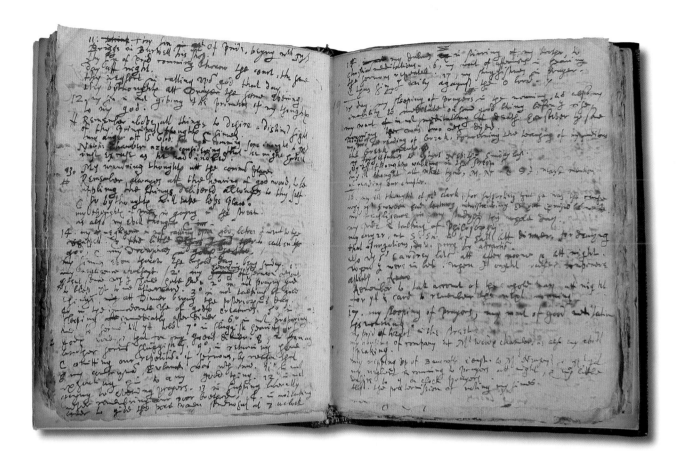

not to eat in the orchard.' Ward also thought he loved wine, beer and laughing too much. He lusted after women and had titillating dreams about 'the grievous sinnes in T[rinity] Colledg, which had a woman which was [?carried] from chamber in the night tyme'.

The diary tells us about much more than these sinful ways, when 'my mind was altogether of my body'. It tells us about the lectures and sermons he attended and from which he took copious notes, about the books he read, and about the daily chores he performed. There are also long prayers he composed for his own salvation. His self-castigation was part of a spiritual training undertaken by many young men at Cambridge during the period. He reveals an engaging personality: he is full of doubt and extremely serious about his education and faith; but he laughs and jokes, is impatient, quick-tempered, and inclined to oversleep. He prefers bowls and tennis to worship much of the time, and is prone to prideful thoughts about his abilities.

Ward's great mentors were the charismatic Puritan dons William Perkins of Christ's and Laurence Chaderton, master of Emmanuel. Perkins' portrait in Sidney's collection of paintings can be explained by this hero-worship. Ward thanked God that he 'came to this college [Christ's], and that in Mr Perkins' time', and was honoured to be asked by the great man to publish one of his major sermons after his death.

As an undergraduate at Christ's, Ward had known James Montagu, who had generously supported him when he was hard up. With Montagu, he had been appointed

Franciscan friars, one of a series of members of religious orders illustrating Psalm 95 from a Psalter, Oxford, c1330. This manuscript was acquired before 1697. Virtually all the faces in the manuscript were defaced by a Protestant iconoclast

one of the translators of the Authorised Version of the Bible in 1604. Ward was a strong candidate for the Sidney mastership when Montagu's short-lived successor Francis Aldrich died at the end of 1609. In early December, six heads of colleges supported his application and Montagu, now Bishop of Bath and Wells, wrote from King James's household in Newmarket to add his endorsement. Ward's appointment was approved by Kent and Harington and he became master of Sidney Sussex on 9 January 1610, three days short of his 38th birthday.

When Montagu wrote to him in November recommending a 'Mr. Damport' (Richard Danford) for a fellowship, but informing him at the same time of the suicide of one of his fellows, John Stafford who 'hath made away with him selfe in his mother's house', Ward may have sensed the job was not always going to be an easy one.

'Obsequies': Death of a Dynasty

It would make a good crime novel or conspiracy theory: the end of the Haringtons came rapidly, suspiciously, and for Sidney Sussex and its new master, almost disastrously. At the time the rumours were, indeed, of deadly Catholic plots and poisonings; even today the sequence of deaths seems extraordinary. As we have noted, Henry, Prince of Wales died on 6 November 1612, unleashing mass national mourning for the loss of the brilliant Protestant white hope of Europe. Following the death of his cousin, the writer Sir John Harington of Kelston, on 20 November 1612, Sir John Harington, the first Lord Harington of Exton, guardian of the prince's sister Elizabeth, took the princess to Heidelberg to settle her there with her husband. He died at Worms on his return journey on 23 August 1613, aged 73. His son John, Sidney's 'glittering prize', succeeded Sir John as Lord Harington of Exton, acquiring his vast debts, only to die at his sister Lucy's house at Twickenham on 27 February 1614, aged 22. Lucy's great friend John Donne wrote a long poem, 'Obsequies to the Lord Harington', with the famous lines:

> Now I grow sure, that if a man would have
> Good company, his entry is a grave.

The former Sidney fellow Richard Stock, a noted anti-Catholic polemicist and ally of James Montagu, delivered a sermon at the younger Lord Harington's funeral that repeated the accusation of poisoning by Catholic agents made in respect of Prince Henry's death. He might also have mentioned that John Tovey, Harington's tutor and father of Nathaniel, who went up to Sidney in 1612, had died in 1614. For good measure, other Haringtons died during this very short period of two years, many of them still young: Sir James, first Baronet of Ridlington; Sir Henry and his son

William; another Sir John; and Lucy's sister Frances. The debts the family faced meant Exton and Burley-on-the-Hill were sold, bringing to an end the family's dominance over England's smallest county.

'Worthies of England': New Sidney Fellows

> He had a moiety of the most considerable Pupills, whom he bred in learning and piety, in the golden mean betwixt superstition and faction. He held a strict-hand over them so that none presumed on his lenity to offend, or were discouraged by his severity to amend. He was an excellent Grecian and generall Schollar; old, when young, such his gravity in behaviour; and young when old, such the quickness of his endowments. He bestowed on his Colledge an hundred pounds for some perpetuall use for the Master and Fellows; and ten pounds for the Library. —Thomas Fuller on Richard Dugard, *The Worthies of England*, 1662

When Henry Grey, Earl of Kent, died on 31 January 1615, at the age of 74, Sidney's founding fathers, and a whole Elizabethan generation, were now gone, and Ward was faced with taking Sidney into an uncertain future, financially, politically and religiously. His new independence had been confirmed in January 1611, when the executors had forfeited their rights over the appointments of masters, fellows and scholars; these were now the responsibility of the College. In 1612, however, the reality of this decision would have been brought home hard to Ward. The executors directed that because much more than the value of Lady Frances' estate had been spent (mainly by Harington) on the buildings, the College could no longer afford to commit to the 10 fellows stipulated in the original statutes. The number was reduced to seven, until further revenues were forthcoming. Ward would have been cheered by the increase in his stipend by £5 and 12 shillings a year, though he was still a poorly paid head of college compared with many in Cambridge. Harington's generous payment towards the cost of paving the Chapel floor with expensive Clipsham stone from Rutland, and Montagu's towards adding wainscotting to the upper part of it, were further welcome enhancements of the College's modest material condition.

There were to be human and institutional changes too. In 1614, Kent's last act as the surviving executor was to amend certain parts of the statutes: Scotsmen and Irishmen could officially be admitted as fellows; senior fellows could be absent for a longer period than previously; the manner of selecting scholars was to be the same as that for fellows; and, most significantly, the

Thomas Fuller, engraving by David Loggan, 1662, frontispiece to The History of the Worthies of England

Fuller came as a fellow-commoner to Sidney from Queens' to study theology under Samuel Ward. His first published work was dedicated to the three sons of the Sidney benefactor Edward Montagu, 1st Baron Boughton, in 1631

statute terminating the tenure of fellowships at seven years after attaining DD was repealed and they were made tenable for life.

The fellowship, as ever, changed over time, though certain faces would become familiar over decades rather than a few years. By now they were mainly drawn from

Lucy Harington, c1620, by an unknown artist, British School. Private collection

Lucy Harington, daughter of Sir John Harington, 1st Baron of Exton, and sister of the 2nd Baron, was one of the greatest patrons of the arts of her time. This remarkable portrait shows her aged nearly 40, in her study at Twickenham. Her pose, with finger pointing to her forehead, indicates an intellectual and melancholy frame of mind. Lucy and her mother bequeathed a remarkable collection of about 180 books to Sidney around 1616. They had been collected mainly by her brother, who had been a Sidney student a decade earlier

the ranks of Sidney undergraduates. In 1610, Cromwell's tutor Richard Howlett was elected into a fellowship, along with Richard Danford, Richard Daggett and Thomas Mascall. In 1611, Richard Garbutt joined the society, as did Paul Micklethwaite. In 1612, Richard Dugard was elected, followed in 1614 by Samuel Buggs and John Denne.

With the exception of Micklethwaite, these are not figures to be found in the *Dictionary of National Biography*, nor even in catalogues of eminent publications, yet their importance to Sidney was often considerable. Howlett and Dugard were typical of the learned and godly men who attracted the sons of the gentry and Protestant aspiring classes. Their intellectual and spiritual strengths were matched by pastoral skills that reassured parents sending their boys, as young as 13 or 14, to Cambridge.

Thomas Fuller's tribute to Richard Dugard as one of his 'Worthies of England' perfectly summarises the desired characteristics of a great tutor. Dugard, from a Huguenot family that had settled in the Midlands, had gone to Sidney in 1606 as a lowly sizar. Later a close friend of Milton, by 1620 he was a highly influential tutor. Dugard's last years were spent as a rector at Fulletby in the Lincolnshire Wolds, in succession to an earlier Sidney fellow, Thomas Pell, and he was buried there in 1653.

Sidney can lay claim to being the first college in Cambridge to award a Scotsman a degree. John Young's Sidney credentials were impeccable. He was the son of King James's former tutor, and after taking an MA at St Andrews, was elected as a fellow in 1606, well before the change to the statutes made by Henry Grey. Like his new employer and patron James Montagu, Young had excellent court connections and became a royal chaplain. Montagu appointed him chancellor of Wells Cathedral and then dean at Winchester. Young was an important intermediary between Samuel Ward and King James during the Synod of Dort in 1618, an event we shall turn to later. He was ejected from his position at Winchester in the Civil War, and like many churchmen retired into obscurity before he died in 1654.

Paul Micklethwaite, who had migrated from Caius to become a Smith's Fellow, quickly became a leading figure in the church as a prominent preacher in Cambridge and London. His lectures at the Temple led to his appointment by King Charles as master there in 1628. In an age extraordinarily sensitive to status and precedence, Micklethwaite's insistence on certain privileges and fees led the benchers to resist his demands vigorously. During the 1630s, although always a Calvinist in theology, he was a loyal High Churchman, becoming a royal chaplain, putting the altar back

John Dee's copy of a Hebrew biblical concordance printed by Alvise Bragadini in Venice in 1564, from the Micklethwaite bequest

Sir William Montagu (c1619–1706), circle of Daniel Mytens, 1639

Sir William Montagu (1632) was the second son of Edward Montagu, 1st Baron Montagu of Boughton, the Sidney benefactor. William's brothers Edward (1631) and Christopher (1633) were also at Sidney. After three years at Sidney, William trained as a lawyer. He was appointed chief baron of the exchequer in 1676 and was a judge for some of the Popish Plot trials in 1678. He later said he 'had never any great faith' in Titus Oates, the 'inventor' of the plot. In 1684 he sentenced to death Alice Welland, almost the last person hanged for witchcraft in England. He died in 1706, aged 87

at the east end of the church and placing burning candles on it during services. To the fury of Puritans, he moved the pulpit from the centre of the church to one side. His promotion of bowing at the altar and his views on the sabbath show why he was a close friend of another former Sidney fellow, the equally haughty Laudian John Pocklington.

Pocklington was notorious for defending royal policy on the sabbath, publishing his *Sunday No Sabbath* (1636) against Puritan opponents of the *Book of Sports*, and for his seemingly friendly attitude towards Rome, a factor no doubt in his favour when he became a royal chaplain in 1637. Such attitudes would have appalled his former master, Ward, and as with John Bramhall, remind us that Sidney was no simple 'nursery of Puritanism'. Pocklington was a fellow when the future Westminster Divine Daniel Cawdrey (1606) was an undergraduate. The two men clashed over the *Book of Sports* in the late 1630s.

Micklethwaite died in 1639, unmourned by most of his legal congregation, but still loyal to Sidney: he left a remarkable collection of 73 Hebrew books, which still survives in the Muniment Room. These include biblical, grammatical, Talmudic, philosophical, mystical and historical volumes. One is from the library of the mathematician and magician John Dee, and many are rare examples of eastern European Jewish printing. Pocklington remained an unrepentant royalist, following the King into the north during the Bishops' War of 1639. He was deprived of his benefices by the House of Commons in 1641, and his books burned in public in London and Cambridge. He died the following year.

Ward would have approved of two great Puritan preachers among his fellowship, however: Samuel Buggs, vicar of Holy Trinity, Coventry and Richard Garbutt, a preacher at Leeds parish church. The worthy and long titles of their publications suggest something of their sympathies: Buggs' *Miles Mediterraneus: A Mid-land Souldier; A sermon preached to the audience (and published at the request) of the worthie Company of Practizers in the military garden of the well governed citie of Coventry* (1622); and Garbutt's *A Demonstration of the resurrection of our Lord and Saviour Jesus Christ; and therein of the Christian religion: Very usefull for the further satisfaction and confirmation of all good Christians; as likewise for the confutation and conviction of those that have a Jewish or atheisticall spirit in them* (1656).

Paten given by William Armine (1593–1651), admitted fellow-commoner 13 March 1609 or 1610

Samuel Ward's Students

While many of Ward's fellows are today fairly obscure figures, quite the opposite is true of his students. Among the sons of the nobility and upper gentry who came as fellow-commoners were Edward Montagu, later 2nd Earl of Manchester, and his

Chapel Court after being gutted for refurbishment in 1970. The old interior dated back to 1628–30

Catholic-convert brother Walter; Montagu, Roger and Robert Bertie; various Wrays, Noels and Wingfields; and the odd Spencer, Lytton and Cromwell.

Much talent came from the more 'middling sort' of pensioners, scholars and sizars. Future churchmen of renown, mostly Puritans, dominate the list and include Jeremy Whitaker, William Price, Thomas Calvert, George Cockayn, Henry Denne, Thomas Dugard and Seth Ward. Thomas Fuller's appointment as a fellow in 1629 reminds us that Sidney produced some important literary figures, such as Charles Aleyn, William Dugard, Clement Paman and Sir Roger L'Estrange. Sidney became a leading college for medical and scientific studies under Ward, and among Sidney doctors, mathematicians and scientists mention should be made of Sir George Ent, John Bidgood, Gilbert Clerke and John Stearne. Lawyers and politicians included Sir William Armine, Sir William Morton, Sir Robert Atkyns and Sir Edward Dering. Morton has the distinction of being the judge who sent the ladies' favourite highwayman, Claude Duval, to the gallows in 1670.

Sidney was a magnet for ambitious parents at a time when Cambridge was at its height of popularity. Ward's student numbers are impressive, rising from an intake of 15 in 1610 to 32 in 1614, and a total population of 117 in 1617, when Cromwell was still in residence. In 1620, the year the Pilgrim Fathers landed in Massachusetts, 40 undergraduates were admitted. Except for plague years, the numbers held at around 25 annual admissions throughout that decade, perhaps a sign of economic pressures on the College chest as well as Sidney's undoubted popularity. In the early 1630s the average numbers admitted each year rose to nearly 40, in part explained by new accommodation. Just before the Civil War, in 1641, the number of admissions was 32. By comparison with many colleges, Sidney was heavily populated.

Ward's reputation as a strict disciplinarian was clear at the outset of his mastership. His commonplace book lists his resolutions as maintaining true religion and learning, and the unquestioned observance of the sabbath. He wanted to promote godly preaching as the prime aim of his scholars. He met stiff opposition from fellows and students to his attempts to ban 'tavern-haunting' and to his insistence that the tutors spring surprise raids on students' rooms. The few admonitions in the College minutes, however, suggest he was largely successful in imposing his will on Sidney.

The academic records for the period are very patchy and anyway extremely misleading. The Tripos *Ordo Senioritatis* frequently reflected the collegiate bias of the examiners and the exams, or disputations, were anyway far from rigorous. Until 1652–53, in fact, Sidney had no examiners, but of the 21 years from 1610 until then, for which there are records, Sidney students were frequently among the top 30: George Goring and Tom May were notable early successes in 1612–13, coming third and fourth respectively.

'For Want of Chambers': New Buildings and Bequests

> Now, whereas some benefactors in repute are *male*factors in effect …, namely such as
> burden and clog their donations to maintain more than they are able, whereby their gifts
> become suckers impairing the root of the foundation, Sir John's gift was so left at large for
> the disposal thereof… —Thomas Fuller, *The History of the University of Cambridge*, 1655

The pressures on Sidney's accommodation were acute, with about 150 students and a maximum of 35 chambers available for all residents in 1625. An account book of the early 1620s describes the problems facing even the fellows: 'In the fellowes parlour for want of chambers there kept Mr. Edmund Eston; after him Mr. Thomas Kaye. Then Mr. Robert Daggett; Mr. Richard Dugard; Mr. Richard Bell; Mr Thomas Wood; Mr. John Land.'

Ward attracted some important benefactors to support the College. In 1618 James Montagu left a rent-charge of £20 a year from his manor at Coppingford, Huntingdonshire; in 1625 Archdeacon Robert Johnson, founder of Oakham and Uppingham schools, left an annuity of £100 for scholars to Sidney, St John's, Emmanuel and Clare. When Sir Francis Clerke of Houghton Conquest, Bedfordshire, came forward as a benefactor in 1627, he did so without connection to the College, but with such munificence that he seemed later to Fuller to have 'exceeded the bounds of benefaction and justly entitled him to be a by-founder'. It was said that Clerke was attracted to Sidney because of its student discipline, dress and diligence in study. Clerke conveyed to Sidney the manors of Pilling Shingay and Pilling Rowsbury and property at Wootton to support four fellowships and eight scholarships, and to increase the value of the foundation scholarship. The Clerke scholarships were limited to boys born and educated in Bedfordshire.

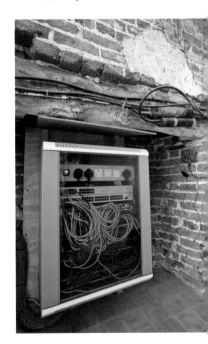

The College computer hub in a fireplace in Sir Francis Clerke's range (Chapel Court), 2009

The new fellows and scholars were to be housed in a new range, paid for by Clerke's bequest, which was built between the southern end of the chapel and Conduit Street, thus completing the 'E' shape of the old front courts familiar to us today. This formed Chapel, then Pilling, Court. The building, with 20 chambers, was completed by 1630 and allowed for at least a further 12 rooms for non-Clerke fellows and students. The Clerke scholars shared rooms 'up 2 pair of Stairs in Sir Francis Clerke's Building and one of his Fellows for their Tutor gratis'. The well-paid Clerke fellows had chambers on the first floor in a building that was pretty much in the style of the two original ranges. According to a guidebook writer of 1803, the Scottish fellow John Young ignored national stereotypes by building 'the brick wall between the second court and the street at his own expense'. The 'fair and firm range of twenty chambers' was gutted for modernisation in 1970, leaving only the outer walls and a red brick fireplace, now housing Sidney's computer hub.

This great addition to Sidney's wealth, fellowship and accommodation was acquired shortly after a College old boy, Sir John Brereton, had left one half of his 'ready money, goods, chattels and credits' in 1626. The income from this was to be dispensed to the College as thought fit by the Lady Margaret and Regius Professors of Divinity. Fuller notes that Brereton was 'as I may term him, one of the aborigines of the College, one of the first Scholars of the House; and afterwards became his Majesty's Sergeant for the Kingdom of Ireland'. With the more than £2,000 pounds left by Brereton, the College purchased Cridling Park in Yorkshire in 1634, which, with its pasturage and feeding for 200 sheep, gave the College an annual income of £143.

What was especially welcome about Brereton's money was that it came with no strings attached, as Fuller noted. In the first year of income, Ward used it to increase all stipends, to institute a new 'Mathematicks Lecture' and an ecclesiastical history lecture. It also funded the Feast of the Foundress, an annual commemoration of Brereton, and an additional manservant for the master.

In 1641 the last of the major gifts to Sidney under Ward came from Francis Combe of Hemel Hempstead in Hertfordshire, who had entered Sidney as a pensioner in 1600. This comprised part of his extensive library and also half of his property at Abbots Langley, the other half going to Trinity College, Oxford, which had been founded by Combe's maternal great-uncle, Sir Thomas Pope. The income was to go towards the education of the descendants of his brothers and sisters, a stipulation suggestive, perhaps, of one of Fuller's 'malefactors'. The manor of Abbots Langley had been given to Henry, Prince of Wales but had become Combe's property some time after Henry's death. Extraordinarily, Combe's family was still disputing the will as late as 1869. The many books Combe left Sidney included Vesalius on anatomy, William Oughtred on mathematics, and the works of St Teresa of Avila.

'Christ Frameth Men by the Word Preached': Samuel Ward and the Synod of Dort 1618

Ward's career was academically distinguished, though he published little. Having been a translator of the *Aprocypha* for the great Authorised Version of the Bible, he was appointed one of five British delegates at one of the seminal theological events of the 17th century, the Synod of Dort in 1618. Inspired by the publication of the new English Bible in 1611, this was an international conference held in Dordrecht in Holland, called by the Dutch Reformed Church, to discuss the challenge posed to orthodox Calvinist theology by the views of the followers of Jacob Arminius. The Arminians took a less severe view on questions of predestination and salvation. Many hard-line Calvinists, such as Ward, saw them as the thin end of a wedge pointing to Rome, at a time of a tense truce in the Spanish-Dutch Wars. The Synod was dominated by Calvinists who rejected the Arminian 'heresy', and by the time the discussions ended in May 1619, it had agreed on 'Five Points' asserting the theological truth of Calvin's ideas: total depravity, unconditional election, limited atonement, irresistible grace, and the perseverance of the saints – often remembered by the acronym TULIP.

The leader of the Arminians at the Synod, Episcopius, considered Ward the 'most learned member' of the British delegates, though Ward fully supported the five points against Episcopius. Johan van Oldenbarnevelt, a political supporter of the Arminians, was beheaded shortly after the Synod had ended, an execution Ward may have witnessed. Another great Arminian, the jurist Hugo Grotius, fled Holland. By the time the Synod had finished, the Thirty Years War had begun, ignited by the

dynastic claims of the Elector Palatine and his queen, John Harington's expensive charge, Princess Elizabeth. Ward could hardly have anticipated how religion and politics were to intertwine so dramatically in his own life 20 years later. The great chest he brought back from Holland, which Sidney still owns, suggests a souvenir from an agreeable and lengthy academic sojourn, rather than the memento of a critical moment in European history. It also reminds us of the regular connections between the College and Holland during the period. The Puritan preacher Julines Herring (1600) escaped the Laudian persecution of the 1630s by becoming minister of the English Reformed Church in Amsterdam; John Morton (1621) set up a baptist church in the same city and was very influential there.

Ward reaped great benefits from his status and connections and, in spite of his stutter and painfully shy manner, was hardly in the mould of less worldly early Sidney fellows such as Thomas Gataker or William Bradshaw. In 1623 Ward, already rewarded for his efforts in the Jacobean church with ecclesiastical offices and livings at Wells Cathedral, Taunton, Great Munden and York, was appointed Lady Margaret Professor of Divinity at Cambridge, succeeding his close friend John Davenant. The sermons and lectures he gave underline his strict belief in predestination, attacking the Arminian tendencies that Charles I encouraged in the 1630s under Archbishop Laud.

To many in the 1630s, Ward would have seemed old-fashioned, if highly principled, in religious matters, at a time when his Calvinist opinions were under attack from the rising Arminian party. He had been condemned in 1630 by the Vice-Chancellor, Matthew Wren, for purchasing the Puritan William Prynne's *Anti-*

Arminianisme (1630), and in the next decade he doggedly opposed 'novelties in both rites and doctrines', defending men such as the Sidney Puritan John Barcroft in 1634 against being 'disgraced and checked'. By then he had told James Ussher that he feared for his position; his resistance to change earning him renown as a man, in John Estwick's words, of 'soundness of faith and integrity of conversation'.

'The Late Usurper': Cromwell Goes to Sidney

> 'Look,' said Julian, 'here comes Mr. Milton.' Mr. Milton was walking on one side of the Master of Sidney, and on the other walked the newly elected city burgesses, Mr. Oliver Cromwell and Mr. John Lowrey. Julian thought Mr. Milton and Mr. Cromwell a strange contrast; the one so neat, trim, elegant, fair and austerely beautiful; the other a great sloven of a man, heavy-featured, red-nosed and unkempt. —Rose Macaulay, *They Were Defeated*, 1932

There were few admonitions of students recorded during Ward's long term as master. However, it appears that 1634 was an uncharacteristically difficult year, with Robert Eccleston admonished for 'his obstinate and disorderly course' and Almeric Butler upbraided in August for 'some immodest speeches against Briggs his wife and base language used'. Eccleston 'migrated' to Magdalene shortly afterwards. Butler was also punished in November for threatening and 'disgracefully pulling by the beard Anthony Meller'. Robert Jarman was punished 'for drinking in Alehouses for 3 or 4 days…'.

Ward's biggest student problems lay in the future, nurtured unwittingly for only a couple of years. Two students who arrived in 1616 and 1618 returned to haunt him, and, in one case, to haunt the College. Oliver Cromwell and Edward Montagu were neighbours in Huntingdonshire and their paths were to intersect in remarkable fashion later in life. It seems likely a Montagu connection was a prime reason for Cromwell's being sent to Sidney, though Ward's mastership was certainly another attraction to an East Midlands Puritan family. Although Sir Sidney Montagu had bought Hinchingbrooke House near Huntingdon from Oliver's debt-laden uncle and godfather in 1627, as young men Oliver and Edward were probably little connected. They just missed one another as undergraduates at Sidney where they were both fellow-commoners.

Edward Montagu was the eldest son of Henry Montagu, first Earl of Manchester, and therefore a nephew of James Montagu, the first master, and Edward Montagu, first Baron of Boughton. His brothers Walter and James also went to Sidney, and we shall hear more about them. As a nobleman's son, Edward was destined for high office and, as it turned out, an extraordinary political career that changed England, and his old College, forever.

Oliver Cromwell's great-grandfather, Sir Richard Cromwell, was one of many beneficiaries of the dissolution of religious houses under Henry VIII, and his grandfather, Sir Henry, bought land in Huntingdonshire on which he built substantial properties. *The Dictionary of National Biography* describes Cromwell's social status, however, as 'ambiguous'.

Cromwell attended the local grammar school in Huntingdon, where he was taught by Thomas Beard, famous for his book *The Theatre of God's Judgements*, published a year after Sidney's foundation in 1597. It gives hundreds of examples of God's wrathful visitations on sinners. Beard's virulent anti-Catholicism is suggested by a book published the year his pupil entered Sidney: *A Retractive from the Romish Religion: Contayning Thirteene Forcible Motives*, designed 'to confirme and strengthen those that stagger, and are weake in the truth' and dedicated to Cromwell's grandfather, who had 'long time' been one of 'the principall auditors of my unworthy ministery'.

We know little about Cromwell's stay at Sidney, which was terminated in the summer of 1617 on the death of his father. He gave a silver 'pott' to the College, as was the tradition for fellow-commoners; rather bathetically it was sold, along with 21 other pieces of valuable plate, barely a year later, when Sidney had to repurchase some land in Sussex Street that it had improperly sold in 1602. Cromwell went up with a number of other wealthy students to a Sidney bursting at the seams, the sixth most populous college in Cambridge at the time. He would probably have shared a room with another fellow-commoner, perhaps John or Henry Savill, from Yorkshire, or Christian Hulsbos, a Netherlandish student.

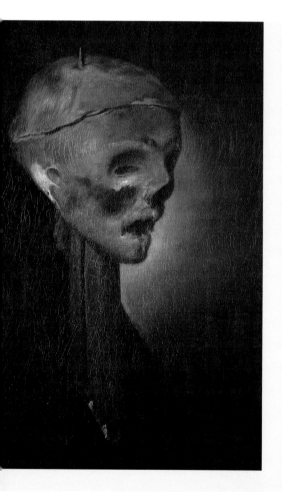

Cromwell's Head

Everyone knows Cromwell's head is buried in a secret location at Sidney. The story of how Cromwell came back to his old college in such macabre fashion is bizarre. Cromwell's body was dug up in January 1661, hung up out of his coffin until sunset and his head decapitated on the anniversary of Charles I's execution. The head was then placed on a pole at Westminster Hall. It is said that one stormy night in the 1680s it blew down and was taken by a sentinel who hid it in his house. In 1710 the German traveller von Uffenbach (who visited Sidney that year) saw it on a wooden staff at a museum of curiosities in London, presumably on loan. It was offered later in the century by the sentinel's daughter's husband to the Sidney master William Elliston, who declined it. It came into the possession of Josiah Wilkinson by 1822 via a London jeweller and three brothers. They had exhibited it in 1799 in Mead Court off Old Bond Street and charged two shillings and sixpence to see it. A narrative was written by the artist John Cranch who also painted the 'shop sign' painting illustrated here that advertised the head. Canon H N S Wilkinson inherited it and gave it to Sidney in 1960, witnessing its solemn burial on 25 March 1960. Scientific examination had shown that it was a 'moral certainty' it was genuine.

Cromwell's head as exhibited by the Hughes brothers in Mead Court, off Old Bond Street, in 1799, by John Cranch

Whether Cromwell gained much academically from his time at Sidney is uncertain. The distinctly anti-Cromwellian biography of 1663 by James Heath, called *Flagellum, or The Life and Death, Birth and Burial of Oliver Cromwell, the Late Usurper*, says he was 'one of the chief match-makers and players at Football, Cudgels, or any other boisterous game or sport'. As football was a banned sport at Cambridge, the implication is that Oliver was already noted as a troublemaker, although as we have suggested he would have played his football at the end of the Sidney gardens. Cromwell's sporting interests are attested by another and more sympathetic source. Cotton Mather, the great New England Puritan, says in a letter that Cromwell claimed 'he could remember the time when he had been more afraid of meeting [John] Wheelwright at football, than of meeting any army since in the field'.

As well as being a formidable football opponent, Wheelwright, a native of Saleby, the Sidney estate in Lincolnshire, was also renowned as a fearsome student wrestler. He entered the College in 1611 and was a mature graduate student by the time he began fouling Cromwell on the football pitch. He became a charismatic preacher, and in 1636, after a conviction for simony, went to America with his large family. He was involved with the Boston church and plunged immediately into its intense religious controversies, coming up against the formidable future governor of Massachusetts, John Winthrop, who had him convicted for contempt and sedition. Wheelwright's incendiary sermons, denying salvation through good works, would no doubt have endeared him to Cromwell, with whom he had an audience after returning to England in the 1650s.

Cromwell's fictional appearance with Samuel Ward and John Milton in Rose Macaulay's historical novel *They were Defeated* about the period in Cambridge just before the Civil War, reminds us that his career for nearly 20 years after his time at Sidney is shrouded in as much obscurity as his College life. He may have gone to Lincoln's Inn briefly after Cambridge, a conventional move for a student of his background. He married in 1620 and eventually had nine children by his wife Elizabeth. In 1628 he was briefly an MP for Huntingdon along with Edward Montagu's younger brother James, who had entered Sidney in 1624. He clearly had a mental breakdown around 1630, followed by a monetary dispute with the Montagus that left him bankrupt. He moved to St Ives to work as a yeoman farmer, and in 1636 inherited a small fortune from his uncle. At this point he had a conversion experience, acknowledging that he was 'chief of sinners' and turning to an extreme Puritan belief that might have pleased his former schoolmaster Thomas Beard. Whether or not it would have gained Samuel Ward's approval is less certain. They were providentially to come across one another in a few years' time.

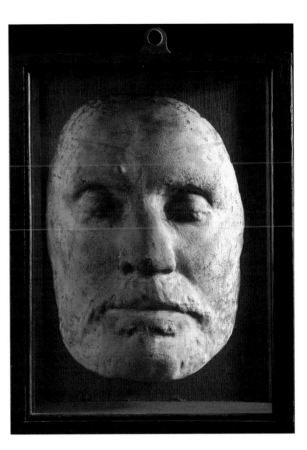

Plaster after-cast of Oliver Cromwell's death mask, presented by H Beresford Jones, 1930

'He That Hath a Paine in his Backe': George Palfrey's Notebook

He that hath a paine in his Backe,
  And would have a Remediato.
Ringo rootes & Mary-bone pyes/
  Red wine & a rich Potato.
An oyster pye & a Lobsters thigh/
  Hard Eggs well steept in Marrow,
Muscadine & an Egge is fine/
  Anchovies Oyle & Pepper,
When [tha]t is spent, you may be content/
  W[i]th an Ounce of Cynnamon water.
—George Palfrey, *Notebook*, 1623

George Palfrey, 'Oration made in the Hall on 8 October 1623, celebrating the return of Charles, Prince of Wales, from Spain', collection of Sheriff D B Smith

One of Cromwell's contemporaries was the sizar Jeremy Whitaker, one of an increasing Yorkshire contingent at Sidney, whose favourite saying – 'I had rather be a Preacher of the Gospel than an Emperor' – might have been lost on Cromwell. He became a teacher at the 'Sidney' school in Rutland, Oakham, and an evangelical preacher in the town in the 1620s. His wife's name, Chephtzibah, suggests a very particular time and place in English history. He fell foul of church authorities in the 1630s for his anti-sabbatarian views. In 1641 he subscribed to a petition to convert Native Americans, and in 1643 preached an influential sermon that helped him to become a prominent member of the Presbyterian Westminster Assembly of Divines that year, along with other Sidney-trained churchmen. Although he refused to swear allegiance to the republic after Charles I's execution, he sent a book as a gift to Cromwell.

A more obscure figure, George Palfrey, who went up to Sidney from Blundell's School as a scholar in 1616, shortly after Cromwell, has left us a priceless insight into the academic studies of a serious student of the time. Palfrey was at Sidney for nine years before returning to Devon as a 'preaching minister'. His tutor was John Hayne, also of Blundell's, now as obscure as Palfrey himself, and to whom we may ascribe some of the knowledge Palfrey reveals he absorbed while at Sidney. Palfrey's small notebook, of about 180 sides, was written in a typical Jacobean hand during the period from 1616 to 1625. It contains notes on, or from, works of natural philosophy, many of them highly traditional in their scholastic emphasis on Aristotle. The Italian anti-papist, republican sympathiser Giacomo Zabarella, the leading Renaissance Aristotelian scholar, is frequently quoted. A favourite author among Protestant scholars, Zabarella wrote extensively on logic and natural science, taking a strong line against newer scientific and pragmatic theories. The notebook also includes rhetorical orations made in the Sidney Hall ('Oratiuncula in Aula Coll:') and in the university halls ('Oratiuncula in scholis publicis'), and is full of quotes from Horace, Virgil, Ovid, Seneca, Plutarch and other classical authors.

Palfrey spends much time on an ethical and political discussion of the relative merits of natural and civilised life and on the nature of the soul, which, he says, takes the form of the body but enters corporeal life through a divine source. He also makes reference to the natural magic of Albertus Magnus and Ficino, and refers to tobacco in a discussion of the effects of medicines. Among various cryptic personal notes one entry is the useful, if daunting, verse remedy for back pain, quoted above.

'Notorious Whores': Walter Montagu and the Spanish Match

> An Envoy of the Duke of Buckingham, one whose name was Montague, having been seized, they found upon him proofs of a league between the Empire, Spain, England, and Lorraine. This league was formed against France. —Alexandre Dumas, *The Three Musketeers*, 1844

The only date in George Palfrey's notebook is 1623: that year witnessed a turning point in English politics perhaps equal to 1605 in its significance. The phrase *Poculum Aureum Plenum Abominationis*, at the beginning of the notebook, has under each word the initial letters 'P A P A' indicated (i.e. 'the Pope'). The phrase itself means 'a cup of gold full of abominations'. Later in the notebook, Palfrey refers to his thanksgiving on 'Octobris 8 1623' for the much-longed-for return of Charles, Prince of Wales from Spain. In a Latin verse he describes the horrors of winter that follow the retreat of Charles's sun. Cambridge welcomes its prince back with piety of heart rather than riches. Palfrey's overblown style, invoking satyrs, fauns and celestial nymphs, celebrates the failure of Charles's mission to Spain. Indeed, on 5 October the bells began ringing in Cambridge and continued to do so for three days. Here, and in Palfrey's admiration for the anti-Spanish hero Sir Walter Raleigh, executed five years previously, the notebook reveals possible republican sympathies.

Other Sidney students, such as William Wolstenhome (1615), a near contemporary of Cromwell, and Humphrey Wheatley (1621), took their Protestant and patriotic duties to their ultimate conclusion: both are recorded in the admissions register as 'interfectus a milite'; that is, they died fighting in the Palatinate wars in 1626–27.

Palfrey's notebook hints at the deep disagreement in England over James's Spanish policy, a combination of proposed dynastic political alliance designed to unite Protestant and Catholic powers against the Holy Roman Empire and to prevent a European war. It was based on deeply suspect concessions to Rome, and brought James into conflict with Parliament when war did erupt in 1621, and when he insisted on going forward with the Spanish Match in spite of strong opposition. Samuel Ward of Ipswich's 1621 print, which we have already looked at, was deliberately published as the political temperature rose. The King attempted to impose a Scottish ally on Sidney's fellowship by royal mandate in 1623, but a lengthy correspondence shows that the College resisted this attack on its independence.

Two Sidney students were directly involved in the most famous and absurd episode in the whole disastrous affair. In an attempt to woo the Infanta, Charles travelled to Spain *incognito* with Buckingham, the pair presenting themselves to the English ambassador in Spain in 1623 as 'John and Tom Smith'. The tragi-comic farce evolved, ending with Charles returning to England having made concessions to the Spanish that he reneged on within days. He then presented himself as a heroic protector of his sister and Protantism, war was declared on Spain, and troops were sent to defend the cause in Europe.

The royal retinue in Spain had included George Goring, one of Sidney's earliest fellow-commoners, by now an MP and an experienced diplomat who had been a courtier to Princess Elizabeth. A member of Buckingham's clique, Goring would have been extremely unpopular with men such as Cromwell for taking part in extravagant court masques and becoming an assiduous collector of royal pensions and offices. Goring was sent from Madrid to the Hague to reassure Princess Elizabeth in exile there that all was well. Once these negotiations had collapsed, Goring turned his attentions to the French Match with Henrietta Maria. This was a successful effort and led to his close attachment to the new queen.

While Goring was a superb diplomat, ducking and diving as the occasion demanded, another Sidney man took an entirely different approach. Walter Montagu, the middle son of Henry, 1st Earl of Manchester, and younger brother of Edward Montagu, Cromwell's later parliamentary colleague, went up to Sidney in 1618 as a fellow-commoner. He then undertook a grand tour in Europe and learned a number of languages, preparatory to entering the court. Like Goring he became part of Buckingham's circle and began to move away from his family's strict Protestant and anti-Spanish position. It was Montagu who acted as interpreter for Buckingham, attending the last private interview between his master and the great Spanish minister Conde-Duque de Olivares at the Escorial.

Lord Goring, etching by S de Wilde and John Cawthorn, 10 April 1812. The Royal Collection

GEORGE GORING.
Earl of Norwich.
from a Picture formerly at Scotts hall & still in the Family.

Etch'd & Pub.d April 10 1812 by S.De Wilde & John Cawthorn, 5, Catherine Street, Strand.

The Shepherd's Paradise

In 1633 Walter Montagu wrote an immensely long pastoral masque entertainment for Henrietta Maria and her ladies-in-waiting, *The Shepherd's Paradise*, for which elaborate sets were designed by Inigo Jones and which was performed at Somerset House. Written at the Queen's request after Ben Jonson had severed his relationship with Jones, *The Shepherd's Paradise* is a five-act drama of bizarre metaphysical complexity. It prompted William Prynne the Puritan to write his celebrated, lengthy and sour *Histriomastix* (1633), attacking it for its use of women actors who were 'notorious whores', defaming the Queen and her ladies and earning him a £5,000 fine and the loss of his ears. The Cavalier poet John Suckling ridiculed the eight-hour performance for its laborious obscurities, although it is thought it was written to teach the Queen and her entourage good English, and marked an important moment in the acceptance of women on stage. Prynne and his supporters above all loathed the implicit link Montagu made in his masque between the beauties of court and those of heaven, a vision accessible only to those of the 'nobler sort'.

Inigo Jones, design for The Shepherd's Paradise, *1633. The Devonshire Collection, Chatsworth, Derbyshire*

Montagu, again with Goring, was part of the negotiations in France for the marriage with Henrietta Maria, reporting in March 1625 that 'the lady should be delivered in thirty days'. He was a well-paid and popular servant of the new Queen and as a result became an important diplomat and secret agent for England in France. Shortly after taking his MA in 1627, Montagu was arrested by Cardinal Richelieu's agents and imprisoned in the Bastille, later receiving payment 'for his Majesty's secret service in France'. This episode led to his appearance in Alexandre Dumas's great novel *The Three Musketeers*. Upon his return he was present at the assassination of his master Buckingham in 1628, surviving that climactic event and continuing his service under Charles in France.

Back in France, Montagu witnessed the famous exorcisms of Ursuline nuns at Loudon (recalled in Ken Russell's film *The Devils* in 1971), which led to his conversion to Catholicism, probably the first such act by any Sidney man. Montagu caused a sensation at court through the distribution of his letter explaining his decision to his appalled father. He was ordained and became Henrietta Maria's chamberlain at Somerset House. In 1641 he was banished by parliament and left for France, returning in a clumsy disguise in 1643, after which he was imprisoned until 1647. From the Tower he wrote a series of religious essays and engaged in theological disputes with the Puritan John Bastwick. In 1649, deprived of all his wealth and estates by Parliament, he returned to France where he continued to write verse, act as mentor to Prince Henry and became Abbot of St Martin near Pontoise. He remained a prodigious plotter and negotiator: Henry's brother Charles, soon to become the restored king, viewed Montagu as 'the queen's evil genius'. His final years were ones of quiet study, writing and devotion. He was buried at Pontoise in 1677.

Frontispiece to Vox Piscis, or The Book-Fish, contayning three treatises which were found in the belly of a cod-fish in Cambridge Market, on Midsummer Eve last, anno Domini 1626, *1627*

Vox Piscis: **Samuel Ward and Providence in Cambridge Market**

I dare not slight that hand of God in sending John Frith's preparation to the Crosse, in the fish bellie to the Universitie of Cambridge, a little before the Commencement. That such a booke, should in such a manner, and to such a place, and at such a time be sent: when by reason of peoples confluence out of all parts, notice might be given to all places of the land, (in my apprehension) it can be construed for no lesse, then a devine warning, and to have this voice with it, England prepare for the Crosse. —Jeremiah Dyke, *Sermon to the House of Commons*, 1628

In 1626 a half-dissolved book wrapped in canvas, stinking, and covered in gelatinous slime, was delivered to John Gostlin, the Vice-Chancellor of Cambridge. It had been discovered in the belly of a fish caught near King's Lynn when it was gutted by a fishmonger in Cambridge market. While townspeople flocked

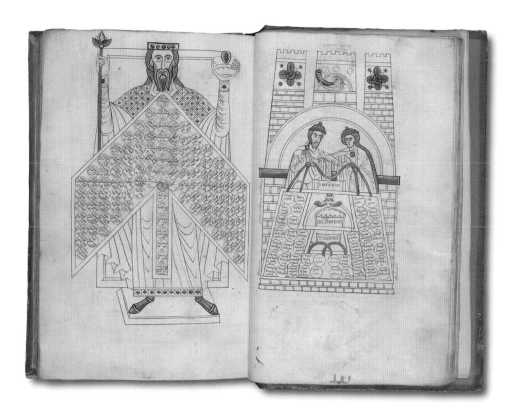

Tables of Consanguinity and Affinity from Gratian's Decretum, *Italian, probably Bologna, c1175–1200. This book belonged to Durham Cathedral and was acquired by the Sidney master Samuel Ward*

around to look at the strange find, Dr Joseph Mede of Christ's, an expert on the Book of Revelation, examined the sextodecimo volume more carefully. He was able to read the table of contents and the titles of two works, *Of the Preparation to the Cross* and *A Lettre Written to the Faithfull Followers of Christes Gospel*. Mede took the book, transcribed and preserved it, and had it washed and cleaned, noting at the time that earthquakes and other strange events seemed unnaturally common in 1626.

While many undergraduates made fun of the discovery – one claiming 'hee would hereafter never count it a reproach to bee called a Codshead, seeing that fish is now become so learned an heluo librorum [bookworm], which signifieth a man of much learning, or skilfull in many bookes' – other senior figures at Cambridge took a far more serious view of its providential significance. One of them was Samuel Ward, who told his friend James Ussher, 'It may be a special admonition to us at Cambridg'. The Archbishop of Armagh agreed and was not alone in his view; as one diarist wrote at the time, it was clearly a 'presage of further misery'.

The original books were identified as important early Reformation Protestant texts from the 1520s written by a Protestant martyr, John Frith. They were re-published as a warning to the nation in 1627. The publisher wrote of the 'Jonah' book as typical of 'strange judgements usually ushered in by strange and prodigious signes', alerting all 'by spirituall prudence in the midst of supposed security, to arme our selves against ghostly dangers which may and doe on every side besiege us'.

The severest Protestant view was that the book and other weird happenings were signs of God's displeasure at the religious and political events of the time: the early dissolution of Parliament, the progress of the Thirty Years' War, the marriage of King Charles to a Catholic, and the rise of Arminianism and ceremonialism. Above all, Cambridge Calvinists saw the book as a divine warning a month after the election of a new university Chancellor, the much-loathed and suspect Duke of Buckingham. Ward had abstained at the election, saying he could not have 'attended without hazard of my health'. England, he feared, was slipping dangerously away from the principles he had helped defend at the Synod of Dort. In 1625 he had, as Lady Margaret Professor, attacked the 'scandalous' writings of Richard Montague, a royal chaplain. His sermon, *Gratia Discriminans*, an attack on Arminianism, was licensed by the man who almost certainly published *Vox Piscis*, Thomas Goad. Ward's demand that 'no one disputes, save in error, against absolute predestination', was met soon after by the King's proclamation requiring 'the peace and quiet of the Church of England'.

Ussher wrote to Ward shortly after the fish book was discovered to urge a closing of the ranks: 'It behoveth you who are heads of Colleges, and (likeminded) to stick close to one another, and (quite obliterating all secret Distasts, or privy Discontenments which possibly may fall betwixt your selves) with joint consent to promote the cause of God'.

In 1628, Sidney's one-time fellow, Jeremiah Dyke, joined in on the side of his former master. Now an Essex preacher of impeccable anti-Catholic credentials, he addressed the House of Commons on the occasion of the public fast. He painted a terrifying picture of the nation's imminent collapse and drew attention to the Lord's wrath, manifested in comets, earthquakes, storms and double tides over the last decade. He was rewarded by the Commons with a handsome silver tankard.

'Dangerous Passages': Isaac Dorislaus in the Master's Lodge

Samuel Ward was always loyal to the crown. However, his Calvinism and German and Dutch connections meant that he was in close touch with men such as the orientalist and mathematician Matthias Pasor, the classical scholar and book collector Isaac Vosius, and Isaac Dorislaus, the scholar and diplomat who was appointed as first incumbent of Fulke Greville, Lord Brooke's new history chair at Cambridge in 1627. They were often republican in sympathy.

Dorislaus was Sidney's first known visiting professor, staying in the Sidney Lodge until he was forced out of office by the efforts of Ward's great opponent Matthew Wren. His first two lectures on Tacitus had challenged the divine right of kings through an account of episodes in Roman history. They were viewed by Wren as republican propaganda 'stored with…dangerous passages'. Ward reported that few other masters were offended, and that Dorislaus's defence was delivered with 'great moderation' in 'defence of the liberties of the people'. Ward was still leading the defence of his house guest in 1631 when the King finally forbade Dorislaus from lecturing again. Lord Brooke nevertheless continued his stipend to the Dutchman, and in 1642 Dorislaus acted as a lawyer for the parliamentary army. He was one of those who drew up the charges against King Charles in 1649, the preamble echoing the language of his aborted Cambridge lectures. During a diplomatic mission to the Hague in 1649 he was stabbed to death by royalists and, like Sidney's Thomas May and Oliver Cromwell later, was buried in Westminster Abbey, only to be disinterred after 1660.

Sidney took on a number of boys from Germany and the Netherlands as undergraduates, including Christian Hulsbos from the Southern Netherlands in 1616, and Samuel Ephron, or Benedictus, from Moravia via Leipzig University, in 1632. John Reede, or Johan van Reede, came to Sidney as a fellow-commoner in 1613, a month after getting married in Utrecht against his parents' wishes. Already a canon at Utrecht, and a political ally of the exiled Elector Frederick and Elizabeth of Bohemia, he acquired the title of Lord of Renswoude in 1623, and became a major political and diplomatic figure. In 1644 he was an intermediary between Charles and parliament and returned to Holland convinced that the latter was to blame for the dispute and likely to pose the greatest threat to Holland's security. In 1652 Reede became President of the States-General and died in 1682.

John de Reede, Baron Reede, etching by Wenceslaus Hollar after Johannes Meyssens, 1650. National Portrait Gallery, London

'His Majesty Wondered Att It': Sidney and the New Science

> [They] shall sit in the Chappel as Questionists used to do, 2 hours a day for 3 days, there to be examined for triall of their sufficiency. And because the University Statute de Bacc. Art. (ie BA) C.7 requires that such be auditors Philosophicae lectionis, Astronomiae, Perspectivae et Graecae linguae; it is judged fit that triall be made of their skill therein, beside other things suited with their degree. —Samuel Ward, regulations for those commencing an MA at Sidney, 1639

George Palfrey's notebook makes no reference to contemporary science, mathematics or medicine. Its intellectual world was dominated by the traditional texts of Aristotle and scholastic theology. The Cambridge fish episode might suggest that Sidney's fellows and students had little interest in the newer academic disciplines, turning their eyes only to the Bible and its interpretation. This was far from the case, however, and 'natural causes' and 'natural effects' were matters of great significance. During Ward's mastership there were growing calls for an expansion of the university syllabus and in particular for an experimental approach to natural philosophy. Many at the time saw scientific investigation as a route to redemption for man, a means of reversing the calamity of man's fall from grace.

Samuel Ward was renowned as a deep investigator of 'God's providences' in human affairs, but he had nearly turned to mathematics as his main course of study as

Carved wooden box containing fragments of the fossilised skull of a child, c3,200 years old, encrusted with travertine, found in Crete, and given by Captain Stevens of Rotherhithe, 1627. It is of importance in the history of palaeontology, being the first fossilised human skull to reach an English collection

a graduate student. A close friend at this time, and throughout his life, was the future Savilian Professor of Astronomy at Oxford, Henry Briggs. The library loans Ward made as a student at Emmanuel show that he read books on geography, optics and astronomy, as well as architecture and physics. At Sidney he established the College's first mathematical lectureship and he also bought navigational instruments, lenses, telescopes, globes and maps. The library acquired books by Tycho Brahe, Johannes Kepler and Francis Bacon, and the Sidney routine drawn up in 1639 by Ward for those commencing their MA examination stipulates attainments in astronomy and perspective.

Some items acquired by Samuel Ward have the quality of a 'providence' about them. An exchange of letters between Ward and the great medical scientist and discoverer of the circulation of the blood, William Harvey, concerns a curious ancient skull belonging to the College. This had been found in Candia, Crete, about 30 feet below ground level and was acquired by Captain William Stevens, a merchant explorer from Rotherhithe and one of the elder brethren of the Trinity House. It may have arrived at Sidney through William Gataker, the former Sidney fellow who was by then a priest in the Thameside parish. Harvey requested that the skull should be sent from Sidney to the King. The skull is that of a child, is strangely encrusted with travertine, and is now thought to date from 1230 BC, and so to be Minoan. Ward wrote to 'his much honoured friend Doctor Harvey one of his Majestys Physitians att his house in Blackfryars' agreeing to send the skull in the 'case wherein we keep it'. Harvey's reply thanked Ward and informed him that 'his Majesty wondered att it & look'd content to see soe rare a thinge'. He also says he considers it 'a kinde of sacriledg not to have retorned it to that place where it may for the instruction of men heare after be conserved'. The skull still sits in the richly carved oak case Ward referred to, a strange *memento mori* from the deep past.

'To Practise Physic': Sidney's First Doctors

Sidney had a reputation as a college producing physicians in the early-17th century. The first on record, Edward Dawson, came up as a pensioner in 1613, was granted a licence to 'practise physic' at Oxford in 1621 and became a fellow of the Royal College of Physicians in 1634. Richard Resbury (1622) was a Puritan vicar at Oundle who practised medicine after 1660 while also preaching as a congregationalist in his own house. In 1624 Samuel Remington, Richard Stanes and George Ent, all entered the College as pensioners and all went on to study at Padua, the traditional destination for English doctors. Of these three, George Ent became the most eminent. Born in Sandwich, the son of a Flemish merchant and probable religious refugee, he attended schools in Veere and Rotterdam. Ent became a scholar at Sidney in 1628 and this date, along with the course of his subsequent career, suggests he would have been familiar with the Stevens skull. After taking his MA in 1631, Ent travelled to Padua and took an MD there in 1636. In Padua he was taught by the celebrated physician J D Sala, and on a trip to Venice met William Harvey, who was travelling with the Earl of Arundel. Harvey was also from Kent, and like Ent had studied at Cambridge and Padua, and the pair may have first met during Ent's time at Sidney. They travelled to Rome together and became close friends and medical colleagues. Ent's first book, *Apologia Pro Circulatione Sanguinis* (1641), was the first major defence of Harvey's theory of the circulation of the blood and emphasised the need for experimental medicine. Ent, by now a fellow of the Royal College of Physicians, made important contributions to physiology through his work on the presence of nitre in air and water, and was the Goulstonian Lecturer at the College of Physicians in 1642. At the same time, he was part of the Oxford-based group that met at Gresham's College and eventually became the Royal Society, of which he was a founder member. During the last days of the Civil War Ent obtained from the royalist Harvey the manuscript of his masterpiece on embryology, *Exercitationes de Generatione Animalium*, edited and prefaced it, and saw it through the press in 1651.

An anatomist of distinction as well as an all-round scientific experimenter, Ent hosted the early anatomical meetings of the Royal Society, enjoyed an immensely successful practice as a physician, and was knighted. One of his last publications, before he died in 1690, was a response to Malachias Thurston's attack on his theories of respiration. Thurston, a Blundell's scholar from Devon, had gone to Sidney in 1645 and was a fellow in the 1650s, before moving to Caius where he was also a lecturer in Hebrew and Greek. Like Ent, Thurston became a fellow of the Royal Society in 1665, but died mad in Exeter in 1701. Another early Sidney doctor, the successful but 'morose and satirical' John Bidgood, was also from Exeter. This connection between Sidney, doctors and Devon continued well into the 18th century.

A less obvious medical connection is with Ireland, the birthplace of one of the greatest figures of 17th-century medicine. John Stearne was born in County Meath in 1624 and arrived at Sidney to study medicine in 1642, in flight from the Irish Rebellion of the previous year. The explanation for his choice of college may lie in family links: his mother was a niece of Ward's friend Archbishop James Ussher of Armagh. Stearne was first a student at Trinity College, Dublin, founded in 1592 with a mission similar to Sidney's. During his time at Sidney, Stearne collected material for *Animi Medela* (1653), which reflects his acceptance of many of the tenets of neo-stoic philosophy, prompted by the turmoil in Cambridge during the Civil War. He returned to Dublin in about 1651 where he became a lecturer in Hebrew and professor of physic.

Animi Medela is an early book on disorders of the mind, dedicated to the Protector's son, the soldier Henry Cromwell, who was made Chancellor of Trinity College in 1653. It makes fascinating reading as it brings together theology, philosophy and medicine; anatomical ideas rub along with those of his favourite authors Seneca and Epictetus. His view of the religious conflicts of the time was tolerant and non-partisan, and no doubt reflects an opinion that they might be a major source of mental illness. For Stearne, sanity lay in a private life and the contemplation of the misfortunes of human society. His approach to life certainly assured him the goodwill of both Puritans and their opponents. A marble plaque in the chapel at Trinity College, Dublin celebrates Stearne as '*Philosophus, Medicus, Summusque Theologicus Ide*'. After the Restoration in 1660, Stearne brought about his greatest achievement, the foundation of the Royal College of Physicians of Ireland, of which he was the first president.

'A Most Magnificent and Munificent Mind': Seth Ward

Of all Samuel Ward's students, Seth Ward, son of an impecunious attorney of Buntingford in Hertfordshire, was perhaps his favourite and the one who most brilliantly combined his master's ideals of great religious and scientific achievement. He was recommended to Samuel Ward as a very promising student by the vicar of Buntingford. Seth went up to Sidney as a sizar in 1632, the same year as fellow-commoner William Montagu, a son of the College benefactor Sir Edward Montagu of Boughton, and later a politician and judge.

In spite, or because, of his low social status, Ward was given lodgings in the Master's Lodge, special tutoring by the master and unfettered access to the library. According to Seth's friend and biographer Walter Pope, Samuel treated him 'as if he had been his one and only son'. He was a studious and quiet boy of 15, of 'low stature and as he walked about the Streets, the Doctors and other grave Men would frequently lay their Hands upon his white Head, for he had very fair Hair, and ask him of what College he was, and of what standing, and such like questions'.

Seth Ward, by John Greenhill, c1673. The Guildhall, Salisbury

Seth took an early interest in mathematics, an unusual focus he later claimed, and at a university disputation in his third year impressed the astronomer John Bainbridge. His official tutor was Charles Pendreth, who had just been elected a fellow and who has left us, no doubt inadvertently, a number of objects found under floor boards in Hall Court in 1997, including a playing card and a love letter. Pendreth was not greatly admired by Ward, and Pope wrote, 'tho' he was a very honest Man, yet was no Conjuror, nor of any fame for Learning. I have often heard the Bishop (i.e. Ward) repeat some of his Tutor's speeches, which never fail'd to make the Auditory laugh.' Ward said he had little instruction in mathematics at Sidney for, although the library contained many

Items found under the floorboards in B5, Hall Court, August 1997, including two inkwells, a playing card, a tailor's bill and scraps of paper that include part of a love letter addressed to Charles Pendreth (1604–57), who matriculated in 1623

books on the subject, he could find no fellow to help him understand them. At the time, mathematics was considered by many as merely a practical subject for builders, ship-builders and carpenters. Ward was made a college lecturer in mathematics by 1642.

Seth Ward left Sidney for Oxford in 1644, during the Civil War, amid the most dramatic circumstances, as we shall see. He was appointed Savilian Professor of Astronomy and became a fellow-commoner at Wadham College. The warden at Wadham was John Wilkins, one of the group of scientists who formed the nucleus of the Royal Society of which Ward was a founder member. During the 1650s, Ward wrote on comets, planetary motion, trigonometry and a defence of the universities against opponents such as Thomas Hobbes, who is believed to have avoided his critic in public at all costs. Ward wrote extensively on proposals for a universal language based on a concept of 'simple notions'.

Pope wrote of his friend that 'his sermons were strong, methodical, and clear, and, when Occasion required, pathetical and eloquent; for, besides his Skill in Mathematics, he was a great lover of Tully and understood him very well'. Ward was also a preacher, loyal to the Anglican church, and became chaplain to the ejected Bishop of Exeter, Ralph Brownrigg, succeeding him in 1662. He was a remarkable administrator of his see and a harsh prosecutor of nonconformists. He went on to become Bishop of Salisbury, restoring the buildings, attending the House of Lords diligently and building a grand house in Knightsbridge so that he could ride in Hyde Park. Regrettably, though his dedication to his old master at Sidney was legendary, it seems that later in life he no longer had the same feelings towards the College: he endowed four scholarships at Christ's in 1681, just when Sidney could have done with such generosity. He died senile in 1689 and his reputation was compromised by widespread accusations of over-worldly 'wavering for lucre and honour sake'.

'A New Country': Sidney Goes to America

> Sir, whether it be true or false, the Saints in these goings down of the Sun had never more light to see why their Father hath thus farre removed them… —Thomas Harrison, letter to the Governor of Massachusetts, John Winthrop, 1649.

Scientific frontiers were not the only ones at which Sidney men pushed in the period before 1640. The 1630s saw nearly 15,000 English men and women emigrate to America, of whom 118 have been identified as 'university' men, three-quarters of them from Cambridge. Most were in flight from the harsh anti-Puritan climate of that decade and hoped to build a 'new Jerusalem' in Virginia or New England. Though Emmanuel dominates the names among those from Cambridge, Sidney claims at least four clergymen who made the transatlantic journey in search of a new life. We have already come across one, Cromwell's friend John Wheelwright.

It is reassuring to discover that Sidney had its fair share of disreputable villains amongst the godly and scholarly. George Burdett, like the physician John Stearne later, came to Sidney from Trinity College, Dublin, in 1624, a contemporary of George Ent. He took an MA and began a tempestuous career. He was a Puritan preacher in the mould of Samuel Ward of Ipswich, ending up as lecturer in Great Yarmouth in the early 1630s, where he was accused by his curate of 'blasphemy', 'raising new doctrines,' and 'not bowing at the name of Jesus'. He refused to offer communion to whoremongers and drunkards, though accused of such sins himself. In 1635 a church court suspended him, and he soon left for New England, leaving an impoverished wife and children behind him.

George Moxon, by an unknown artist. Private collection

Burdett arrived at Salem, Massachusetts, from where he wrote to Archbishop Laud complaining of the manner of his departure from England. Yet by 1638, as a preacher in Pascataquack (now Dover), New Hampshire, he was writing to Laud denouncing the clergy of Massachusetts, where he had been made a freeman, for unorthodoxy and sedition. John Winthrop, governor of the Massachusetts Bay Colony and also an adversary of John Wheelwright, exposed Burdett as a spy in the pay of Laud, as Winthrop believed, who was seeking evidence of 'our combination to resist any authority in England'. Burdett was disliked in Pascataquack for his domineering manner, and by 1639 he was in Agamenticus (now York), Maine. Here he led a life of remarkable dissoluteness, 'drinkinge, dauncinge and singinge scurrulous songes'. In 1640 he brought before the court in Saco, Maine, three suits of slander against neighbours who accused him of adultery – but was instead himself indicted 'for a man of ill name and fame, infamous for incontinency, a publisher and broacher of divers dangerous speeches the better to seduce that weake sex of women to his incontinent practises'. For these and other activities such as 'deflowring Ruth the wife of John Gouch', the husband being 'minded to shoot Mr. Burdett', he was fined £40. Winthrop gloated that Burdett returned to an England no longer sympathetic to his religious views, whatever they may have been, and was imprisoned. Yet this Sidney ne'er-do-well became Dean of Leighlin in Ireland after the Restoration.

Burdett's spiritual opposite must surely be George Moxon, a farmer's son from Yorkshire, who arrived at Sidney as a *pauper scholaris* in 1620, a pupil of the tutor John Bell, and noted for his Latin lyric poetry. After 12 years as curate at St Helen's, Chester, Moxon was cited for nonconformity, sailed from Bristol in disguise in 1637 and arrived at Dorchester, near Boston. In 1638 he became a member of his close friend and business principal, the furrier William Pynchon's famous settlement at Agawam (now Springfield), Massachusetts. The 40-foot meeting house he preached in was filled with settlers brought to it by the beating of a drum 'at 10 of the clock on lecture days and at 9 of the clock on the Lord's days'. Moxon was an enormously popular preacher of 'sermons of love' who claimed that 'we are in a new country, and here we must be happy, for if we are not happy ourselves we cannot make others happy'. His stipend was '6 pence in wampum [a string of shell beads], of every family, or a pick of Indian corn, if they have not wampum'. This 'happy-clappy' preacher was less keen on the Native Americans, of whom he had a low opinion, but by Pynchon, Winthrop and his congregation, he was counted a great, and indeed overweight, blessing. In spite of a few hiccups, such as accusations that his daughter's 'fits' were a sign of witchcraft, verses written in his honour at his departure for England in 1652 show the affection in which he was held:

> As thou with strong and able parts are made,
> The person stout, with toile and labor shall,
> With help of Christ, through difficulties wade.

The real blow came just before this, when Moxon was forced to leave Massachusetts in the wake of his mentor William Pynchon's indictment for heresy. When he returned to England he found preferment under Cromwell's regime in Cheshire, acting as a 'trier' to ensure prospective ministers did not encourage dancing or play-acting. At the Restoration, like many of his persuasion, he was deprived of his position and lived an underground, hand-to-mouth existence, preaching in barns and farmhouses.

Our final Sidneian in early America was Thomas Harrison, a native of Kingston-upon-Hull who, as a prosperous merchant's son, went to Sidney as a pensioner in 1634 along with the legendary Sir Roger L'Estrange. In 1640, Harrison arrived at Sewell's Point, Lower Norfolk, Virginia as a Church of England minister and by 1645 received a payment in the form of 1,000 pounds of tobacco for conducting a burial service. He was also by that time a Puritan convert and his churchwardens complained against him for not reading 'the booke of Common Prayer and for not administering the Sacrament of Baptisme according to the Cannons'. He formed a congregation in Nansemond County, and his correspondence with the Governor of Massachusetts,

John Wheelwright, a copy of a portrait in the State House, Boston, Massachusetts. Exeter Historical Society, New Hampshire

John Winthrop, reveals his pleasure at conversions he had made in conformist Virginia. Harrison was banished to Boston in 1648, amid great controversy in Virginia and London, and by 1650 was back in London preaching at St Dunstan-in-the-East, where Cromwell attended his sermons. His first publication, a sermon of 1655 entitled *Old Jacobs Accompt Cast up and Owned by One of His Seed, a Young Lady*, commemorated the death of Lady Susanna Reynolds and considered the bad times that affected the saved and damned alike.

In 1655, and perhaps suggesting a connection with our stoical doctor John Stearne, Harrison was chaplain to Henry Cromwell in Ireland, and reported dissidents to the Protector's spymaster John Thurloe. In 1659 he was among the examiners of a shipment of Quaker books that was ordered to be burnt. His popularity was such that his salary was the enormous sum of £300 per year, many times that of the Sidney master. After 1660, back in England, Harrison was now a marked man and arrested and fined in 1665. He was later arrested again for holding illegal conventicles in Cheshire. Harrison returned to Ireland where he began writing an ambitious theology system and died in Dublin in 1682. Edmund Calamy, the historian of nonconformity, wrote of Harrison's great oratorical skills, probably learned in the Sidney chapel, and his 'extraordinary Gift in Prayer' and 'peculiar Flights of Spiritual Rhetorick'. One patron, says Calamy, 'often us'd to say, that he had rather hear Dr. Harrison say Grace over an Egg, than hear the Bishops pray and Preach'.

CHAPTER 4

'Storms and Tempests' 1643–1660

'Leave me all other business but teares,
A sadder business than both houses feares,
And a much holyer concernment, Cou'd
Our eyes but wash our hands and purge that blood
Which stained Edgehill, where some of our men lye,
And what should save the rest, our Charity.
Compassion dide there gasping in a wound
And stretch'd out in a sinew, where she found
Death and a grave, while the cold gore relents
And weeps ageal'd into her Monument.'

—Clement Paman, 'The Teares', 1642. (Paman, from Suffolk, matriculated at Sidney in 1627. He was a Royalist, chaplain to the Earl of Strafford, and an accomplished poet. He was ejected from his living in Thatcham, Berkshire in 1653 and died as dean of Elphin, Ireland, in 1664.)

WHEN KING CHARLES I raised his standard at Nottingham in August 1642, he set in train events that changed Britain for ever. The religious and political tensions of the previous 15 years erupted into civil war, following the recent arrest of Archbishop Laud and the execution of the King's chief advisor, the Earl of Strafford, at the behest of parliament the year before. Sidney men, past and present, were plunged into years of turmoil that found only fragile resolution in 1649 with the King's execution, and the establishment of a Commonwealth and then a Protectorate under Oliver Cromwell, and then again in 1660 with the restoration of the monarchy.

OPPOSITE: *Oliver Cromwell, after Sir Peter Lely, probably from the collection of Richard Cromwell*

Scottish pistol, made for Hugh Campbell, dated 1647, and given by Mr William James Smith (1906), one of whose ancestors reputedly captured the pistol at the battle of Worcester in 1650

Sidney students fought on either side of the conflict, maintained their estates if allowed to, practised as doctors and lawyers, attended parliament as peers or MPs, acted as army chaplains, made a living as Presbyterian and independent ministers, or survived in obscurity or even exile abroad as ejected Anglicans. The College managed to continue its day-to-day work, and with the exception of 1643, maintained its numbers remarkably well over the next two decades. A slight decline in the later 1630s was reversed in 1640–42, when there were over 30 new undergraduates a year. However, a note in the College register for November 1642 reads, following the names of John Stearne and Thomas Richardson, the future Lord Cramond: '*Grassante bello civili cesserunt armis togae, nec plures hoc anno admissi sunt*' ('Civil war being in progress, gowns gave way to arms, and no more were admitted this year'.)

'A Dangerous Distemper': Samuel Ward's Final Days

St. John's College was made a Gaol by the Parliamentary Forces, commanded by the Earl of Manchester; and amongst the rest Dr. Samuel Ward, Master of Sidney College, was imprisoned, whither Mr. [Seth] Ward accompanied him voluntarily, and submitted to that confinement, that he might assist so good a Man and so great a Friend in that Extremity. I have heard him say that Imprisonment seem'd at first to him very uneasie, but after he had been a little time used to it, liked it well enouf…The great Inconvenience of so close a Confinement, in the heighth of a hot Summer, caused some of Doctor Ward's Friends to mediate for his Removal, at least for some weeks, which was granted, and in the beginning of August the Doctor was permitted to go to his own House, to which also Mr. Ward accompanied him. —Walter Pope, *Life of Seth Ward*, 1697.

The born-again Puritan Oliver Cromwell came back to haunt his old master. By now a successful local politician and businessman, and so-called 'Lord of the Fens', Cromwell had been granted freedom of the borough of Cambridge at a celebration at the town hall, at which he appeared 'arrayed in a scarlet coat with a broad gold lace', and for which he provided a 'good quantity of wine' and 'confectionery stuffe, which was liberally filled out, and as liberally taken off, to the warming of most of their noddles'. He had been elected MP for Cambridge in 1640 and again in 1641–42, and lived in the city, in a house near St Clement's Church, halfway between Sidney and Magdalene.

King Charles returned from Scotland after the Second Bishops' War in November 1641, the event celebrated in verses by Cambridge men, including the loyal Samuel Ward, the young Edward Dering (1640), who was to join his father with the King at Nottingham the following year, and the fellow Joseph Haine. Such acts of loyalty were rewarded with words of future support from the King and a request for plate and money on loan at eight per cent interest.

The *Acta Collegii* record: 'July yᵉ 2, 1642. It was ordered by yᵉ M[aste]r, Mr. Garbut, Pendreth, Haine, Ward, being yᵉ major part then present, [tha]t a £100 should be taken out of yᵉ Treasury for yᵉ Kg's use, and so much plate as hath been given to yᵉ M[aste]r & ffell[ows]; for admissions of ffellow-commoners should bee set apart in lieu of it, till it bee repaid.'

Given the loan of £150 made by St John's, this was a very generous offering for a poor college. However, when a request from Charles for plate came a few weeks later, it seems Sidney did not contribute to the nearly £10,000 worth collected and sent with great haste to Nottingham.

Cromwell had intercepted some of the plate and 'seized the magazine in the Castle in Cambridge'. Three heads of colleges were imprisoned in London and on 17 August Cromwell was sent instructions to 'exercise and train all the Train Bands and Volunties in the Town of Cambridge…to defend it from all hostile attempts,…to disarm all Popish Recusants and other ill-affected persons'. Many college members were harassed in the streets by soldiers, and the House of Lords in March 1643 had to offer its protection to the university to ensure the 'quiet and studies of Scholars'.

Monument to Thomas Fuller, Cranford church, Middlesex. The brass plaque shows that the Sidney master G A Weekes and the fellows restored the monument in 1937

William Wilmer

Most Sidney royalists had land and wealth seized. William Wilmer entered Sidney in 1598 at the advanced age of 20. The following year he was admitted to the Inner Temple, and later married Anne Andrew, daughter of a local worthy, and had four children. Wilmer became Sheriff of Northamptonshire and was knighted in 1617. During the Civil War he suffered severely. Wilmer died of natural causes in 1646 and his will refers to the loss of his considerable estates and fortune: 'and touching my worldly goods which since these sadd times have been almost all taken from me, soe that I cannot remember my particular friends and kindred as I would'. His executors were obliged to compound for his estates in the sum of £500.

Fortunately for Sidney, in 1613 Wilmer had given to the College library a number of valuable and beautifully leather-bound books, which have his coat of arms embossed on the cover and book plates inside, proudly announcing 'qvondam. pencionary. in. ista. domo. viz.in.anno.domini.1599 ('Sometime pensioner in this house, namely in the year of our Lord 1599'). The books were Jesuit theological writings, published in Cologne in 1612. Strangely, a descendant, Clive Wilmer, became a fellow at Sidney in 2005.

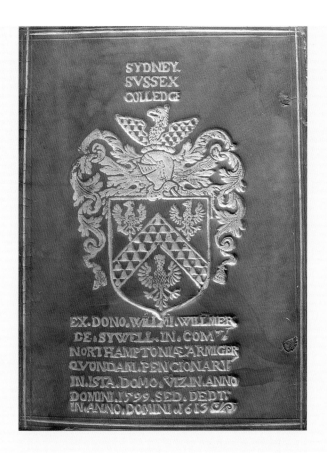

The unruly soldiers were part of the parliamentary Eastern Association, a military alliance of eastern counties based at Cambridge, with their headquarters very near Sidney, at the Bear Inn on the site of Market Passage. The leading figures in the Association, appropriately, were Sidney's Colonel Oliver Cromwell and Edward Montagu, 2nd Earl of Manchester, who ensured the town's security. The governor of the castle reported to the Commons in July 1643 that 'Our Town and Castle are now very strongly fortified, being encompassed with breastworks and bulwarks'.

1642 saw the closure of the theatres in London and the indecisive Battle of Edgehill. In 1643 a parliamentary ordinance ordered the confiscation of royalist estates. On 30 March 1643 the university was asked to contribute to the parliamentary coffers, 'so to redeem their forwardness in supplying the King'. The reply from the venerable heads of college was that such a contribution would be 'against true religion and a good conscience'.

The 71-year-old Samuel Ward was among those who, as a royalist source claimed, 'in the Convocation House, when all the Members of the University there assembled (many of them 60 years old and upwards) were kept prisoners in the Public Schools on an exceedingly cold night till near one in the morning, without any accommodation for food, firing or lodging; and, to complete the outrage, it was done on Good Friday…' The heads refused to buckle under the pressure and Ward held out despite a personal plea from Cromwell. He was thrown into the gaol constructed at St John's, accompanied by Seth Ward. His life was rapidly drawing to a close. 'Within a Months time after his Inlargement, the good Old Man fell into a dangerous Distemper, caused by his Imprisonment, whereof he died the seventh of September following in the year of our Lord 1643.' Seth Ward says that his master's final words were 'God bless the king and my Lord Hopton'. He was buried in the College chapel.

Thomas Fuller, now a chaplain in Lord Hopton's army and another devoted fellow of Samuel Ward's at Sidney, described him in his history of the university of 1655 as a 'Moses, not only for the slowness of his speech, but, otherwise, meekness of nature'. Fuller saw Ward as a wise moderate, seeking to protect his college and its mission from the tumult gathering around it: 'He was counted as a Puritan before these times, and Popish in these times; and yet being always the same was a true Protestant at all times.' His description of the nature of Ward's fate is deeply touching: 'Now, as high winds bring some men the sooner into sleep, so I conceive the storms and tempests of these distracted times invited this good old man the sooner to his long rest, where we may fairly leave him and quietly draw the curtains about him.'

'Violently Pluck't': Richard Minshull's Election

> Before ye election of Mr Minshull to be Maister of ye College, Mr Seth Ward in ye presence of Mr Garbut, Minshull, Pendreth, Lawson, Hodges, Seyliard, Gibson, Matthewes, Bertie, made a protestation against ye election (which was by Statute to bee perfected before 12 of ye clock at noone [tha]t day) because Mr Pawson was taken away by souldiers sent from ye Committee, so that he could not give his voice with others: notwithstanding ye rest of the ffellowes proceeded on and Mr Minshull was elected, and admitted before 12 of ye clock [tha]t day. —*Acta Collegii*, 13 September, 1643.

Sidney had to elect a new master, a process about which the College statutes were detailed and strict. These were not times, however, for such pedantic regulation. Less than a week after Ward's death, the fellows assembled in the Chapel at 5 a.m. on 13 September 1643 to elect his successor. The applicants were the royalist Herbert Thorndike, a fellow and senior bursar of Trinity, and the Sidney fellow Richard Minshull, who had been an undergraduate in Cromwell's year and was loyal to parliament. During the service preceding the election, a group of parliamentary forces, under Manchester's ultimate command, broke into the chapel and seized one of the fellows, John Pawson, who, according to a royalist account, 'was violently pluck't from the Communion as he was ready to receive that Holy Sacrament…and thrown into Gaol to the great disturbance of the Election'.

John Pawson, a Yorkshireman who had been at Sidney since arriving as a sizar in 1636, though a royalist in 1643, soon afterwards took the parliamentary covenant and was elected a fellow of St John's in 1644. He died as the rector of nearby Newton in 1654 at the age of 34. His son Thomas went up to Sidney as a pensioner in 1667, perhaps mindful that the fellows had paid his father in full for the year he was without a fellowship.

The *Acta* describe the actual votes cast. There were six voters: James Garbutt, Richard Minshull, John Lawson, Thomas Seyliard, Robert Bertie and William Hodges. The last abstained while the others voted for Minshull. Those who, 'refusing to repair to the Chapell againe', absented themselves entirely, were Charles Pendreth and his former student Seth Ward, along with Edward Gibson and Edmund Matthews.

Seth Ward went to Oxford to get a mandate from the King commanding Minshull and the Sidney fellows to go to Oxford to give an account of the election. This was pinned to the chapel door by a Dr Linnet, an ally of the defeated Thorndike.

Robert Bertie also went to Oxford, however, to get an order from the King confirming Minshull's appointment. He got a broad seal for the order and Thorndike and his supporters accepted it. Minshull paid his surviving Sidney colleagues 'about a hundred pound' for their troubles, according to Walter Pope. Interestingly, Bertie had been appointed a fellow in December 1642 by royal mandate.

Montagu Bertie

The actions of Robert Bertie (1635) in seeking royal approval for the parliamentarian candidate can be seen against an intriguing backdrop of family and military events and attempts to hold the peace. Robert was the fifth son of Sir Robert Bertie, first Earl of Lindsey, and the younger brother of Montagu Bertie, the second Earl of Lindsey from 1642, and of Roger, both of whom had gone up to Sidney as fellow-commoners in 1623. Their father, Lord Lieutenant of Lincolnshire and a general on the royalist side, had died in Warwick Castle of wounds incurred at the Battle of Edgehill on 23 October 1642. Montagu Bertie, a royalist captain, had made a famous attempt to rescue his father on the battlefield (a scene popular with Victorian artists) and had tended to him in his final hours at Warwick. Bertie was held captive until July 1643, when he was released in an exchange of prisoners. He returned to the King's forces and fought at various battles including Naseby, where he was wounded. As a diplomat he urged Charles to reach an agreement with parliament. He accompanied the King's body to its grave in 1649. He lost his estates, which, however, were restored in 1660. His second marriage during the Civil Wars was to the daughter of fellow Sidneian, Edward Wray, the musical groom of the bedchamber. He died in 1666.

Montagu Bertie, 2nd Earl of Lindsey, by William Dobson, c1644. Private collection

'Reformation of the University': Manchester and the Sidney Dons

'Wee'l down with all the Versities
    Where learning is professt,
Because they practice and maintain
    The language of the Beast;
Wee'l drive the Doctors out of doors,
    And parts what ere they be;
Wee'l cry all Arts and Learning down,
    And hy then up go we'.
(Anon, 'The Roundheads', 1653)

Edward Montagu, 2nd Earl of Manchester, engraving by an unknown artist, 1647. National Portrait Gallery, London

Manchester is shown here as the 'Major General of the [Eastern] Association', after his fall from grace with the increasingly powerful Cromwell. His post-Restoration portraits are far grander images

A parliamentary report on Cambridge in 1641 had little to criticise Sidney for in terms of religious practice, though some errors were noted: 'Some in this Colledge bow towards the Elements at the sacrament tyme. Mr Rodes sometime Deane used some violence to bring the schollers to the observation of some rites, not in practise there before, as standing up at gloria patri and the Gospell and bowing at the name Jesus.' In the main, however, Sidney was conformist as far as the House of Commons was concerned.

In early 1644, the Earl of Manchester had sought successfully to defeat a proposal by parliament that the colleges that had given plate to the King should have their lands sequestrated. However, parliament insisted that Manchester be given power to eject masters, fellows, and students, as 'he shall think unfit for their Places and to place other fitting persons in their Roome, such as shall be approved of by the Assembly of Divines sitting at Westminster'. This meant an attack on all the signs of 'superstition and popery' that had been encouraged by Laud.

Manchester visited Cambridge in February to undertake a 'reformation of the University' with a zealous Committee of Visitors. Their meetings were held at first at the Bear Inn and then at Trinity. Though renowned for his moderation and good manners, Manchester ordered Sidney to send him a copy of the statutes, together with the names of all college members, stating who was absent and present. His next order demanded all members to 'be resident at your said Colledge the tenth day of March next ensuing, to give an account wherein they shall be required to answer such things as may be demanded by mee…' He then asked for records of all college acts passed during the previous 12 years.

Manchester's initial demands for attendance might have referred to those he suspected of being with the King's army many miles away from Cambridge, but in fairness he deferred the meeting for a month. One Sidney fellow was ejected for failing to turn up, and four more were later turned out for refusing to take the covenant swearing allegiance to Parliament.

The five ejected fellows were Seth Ward, who, as we have seen, eventually went on to Oxford and had a glittering career; John Pawson; Edward Gibson, a native of Rutland and former sizar from Uppingham School who went into clerical obscurity in Bedfordshire; and John Lawson, a Yorshireman who, like Pawson, died young, at 30, and was buried in Cambridge in the following January. The deaths of Pawson and Lawson cast light perhaps on Fuller's concern about how those ejected survived the grief, citing the Greek proverb, 'He is either dead or teacheth school'. Finally, caught in the crossfire, was the unfortunate Robert Bertie.

'These Sadd Times': Sidney versus Sidney

It cannot but have struck our readers, that there have been two or three of the stoutest royalists, and two or three of the stoutest republicans in the country, of this College.
—George Dyer, *A History of the University of Cambridge*, 1814

Mary (Talbot), Lady Armine, engraving by Frederick Hendrick van Hove, 1683. National Portrait Gallery, London

Mary was the devoutly Puritanical wife of the parliamentarian Sir William Armine (1610). Their son Theophilus was killed fighting for parliament in 1644

The Honourable the Lady Mary Armyne. F.H. Van Houe. sculp.

While the small and relatively peaceful world of academia was turned upside down by the Civil War in the early 1640s, many Sidney students were fighting on battlefields across England, frequently against one another. Others were engaged in political manoeuvres that saw a criss-crossing of destinies and allegiances. We know much about the war fought by major parliamentary figures such as Cromwell and Manchester and royalists such as Edward Noel, Viscount Campden and Montagu Bertie, Earl of Lindsey. There are others, though, whose experience is significant in Sidney's history as they crossed paths, words and often swords.

Sir William Armine of Osgodby, Lincolnshire, who had gone up to Sidney as a fellow-commoner in 1610, was a wealthy landowner with estates across the Midlands and Yorkshire. He was a staunchly parliamentarian MP who was sent to Oxford to discuss terms with the King in 1643. In the same year Baptist Noel, Viscount Campden, who had taken his MA at Sidney in 1628, sacked and burned Armine's house at Osgodby. The King's senior advisors included the Earl of Norwich, George Goring, one of the earliest fellow-commoners at Sidney, whose son was one of the most dashing, brilliant and erratic of the royalist commanders. The younger Goring, who was to die in exile in Madrid in 1657, led a magnificent rout of one wing of the parliamentary army at Marston Moor in July 1644, only to be let down by the right flank of Prince Rupert's army, allowing Cromwell to sweep round and achieve a decisive victory. His father survived him and was buried in Westminster Abbey, a replacement, so to speak, for the body of his enemy Cromwell. Armine declined to sit in judgement on the King in 1649, but when he died

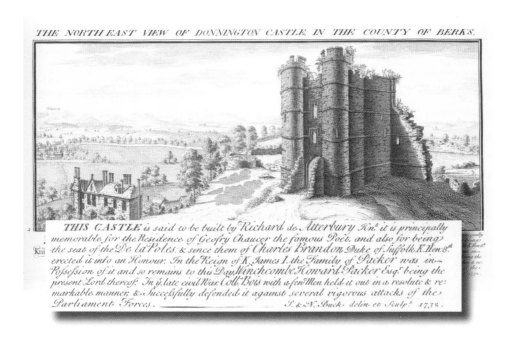

THE NORTH EAST VIEW OF DONNINGTON CASTLE, IN THE COUNTY OF BERKS.

THIS CASTLE is said to be built by Richard de Atterbury Kn.t it is principally memorable for the Residence of Geofry Chaucer the famous Poet, and also for being the seat of the De la Poles. & since them of Charles Brandon Duke of Suffolk K.Hen.8.th erected it into an Honour: In the Reign of K. James I. the Family of Packer was in-Posession of it and so remains to this Day, Winchcombe. Howard. Packer Esq.r being the present Lord thereof: In y.e late civil War Coll. Bois with a few Men held it out in a resolute & re: markable manner; & Successfully defended it against several vigorous attacks of the Parliament Forces. ———   J. & N. Buck. delin: et Sculp.t 1732.

LEFT: *Donnington Castle, engraving by L & N Buck, 1732*

BELOW: *Tomb of Baptist Noel (MA 1628), 3rd Viscount Campden, by Grinling Gibbons, Exton Church, Rutland, 1682*

Noel was commissioner of array for Rutland where the main Civil War conflicts were between the parliamentarian Haringtons and the royalist Noels. He looted the house of fellow Sidneian Sir William Armine at Osgodby in Lincolnshire. Noel's fourth wife, Elizabeth, interred here with him, was one of Montagu Bertie's daughters, a further Sidney connection.

intestate in 1651, Parliament decided not to sit as a mark of respect, and the Council of State, of which he had been a member ordered all members to attend the funeral in Lincolnshire. His son was killed as a parliamentary colonel in 1644.

John Boys, eldest son of Sir Edward Boys of Bonnington, Kent, is the first of three Sidney murderers from that county in the 17th century – he killed a vagrant, Thomas Alcock, with 'a blow on the head with a fire pan' in Canterbury in 1630, but was pardoned. This was a few years after taking his degree in 1626 and shortly before he spent the 1630s as a soldier in Ireland. He was a captain in the King's army against the Scots in 1640, and in 1642 was a lieutenant-colonel in a royalist foot regiment.

In 1644 he came up against the forces of Manchester, who had been at Sidney just a few years before him, at the siege of Donnington Castle, Berkshire, of which he was governor. Boys built earthworks around the castle and fought off two major assaults on it. He was knighted for this bravery before the second battle of Newbury, made a colonel, and then fought off a further attack. In spring 1646, Parliament staged a final siege of the castle and Boys was instructed to surrender.

Boys fled to Holland but returned to England in 1648 to take part in the Kentish uprising after Parliament's misjudged attempt to abolish traditional Christmas celebrations. He was captured at Deal after a skirmish in which he was shot, and escaped with sequestration. Ever the fighting man, Boys was arrested twice in the 1650s on suspicion of plotting armed insurrection. His fame and reputation as a war hero were

'The Battayle of Nasbye'

Naseby was the decisive battle of the English Civil Wars. Sidney's leading parliamentary soldiers that day included Oliver Cromwell and Edward Rossiter. For the royalists, Montagu Bertie commanded the rearguard and Thomas Fuller was chaplain to Sir Edward Hopton's regiment.

The Description of the Armies of Horse and Foot....at the Battayle of Nasbye, engraving by Robert Streeter, 1645

considerable, Clarendon saying that he was 'as fit a person to be Major General… as any man', and Pepys declaring him 'a fine man'. During 1660 Boys was one of those who went back and forth across the Channel with correspondence between the King and the naval commander Edward Montagu, 1st Earl of Sandwich, fighting off attempts by republicans to turn local opinion in Kent against the Restoration. This Edward Montagu was a cousin of Edward Montagu, who was now serving in the navy under him and had been at Sidney in 1652. The Sidney man had been instrumental in persuading his republican cousin to defect and help with the negotiations to restore the monarchy. He died fighting for the Earl of Sandwich, then Admiral Montagu, at Bergen in 1665 during the second Anglo-Dutch War. John Boys seems to have had a cousin, also John Boys, who went up to Sidney in 1623 and was an MP for Kent in the 1650s – perhaps he was one of the republicans of his county.

Edward, 2nd Lord Montagu of Boughton (1631), by Robert Walker, c1650s. Collection of the Trustees of the 9th Duke of Buccleuch's Chattels Fund. Montagu opposed the regicide and was sidelined politically in the 1650s. He died in 1684

Sidney royalists seem also to have suffered worse fatalities than their parliamentarian opponents. Ferdinando Stanhope (1635), son of the Sidney benefactor the Earl of Chesterfield, was slain at Bridgford, Nottinghamshire, in 1643. Richard Cholmley, of Whitby, Yorkshire, was admitted as a fellow-commoner in 1635, when his mother, no doubt embarrassingly, had come up with him 'and boarded her selfe with in a mile that she might bee neare to look after him being a very indulgent, carefull Mother'. He was killed besieging Lyme Regis as a Colonel in 1644, aged 27. Salvin Carleil, another Yorkshireman, admitted in 1639, was killed at Scarborough Castle in 1645 aged 29. Sir Shilston Calmady, of Devon, a fellow-commoner in 1601, died during the siege of Ford in that county in 1645; his splendid tomb still stands by the screen in Membury church.

'Disgrace to Rebels, Glory to the King': Sir Roger L'Estrange

> I am the bird whom they combine,
>   Thus to deprive of liberty;
> And though they my corps confine,
> Yet maugre hate, my soule is free:
> And though imur'd, yet here I'le chirp and sing,
> Disgrace to rebels, glory to my King.
> —Sir Roger L'Estrange, 'Mr. L'Estrange his verses in the Prison at Lynn'

One Sidney royalist stands out above all the others. Roger L'Estrange was the third son of Sir Hamon L'Estrange, the author and MP, and was born at Hunstanton Hall in Norfolk. After schooling at Sedgeford, Westminster and Eton, he arrived at Sidney in November 1634 as a pensioner under the tutorship of William Flathers. L'Estrange's Sidney contemporaries, or near-contemporaries, are interesting figures. They include later royalists such as Seth Ward; Robert Mawdes, who was killed at the siege of Newark; Sir John Bale, whose house at Carlton Curlieu in Leicestershire became a garrison for the King's army; Robert Bertie; Colonel Jarrard Salvin, killed at Northallerton; Anthony Byerley, colonel of a regiment under the Marquess of Newcastle; and Major William Lutton. Among prominent parliamentarians were Edward Montagu, 2nd Baron Montagu of Boughton, who strongly disapproved of the regicide; Sir Robert Atkyns, later one of the leading Whig lawyers and political theorists of Restoration England; the MP Sir Edward Rossiter; and Brian Stapleton, commissioner for Scotland. Independent churchmen, such as Thomas Harrison, the early settler in Massachusetts we

'Noll's fidler running from the parliament', design for a playing card, drawn by Francis Barlow, 1678–80, showing Sir Roger L'Estrange in flight after publishing The History of the Plot, *1679, and other pamphlets in 1680, in which he expressed his disbelief in the evidence of Titus Oates during the Popish Plot. British Museum, London*

have already considered, and George Cockayn, who was chaplain to Colonel Charles
Fleetwood and who gave a famously prophetic sermon in the House of Commons in
1648 shortly before Pride's Purge, also stand out. Such men L'Estrange would have
cordially loathed. From the outset he was an ardent royalist. His three years at Sidney
gave him the education he required to become one of the greatest and most vitri-
olic political journalists of all time; 'Mr. Filth', the nickname given to him by John
Bunyan, gives some idea of his fame and infamy.

Like many Cambridge contemporaries of his era and rank, L'Estrange entered
Gray's Inn in 1637, without having taken a Cambridge degree. In 1639, aged only 23,
he joined his father in the First Bishops' War against the Scots and in the early years
of the Civil War he fought at Newark and at Edgehill. His military fame, or notoriety,
rests on the campaign around King's Lynn, a town close to his family home, which he
seized in August 1643 and then withdrew from in September. In November he was
ordered to regain the town by bribery. He was betrayed by an accomplice, arrested in
an ale-house in his slippers, and sentenced to death by parliament. Reprieved from
execution, he was imprisoned in Newgate from where he began his writing career
with two appeals for release. He absconded in 1648, was involved in the unsuccessful
royalist uprising in Kent, and, once again sentenced to death, fled to Holland. Here
he obtained the patronage of Edward Hyde, later Earl of Clarendon, and may have
travelled on as far as Rome.

When he returned to England in 1653, fellow Sidneian Oliver Cromwell nulli-
fied L'Estrange's sentence of death. Cromwell's interest in L'Estrange's skills as a viol
player earned him the nickname 'Noll's Fiddler', and Thomas Fuller, a Sidney fellow
during L'Estrange's undergraduate days, dedicated his political fable *Ornitho-Logie, or
The Speech of Birds* to him in 1655.

When Cromwell died in 1658, L'Estrange was one of a cabal of royalist pamphlet-
eers arguing for the dissolution of the Rump Parliament and the election of a free
one. His *No Blind Guides*, written in 1660 against a tract by Milton, gives some idea
of his extremely aggressive, *ad hominem* style. After the Restoration L'Estrange was
the leading propagandist for the most vindictive royalists, relishing the disinterment
of Cromwell and that other great Sidney parliamentarian, the writer and historian
Tom May, and seeking the execution of the regicides. With Clarendon's support,
L'Estrange became first a government pamphleteer, then an informer against seditious writers and printers, and finally Surveyor of the Imprimery, a role he held, with
interruptions, until 1688. This role, joined with that of Licenser, made him a greatly
feared, respected and hated figure, for a quarter of a century.

Through the Act of Uniformity and the Licensing Act of 1662, L'Estrange was
given enormous power over all publishing and printing in England, empowered to
enter and search any property (other than peers') simply on suspicion that it contained seditious books and those 'contrary to…the doctrine of the discipline of the
Church of England'. Men such as the clergyman George Cockayn, a Sidney contemporary mentioned earlier, were the targets of L'Estrange's efforts as censor and
enforcer. He also had sole privilege of 'writing, printing and publishing all narratives
or relations not exceeding two sheets of paper and all advertisements, mercuries,

diurnals and books of public intelligence': in other words, the daily press as it then existed. Add to that the licensing power over all books except those on law, divinity, 'physick' and philosophy, and one gets a picture of a man with dictatorial discretion beyond comprehension in Britain today. His imprimatur is a familiar and chilling reminder of his influence as the scourge of free speech; it appears on countless books of the time. As Macaulay later wrote: 'from the malice of L'Estrange the grave was no hiding place, and the house of mourning no sanctuary'.

A Divine Assembly

J R Herbert, The Assertion of the Liberty of Conscience by the Independents at the Westminster Assembly of Divines, 1644, *c1844. Palace of Westminster Collection*

Herbert, a Catholic convert, probably painted this at the time of the 200th anniversary of the Westminster Assembly. The picture includes two of the Sidney men at the Assembly, Thomas Gataker (4) and William Price (3), as well as Edward Montagu, the Earl of Manchester (1). Herbert's painting also includes Oliver Cromwell (2) who, along with John Milton, was not actually present but made the image more familiar to Victorian viewers. Other Sidney men at the Assembly were Daniel Cawdrey and Jeremy Whitaker. Sidney's master Samuel Ward was invited but refused to attend.

'The Saints That Walk With God': Sidney's Puritan Chaplains

I know nothing you have that is long-lived but Jesus Christ…even the Kingdom of heaven, so far as it is made up of forms and administrations, shall wither and die, but the Kingdom of God shall never be shaken.
—George Cockayn, 'To all that live Godly in Christ Jesus', 1646

The kinds of Sidney men L'Estrange especially loathed were godly ministers like Henry Root and George Cockayn, who provided the parliamentary army's spiritual needs during the Civil War. Inevitably, Sidney had more than its fair share of such 'saints in arms', eight of them entering the army records.

Henry Root, who matriculated in 1606, was typical, and is the kind of Puritan minister Sidney is most associated with. In 1643 he moved to Halifax, Yorkshire, where he formed the first Independent congregation in the town. Despite quarrels with local Presbyterians, he was appointed chaplain to the regiment of foot Cromwell raised in Lancashire in 1650 for the Scottish campaign, which was used to help Lilburne's forces against those of Derby. A prominent and pacifying figure in Yorkshire religious politics in the 1650s, Root preached to Lilburne's troops at Manchester after the defeat of Booth's rising. An influential preacher at Sowerby after 1660, he was ejected when his chapel was used for a Congregationalist conference to discuss the impending Act of Uniformity, the kiss of death for nonconformists like Root. He was imprisoned at York Castle. He died a radical in 1669, his funeral marred by abuse of his character and his family by many locals.

George Cockayn came from the Puritan heartlands of Bedfordshire, his father, according to the approving Bulstrode Whitelocke, in 'the mediocrity & middle estate & condition…' He went up to Sidney as a pensioner in 1636, a near-contemporary of the royalist fatality Richard Cholmley, the parliamentary colonel Sir Edward Rossiter, and many others involved in the conflict. A popular radical Independent preacher in London, he was chaplain to Fleetwood's regiment in 1643. His congregation followed him around London, settling at St Pancras, Soper Lane, which was destroyed in the fire of London in 1666. His supporters there included various city grandees, such as Robert Tichborne and John Ireton.

In 1648 Cockayn preached an explicitly political sermon before the House of Commons, a week before Pride's Purge. Hinting at what was about to happen, he quoted from the *Book of Isaiah*: 'And I will turn my hand upon thee, and purely purge away the dross, and take away all thy Tin', urging his listeners 'to 'delay not to do Justice' and 'think not to save yourselves by an unrighteous saving of them, who are the Lords and the Peoples known Enemies'. Cockayn saw the millennium approaching: 'The Saints that walk with God in Union with

George Cockayn, Flesh Expiring, and the Spirit Inspiring … A Sermon, title page, 1648. Corpus Christi College, Oxford

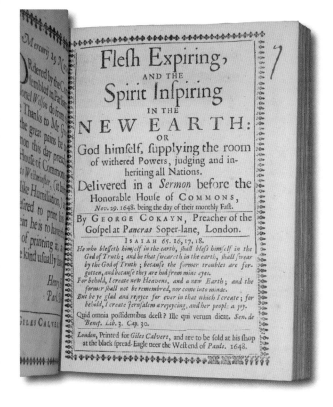

Holiness and Righteousness are the men by whom God at last will judge all the causes of the sons of men.' In 1651 Cockayn was with Fleetwood's regiment in Scotland, and the following year was involved in the millenarian agitation in London, associating himself with the Fifth Monarchists. He was in discussion with republican officers who were disgruntled at Cromwell's proclamation of the Protectorate, though he also provided Cromwell's spymaster John Thurloe with intelligence about dissidents. At the Restoration he lost his ministry in London and in 1662 co-authored books of 'prodigies' showing that 'God doth from Heaven testifie against the Prophane, Superstitious, Apostatising and Persecuting Spirit of the Day'. As late as 1683, by now a close associate of John Bunyan, he was convicted at the Old Bailey for unlawful preaching.

We have already encountered two chaplains, Thomas Harrison and George Burdett, in America. Harrison was Henry Cromwell's chaplain in Ireland and Burdett was chaplain to Colonel Tyrrell's regiment of foot in the Earl of Essex's army in 1644. After time in gaol in Cambridge as 'a man of evil report and a very dangerous man', Burdett was commissioned chaplain to Robert Lilburne's regiment of horse in 1650. He was a signatory of the letter on behalf of Lilburne's and Lambert's regiments demanding a general fast to support the Scottish campaign and, no doubt, travelled to Scotland on Cromwell's campaign.

'Nothing There to Be Amended': Sidney in the 1640s

At Sidney things were not as bad as might have been expected; even the plague outbreaks in 1646 and 1647 had only a minor impact on life there. The great Puritan iconoclast William Dowsing – who had gone through East Anglia in 1643 and 1644 methodically 'reforming' churches by smashing stained glass, ripping up monumental brasses, destroying altar rails and crucifixes, and knocking the heads off medieval sculptural saints – visited the Cambridge colleges and wreaked similar destruction. It was payback time for Laud and his followers, and the Church of England was dismantled as ruthlessly as Thomas Cromwell and Edward VI had destroyed the old Catholic church a century before. Dowsing arrived at Sidney chapel on 30 December 1643 and recorded in his diary: 'We saw nothing there to be amended'. The plain white walls and wainscot and cold stone floor made a perfect reformed religious space. The decoration and furnishing were in fact quite rich, with a wall-fixed pulpit, a desk and communion-table carpets and damask cloths. There was, however, nothing heretical or superstitious, as there was at Pembroke, King's and Peterhouse.

The following year, Manchester asked the surviving rump of Sidney fellows and their new master to send him the names of scholars most suited to fellowships. There were, following the recent putsch, five vacancies to be filled. One was suspended to pay a Mr Lukyn for the 'detriments' of John Lawson's beer bill. The remaining

*'Cromwell's Chair',
once in the possession of
Oliveria Cromwell, the last
Cromwell descendant of
the Protector, but probably
later than the date of 1653
carved on the back*

four fellowships went to Francis Quarles, John Rowlett, William Wells and George Thorne, none of whom have left much to remind us of them. With the approval of the Westminster Assembly of Divines, they all had to swear to uphold the covenant. The Assembly, comprising 121 Divines and a number of lay members, including Manchester, convened in 1643 to agree a new religious order in England, mainly based on Presbyterian principles. It included a disproportionate number of Sidney men, all considerable figures in largely nonconformist traditions: Daniel Cawdrey, Thomas Gataker, William Price, Jeremy Whitaker and, ironically, Samuel Ward. Ward, understandably, refused to attend.

'Ambling Along': Sidney in the Commonwealth and Protectorate

> Dr Minshull, though he joined first with the rest, crept at night into their lodgings and put his hand to the parchment, his whole College ambling next day in the same step. —Samuel Dillingham of Emmanuel, on Richard Minshull's subscribing to the Engagement, 1644

On 23 April 1645, Minshull wrote Manchester a rare surviving letter, which suggests some favour shown to Sidney by its former student, who was now one of the most powerful men in England. It seems to refer to a payment made to the College by the Earl of Manchester at a time of great economic distress. 'This College is truly sensible of its own happiness in having this relation to you; it is the first money we have received this last half-year for our subsistence from any, and indeed it stops the mouths of the clamorous. The Committee [for the regulation of the university] here have called me before them, upon some complaint made to them that I refused to pay our new Fellows; but there was no such matter; only I had not received any for the time that they could command any, and so thought myself disobliged from payment till such time as our tenants brought it in. But my answer was not well relished, which I think was very reasonable, without fraud, and which I will justify before any that is not prepossessed with prejudice. This I thought good to make your Honour acquainted with, to see what hard task I have to give content in these times; but if men will not be pleased, my conscience doth comfort me, whatsoever malevolent fame may render me.'

Manchester, who had fallen out with Cromwell after the Battle of Marston Moor in 1644 because of his unwillingness to prosecute the war more aggressively, and who in 1649 had strongly opposed the ordinance for the King's trial, retired from the sharp end of political life. He was made Chancellor of the University of Cambridge in the same year and was immediately faced with a major political challenge. Parliament passed an act that required heads, fellows and college officers to subscribe to the Engagement and thereby required allegiance to a Commonwealth established without a king or House of Lords. Assessed by a Committee of Engagement sitting at the Bear Inn, many heads and fellows refused to sign and were ejected. As might be expected, Minshull dissembled, sloping off in the dark to the nearby Bear Inn, as Samuel Dillingham of Emmanuel noted sarcastically.

'A Cage of Unclean Birds': Sidney Men and Quaker Women

An incident in 1653 suggests the heightened religious tensions of the time and perhaps also the growing indiscipline among many Sidney undergraduates that became so disruptive after the Restoration. Two Quaker women from Yorkshire, Elizabeth Williams and Mary Fisher, came to Cambridge that year and began preaching outside Sidney, quickly eliciting a noisy response from the undergraduates. Joseph Besse's *Sufferings of the Quakers*, written a century later, tells how the women, 'discoursing with some Scholars of Sidney Sussex College concerning Matters of Religion, the Scholars asked them How many Gods there were? The Women answered, But one God, and told them, they had many whom they made God of, reproving their Ignorance of the true God and his Worship. Whereupon the Scholars began to mock and deride them: the Women observing the Froth and Levity of their behaviour, told them they were Antichrists, and that their college was a Cage of unclean Birds, and the Synagogue of Satan.' The women were reported to the mayor of Cambridge and a constable was sent to interrogate them. In reply to a request that they

divulge their names, they said they were 'written in the Book of Life', and when asked their husband's names they replied, 'they had no husband but Jesus Christ, and he sent them'. The mayor called them whores and ordered they be whipped at the Market Cross 'until the Blood ran down their Bodies', a punishment they endured with 'Constancy and Patience', praising the Lord for thus honouring them and praying for their persecutors.

As Besse points out, this was the first occasion on which any Quaker had been flogged in public and is a legendary incident in the sect's history. Mary Fisher became a missionary in the Americas and Turkey, attempting to convert the Sultan Mahomet IV in Adrianople and speaking to him through an interpreter. He listened with far more grace and attention than her Sidney tormentors and at the end of the meeting proposed an escort back to Constantinople, an offer she refused, preferring to walk. Always believing her Turkish mission had been successful, she died in Charleston, South Carolina in 1698.

In fact, even Manchester objected to the Engagement and was removed from office. Cromwell, like Manchester, seems to have looked fairly kindly on his old college; it was claimed by royalists at the time that the College was never 'rifled' for its plate and other wealth. There was other good news. The acquisition of the College's first 'advowsons', or right to church livings, was a major improvement in Sidney's financial affairs during the period, and made it more attractive to prospective fellows. Wilshampstead in Bedfordshire was acquired in 1649, through an ally of the Montagus, James Risley of St Andrew's, Holborn. Peasmarsh in Sussex was acquired in 1654, through the generosity of 'Mr. John Gyles', a former sizar from Sussex who had entered the College in 1602 and became a priest.

Thus Sidney survived the tumultuous times, but it seems likely its connections with Cromwell, Manchester and Puritanism stored up resentment for the future. Its character was changed permanently, losing most of the social cachet it had and becoming, instead, a place of mainly quiet scholarship rather than loud public profile.

'Our Soul is Escaped': The Enigma of Edmund Matthews

OPPOSITE: *Edmund Matthews, by an unknown artist, 1653*

What was it like to be a fellow in 1653, with Quaker women outside engaged in slanging matches with the undergraduates? One of Sidney's finest and most intriguing early

Anno Dñi 1653
Aetatis 36

portraits, painted that year, is of Edmund Matthews, a fellow who survived not only the Civil War, but the Commonwealth and Protectorate, and the reigns of Charles II and James II. He died in William and Mary's reign in 1692. He was at Sidney for 60 years, and a fellow for 51 of them, creating a remarkable record of loyalty and endurance. Yet little is known about the man behind this haunting painted face.

Matthews was born in 1616, the year of Cromwell's admission, and was the son of a barber-surgeon in Bishop's Stortford, Hertfordshire. He came to Sidney as a sizar in 1632, a contemporary of Seth Ward. In 1641 he was elected to the fellowship left vacant by Richard Dugard's departure. His early experience as a fellow was, to say the least, unsettled. Samuel Ward's death, the imposition of Minshull and the ejection of various fellows left him one of only a few pre-war fellows at the College. Matthews' name is missing from those who approved Minshull's election, yet he stayed at Sidney and signed the Covenant and Engagement. Whether this was on principle or out of caution is unclear. It is true to say, however, that the constancy of men such as Matthews kept the College going. His students included John Warren (1641), the congregationalist and close friend of the great Puritan Richard Baxter; and the 'Seaman's Preacher', John Ryther (1650), convicted for preaching to sailors in Wapping in 1670.

His portrait was painted when he was 36, the year the Protectorate was established. His long hair is distinctly not 'Roundhead', and his moustache and small tufty chin beard are even a little raffish. His black cap and clothing are those of his clerical profession. On the table to his right are several books, while he holds the *Septuagint* published by Daniel Rogers in the year of the painting, open to show Psalms 120 and 121 on the left and Psalms 124 and 125 on the right. His index finger points towards the end of Psalm 124. This is the 'song of deliverance' often used to celebrate victory or rescue at sea by the Royal Navy. The singing of metrical Psalms was about the only music allowed in Sidney's chapel at this time.

After claiming the protection of Israel by the Lord against the 'deep waters of the proud', the Psalm ends:

> Our soul is escaped even as a bird out of
> the snare of the fowler: the snare is broken,
> and we are delivered.
> Our help standeth in the Name of the
> Lord: who hath made heaven and earth.

The first Anglo-Dutch War had begun in 1652, and in 1653 England had scored three notable victories over the Dutch, ending the war with the Battle of Scheveningen on 10 August at which the great Admiral Tromp was killed. Matthews's portrait perhaps alludes to these military events; we cannot be sure. It may be that the reference is to immediate political and academic warfare. Or, it may be that the picture invokes both, and even a more private meaning.

In 1653 there was a violent debate in pamphlets, sermons and the House of Commons about the future of the universities and the training of ministers. The

Anabaptist master of Caius, William Dell, took an extremely anti-academic view, arguing that learning was dangerous to spiritual health but also proposing that all large towns should have universities. There was also an attempt to take the colleges' rents away. Cromwell's armed intervention ending the Long Parliament in April that year put an end to the threat to Oxford and Cambridge, but the dispute had been intense and alarming.

There may be interesting connections between Matthews, Seth Ward and the universities debate. In 1654, Ward and his new Oxford colleague John Wilkins wrote a defence of the universities, *Vindiciae Academiarum*, against Dell, Thomas Hobbes, who had criticised Oxford and Cambridge in his *Leviathan* in 1651, and the sectarian army chaplain and occultist John Webster. Webster's *Academiarum Examen* was the kind of visionary tract that proliferated at the time. Ward defended the universities against accusations of an anti-scientific bias, pointing to the new learning and the private laboratories sprouting up around him. As Ward's contemporary, Matthews' views on the debate and on his colleague's new life in Oxford would be interesting to know; the Psalm he points at may suggest some reference to his views on the matter. It was a difficult time to keep a job; between 1646 and 1660 no fewer than 22 Sidney fellows were ejected. While Matthews led a career of quiet obedience and obscurity, Ward's rapid ascent after his brave move followed the very opposite trajectory.

Descartes, Witches and Spot-Dials: The Strange Career of Gilbert Clerke

One alternative to Matthews' approach was to go it alone elsewhere as a scholar and entrepreneur. In 1655 Gilbert Clerke resigned his fellowship at Sidney when he was due to take his Bachelor of Divinity degree. Son of the headmaster of Uppingham School, Clerke had arrived at Sidney as a sizar in 1641 aged 15, just in time to witness the next few years' dramatic events in College, the university and across the country. He was elected a fellow in 1648, became a tutor, and in 1652 was Sidney's first university proctor, a disciplinary and examining role. He took Presbyterian orders in 1651. He claimed to have been one of the first to introduce the new Cartesian philosophy and the more theoretical study of mathematics to Cambridge, and wrote books on that subject inspired by Descartes. Philosophically, he attacked his former colleague Seth Ward, as well as Thomas Hobbes and others, who believed a vacuum could exist in nature.

The University Library at Cambridge has a notebook belonging to one of Clerke's tutorial students, the sizar Thomas Clark of Yorkshire, who went to Sidney in 1650. It contains notes, mainly in Latin, which he took up to 1654. It shows that Clerke had introduced his students to the ideas of Descartes and his opponent Henry More at an early stage in the debate between Cartesians and the Cambridge Platonists. It is dominated by considerations on the relation of mind and body. One quotation in English about the nature of matter reads: 'If parts were actually in the whole then quantity would be composed of Indivisibles 1654'. The notebook is also fascinating for the light it casts on the undergraduate mind of the Cromwellian period. The

The Unknown Man

This mysterious painting is not recorded in Sidney inventories until 1813 when it was mistakenly thought to be a portrait of Ralph Symons, the College's first architect. It shows a man in a long buff coat, a knotted cravat with wide lace end and large black knots on each shoulder; the dress suggests a date of about 1670. He holds a backstaff with a double quadrant in his left hand, and a pair of dividers in his right hand, his right arm resting on a globe. On the table are a watch and book with clasp binding. The double quadrant was a navigational instrument invented by the Elizabethan navigator John Davys and was used to measure the sun's meridional altitude and thus establish latitude at sea. A barely legible set of inscriptions includes the dates 1592 and 16.8 (1668 or 1698 have been suggested), the letters 'Joh' or 'Jon' and, under infra-red investigation the name 'DAVYS'. The subject of this portrait is too young to be Davys, however, and the connection remains tantalisingly obscure. Davys tried to reach the South Pacific via the Magellan Straits in 1592, the year Emery Molyneux completed a pair of globes, the terrestrial one incorporating discoveries Davys had made in the Arctic. The painting may be of a Sidney man or of someone with connections with the College.

'The Navigator', portrait of an unknown man, by an unknown artist, c1670, first recorded in the College collection in 1813

words 'kill kill' are next to the name 'Simon Stout', and there are various bits of verse addressed to an unknown 'ladye': 'Your all ethereal, there's in you no drosse, nor any part that's grosse', wrote Clark. Another poem is a dialogue between his lady's lips and eyes 'disputing which is the finer'. Clark left Sidney in 1655, the same year as his tutor, and we know nothing more about him or his 'ladye'.

Gilbert Clerke left Sidney after 14 years' residence, for religious and political reasons, and was evidently a fellow Sidney would have done well to keep. Minshull, who lasted an extraordinary 43 years as master, left little mark and what excellence arose during his term seems almost in spite of him. Had Sidney elected Herbert Thorndike in 1643, the next half-century might have been very different. Thorndike was a biblical scholar and theologian of note with strong interests in oriental languages. Like Clerke he was a Presbyterian but he defended the Book of Common Prayer, was considered dangerous by parliament, and was ejected from Trinity. He soon found employment with the learned royalist Sir Justinian Isham at Lamport in Northamptonshire. In the early 1660s Isham was also Clerke's employer, and one wonders if Clerke and Thorndike were in fact close associates.

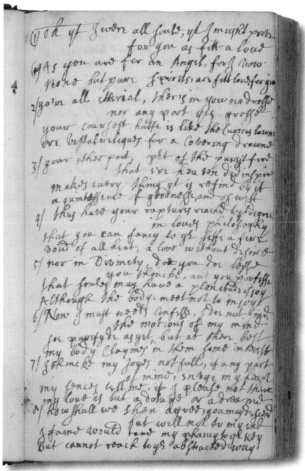

Page from Thomas Clark's notebook, 1650–54. Cambridge University Library

Clark's notebook is full of quotations from the Cambridge Platonist Henry More. This poem to a lady draws on the problem of desire and love, body and soul. While the object of his desire is 'all etherial' with no 'part that's grosse' and 'fit for an Angel', Clark does not 'find the motions of my minde as purifyde as yet'. It was an old theme given a specific modern gloss

Clerke dedicated one of his Cartesian books to Isham in 1662, by which time he was living near his patron in Loddington in a house that he filled with books, elegant scientific instruments and 'strange curiosities'. He was tutor and mentor to Isham's children and also ran the family's large estate at Lamport. He ran a small pipe works, experimented with telescopes and speaking trumpets, and undertook studies in latitude. He invented a form of sundial, a 'spot dial', about which he wrote two books and which he installed in the grounds at Lamport, the extensive landscaping of which was also his work. Of this, only a stone cockpit, the walls of a kitchen garden, and raised banks survive.

With the Ishams, Clerke shared a sceptical interest in witchcraft. Shortly after leaving Sidney, and during a high point of obsession with witches in England, he investigated a possession and poltergeist 'about May-Day 1658' at a house near Daventry, which was later published in the famous compilation on witches and apparitions *Saducismus Triumphatus* (1681) by Joseph Glanvill and Henry More, a book dedicated to Seth Ward. Clerke wrote to the publishers saying his account of the Daventry incident will 'fit Mr. More gallantly' and that 'this story which I had to the full, and in which I could not but acquiesce, though otherwise I am very chary' concerned a grandmother 'Widdow Cowley', a mother 'Widdow Stiff', and her two daughters and sister. Witnessed by 500 people, the subjects were very 'civil and orderly people'. A daughter 'vomited 3 gallons of water…stones and coals', some of which 'weighed a quarter of a pound, and were so big as they had enough to do to get them out of her mouth'. This went on for two weeks and was followed by the unaccountable blazing of flax, bed clothes thrown off, milk flying off the table and stones whirling about the room. One of the women was sent to gaol, and Clerke concluded that the evidence was hard to deny.

Clerke had a correspondence with the Puritan Richard Baxter and increasingly turned to a Unitarian position on God, refusing to subscribe to the Thirty-Nine Articles. His attitude can be seen in his writing against Bishop Bull's *Defence of the Nicene Faith* and these views clearly influenced the unorthodox religion of his private pupil William Whiston, who went on to succeed Newton as Lucasian Professor of Mathematics. Clerke was an early reader of Newton's *Principia Mathematica* (1687) and wrote to the author to complain about his obscure language. He died at North Luffenham in Rutland, the 'Sidney County', in about 1697.

'Horrid and Detestable Murder': Sidney's Kentish Killers

The 1640s saw much military violence across Britain, of course. For Sidney, the following decade also witnessed two widely reported episodes of extreme domestic violence, both in Kent. Sidney's Kentish royalists were an extraordinarily violent lot, though Sir Edward Dering, also from the county, who briefly left Sidney to join the King at Nottingham in 1642, was a moderate who sought refuge in a literary life and travel during the Interregnum. All these men knew one another well.

As we have seen, John Boys, the Sidney royalist colonel, also of Kent, had killed a man in 1630. Another Kentish man, Adam Sprakelinge, went up to Sidney as a fellow-commoner in 1622, a contemporary of Montagu Bertie, William Dugard and George Palfrey, among others. He inherited Ellington House in St Lawrence (now part of Ramsgate) on the Isle of Thanet, and in 1632 made an advantageous marriage to Katherine, daughter of Sir Robert Lewknor, a local knight. Like John Boys, Sprakelinge was a militant royalist. Giant-like in stature, he was also clearly a monster: idle, drunken, quarrelsome and wildly violent. He murdered his wife Katherine in a vicious, alcohol-fuelled attack in December 1652. In spite of elaborate attempts to cover up the crime, he was arrested and put on trial in Sandwich.

Once Sprakelinge was caught, people came forward to tell of other evil deeds, all with a political complexion to them. One witness had seen Sprakelinge beaten in a fist-fight with Robert Lister. Sprakelinge went to a local thug, Corslet, and paid him to beat up Lister. Some law officers said that Sprakelinge had fired off his pistols at them when they had been to investigate complaints against him. In 1648, Sprakelinge and Robert Langley had quarrelled and, as Langley rode away, Sprakelinge went after him and shot him in the back, killing him. At the end of the trial, the jury took only a short time to find Sprakelinge guilty of murder, and the judge sentenced him to death.

In his cell, Sprakelinge refused to see a priest and, putting on his long flowing cloak, he went to the scaffold. After the hanging, his body was put in a coffin and rowed back

to Thanet. The only transport available at Cliffsend was a sea-weed wagon, which carried his body to St Lawrence Church, where he was buried in an unmarked grave. A skeleton nearly seven feet tall was found in 1888, thought to be Sprakelinge's, and the only physical remains of a ghost once said to haunt the churchyard.

Two years later, in 1655, there was another shocking murder by a Sidney man in Kent. To the south of Faversham is the imposing 17th-century house, Lees Court, Sheldwich, now a set of luxury apartments. The 'new range', with its exaggerated eaves and 13 classical bays decorated with giant pilasters, is one of the finest buildings of the Interregnum in England, supposedly after a design of Inigo Jones. This was the home of the royalist knight Sir George Sondes, MP and Sheriff of Kent, who completed the new wing in 1654 after being confined to his estates in 1650.

Sir George, a contemporary of Cromwell's at Cambridge, and nephew of Sidney's first master James Montagu, had married Jane Freeman, two of whose aunts were married to sons of Sidney's Lord Montagu of Boughton. They had two boys, Freeman and George, the first of whom died young. The next son was named Freeman after his dead sibling, a few years before his mother died in 1637. Sir George did not remarry and instead looked after his estates. By the law of primogeniture the elder son, George, became sole heir to his father's enormous wealth. During the Civil War, as a loyal though non-combatant servant of the King, Sir George was imprisoned in the Tower and had his estates sequestered by parliament, leaving his young sons without a parent for seven years. Released in 1650, Sir George faced further

Lees Court, Faversham, Kent, showing the grand new garden front where Freeman Sondes murdered his brother George in 1655

Frontispiece by William Faithorne to Saducismus Triumphatus (Part the Second), *1681, by Joseph Glanvill and Henry More. British Library, London*

brief imprisonment over the next decade during the rebellions in Kent. By 1652 he moved into the nearly complete Lees Court with his family, his sons having recently come down from Sidney.

George and Freeman Sondes, though more than two years separated them, went up to Sidney months after the King's execution in 1649, where they both stayed for two years. Freeman's tutor was Edmund Matthews, described later by Sir George as 'a religious, godly and learned man'. Freeman contracted smallpox at Cambridge, which may have disfigured his face. Both boys lived in London after finishing at Sidney, continuing their education in mathematics as well as in the gentlemanly pursuits of singing, dancing and fencing. They seemed to have enjoyed their metropolitan lives in ways their pious father found unsettling, in particular their fondness for cockfighting and gambling.

Following their return to Lees Court in 1652, George began a relationship with a cousin and may even have married her secretly. His father brought the affair to an end and thereby divided family loyalties. His brother Freeman, doing nothing at home in Kent and refusing to take up law as his father wished, subsequently also fell in love with the girl. This caused in him a 'melancholy passion', and his frustrated longings for her and jealousy towards his older and wealthier brother began seriously to affect him; Sir George later described his exasperation with his 'cross-grained' son. When Freeman argued with George over a doublet, and his father severely reprimanded him, the seemingly trivial incident sent him into a silent sulk lasting five hours.

One evening in August 1655, following a running match at Faversham, and after prayers in the chapel at Lees Court, Sir George and his two sons went to bed. Early the following morning Freeman took a cleaver from the kitchen he had secreted in his room, along with a dagger bought in London, and went to his brother's room. He hit George five times with the cleaver and, because his brother was still alive, writhing and groaning, he stabbed him seven times with the dagger. Freeman ran to his father's room and announced: 'Father, I have killed my brother', to which Sir George replied, 'Why, then you must be hanged'. They went back to the murdered George's room where the victim was still just alive, weltering in his blood. George died and Freeman was locked in his room.

Freeman was put in gaol and sent to the Assizes at Maidstone a few days later where he pleaded guilty to murder and was sentenced to death. During the period of confinement before his hanging, various Cambridge-educated clergy attended him and his quiet and godly behaviour impressed even his father. They pleaded successfully for a deferral of execution in order to prepare his soul for eternity. By prayer, bible- and psalm- reading, and earnest confession, Freeman eased his guilt and misery and was ready to die for the 'horrid and detestable murder which I have committed upon my late dear brother…'. He was hanged at Penenden Heath, a priest praying to God for his 'sad and mourning soul', and buried at nearby Bearsted.

The crime, trial and penitence of the murderer were widely discussed and debated in print across England, the motives, behaviour and political and religious leanings of the father, sons and priests coming under intense and often critical scrutiny. Sir George, probably guilty in some ways at his treatment of his younger son, feeling under attack from local enemies, and with his life's work shattered, wrote an account of the whole affair. Its conclusion begins: 'No man's sorrow like to my sorrow! No affliction to be compared to mine in all the divine writ. Nor any wickedness like unto that of my son.'

'Almost Creepy!' Sidney and the Dugard Family

> My husband is become friendly enough with Mr. Dugard, an excellent printer, who was also formerly Master of the Merchant Taylor's School. When another printer stole the copyright of one of Mr. Dugard's books (upon a disease called the Ricketts) my husband brought a complaint before the Council and justice was done. But latterly his friendship for Mr. Dugard, who prints whatever he can sell, has led him into trouble; for, in a heedless mood, he licensed him to print a book which, upon a petition of ministers, a Committee of Parliament examined and found 'blasphemous, erroneous, and scandalous', and ordered copies of it to be publicly burned in London and Westminster, under direction of the Sheriffs. —Mrs. Milton, in Robert Graves, *Wife to Mr. Milton*, 1942

When the eminent international jurist John Dugard first came to Sidney from South Africa in 1963 to study law, he had no idea that it was the College of two famous ancestors. John arrived in England on a British Council grant and had the university and college chosen for him by the Council; indeed, he had never heard of Sidney Sussex. It was his mother who noticed the connection. It was, as his sister Jane said later, 'a most remarkable coincidence. Almost creepy!' A major figure in human rights legislation, and friend and advisor to Nelson Mandela, John Dugard was delighted to discover both his connection with Sidney's 17th-century history, and the College's strong South African connections over the last 150 years. He was a Professional Fellow at Sidney in 1995–96.

The Dugards were a Huguenot family who probably came to England in the wake of the 1572 St Bartholomew's Day Massacre of Protestants in Paris, the kind of event the founding of Sidney was intended to prevent. Henry Dugard, born at Grafton Fliford, Worcestershire, attended Emmanuel in 1588, and later lived in Lickey, Bromsgrove, also in Worcestershire. Two of his four sons were sent to Sidney, William in 1622 and Thomas in 1626. The choice of college is easy to explain: not only was Sidney, like Emmanuel, suitably hard-line Protestant, but the boys' uncle, Richard, was a celebrated fellow there.

Of Richard's two nephew-pupils, William (1606–62) is the more fascinating. After Sidney, where he was also a sizar and attained his BA in 1627, he became a successful schoolmaster at Oundle and then at Stamford, where he married his first wife Elizabeth. Following a dispute he moved to Colchester School, again leaving after a disagreement. In 1644 he was appointed chief schoolmaster of Merchant Taylors' School, London, where he introduced innovative teaching methods and reorganised the school's management. Influenced by the great educational reformer Comenius, William wrote Latin and Greek composition text books and in 1648, having been invited to correct the Stationers' Company's schoolbooks, set up a number of printing presses that greatly extended his impact on English schooling. The range of publications included works on science and history, as well as political tracts. The Merchant Taylors were not happy with these activities, but Dugard held on to his position.

He was a royalist at the start of the Civil War and famously published the *Eikon Basilike* (1649), a defence of the divine right of the monarchy. In 1650, the parliamentary Council of State punished him for printing the anti-regicide *Defensio Regia* by Claude de Saumaise by confiscating his presses, dismissing him from Merchant Taylors', and jailing him in Newgate. He was released after a month on the intervention of two republicans, his friend Sir James Harington and John Milton (perhaps through his connection with his uncle Richard). His presses and school post were

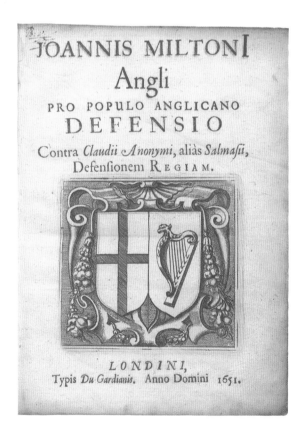

John Milton, Pro Populo Anglicano Defensio, 1651, title-page, published by William Dugard. The Robert J Wickenheiser Collection of John Milton, University of South Carolina

returned to him. This led to his rapid, even remarkable, conversion to republicanism and he became a 'printer for the state' of books supporting the Commonwealth. Ironically, he published Milton's reply to Saumaise, the *Pro Populo Anglicano Defensio* (1651).

The remaining ten years of his life were typically controversial: he published the *Racovian Catechism* (1652), an anti-trinitarian work that was burned in public, but he was allowed to continue printing and publishing for the Commonwealth. This exacerbated his relations with the authorities at Merchant Taylors', and he was dismissed in 1660. He set up his own school in London, a successful venture, and avoided punishment for sheltering his former saviour, Sir James Harington, from the Restoration government. He died in 1662.

William's younger brother, Thomas (1608–83), entered Sidney in 1626, also as a sizar, suggesting little family wealth, and graduated BA in 1630. He too was a schoolmaster and became master at Warwick School through the patronage of Robert Greville, Baron Brooke, to whom he had been introduced by one of Sidney's greatest early fellows, the Puritan clergyman and classical scholar, Thomas Gataker. He was ordained in 1634. His diary, kept between 1632 and

[John Gauden],
Eikon Basilike: The
Pourtraicture of His
Sacred Majesty, *1649,*
frontispiece engraved
by William Marshall,
published by William
Dugard. British Library,
London

1642, gives a particularly interesting and full picture of a Puritan clergyman in the decisive years of the personal rule of Charles I. It describes the life of preaching, religious discussion, pulpit-swapping, and political wrangling of those ministers in opposition to the Laudian High Church reforms in the Church of England. Thomas was close to a number of important leaders of the Puritan faction and to parliamentary opponents of Charles's rule, and through these connections acquired the wealthy living of Barford, near Warwick, where, during the 1650s, he was a Presbyterian conformist who preached against the rise of radical sectarianism. In other words, he was a loyal follower of fellow Sidneian, Oliver Cromwell.

Like his brother, Thomas changed with the times, though in the opposite direction politically, turning his back at the Restoration on colleagues who were now nonconformist. He conformed to Charles II's Act of Uniformity in 1662 and in 1664 published a collection of poems eulogising Charles I and various powerful bishops. His diary, an important historical document, reveals a cautious and rather pedantic man whose conventionality was quite at odds with his brother's more adventurous spirit. He married three times, leaving a substantial estate and having been enrolled among the Warwickshire gentry.

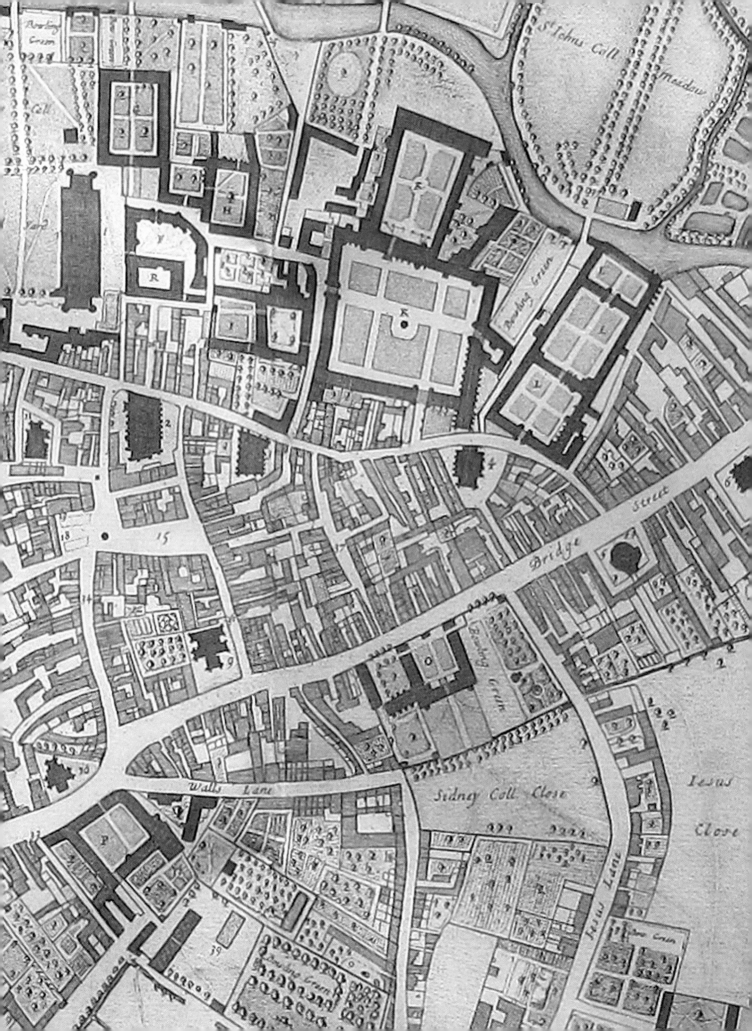

St Johns Coll Meadow

Bowling Green

Bridge Street

Bowling Green

Walls Lane

Sidney Coll. Close

Jesus Lane

Jesus Close

CHAPTER 5

'Small but Handsome' 1660–1746

I have no excuse for Dr. Minshull, the Master, who suffered all this, unless that by thrusting himself, as he had done, illegally into his office he was all his life long obnoxious and never his own master.

—Francis Sawyer Parris, Master, 1746–60, on Richard Minshull, Master, 1643–1686

Politics and religion had catapulted Sidney into national prominence before the Civil War. At the return of King Charles II in 1660, however, the College found itself in a new and far more hostile world. The exhumations of Cromwell and Tom May from their grand tombs in Westminster were a sign of this change in fortune. Identified with the theology, and even politics, of the Cromwellian regime, the College was financially insecure and run by a man who was by some accounts second-rate. That Richard Minshull, one of only two masters of Cambridge colleges not to resign or to be ejected after the Restoration, lived for another 26 years was for many Sidney's misfortune, though Fuller wrote warmly about him as the first Sidney-educated master 'much meriting thereof by his providence', and others respected his caution.

Minshull no doubt owed his survival to Manchester, who had been reinstated as Chancellor of the university. Manchester had become a powerful man again under the new monarchy, and he probably took a favourable view of his old Sidney acquaintance. Parris's words (quoted above) were written at the moment nearly a century later when Sidney entered a period of overdue renewal. The intervening years were difficult ones. When a Catholic master was intruded into the College by James II in 1687, Sidney's founding ancestors would have been collectively turning in their graves.

'Ex Mandato Regio': Sidney in Restoration Cambridge

Restoration Cambridge was royalist, complacent and often corrupt. Although it was the age of Newton, Bentley and other eminent men, the university was institutionally

OPPOSITE: *Map of Cambridge (detail), 1690, by David Loggan. The Sidney fellows' bowling green is clearly marked, as is the layout of gardens, trees and outbuildings*

and intellectually lacking in dynamism and direction. The stagnation is reflected in undergraduate numbers. An immediate post-1660 graph shows a marked increase up to 1670; thereafter numbers declined steeply, and by the mid-18th century small colleges such as Sidney might have fewer students entering each year than the total number of fellows. Thus, Sidney's student population of 122 in 1672 had dwindled to 27 by 1732. It was no longer the case that virtually all the movers and shakers in English society had been through one of the two ancient universities. Although Sidney, along with Magdalene and Emmanuel, was admitted in 1661 to equal privileges in the election of proctors, this enhanced university status was hardly matched by any great blossoming of learning.

The 1662 Act of Uniformity required all professors, fellows and heads of colleges to swear allegiance to the Anglican liturgy, to disclaim the right of resistance to the monarch, and to declare the Solemn League and Covenant illegal. Most did, including Minshull, who nonetheless may have felt uncomfortable in his survival, given the circumstances of his election.

The greatest source of corruption was the prevalence of degrees, fellowships and even masterships decided by royal mandate. This meant that the interests of the court, enhanced by the pro-royalist burgesses returned to parliament during the period, dominated the university and town. Sir Roger L'Estrange would have been delighted by this great turn of events, not least in 1681 when Cambridge graduates raised a subscription in his honour. The second Duke of Buckingham's succession to Manchester as Chancellor in 1671, followed by the Duke of Monmouth in 1674, and

The Art of Trolling

Robert Nobbes, son of a Northamptonshire rector, went up to Sidney as a pensioner in 1668. He became a priest, but was also a poet and keen angler. *The Compleat Troller*, or *The Art of Trolling* (1682) concerns pike fishing by means of drawing baited lines behind a boat. Nobbes believed 'our simple Art composes the soul to that quiet and serenity, which gives a man the fullest possession and fruition of himself and all his enjoyments. This clearness and equanimity of spirit being a matter of so high a concern, is of much value and esteem in the opinion of many profound philosophers.' Nobbes' 'melancholy art' was close to Izaak Walton's idea of fishing as a contemplative sport, made famous in his *The Compleat Angler* (1653). Nobbes included in his book a poem on the beauties of England's rivers, and a 'Receipt to dress a Pike', a recipe including salt, claret, marjoram, thyme, fennel, anchovies, horse radish, garlic and lemon. Nobbes died as vicar at Sausthorpe, Lincolnshire, in about 1706.

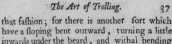

A page on hooks from Robert Nobbes, The Compleat Troller, or The Art of Trolling, *1682. Bodleian Library, Oxford*

The Duke's Bagnio

Samuel Haworth, son of a Hertfordshire congregational minister, entered Sidney as a sizar in 1677. In 1680 he is recorded practising medicine in London, writing on anatomy and selling 'excellent and effectual tablets' for scurvy. He began to move in court circles and attracted the admiration of Charles II. Based in Brompton, London, Haworth wrote *A Description of the Duke's Bagnio* (1683), dedicated to the Duke of York, and describing a Turkish bath and medicinal establishment he had established in Covent Garden. The 'bagnio' provoked controversy and Haworth was dismissed as a quack by many doctors. The building with its cupola roof, had a coffee house, plunge bath, mineral bath and spa, and Haworth's book explained various methods of sweating, rubbing and bathing, as cures for many ailments.

Samuel Haworth, A Description of the Duke's Bagnio, *1683, frontispiece engraved by R White. The Wellcome Library, London*

then the Duke of Albemarle in 1682, all royal favourites, underlines the hold the monarchy had over the university.

At Sidney, royal interference was as bad as anywhere. Fellows appointed *ex mandato regio* between 1660 and 1685 included George Downing, Thomas Freeman, Ralph Barker, David Jenner, the future master James Johnson, Edward Condy, Edward Alston, Thomas Towler, Richard Reynolds, John Grant and William Scott. The list highlights the fellowship's mediocrity. With a few exceptions, such as Jenner and Reynolds, none of these men was academically distinguished, nor did they go on to achieve eminence in the world at large. They may possibly have been good tutors and pious Christians, but they have left little trace of their lives by which they might be judged.

Minshull, or more likely his colleagues, occasionally tried to resist these interferences, as a careful reading of College minutes reveals. John Fuller, son of the great Sidney fellow Thomas Fuller, who had died in 1661 and had had the pleasure of seeing the monarchy restored, was appointed by King Charles. The *Acta* for 21 January 1663 record that 'Mr John Fuller was admitted Fellow by virtue of the King's mandate. Mr. Luke protested against his admission in behalfe of S[ophiste]r Green and S[ophiste]r Sacket. The M[aste]r, Mr Matthews, Mr Frere, Mr Brace, Mr Moore were for his present admission. Mr Luke, Mr Kitson, Mr Nethercot, Mr Johnson, Mr Jenner were for petitioning to the King for a free election.' Minshull, always unlikely to make a stand on anything, had the casting vote; predictably it went to Fuller.

Tankard, with cover, London, 1683–84, given by Cyril Arthington, admitted as a fellow-commoner on 29 June 1683

Cyril Arthington, son of a Yorkshire gentleman, entered Sidney from Wakefield School in 1683. He became a JP in the West Riding and MP for Aldborough, and built Arthington Hall, Leeds, where he conducted various scientific experiments, undertook archaeological excavations and entertained his friends among the famous 'Yorkshire Virtuosi'. These included Sir Godfrey Copley and Ralph Thoresby, who, like Arthington, were freemasons. Arthington was elected a Fellow of the Royal Society in 1701 and died in 1720.

It is notable among the objectors that David Jenner, himself a royal appointment, and John Luke, who had been a fellow since 1654, were the only two men of any distinction among the voters. Jenner, a Trinity sizar in 1653, became a royal chaplain; he wrote a celebrated sermon on the martyrdom of Charles I in 1681, and an orthodox attack on dissenters and liberty of conscience in 1683. His accusation of anarchy and treason in this last work against his opponent, Dr Daniel Whitby, indicates the conventional line expected of a royal appointee. In 1683 he also wrote *The Prerogative of Primogeniture*, dedicated to James, Duke of York, attacking Whig attempts to exclude the future king from succeeding to the throne. John Luke, who entered Sidney as a pensioner in 1649, went on to become chaplain to the Levant Company and professor of Arabic at Cambridge, a position established in 1668 through the beneficence of a Sidney old boy, the woollen draper, merchant and Lord Mayor of London, Thomas Adams. (Adams, a pragmatist during the Civil War, died following a fall from his coach; his autopsy revealed, in Samuel Pepys' words, a kidney stone 'bigger than my fist' weighing 'above 25 ounces'.)

'The Time of Ye Sickness': Plagues and Delapidations

In the 1660s and 1670s Sidney members might have been forgiven for thinking the College was facing disaster on most fronts. The great plague outbreaks of 1665 and 1666 were in fact repetitions on a larger scale of epidemics that had swept across the country in 1610 and in the 1620s, 1630s and 1640s, claiming many lives in Cambridge, including some Sidney undergraduates. Most members of colleges left the town during plagues, but not all did, and of course a number of college servants were required to stay put. Booths were put up on Jesus Common for the reception of the stricken and in 1665 a grace was passed by the Senate for discontinuing sermons at St Mary's and exercises in the Schools. In the summer of 1666 all public meetings in the town and university were suspended.

A minute in the Sidney *Acta* of 17 June 1666 refers to the steps taken to deal with the problems during 'the time of ye sickness'. The maniple Thomas Wood, the porter Henry Smith, his wife the laundress and his son the servant, along with the bedmaker Goodwife Hooper, the cook Thomas Tracy, and the kitchen maid Mistress Abbott, were all to stay in College while the academic members left Cambridge to 'retire into yᵉ country wth all convenient speed and onely two sisars besides yᵉ Master staying behind'. The fellows and students 'shall not be accounted for their discontinuance'.

It was not only bodily fabric that was under threat. Although the College managed to make a donation of £10 'towards yᵉ rebuilding of St Paul's Church in London' after the Great Fire of 1666, it could scarcely afford such generosity. Sidney was faced with constant repairs to its own buildings, and College plate was sold off to pay for them. In 1670 a mason was employed to re-tile the roof of the library, hall and the northern and middle ranges. On 29 July 1671, for instance, the following rather melancholy order was announced:

'The M[aste]r and all yᵉ ffellowes at home agreed that Mr Urlin should have these peices of Plate, viz., Mr Thomas Power's [and eight other Fellow-Commoners']

Pots, Mr Shilston Calmady's broaken boal, a broken Salt and two broken Spoones…
weighing in all 191 ounces…for the summe of fourty-five pounds seventeen shillings
and six pence, which have been laid out for tiling and other repaires of the Chappell
roofe and thereabouts.'

A further quantity of old and broken plate was sold in 1679 to pay for new slating.
The names of those whose plate was melted down in 1671 and 1679 was a poignant reminder of Sidney's turbulent history so far. Shilston Calmady was a royalist
fatality in the Civil War; George Sondes, as we have seen, had been murdered; the
Wingfields and Ayscoughs had sent many boys to Sidney; Edward Dering had been a
royalist exile, a poet in the circle of Katherine Philips and now a politician in Ireland
who was implicated in the Popish Plot; James Montagu was of the great Sidney
founding family.

'Outragious Insolences': Sidney's Restoration Bad Boys

When we were met I declar'd unto them the cause of my calling them, which was this. A
discovery was made to me of a robbery that was committed in S[ophiste]r Charles Pym's
chamber by Thornton and Huggins: Woodall (as he confessed to his Tutor) knew of the
same. Thornton also by the confession of Huggins told Berry that Thornton had been with
him severall times to attempt the same on the M[aste]r; but he would never consent to him
nor for the world endeavour it. Likewise Berry and Taylor senior were told by Avis the Joyner
last week that Thornton and Woodall had been with him now and then above a quarter of
a yeare to assist them in the same, but he denied them; whereupon (as Woodall confessed
to his Tutor) Thornton and Woodall endeavoured the breaking open of my doore and cut
the holes which were found there, and Woodall told them since that Thornton gave him
money to buy the instrument with which they did it. —*Acta Collegii*, January 1681

By 1680 Sidney was suffering from a worse problem than the relinquishing of plate.
Under Montagu and Ward discipline was strict and earned the College a reputation
that recommended it to many parents. Sidney was hardly alone after 1660 in seeing
a great collapse of manners and discipline during a period notorious for its licen-
tious and chaotic social mores. Nevertheless, the great centre of moral rectitude
and sober behaviour was clearly under intense pressure from many of its members,
both undergraduates and fellows. Daniel Naylor, later a vicar at Exton, was one of a
number admonished or deprived of their fellowships. Naylor, 'having been diverse
times statutably admonished and not reforming his manners', was expelled in 1663
for 'ill manners'.

In 1669 there is a long minute in the Order Book detailing the severe problems
posed by a dangerously unruly graduate:

'April 15ᵗʰ, 1669. Memorandum. That William Butler Bach: Arts of the Second
Year and Schollar of Mr. Peter Blundell's foundation having been divers times statutably admonished and not reforming his ill manners and having on the day of the
date hereof for high misdemeanours then committed been summon'd to appear
before the Master and Fellowes and refusing to come, and with his sword and pistol

69

Dec: 10th 1677:

Memorand: yt Charls Creed on ye 6th of Decemb: last past was out of ye Coll: at ye Dolphin where he distempered himself by excessiue drinking & came not into ye Coll: till 12 of ye Clock at night to ye disturbance of ye same: for which he was solemnly admonished to ye Master in ye presence of ye Sen: fellow & Dean

Ita testamur   Ri: Minshull
                Edm: Matthews.
                Ri: Lake, Decan.

Memorand: yt on ye same day Mathew Munday on ye 6th of Decemb: last past was out of ye Coll: at ye Dolphin where he distempered himself by excessiue drinking & came not into ye Coll: till 12 of ye Clock at night to ye disturbance of ye same: as also yt ye next night he was at ye same place till nine of ye Clock & came into ye Coll: distempered & did swear fiuen oaths yt were publickly heard for which fault he was solemnly admonished by ye Master in ye presence of ye Sen: fellow & Dean; & ordered at ye same time to read a publick Recantation in ye Hall.

Ita testamur   Ri: Minshull
                Edm: Matthews.
                Ri: Lake Decan:

Memorand: yt Thomas Myers on ye same day was admonished by ye Master for comeing in & being guilty of ye same crimes with Charls Creed & also for other misdemeanours: in ye presence of ye Sen: fellow & ye Dean

Ita testamur   Ri: Minshull
                Edm: Matthews
                Richd Lake Decan:

Memorand that Aug: 21. 1678 Henry Bee, John Allen, Theodore Parbo, Matthew Munday, & Jos: Pridham were admonished for being distempered with drinke, & assaulting Wilson son Sophister of this Coll: strikeing & threatning him & other misdemeanours comitted by them in the presence of the Sen: Fellow & Dean.

Ita testamur   Ri: Minshull
                Edm: Matthews
                Edw: Alston. Decan.

memor: ye Nov: ye 30. 1678 Matthew munday was suspected between 8 & 9: of ye clock at night to have thrown ye stone wch came in at mr Alston's study window & was likely to have done him a mischiefe, ye sd munday being out unseasonably neare ye Coll: at ye time when it was throwne & comeing in not long after & ye next night after ye forsd dareing to be out about ye same houres was convicted before me, mr Matthews mr Alston, mr Crosse & mr scot ye Deane of ye Coll: but stifly denying ye fact to have been done by him or any other upon his instigat or knowledge was notwithstanding warned by me to observe statutable houres & in case he did not I assur'd him he should be convicted before ye Society, & this I did in ye presence of ye foure abovenamed.

memor: ye Ds Cock & Ds Abbot for being out disorderly, & brought by ye Coll: by ye Proctor betweene 10 & 11 of ye Clock last night, were both admonished. but they for promising to amend, it was so far indulg'd them, yt his admonition should not preiudice him. & they amended according. Ita testamur   Ri: Minshull
Aug. 4. 1680.   Edm: Matthews
Jos: Moore [?]

threatening some and assaulting others, was by the unanimous consent of the Master and Fellowes deprived of his Schollarship and expelled the Colledge.'

Butler, whose father Almeric had been one of the few bad boys at Sidney in the 1620s, was backed by one of his peers, the Yorkshireman John Burgess, who expressed his solidarity in memorable fashion. He 'distempered himself with drinks and committed outrageous insolences against the Dean in breaking his Windowes with Brick-batts' and 'publickly defied all the censures of the Society by throwing off his gown'. Unlike his comrade, Burgess actually took his BA in 1668–69.

In the mid- to late-1670s the situation seems to have got out of control, and not only among students. Minshull wrote in 1674 that 'William Beale our Cooke had an admonition given by me in the Hall after dinner before the Society for going away without leave and staying eleven dayes wandring whither we know not'. Beale was at it again soon after for 'misbehaving in yᵉ Mill Inne' and again in 1676. In 1681 he 'had a publicke and his last admonition for his intolerable extravagancies', and in 1683 he was given 'another ultimate admonition'. Presumably this really was his last: either Minshull was a very weak man, or Beale was a very fine cook.

Students easily matched Beale's excesses. The year of the Popish Plot, 1678, proved especially troublesome. In 1677, Thomas Walker, Richard Payton and Francis Browne had been admonished for 'being chief sticklers in an assault made upon yᵉ B.A.s in the buttries'. The Londoner Browne got his BA shortly after and became a doctor. Walker was admonished again in 1678 for drunkenness and 'telling lies to the Dean'. He was later elected a Sidney fellow and became a rector in Buckinghamshire. Payton, son of a Berkshire yeoman, was obviously a major problem, facing admonition in 1678 for 'drunkenness, intolerable Impudence, making a disturbance in the Town, coming in after twelve o'clock and then making a disturbance in the Colledge, and very seldom in his chamber when the Dean visited'. He got his BA that year, however, and became a priest.

Matthew Munday, son of a Devon clothier and a Blundell's pensioner, was a notable miscreant. He excelled himself in the same year 'at yᵉ Dolphin where he distempered himself by excessive drinking and came not into yᵉ Coll. till 12 of yᵉ Clock at night to yᵉ disturbance of yᵉ same: as also [tha]t yᵉ next night he was at yᵉ same place till nine of yᵉ clock and came into yᵉ Coll. distempered and did swear divers oaths [tha]t were publickly heard; for which fault he was solemnly admonished by yᵉ Master in the presence of the sen: fellow and Dean; and ordered at the same time to read a publick Recantation in the Hall'. This humiliation did not prevent Munday from getting drunk and 'assaulting Wilson, senr Sophister of the Coll., and other misdemeanours', nor, three months later, throwing a stone 'which came in at Mr. Alston's window and was likely to have done him a mischief'. In assaulting the unfortunate Wilson, Munday was assisted by the future Suffolk rector Henry Bee, the Rutland-born sizar John Allen, the 20-year-old Theodore Parker, previously thrown out of Balliol, Oxford, and another Blundell's boy, Joseph Pridham. Munday took his BA the next year, followed that with an MA and became a rector in Somerset.

At the Dolphin the Somerset yeoman's son Charles Creed distempered himself in December 1677, as did the Yorkshireman Thomas Myers the same night. However, such drunken larks paled into insignificance when compared with a dastardly attempt to break into the Master's Lodge by John Huggins, a London shoemaker's son, the Yorkshireman Robert Thornton and the farmer's son John Woodall in January 1681. Minshull gave a detailed account of the emergency College meeting in the Lodge to discuss the matter with the fellows. 'Upon this information the Society proceeded to the expulsion of Huggins, Thornton and Woodall, and expell'd they were the day above written by unanimous consent.' Thornton, a pensioner, took an MA at University College, Oxford, became a fellow of Magdalen and was a naval chaplain. The sizars Huggins and Woodall are not heard of again.

A fascinating further postscript to this story is that Sir Charles Pym, whose room the three villains first broke into, was the grandson of the great parliamentarian John Pym, and was killed by a rapier thrust in a brawl in the Swan Tavern on Fish Street Hill, London in 1688, just before the Glorious Revolution. The trial of his three attackers (no Sidney connections as far as we know) at the Old Bailey was a sensational story in its time, the jury being instructed by the judge to deliver a verdict of manslaughter during what he called 'an ungoverned storm'.

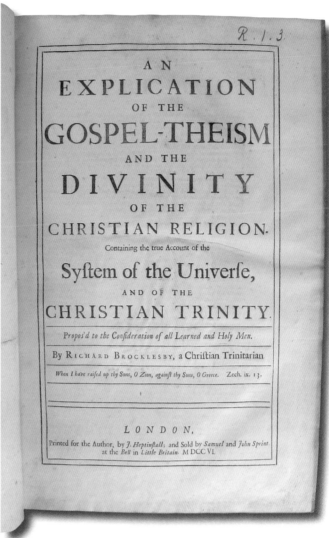

Title-page to An Explication of the Gospel-Theism..., *by Richard Brocklesby, 1706*

'Private Holes and Corners': Sidney's Restoration Churchmen

It certainly wasn't all drink and violence at Sidney in the second half of the 17th century. Indeed, some of the College's most impressive students of all time managed to avoid the flying bricks and bottles, the leaking roofs and drunken cooks, to achieve great things; though usually elsewhere, it must be admitted. Though Minshull and his fellows were hardly men of great reputation, Sidney's record in the *Ordo Senioritatis*, despite its imperfections and even absurdities as a guide to academic attainment, shows a college whose students were capable of the highest achievement. Between 1660 and 1686, when Minshull died, the College featured regularly in the lists of the top 30 students, Richard John Sykes, in 1674–75 being the first Sidney man, on record at least, to be top of the table. Indeed, although that decade reads badly in disciplinary terms, it was evidently a time of great success in the Tripos. The following year Wale was also top and in 1676–77 David Acklam was second. Many years record three or four Sidneians in the *Ordo*.

*Thomas Comber, by an
unknown artist. Durham
Cathedral*

Sidney, naturally, still produced some major
figures in theology and the life of the church.
The 1650s had produced two very private men
who feature in any serious history of English religious life in the second half of the 17th century:
the nonconformist Edmund Calamy, and the
influential and eccentric theologian and philanthropist Richard Brocklesby. Calamy's convictions led him to reject the Act of Uniformity in
1662, forcing him, as he said, to 'disguise himself
and skulk in private holes and corners, and frequently changing his lodgings'. His son, Edmund,
was a Presbyterian minister and became the great
historian of nonconformity. He stipulated that
there should be no gifts at his funeral but simply
sprigs of rosemary for his friends.

Richard Brocklesby, who took his MA in
1660, retired on a matter of principle to Stamford
in his native Lincolnshire, and wrote the massive and heterodox 1,100-page theological treatise *An Explication of the Gospel-Theism and the
Divinity of the Christian Religion, Containing the
True Account of the System of the Universe and of
the Christian Trinity* (1706). Full of neologisms
and covering a bewildering range of concepts
and sources, the book was a major influence on the Deist and Newtonian William
Whiston.

As Brocklesby entered his last year at Sidney, Thomas Comber, the son of Kentish
royalist parents who had been exiled in Flanders, arrived as a sizar in 1659. Under
his tutor, Edmund Matthews, the gifted Comber studied music, painting and oriental
languages, indicative of the extra-curricular move away from traditional scholastic
studies at this time. Comber's subsequent career in the church was meteoric: he
was priested by the Archbishop of York within a year of taking his BA in 1663, and
quickly became renowned for his extempore preaching. His enormously successful
and influential masterpiece, the seven-volume *A Companion to the Temple and the
Closet* (1672), of which Sidney still has a copy, is a detailed commentary on the new
Book of Common Prayer, aimed at promoting its use and understanding. Comber was
a dedicated loyalist of the revived Anglican Church, and wrote important attacks on
Catholicism and Quakers. His popularity with the King and the church establishment led to significant preferments. Princess Anne received him at court, having
read the third part of *A Companion* for her first communion, and later made him
a chaplain. Comber wrote for the Tories during the Exclusion Crisis in 1681 and
attacked those in the church he considered to be disloyal. In 1687, Comber vigorously opposed James II's Catholic policies in Yorkshire. In 1691 he became Dean of

Durham Cathedral; he was chaplain-in-ordinary to William of Orange in 1692 and by this time seems to have become a pragmatic Whig.

Benjamin Calamy, half-brother of the nonconformist Edmund, held many of the same views as Comber, whom he would have met when he arrived at Sidney in 1661. He migrated to St Catharine's, where he became a fellow. He was a friend of Judge Jeffreys and a chaplain to Charles II. He wrote and preached tirelessly against nonconformity, which he saw as a treason that undermined the parish churches and hence the unity of the realm. His ruthless pursuit of a Baptist opponent, Thomas Delaune, led Daniel Defoe to characterise the court-favoured Calamy as a villain, a view held by many into the 19th century.

Frontispiece to The Excellent Woman, *1692, by Theophilus Dorrington, engraving by J Sturt. Bodleian Library, Oxford*

The kind of man Comber and Benjamin Calamy opposed was the Presbyterian minister and tutor Joseph Hallett, a west-country man who was taught by his father Joseph, a celebrated nonconformist and classical scholar, before arriving at Sidney aged 20 in 1676. Subsequently entering a world Edmund Calamy would have recognised, he was ordained in secret in 1683 before moving to Leiden to study. Following this he returned to England in 1687 where he became his father's assistant at the new James Meeting House in Exeter, Devon. He became pastor there in 1714. From 1690 he ran an important academy in Exeter that prepared young men for the ministry and that was also open to laymen, teaching theology, classics and Hebrew. The students who passed through the academy included many leading preachers, theologians and doctors.

It was usually a hard life on the pioneering frontiers of nonconformity, and many who began life there turned eventually to the established church. Theophilus Dorrington was the son of a nonconformist London clothier and a student at Merchant Taylors' School, where William Dugard had been master. He went to Sidney in 1670, and later became a Presbyterian minister in London, a lecturer at a wealthy merchants' coffee house in Exchange Alley, and a medical student in Leiden in 1680. Dorrington returned to England and took Anglican orders. A well-travelled, cultured and refined man, he soon became a fierce critic of dissenters. His assaults on immorality, schism and sedition included advice to ladies on proper conduct, to gentlemen on discipline and devotion, and to the lower orders on the catechism and meditation in the home. These works were immensely popular.

While Dorrington attacked Protestant dissenters, especially Baptists and Quakers, he also toured Europe to gather information for a book warning against superstition and Jesuit infiltration of England. His later works were aimed at a general audience, exhorting organised prayer in such books as *The Plain Man's Gift of Prayer* (1703), and *Family Instruction* (1705), and describing dissenting academies, such as Hallett's in Exeter, as 'nurseries of error and schism'.

'Passionate and Fiery': Two Sidney Politicians

Sidney, like all Oxbridge colleges, remained primarily an establishment with a central religious mission until the 20th century, and it is no surprise to find it producing so many important figures in Britain's religious history. Its early influence on the political life of the country, however, was barely sustained after 1660. The Interregnum had produced men such as Sir Thomas Meres (1651), a 'country Tory', and the political writer Peter Pett (1645), but there were to be no more Cromwells or Manchesters.

A Whig answer to Sir Roger L'Estrange was John Thompson, later Lord Haversham, son of a wealthy London nonconformist merchant who went up to Sidney in 1664 as a fellow-commoner following a year at Lincoln's Inn. A short, stout, red-faced, John Bull type, Thompson entered political life like a whirlwind, speaking his mind and stirring up controversy at every opportunity. He inherited property in London, Buckinghamshire, Ireland, the Americas and the Caribbean and was a member of the East India Company by 1676.

During the Rye House Plot of 1683 Thompson was considered a dangerous radical and in 1685, at the accession of James II, went to Utrecht, reportedly laden with an immense fortune in jewels. He hosted those connected with Monmouth's Rebellion and was in regular contact with William of Orange prior to the Glorious Revolution. After William's accession Thompson, a bluff country Whig rather than a 'Kit-Kat' metropolitan type, opposed place-holders, became an outspoken critic of corruption and of proposals for a standing army, and saw William as 'the best of Kings'. Yet in 1695 he changed his position and voted with the Whig 'Junto', leading to his elevation to the peerage as Lord Haversham in 1696, still, in John Macky's words, 'very eloquent, but very passionate and fiery, a Dissenter by principle, and always turbulent'.

Haversham was immortalised in a cartoon of 1702 satirising the Earl of Anglesey's death. By 1705 he had moved close to the Tories. This created enmity all around him and his speech-making and whoring were satirised in the poem 'The Dog in the Wheel' that year. It shows, under the figure of a turnspit dog, how a noisy demagogue can become a very quiet placeman.

Haversham was also engaged with Daniel Defoe, 'a mean and mercenary prostitute' as he called him, in a long-running dispute, the great writer referring to Thompson as a dog baying at the moon, 'laught at by everybody'. In 1709, after he married his housekeeper, he was also attacked by the female Tory writer Delarivier Manley as the 'old-out-of-fashion-lord', the father to the incestuous siblings in the satire *The New Atlantis*. He died the following year, wealthy but exhausted.

Tankard, with lid, London,?1681–82, given by John Thompson, admitted as a fellow-commoner in 1664 and created Lord Haversham in 1696

At the other end of the political spectrum from Haversham was the Irish-born Nathaniel Hooke. A Jacobite, he was that rare thing, a Sidney Puritan convert to Rome. He entered Sidney as a 17-year-old sizar in 1681, the same year as the ill-fated Charles Pym. He left without taking a degree. In 1685 he landed with the Duke of Monmouth as the duke's chaplain. He was captured on a secret mission to London, but pardoned after discussions that his enemies described as 'treachery'. He experienced a miraculous conversion to King James's cause and became a Catholic. Captured by Williamites and put in the Tower, he was then released and served in the Jacobite army at the Battle of the Boyne in 1690. Hooke pursued a dangerous career as an army officer, fighting with the French against Marlborough while con-ducting under-cover negotiations with rebels in Scotland. His loyalty earned him the title Lord Hooke in the Jacobite peerage. By 1710, though, he was corresponding with the English and took no part in the great Jacobite uprising of 1715; however, he was a spy for his masters in Paris. He was naturalised as a Frenchman in 1720 and married a Frenchwoman shortly before his death in 1738. Like Walter Montagu before him, he died an exiled Catholic in France.

'Historiographer to the King': Thomas Rymer

> You are not to expect truth from an historiographer royal, it may drop from their pen by chance, but the general herd understand not their business; they fill us with story, accidental, incoherent, without end or side, and never know the government or policy of what they write. Even the Records themselves are not always accurately worded. —Thomas Rymer, *A General Draught and Prospect of the Government of Europe*, 1681

Minshull's term as master produced two outstanding literary figures: Thomas Rymer and William Wollaston. Rymer was from Yorkshire gentry stock with strong Puritan beliefs; his father was executed after the Presbyterian uprising of 1663, giving his son an unpleasantly violent start to his adult life; the father's head was left rotting in public in Doncaster to bear witness to the family disgrace. Rymer had entered Sidney in 1659, a contemporary of Thomas Comber, and left in 1662 without taking a degree. After his father's execution, he entered Gray's Inn and became a barrister in 1673; so far this was a conventional route taken by many Sidney men. In

Thomas Rymer, engraving after an unknown artist, 1819. National Portrait Gallery, London

1674, however, he published a translation of René Rapin's French version of Aristotle's *Poetics* and began life as a professional writer and scholar. He published the verse tragedy *Edgar* in 1677, and the following year *The Tragedies of the Last Age Consider'd* in which he analysed plays by Beaumont and Fletcher and Shakespeare from a strictly neo-classical angle. He demanded plausibility in plot, stereotyped characters, the reward of the good and punishment of the bad, and a strong moral conclusion. Dryden described the book as 'the best piece of Criticism in English' and the two men became close friends. While respectively considering his views to have 'ferocity' and to be 'rather too severe', both Pope and Johnson regarded Rymer very highly. T S Eliot said he had never seen a 'cogent refutation to Rymer's objections to *Othello*', a tragedy which Rymer had notoriously written off as 'a Bloody Farce' in *A Short View of Tragedy* (1692).

Rymer was a poet and also a critic of contemporary verse, his friend the Earl of Rochester's 'Satyr upon Man' offering him an opportunity to contrast Rochester's masculine English style with the effeminate efforts of the great French writer Boileau: 'My Lord *Rochester* gives us another Cast of Thought, another Turn of Expression, a strength, a Spirit, and Manly Vigour, which the *French* are utter strangers to.'

Rymer's fame rests, however, on his pioneering work as an historian. With Tom May and Thomas Fuller, he is a harbinger of Sidney's later achievements in historical studies. A friend of the great 'Kit-Kat' Whigs Lord Somers and Charles Montagu, Rymer was appointed historiographer to the King in 1692, on a salary of £200 per annum. Montagu and Somers sponsored *Foedera*, Rymer's *magnum opus*, a collection of transcriptions of all the public alliances, treaties and confederacies of England with other countries since 1101. His salary never covered his costs, and Rymer died in poverty in 1713, forced to sell books to buy food. The immense work, having reached the year 1543, was unfinished at the 15th volume of the 20 Rymer planned. Rymer was in correspondence with the great German scholar Gottfriend Leibnitz in preparing *Foedera*, and the work has an international reputation to this day.

'Driven by the Tyranny of Fate': William Wollaston

> Often thought I, this once I'll turn, and feed my eyes
> With those blest piles that yonder grow:
> My parting sight this once
> Shall kiss the stones,
> That from the sacred turf do rise:
> Yet still repeat my glances as I go,
> Till, sinking with the sky,
> Behind the earth's convexity,
> Cambridge in my horizon set
> And left me in the dark my fortune to regret.
> —William Wollaston, from an unpublished memoir, 1709

William Wollaston came to Sidney as a pensioner in 1674 at the height of the College's disciplinary meltdown. A contemporary of Browne, Payton, Munday and other bad boys, he was still at Sidney when Huggins, Thornton and Woodall broke into the Master's Lodge in 1681. His family were royalist Staffordshire gentry who had fallen on hard times; a wealthy uncle sponsored his entry to Sidney, where his schoolmaster's brother was probably the fellow David Jenner. Unfortunately for Wollaston and for Sidney, Jenner left two years later and his successor was a dunce. Wollaston later recalled that he chose this unfortunate person 'not upon the score of his learning and ingenuity, of which God knows he had little, but because the rest of my fellow pupils generally took him, as being the only senior fellow that did take pupils. The truth is, we thought by this to have compounded with him, as it were, not to hurt us; but this project did not succeed equally to all. He was a partial man, mighty inquisitive after little things, and one who (I believe) at his heart did not love a scholar.... My allowance was short, and, which troubled me most, I had scarce any books or materials to work with, no assistance or direction from any body, nor sufficient confidence to supply that defect by inquiries and examining others; yet I

William Wollaston, by an unknown artist

happened so to order my studies that I was not reckoned no scholar either, but indeed had such a degree of reputation as hath since been a matter of amazement to me who remember my own circumstances.'

Wollaston was a wit and eventually suffered for his cheeky attitude to his seniors. On one occasion he gently ridiculed the Sidney dean during a *viva voce*:

'The man immediately took fire, and his passion was not to be extinguished. Not contented to punish me in the usual methods of the College, he suborned a parcel of illiterate, scandalous fellows, that were already enemies on that account to the best of my year, to blacken us all, and especially me, with lies, and many stories that had not the least foundation in truth.'

It is an incident that casts further sorry light on Minshull's regime. Later, Wollaston was among students who wrote verses in commemoration of a fellow who had recently died but was tipped off about a plot by some fellows 'to put some affront upon me'. Uncertain whether to withdraw from the exercise and be in 'contempt of the Society', or to go ahead and risk the assault of 'buffoons and enemies', Wollaston at last decided 'to make some Hebrew verses, which my enemies none of them understood…. Carrying my performance at the time appointed to the lecturer's chamber, I found there an assembly of my censors all laughing. But when they had opened my paper, and found themselves disappointed, their countenances changed; and…it was my turn to laugh.' Perhaps surprisingly, Wollaston loved Sidney dearly and was devastated to leave Cambridge, unable to gain a fellowship in a society he believed had conspired against him and left him to 'the Tyranny of Fate'.

In Wollaston's case Sidney's loss was philosophy's gain, although his life was fraught with ill health, sadness and complication. After a career as a schoolmaster, he began writing seriously in 1690, publishing an annotated version of the *Book of Ecclesiastes* in verse. At about this time, he inherited a respectable fortune and became engaged to Alice Coborne, who died on the day of their intended marriage in 1689. A long inscription in Latin by Wollaston adorns her monument at Stratford-le-Bow church. He married later and moved to Charterhouse Square, London, where he remained for the rest of his life, fathering 11 children, yet living a reclusive existence of strict regularity. Although he wrote extensively on language, philosophy, theology and history, he burned many of his papers in old age. It was during these years, however, that he wrote *The Religion of Nature Delineated*, printed privately in 1722 and then published shortly before his death in 1724. According to George Dyer, he died a 'dissenter'. The book was a huge success, selling 10,000 copies within a few years and going through many editions during the 18th century.

The book sought to answer the question as to whether there is a natural religion. Confirming the proposition, Wollaston argued that religion and morality are the

Queen Caroline's Hermitage

The exterior of this now-vanished early 'Gothick' building in Richmond was deliberately rough in appearance in order to give a natural and aged character. It was covered in ivy, moss and brambles that clung to 'the solemn grot', as a 1738 poem put it, the whole set in a wild and bushy mound. The busts placed in niches inside the smoother rococo interior were intended to glorify the inspiration of Newtonian philosophy and Latitudinarian theology, bringing together religion and science in a uniquely English form. The Queen appointed a hermit to inhabit the 'grot', the naïve poet Michael Duck, whose untutored rustic simplicities were intended to complement the sophistication of the five heroes. Wollaston's bust is now on view at Kensington Palace, London.

Queen Caroline's Hermitage, Richmond, by William Kent, 1730. Sir John Soane's Museum, London

same thing, their purpose being the pursuit of happiness by the practice of truth and 'right reason'. For Wollaston, moral evil is the practical denial of a true proposition, whereas good was its affirmation. He was considered an advanced free-thinker in his time and his celebrity was such that Queen Caroline included his bust executed by Michael Rysbrack, along with those of Robert Boyle, John Locke, Isaac Newton and Samuel Clarke, in her famous contemplative 'hermitage' built by William Kent at Richmond.

'Mongrel Papist': Joshua Basset, Intruded Master

> As to his government, we found him a passionate, proud and insolent man, whenever he was opposed, which made us very cautious in conversing with him, who saw he waited for and catched at all ocassions to do us mischief in what concerned our religion. I don't deny, that he had learning and other abilities to have done us good, but his interest lay the contrary way. —John Craven, Master of Sidney 1723–28, on Joshua Basset, Master 1686–88, 1725

Following Richard Minshull's death on 31 December 1686, after 43 years as master, James II imposed a Catholic master on Sidney in 1687 as part of his strategy to intrude Catholics into prominent positions. Such was the uproar over this appointment that even the powerful figure of Isaac Newton became involved.

King James, who had come to the throne in 1685, sought to exert his authority at Oxford and Cambridge through some high-profile appointments. He changed the law so that he could ignore the anti-Catholic statutes of colleges, and installed a Catholic as dean at Christ Church, Oxford, in 1686. A few days after Minshull's death, the King wrote to the fellows of Sidney recommending Joshua Basset as his replacement. Basset, a fellow of Caius with strong court connections, had recently converted to Rome and published an anonymous defence of his decision called *Reason and Authority*, expressing concern at 'how grievously our poor nation was… torn and divided with such sects and schism'. The Sidney fellowship replied that he would be acceptable if he took the customary Anglican and loyal oaths, to which the King replied that these should be suspended. The fellows played for time and a month later the Protestant Isaac Newton remarked in a letter about their indecision: 'I wonder that the good men of Sidney do not elect their Master. An honest courage in these matters will secure all, having law on our sides.'

Edmund Matthews returns to view at this stage, now the senior (i.e. oldest) fellow and thereby the College president. He was far older than his colleagues, and his experience suggested to him that acquiescence to James would be the best approach. He was hotly opposed by the third senior fellow, the Yorkshireman James Johnson, who had come up as a pensioner in 1655 and was appointed a fellow by royal mandate in 1662. Johnson was described by the Presbyterian diarist Roger Morrice as a man 'of rough and somewhat boisterous behaviour'.

Sidney's fellows were royalist in sympathy and their colleague Thomas Walker's eulogy to James at his accession expressed entirely conventional Tory sentiments:

'Cease, faction, cease, and smooth thy angry brow;
No more the blasted seeds of treason sow:
Let no disloyal murmurs stain
The long, and ever-peaceful reign
Of James, the Martyr's son.'

Royal appointments were nothing new, and indeed Sidney's fellowship since 1660 had received more appointments by royal mandate than most colleges. But such appointments had to be Anglican and Walker, Johnson and the others wished to defend the College statutes. Their legal position, however, was weak, and although College records show they did not formally elect him, Sidney accepted Basset; he took up office on 7 March under the imposing protection of the King's assize judges. Matthews, described as 'the old man of Sidney' by the Bishop of Ely, probably decided this outcome.

Basset's most provocative act in his first year was to lock the Chapel door to prevent the traditional (anti-Catholic) Gunpowder Plot service from taking place on 5 November. Basset set up a private chapel in the Lodge with an altarpiece with 'IHS' in a glory and cherubims, a feature that survived over the Audit Room door into the mid-18th century. This chapel was used by Catholics from across Cambridge. Basset also admitted a Benedictine monk, Alban Francis, as a fellow-commoner, a man who dined at Sidney in his habit and was reputed to be Basset's chaplain. Francis was denied

Pages from the Sidney statutes with anti-Catholic provisions deleted, as ordered by James II's Commission for Ecclesiastical Causes, 1687

an MA by the university in spite of Judge Jeffreys' attempts to intimidate it, a sign of Cambridge's growing opposition to the King. Basset's own version of Catholicism was deeply unorthodox; Joseph Craven called him a 'mongrel papist, and had so many nostrums in his religion, that no part of the Roman Church could own him'.

Sidney's mainly youthful fellows were not as supine as Newton and others believed them to be, in spite of the ageing Matthews' behaviour. Emboldened by the refusal of Magdalen College, Oxford, to accept a Catholic nomination by the King in April 1687, they tried to fight back immediately. John Laughton, master of Trinity College, Cambridge, wrote to Arthur Charlett, president of University College, Oxford:

'I have communicated what you relate concerning the brave resolution of Magdalen to my friends of Sidney College here, and perhaps you'll hear very shortly good effects of it, for they are already seriously intending to take such a course as probably may retrieve the unhappy miscarriage of their weak and timorous President [i.e. Edmund Matthews] who is now removed to the country very much discontented and disturbed in mind for the irreparable scandal and mischief his wretched frailty hath brought upon us all.'

In April 1687, Roger Morrice reported that the fellows were planning to depose Basset on the grounds that he was in breach of specific Sidney statutes. Morrice wrote in his 'Entring Book', that the master was required 'every month [to] collate in the College upon some point in defence of the Reformation against Popery and that he shall in the public schools once a month or two defend some point of the like kind'. Basset had obviously 'neglected, forborne and refused' to undertake this requirement, and the fellows were determined to expel him. 'But it seems he had notice (by some false brother among them) of their purposes', and rode by horse to London to inform the King. Sidney's statutes were revised, following Basset's recommendations, and the offending anti-popery lines of the statutes were crossed out by the Ecclesiastical Commission.

James II was faced with the threat of William of Orange's Glorious Revolution by the end of 1688 and, in an attempt to appease his opponents, rescinded much legislation, including the new Sidney statutes. The fellows were authorised to elect a new master, and in December James Johnson became the sixth master of Sidney, two days before James II went into exile. Basset fled Cambridge, and in violent anti-Catholic riots the Master's Lodge was attacked. The temporary chapel was destroyed and the papist vestments burned. The College accounts record the expenditure of 11 shillings for 'mending the chamber broken by the rabble'.

Basset later tried to retrieve his belongings from Johnson, but 'was roughly made to understand' by his successor 'that if he did not desist he would be informed against as a Popish Priest'. These belongings included a shovel, bellows, tongs and furniture such as a cupboard worth eight shillings by 'Hall the joiner', several new wineglasses, earthenware chamber pots, and coal from the cellar of the Lodge. Basset also claimed back trees in the garden, having made some significant changes to the College grounds that may be visible in Loggan's print of 1690 (see page 128). Basset moved to London where he lived in poverty and was perhaps the author of *An Essay towards a Proposal for Catholic Communion* published in 1704, shortly after James

Johnson died. He died sometime after 1714 when he presented a copy of his latest publication to the College library. After Basset's sudden departure, Sidney was to have no Catholic among its masters or fellows until 1904.

'Ruinous Condition': Sidney 1688–1746

> Whereas the College of the Lady Frances Sidney Sussex in the University of Cambridge is at present in a ruinous condition as to its buildings, which cannot be put into tolerable repair without very great charge & expence, & whereas there are great arrears of Rent due to the same, part of which will in all probability never be recover'd, & whereas it is at present engaged in a tedious and expensive Lawsuit concerning S[i]r Francis Clark's foundation, whereby £140 per annum are not only detain'd from it, but it is likewise oblig'd to be at great charges in carrying on the said Lawsuit, we the Master and Fellows of the same by a power committed to us by the 19th statute of the said College, do agree, order & determine that the fellowship of the foundation now vacant by the resignation of Mr. [Thomas] Harrison shall not be fill'd up or chose into (until the affairs of the College shall so alter as to make it reasonable to take off this suspension), and that in the mean time twenty pounds each Audit shall be paid out of the profits of the said fellowship into the treasury in order to defray the necessary expences of the said College.' —*Acta Collegii*, 7 November 1729.

William and Mary's accession made England an Anglican nation once again. In the universities, masters and fellows were required to swear allegiance to the monarchy and the Church of England. This was difficult for some who could not support claims for the new King and Queen's legitimacy. These Nonjurors, as they were called, came from a variety of positions, some of them, such as Sidney's Nathaniel Hooke, becoming militant Jacobites and supporting 'The Pretender', James III. Many Tories either were, or were suspected of being, Jacobites or sympathisers of the 'Old Cause'.

The age of political parties had begun, with Whigs and Tories dominating the political scene for over a century. Life in Cambridge reflected these changes and conflicts and in 1734 Sidney was described to Horace Walpole by the poet Thomas Gray, while an undergraduate, as a Whig college: 'Thus the men of Peterhouse, Pembroke and Clare Hall of course must be Tories, they of Trinity rakes, of King's scholars, of Sidney Whigs…'

Royal intrusion into university affairs declined notably, along with student numbers. Between 1690 and 1750 university matriculations continued to drop sharply, from about 250 a year to about 150. In the 18th century, Sidney's undergraduate intake could be as low as three or four students, a tiny number compared with the days when its popularity led to fellows sharing rooms.

Splendidly corpulent and bluff as he looks in his wig, James Johnson managed to improve the learning of the fellowship and the achievements of the dwindling student numbers after the two previous lacklustre masterships. His successors continued the improvement. From 1688 until 1746, when Francis Sawyer Parris was elected master, Sidney's record in the *Ordo Senioritatis* was very good; for such a small college it was quite outstanding. Virtually every year saw one or two students in the list and often there were three or four. On three occasions, admittedly when a Sidney examiner presided, they were top: Christopher Ewings in 1713–14; William Denstone in 1723–24 and Robert Baynes in 1733–34.

In an age of new building in Cambridge, however, Johnson and his successors did not expand Sidney's accommodation or beautify its existing buildings. The German traveller and scholar Zacharis Conrad von Uffenbach described the College in 1710 as 'an old and tolerably fine building'. Under Johnson, income was increased by building a mill at Saleby and selling wood from the estates at Abbots Langley. Johnson's main financial contribution was to leave Sidney £1,200 in his will in 1703 to purchase advowsons, or church livings, and this was spent on livings at South Kilvington, Yorkshire, in 1706, and Swanscombe in Kent in 1710. Johnson also left the advowson of Rempstone, Nottinghamshire, and estates at Cherry Hinton were bought with his legacy. The latter are remembered by Sidney Farm Road in Cherry Hinton. Johnson's generosity was marred by legal difficulties because his will had not been witnessed; nonetheless he increased the College's wealth.

Among students who went on to gain distinction at this time was Richard Reynolds, son of a Cambridgeshire rector, who entered in 1689 as a pensioner and became a scholar the following year. After his graduation he migrated to Trinity Hall, became a chaplain to George I and then Bishop of Bangor. In 1723 he became Bishop of Lincoln. He refurbished the cathedral there and was an active reformer of clerical education, as well as a generous philanthropist, supporting local charity schools as a first line of defence against Catholicism. In the Lords he opposed Robert Walpole vigorously throughout the 1730s and 1740s.

Another eminent churchman was Thomas Jekyll, an Oxford graduate from a Presbyterian background in London, who took his DD in 1694 at the age of 48. He was a renowned preacher in Westminster, famous for his attacks on the refined irreligion of the times and the rise of party politics. He was a Whig who was well placed to benefit from the system he attacked, but prudently distanced himself from the more radical tendencies in the party. Like Reynolds, Jekyll was concerned about the rise of Catholic schools under James II, and founded an Anglican school for 50 poor children in Westminster. Jekyll was a strong exponent of philanthropy and of moral reform in the 1690s. His catechism for the new school he founded was published in 1690 and went through many editions. He died in 1698.

The College was a quieter and more disciplined place than in the previous 30 years; the *Acta* reveal few punishments. Thomas Hutchinson, a pensioner from Pickering, Yorkshire, was admonished for drunkenness, swearing and 'taking the keys of the back-gate from the Porter by violence' in 1690; and the manciple was expelled in 1694 after running into debt with the College brewer. Inevitably, Hutchinson went on to ordination and priesthood.

Sidney comprised, in von Uffenbach's words, a 'small but handsome set of buildings in very fine gardens'. Books were constantly added to the library, which Uffenbach admired, for 'though high up under the very roof of the chapel', it was 'tolerably good and well lighted and the books though not numerous were still in

a good state'. In 1707 James Beeverell in his *Les Delices de la Grande Bretagne et de l'Irlande*, described Sidney as having seven fellows under the master and 20 '*Ecoliers*'. He also described the gardens as '*fort agréables*' with their parterre, '*boulingrin*' and '*belles promenades*'.

However, Sidney's condition was not as good as this might suggest. Its buildings were in an increasingly poor condition, and when the new master John Frankland, fellow and dean of Gloucester and later of Ely, came into residence in the Master's Lodge in 1728, he was shocked by dwindling student numbers, rent arrears,

David Loggan's 1690 print of Sidney reduced and adapted in Les Delices de la Grande Bretagne et de l'Irlande, *1707, by James Beeverell. Private collection*

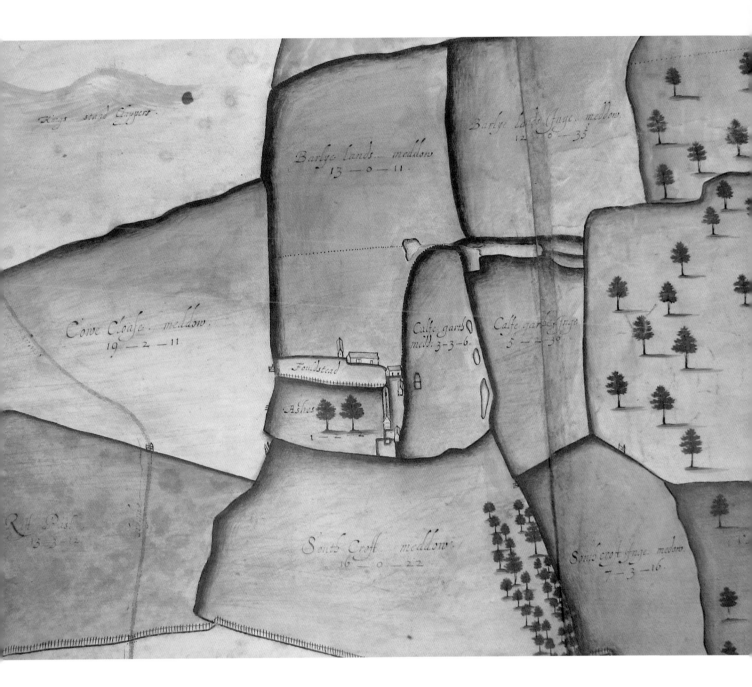

outstanding legal wrangles and the disrepair of the courts. He took decisive if regrettable action and suspended a fellowship to pay for repairs.

In 1730, the year of his death, Frankland recorded 'the ruinous and miserable condition of our College is in as to its buildings' and the need to borrow £200 to be repaid over six years, as well as the fixing of a seal to a bond given to 'Frederick Frankland Esqr., of Westminster'. Sidney seems once again to have had to fall back on family connections.

Detail of a map of the College estate at Cridling Park, Yorkshire, 1635

'Ancient Christianity': Richard Allin and William Whiston

> Mr. Mogridge has given me an imperfect relation of your friend Mr. Whiston, as if he were about to write against some fundamental doctrine of Christianity, if so, I am sorry for the man. —Dr John Allen (1691–92), Fellow of the Royal Society, to his friend Richard Allin

One of Sidney's most interesting fellows under James Johnson was Richard Allin BD, a scholar who came up in 1693 and was elected a fellow in 1701. He lectured in a wide range of subjects, including classics, mathematics, chemistry and theology.

Allin was an inveterate bibliophile, list-maker, and chronologist, and a prodigious correspondent with scholars such as the mathematician and theologian William Whiston, the French mathematician Abraham de Moivre and the heretical churchman John Jackson. He seems to have conformed to a type of scholarly and sedentary don, but with distinctly heterodox interests and a nonconformist tendency in his religious thinking. Allin was also poor. He wrote to Whiston in 1711 that he was unable to accept an invitation to meet in Ampthill, Bedfordshire, because 'I have neither boots nor any riding furniture, having not had occasion to get on horseback for almost seven years last past; nor indeed have I now so much as a coat nor any other upper garments but gowns and cassocks'.

Whiston, who had succeeded Newton as Lucasian Professor of Mathematics in 1703, was best known for his heretical religious opinions, which earned him expulsion from the university in 1710. In the late 1690s he told Allin about his idea that the deluge was caused by a comet hitting the Earth, and thanks his Sidney correspondent for his suggestions and criticisms in developing these ideas. By 1715 Whiston had founded a 'Society for Promoting Primitive Christianity', which opposed the orthodox creed and sought to renew Christianity through a reading of the 'Apostolical Constitutions'. His anti-trinitarian views were highly controversial and may have been a reason for Allin to turn down Whiston's request that he should stand godfather to his son in 1711. In his letter, Whiston said, 'we are all to be of yᵉ ancient Christian perswasion', but in reply Allin explained that he had 'some reasons which restrain me, which if you had been here, I should have communicated to you. Pray be not displeased with me on this account, but still continue to me yᵉ same part in your friendship as hitherto.' Whiston named Allin as godfather anyway, 'though none but my self & Wife know a word of it'. Allin was incensed at this, rebuked Whiston in his reply, and said: 'You say that there is hardly one general council that has not quoted yᵉ constitutions as ancient, sacred and apostolical. Whereas I do not remember that yᵉ Councils do at all quote yᵉ constitutions, but only allude to 'em sometimes; much less do they quote 'em as sacred and Apostolical, or constantly own

'Linens and Stockings'

Allin was a keen accountant of his expenses. In 1696 he recorded payments for books such as Diodorus Siculus, Robert Boyle on chemistry, Clarke's *Physicks*, and Cowley's poetry, as well as expenditure on his periwig, coal and sedge, a barber for 'washballs and shaving his head', 'linens and stockings' from 'Mrs Jolley', a nurse 'in his sicknesse', an apothecary's bill, and the washing of his linen 'when he had small pox'. Frequently the payments were made in clipped money. The books were from Cambridge booksellers such as Dickinson and Webber, and also from Stourbridge Fair where Allin went most years. At his graduation in 1697 he paid for supper for the fellows and, curiously, bought his father a pair of gloves. Other payments include ones to the porter, to the master for a 'banket', his tutor for breakfast, and his father for a dinner.

'em as undoubtedly canonical…. I am afraid you have in these instances carried on your contradiction to yᵉ Convocation so far, as not to be able to justify it.' However, Allin's friendship earned him the reputation of being a follower of Whiston, some anonymous opponents referring to him as his 'Friend' and 'Brother'.

When Joseph Craven died as master in 1727, Whiston thought his friend would make an excellent replacement. He told Allin, 'I heartily wish yᵉ publick or private affairs of yᵉ Nation & of your College would admit of yᵉ hopes of your succeeding him. But since I greatly fear that things are not yet in so good a State, I think it greatly behoves you to endeavour that such a successor may be best chosen as may best deserve to be fit for that place, & such an one as may not endeavour to crush you or obstruct yours or others fair & free enquiries into ancient Christianity.' Whiston recommended the new Regius Professor of Modern History, Samuel Harris, while acknowledging that Sidney's statutes 'are very tender in such a point'. Allin was not a successful candidate and the Etonian John Frankland DD, a near contemporary who died two years later as a royal chaplain and dean of Ely, was appointed.

'The Grossest Absurdities': Thomas Woolston, Heretic

> Among the moderns, Thomas Woolston, a learned member of the University of Cambridge, appears to me to have been the first who ventured to interpret the Gospels merely in a typical, allegorical, and spiritual sense, and boldly maintained that not one of the miracles of Jesus was actually performed.
> —Voltaire, 'Miracles', in *Dictionnaire Philosophique*, 1751–66

Thomas Woolston was the most remarkable fellow at Sidney at the turn of the 18th century, a religious controversialist whose eccentric views and robust humour led to personal tragedy. The son of a prosperous Northampton currier and tanner, Woolston entered Sidney as a pensioner in 1685, where his tutor was James Johnson and his close friends included Richard Allin and the future masters Bardsey Fisher and Joseph Craven. He graduated shortly after James Basset's hurried departure. Woolston was elected a fellow in 1691 and then took holy orders.

Like Allin and other Sidney contemporaries, Woolston was fascinated by early Christian writers, and read Origen particularly closely. From this reading he developed ideas that proposed the Bible be interpreted in a figurative or allegorical, rather than a literal, spirit. When he expressed these views in Latin and English sermons required for his BD in 1699, he shocked many listeners and marked himself out as a potential Deist, an accusation he always refuted. The Latin sermon, published much later in 1720 as *Dissertation on Pontius Pilate's Letter to Tiberius about the*

Thomas Woolston, c1700–25, by Jan Van der Gucht, after an engraving by Bartholomew Dandridge. National Portrait Gallery, London

This print can be seen reversed in Plate 2 of Hogarth's Harlot's Progress, 1732 (see page 158)

THOMAS WOOLSTON B.D.
Sometime Fellow of Sidney Colledge Cambridge.

Bardsey Fisher, Master 1704–23, by John Verelst, 1706

Bardsey Fisher, son of a Nottinghamshire rector, entered Sidney as a pensioner in 1673–74, an exact contemporary of William Wollaston. He was elected master in 1704, was Vice-Chancellor in 1705 and died in 1723

Acts of Jesus Christ, and the English sermon, published in 1722 as *The Exact Fitness of the Time in which Christ was Manifested in the Flesh*, gained him widespread notoriety.

In 1705 Woolston published *Old Apology for the Truth of the Christian Religion*, which developed his idea that even though Pilate's letter was probably spurious, he would have sent such a letter, and that it communicated a request by Jesus that the Romans worship him as the god of a conquered nation, their normal practice. Woolston condemned Pharaoh and the Romans for denying their subjects the right to practise the true faith, while praising English kings for forcibly converting the nation to Protestantism. Printed by Cambridge University Press, on whose board Woolston sat, the book unleashed a furious reaction, which, he said, made him consider 'an exit out of this world [for] shame'. He was dismissed by many as suffering from a 'disorder'd mind', and in response to the accusation, in his friend William Whiston's words, 'he grew really disordered and…was accordingly confined for a long time'. Sidney remained loyal to its wayward fellow, and Fisher and then Craven continued paying his stipend through friends until 1724. They only stopped doing so when he denied the existence of the 'bodily distemper' that allowed the payments to be made.

Woolston was released from confinement by 1720 and immediately began to defend himself against the accusations of insanity and heresy, writing letters to friends and celebrities claiming the so-called madness he suffered from was a smear spread by those unable to argue against his beliefs. He earned an income by publishing pamphlets about his figurative reading of scripture, and his notoriety was such that his portrait was included in one of the plates of William Hogarth's *Harlot's Progress* in 1732.

In 1725 Woolston joined a controversy between the Deist Anthony Collins and the established clergy. In a work of 1724 Collins had challenged the church to prove that Christ had realised the Old Testament prophecies. Woolston exploited the debate and published his *Moderator between an Infidel and an Apostate*, dedicated to the Archbishop of Canterbury. He attacked the literal interpretation of Jesus' miracles, the resurrection and the virgin birth, arguing that the clergy had sacrificed the spirit for the letter. Whiston managed to prevent Edmund Gibson, the Bishop of London, sending Woolston to jail for blasphemy, although the King's Bench had convicted him. It was during this dispute that he lost his Sidney fellowship and that his brother gave his paranoid sibling £30 pounds a year to live on.

Woolston's sad end was precipitated by the publication of his six *Discourses on the Miracles of our Saviour* (1727–29), written as if by a rabbi, each of which opened with a mischievous dedication to a prominent bishop. Intending to restore 'ancient Christianity', he attributed his readings of the miracles to the early Church Fathers and in doing so misquoted, or even invented, words to suit his argument. For Woolston, miracles might be harmful, such as Christ's turning water into wine for those already inebriated; innocuous, such as the divining of the Samaritan woman's five husbands; healing, such as curing the blind man; and resurrectional, like that of Lazarus. The miracles, he said, made Jesus look like a 'juggling imposter' and 'strolling fortune-teller', and taken literally they 'imply improbabilities and incredulities, and the grossest absurdities, very dishonourable to the Name of Christ'. Woolston claimed Jesus' resurrection was spiritual, not physical, and that his disciples had got the guards outside the tomb drunk and taken his body away secretly – 'the most bare-fac'd imposture that ever was put upon the world'. He also described two mystical journeys he had himself made to heaven in order to discuss with Elijah and the Church Fathers the nature of the transfiguration.

The whole tone of the *Discourses*, which sold in tens of thousands, was satirical and gave the impression that Woolston was trying to undermine Christian faith. Sixty replies from his ironical dedicatees and many others preceded the inevitable prosecution for blasphemy. Woolston was sentenced to jail in Southwark prison. He refused to recant and his sentence was increased until he would agree to conform. Woolston wouldn't back down and was supported by the anti-trinitarian philosopher Samuel Clarke. He bought the 'liberty of the rules', enabling him to live in the City, and continued to publish pamphlets. Woolston's enormous popularity was noted by Jonathan Swift, who wrote: 'He is much caressed by many great Courtiers, and by all the Infidels, and his books read generally by the Court Ladies.' His presence in the chapter coffee house near St Paul's got him imprisoned again by offended clergymen, but he was soon back in the City, this time in Birdcage Alley in the Mint, where he died of influenza in 1733. Woolston's alleged last words, typical of this principled but mild-mannered man, were, 'Here is a battle that all men are forced to fight and that I fight, not only with patience but willingly.' A later member of the College was unimpressed, adding to Woolston's entry in the College Register a sentence in Latin that attacked him as 'that Heretic who in the year

Elizabeth, second wife of Bardsey Fisher, by John Verelst, 1706, one of only two surviving portraits of a Sidney master's wife

The Harlot's Progress,
Plate 2, 1732, etching
and engraving by William
Hogarth. Woolston's
portrait is on the wall
between the two main
figures. British Museum,
London

1728–29 did not blush to attack openly the miracles wrought by his Saviour…'. The Norrisian Professor of Divinity in the second half of the century, the Sidney fellow John Hey, wrote a more considered response: 'I feel more compassion, when I think of Woolston, than indignation. He was a man of learning and probity; nay, of wit and humour, however misapplied. It would have reflected more honour upon our religion and upon our civil government to have committed him to the care of his relations and friends…'

Woolston's influence on free thinkers and atheists, as well as less orthodox Christians, has been considerable, although his ideas are often misunderstood. He was much admired by Voltaire, who was exiled in England between 1726 and 1729. Voltaire wrote that 'never was Christianity so daringly assaulted by any Christian'. David Hume's sceptical attack on miracles later in the 18th century owes much to Woolston's bold and anti-clerical interventions and, very recently, the radical writer Raoul Vaneigem admired his 'corrosive humour', 'irreverence and misfortune' in his work *The Resistance to Christianity* (1993).

The Female Tatler: Thomas Baker, alias 'Phoebe Crackenthorpe'

But others will swear that this wise Undertaker
By Trade's an At---ney, by Name is a B---r,
Who rambles about with a Female Disguise on
And lives upon Scandal, as Toads do on Poyson.
—*The British Apollo*, on Thomas Baker, editor of *The Female Tatler*, 1709

The masters who steered Sidney from the end of James II's reign in 1688 to the early years of George II's in 1730 – James Johnson, Bardsey Fisher, Joseph Craven and John Frankland – were all contemporaries or colleagues. The sense of friendship and loyalty is discernible in their interactions; and though Sidney, like most of Cambridge, was in a state of decline at this time, there was an atmosphere of freedom and change in the College that produced some fascinating students and fellows and paved the way for a major revival of energy and activity in the middle of the 18th century. Woolston's writings are very much of the period, sceptical, forceful and indicative of changes that could not be stopped from developing, whatever the universities might wish.

Something of the growing liberality of the College, and the strange cross-dressing imagination of the period, may be discerned in the admission of the comic playwright Thomas Baker to take an MA in 1709. Baker, from Herefordshire, had attended Brasenose College and Christ Church, Oxford from 1697 to 1700, and then moved to London where in 1701, while training as a lawyer, he premiered his first play, *The Humour of the Age*, at Drury Lane. It was a great success and led to a second play in 1703, *Tunbridge Walks: or the Yeomen of Kent*, which was performed many times in the 18th century. Baker's third play, *An Act of Oxford*, was probably objected to by the university for its satire, and was performed instead as *Hampstead Heath* in 1705. This play was followed in 1708 by his final effort, *The Lady's Fine Airs*, which seems to have been far less popular than his previous plays. As a result of this failure, and a feeling that he should do something 'which may prove more serviceable to the Publick, and beneficial to myself', he decided to enter the church. Baker chose Sidney Sussex to study for his MA in 1709.

While enrolled at Sidney, Baker inaugurated Britain's first women's 'lifestyle' magazine, *The Female Tatler*, in July 1709, conceived as a tri-weekly answer to Richard Steele's male-orientated news and gossip journal *Tatler*, which had begun in April. The two publications were published on alternate days of the week. Baker edited his journal as 'Phoebe Crackenthorpe', a 'Lady that knows everything', as the title page announced. *The Female Tatler* published satirical portraits, theatre gossip and mock advertisements and offered sound advice to fashionable young ladies through the voice of Mrs Crackenthorpe. The journal lasted nearly a year and came under fierce attack from a rival, *The British Apollo*, which claimed Baker 'poses as a woman and some may by this be taken in'.

Baker was probably assisted as editor by the female writer Delarivier Manley, whom we met earlier, satirising Sidney's Lord Haversham. Like Steele's magazine,

The Female Tatler acted as a commentary on contemporary manners and ethics and Baker's feminine alter ego sought to promote genteel frugality, prudence and tasteful restraint. Full of the views of gossiping ladies such as 'Artesia', 'Rosella' and 'Sophronia', and targets such as 'Lady Meanwell' and 'Lady Bumfiddle', it circulated in the small world of ladies' India houses, where tea was drunk and where everyone knew each other. *The Female Tatler* was socially conservative in its emphasis on dressing and behaving according to rank, in particular targeting the *nouveaux riches* or 'mock-genteels'. However, it also had a distinctly feminist edge in its comments on the constraints of beauty and women's education. Mrs Crackenthorpe, who announced early on that she was no beauty, wrote in number 88: 'How can people in their senses think that the fine clothes, and all the trinkets that are given

Front page of The Female Tatler, *number 23, August 26–29 1709. Bodleian Library, Oxford*

us are bestowed upon the sex any other ways than playthings are given to children, to amuse, keep their thoughts employed and their hands from doing of mischief.' Women, she continued, should control their husbands by feminine wiles and sensuous charm. She called marriage a 'fatal snare'.

Baker attacked the growing cult of celebrity preachers, noting that 'if the divine expected happens not to preach, half the church empties at a strange face'. It might have been the Sidney fellowship writing, and one wonders what Baker's tutors would have thought of his journalism; indeed, might they have encouraged much of his thinking and might issues of the *The Female Tatler* have been read in the College Parlour?

The Female Tatler ceased publication in March 1710, but Mrs Crackenthorpe had resigned in November 1709 when Baker announced 'she' was resigning in favour of 'a Society of Modest Ladies', no doubt a coded reference to his entering the church. Baker became rector of Bolnhurst, a few miles north of Bedford in 1711 and vicar of Ravensden, a few miles south of Bolnhurst, from 1716 until 1731. At his death in 1749 he left money to found a school at Bolnhurst.

'The Criterion of Virtue': The Philosophy of John Gay

Sidney produced theologians and churchmen by the score in its first 200 years. However, men who can be identified more strictly as philosophers in the modern sense are less common. An important exception is John Gay, cousin of the more famous eponymous poet who wrote *The Beggar's Opera* in 1728. Sidney's John Gay, the son of a Devon vicar, attended Blundell's School and entered Sidney as a scholar in 1717. This was the year after the College determined its new election procedure for fellows should consist of examination in the Hebrew Psalter, Homer, Aristotle's *Rhetoric* and *Logic*, Virgil's *Georgics*, and physics. Gay was always going to be a strong candidate for a fellowship, and in 1724 he was elected a fellow and acted as Sidney's Hebrew, Greek and ecclesiastical lecturer. Edmund Law, a fellow of Christ's, devoted follower of John Locke's ideas and a future Bishop of Carlisle, said that no one in Cambridge could match Gay's knowledge of the Bible and of Locke's writings. Gay represents both a continuation of the predestinarian traditions Sidney had been founded on and a powerful break with them; he was in the mould of William Wollaston.

In 1731 Law, a Whig and latitudinarian churchman who nevertheless grounded his faith in the evidence of the biblical miracles, published his translation of William King's *Essay on the Origin of Evil*, which was prefaced and counter-balanced by Gay's anonymous essay *Concerning the Fundamental Principle of Virtue or Morality*. Gay's brilliantly succinct essay, developing his ideas from John Locke's theories, provided the first systematic attempt to construct a utilitarian theory of morality. His argument, put simply, was that happiness is pleasure and the avoidance of pain, and that, paradoxically, virtue is conformity to a way of life that seeks the happiness of others:

'Now it is evident from the nature of God, viz. His being infinitely happy in Himself from all eternity, and from His goodness manifested in His works, that he could have no other design in creating mankind than their happiness; and therefore He wills their happiness; therefore the means of their happiness; therefore that man's behaviour, as far as it may be the means of the happiness of mankind should be such.'

The argument influenced much subsequent thinking, such as the associationist psychology of David Hartley, a doctor and fellow of Jesus College from 1727, whose *Observations on Man* of 1749 drew on Newton for his theory of physical vibration, and on Gay for his idea that sympathy and conscience are developed by means of association from selfish feelings. Other thinkers indebted to Gay include Abraham Tucker, William Paley and the great Utilitarians Jeremy Bentham and James Stuart Mill. Gay also made an impact on Samuel Johnson who, in chapter 22 of his 1759 novella *The History of Rasselas, Prince of Abyssinia*, satirises a philosopher of nature. The philosopher proclaims that 'the way to be happy is to live according to nature, in obedience to that universal and unalterable law with which every heart is originally impressed; which is not written on it by precept, but engraven by destiny, not instilled by education, but infused at our nativity'. When the truth-seeking Rasselas asks what he means, the philosopher replies: 'To live according to nature, is to act with due regard to the fitness arising from the relations and qualities of causes and effects; to concur with the great and unchangeable scheme of universal felicity; to co-operate with the general disposition and tendency of the present scheme of things.' None too helpful advice, Rasselas feels, and his inventor agreed. Johnson had inverted Gay's views to parody philosophical gibberish and certainly would have agreed with Gay's philosophy, which sought the 'Criterion of Nature', a phrase Johnson himself used. The author of *The Vanity of Human Wishes* would have wholeheartedly concurred

Wilshampstead church, Bedfordshire, the Sidney living where John Gay, the rector, was buried in 1745

with Gay's opinion about the thirst for knowledge, fame, the delight in reading, building, planting 'and most of the various exercises and entertainments of life': 'These were at first entered on with a view to some further end, but at length become habitual amusements; the idea of pleasure is associated with them, and leads us on still in the same eager pursuit of them, when the first reason is quite vanished, or at least out of our minds.' It is thoroughly appropriate that Dr Johnson made a memorable visit to Gay's college over 30 years after the essay was published. Indeed, in 1758, the year before *Rasselas* was written, the essay was published under Gay's name for the first time, the title page referring to him as 'of Sidney College'.

Gay was already long dead, having died at the age of 46 at the Sidney living of Wilshampstead, Bedfordshire in 1745, where he had been rector since the essay was published.

'Moral Depravity': The Poetical Career of William Pattison

'So died in the twenty-first year this talented but reckless young man.…From the extreme licentiousness of his poetry the world was a gainer by his death, and Sussex can take little credit for having given him birth. Most of his poems were written before he was nineteen, and they show a moral depravity quite remarkable for that early period of life…'.

Thus wrote Mark Antony Lower in his *The Worthies of Sussex* in 1865. The 'reckless' young man was the libertine poet William Pattison (1706–27), the son of a farmer in Peasmarsh, Sussex, where Sidney held the advowson of the church. He arrived at Sidney in July 1724 and left two years later, having excised his name from the College register and left on his cut-up gown the following verses:

Whoever gives himself the Pains to stoop,
And take my venerable Tatters up;
To his presuming Inquisition I,
In Loco Pattisoni thus reply:
'Tir'd with the senseless Jargon of the Gown,
My Master left the College, for the Town;
Where, from Pedantick Drudgery secur'd,
He laughs at Follies he once endur'd;
And scorns his precious Minutes to regale,
With wretched College-Wit, and College-Ale;
Far nobler Pleasures open to his View,
Pleasures for ever Sweet! For ever New!'

Pattison had fallen out with his strict tutor, the Yorkshireman John Bell, who was a fellow from 1721 to 1730, and whose discipline he said was 'not easy to brook'. Fearing that he might be sent down, Pattison left of his own accord to lead the precarious life of a poet in London. The reasons for his dispute with Bell seem to be that he was, as his biographer wrote, more likely to be found 'Versifying at Sidney

College' or 'Angling on the Banks of the River Cam', than studying and performing the public disputations he so loathed.

A fascinating correspondence between Pattison and his Cambridge friends survives, which shows that they and some of the fellows were keen for him to return, but that Pattison's love of London's literary life and Bell's hostility prevented this happening. His undergraduate friends included William Foord from Scarborough, who became a fellow in 1729, and Nathaniel Hodgson, who went on to become a priest in Yorkshire. Among the fellows who supported his return were the future master John Adams, elected to the fellowship in 1714, and John Gay. A St John's friend, John Dickinson, wrote to Pattison that he had 'heard by chance, that your College would admit you again…' Nothing came of it, and another friend, Benjamin Wase, wrote to Pattison later: 'I was inconceivably grieved at Hulse's account of your tribulation and confusion, after I parted from you, and wish I could have contributed to your Relief: Here hath been vast Enquiries made about you by the Fellows, but none of them seems to be touched with so much pity and concern as Mr. G-y;…I advise you to send him a decent Epistle, and one to the Master [William Craven], with an impartial account of the Ill treatment which you have met with under B---, display therein his severe Usage, in moving Terms, and urge that he was the chief cause of your abrupt parting hence.' Bell had Pattison's belongings seized 'for his own security', as Wase commented ironically, and Pattison was seen no more, though the College kept his exhibition open for him. Gay's concern for Pattison suggests some considerable sympathy between the young philosopher of happiness and his pleasure-seeking student.

Pattison's letters and poetry are full of carnal matters. He wrote to Wase: 'Yesterday I fell in Love with a Lady in the Park; I took the Freedom of the Place, offered my Addresses, which at first she received coily, but awaiting upon her to her Lodgings, I found after some modest struggles of Honour, that, to speak poetically…'. He goes on in verse to describe his successful seduction and the resulting 'vast sea of Extacy' he and his new love enjoyed. Many of his poems describe in detail his amorous exploits and fantasies, with

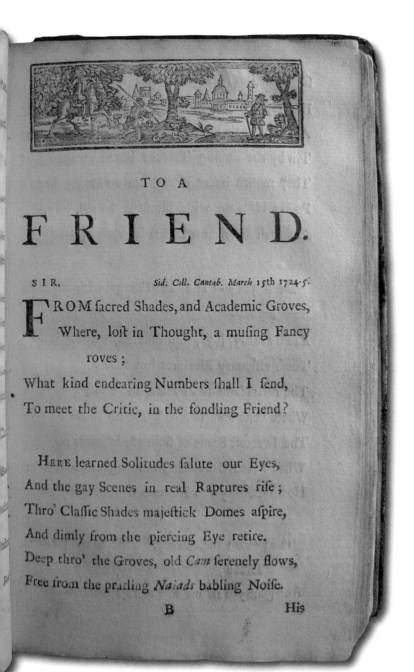

A page from William Pattison's Poems, *1728*

This painting was rediscovered in a furniture storeroom in Sussex House in 2003 by the fellow curator of pictures, Jonathan Conlin. It shows Diogenes in his barrel gesticulating at Alexander the Great. It was first recorded in an inventory of 1760 and once hung in 'the Room over the Bedchamber' of the Master's Lodge and was in 'the Anteroom', by 1807. It had been badly neglected for over a century. Jonathan Conlin believes it may have been painted by the architect, designer and painter William Kent in Rome in the 1710s. Kent designed the Hermitage at Richmond that housed a bust of Sidney's William Wollaston (see page 145). It is not known how the painting came to Sidney, however.

Diogenes and Alexander, possibly by William Kent

their 'panting Bubbies', 'pretty dying eyes' and 'fierce Transfusion of exchanging Hearts'.

Pattison's career in London was at first very promising and he was admired by Alexander Pope, a subscriber to his posthumous *Poetical Works* of 1728, which were dedicated to the Earl of Peterborough. Other subscribers included over 30 Cambridge contemporaries, among them Sidney's Wase and Stephen Soames, by then a lawyer. Wase advised Pattison: 'You had better mention Sidney-College immediately after your own Name on the Title-Page than not; it will look more Ornamental too, tho' cannot enhance the intrinsic value of your Poems'. Pattison followed the advice and it is believed over 3,000 copies of the book were sold, a very impressive sales figure for a new talent.

Within a year, however, his letters show a broken young man, reduced to poverty and writing in desperation to Lord Burlington: 'Sir, What I am, my Proposals will inform you; What I have been, Sidney College, in Cambridge, can witness; but what I shall be some few hours hence, I tremble to think…' He describes sleeping on benches in St James's Park and his fears for his health. Pattison eventually contracted smallpox and died in the famous publisher James Curll's house in the Strand in July 1727. He was buried at St Clement Dane's, according to his sister 'in the best part of the Upper Church Yard', unlamented by a cold-hearted father. Her own final judgement on her brother was a counsel of pity for a wasted talent: 'We ought to draw a veil of Forgiveness over his Imprudencies; and it is to be hoped, that the Fatality of his Example, will have some influence over all such Youth who by running counter to the advice of their best friends, let their Heat get the better of their Judgement, and fall victims to their own folly.' The Cambridge historian George Dyer referred to Pattison in 1814 as 'another Chatterton'.

Charlton Wollaston's teapot and stand, London, maker Anthony Nelme, 1708. Charlton, admitted as a fellow-commoner in 1708, was the son of the philosopher William Wollaston

'Mortify Therefore Your Members': Bishop Garnett and Joseph Greenhill

I beseech you therefore, brethren, by the Mercies of God, that ye present your bodies a living sacrifice, holy, and acceptable to God: which is your reasonable service. The worst enemies you have are those of your own household, your lusts and passions, which war against the soul; get it but the better once of these, purify only those temples of the living God, from all the corruption of sensual appetites, and his blessed spirit will come in, and make his abode with you. Mortify therefore your members, which are upon the earth, fornication, uncleanness, inordinate affection, evil concupiscence, and covetousness, for which things sake, the wrath of God cometh upon the children of disobedience.

—John Garnett, *A Sermon Preached before the University of Cambridge, on Wednesday February 17, 1747–48*

Sidney's chief aim in the early-18th century was still to produce priests, not poets and moral philosophers, and thereby to maintain the place of the clergy in the state. While John Gay's intellect was appropriately rewarded as far as the College was concerned, William Pattison's talent and temperament brought him to physical and moral disaster. An ideal near-contemporary of Pattison's might have been the grammarian and headmaster William Ward (1727), whose books on English grammar were both highly original and influential on generations of schoolboys. Like those of all Oxbridge colleges, most Sidney undergraduates went into country parishes and led quiet and obscure lives ministering to their congregations. It was hoped by the College that their sentiments while at Sidney would reflect those of Pattison in his 'College Life':

Wak'd by the promise of a day we rise,
And with our souls salute the dawning skies:
All summon'd to devotion's fane repair,
And piously begin the day with prayer;
Thence, led by reason's glimmering light, descry
The dark recesses of philosophy;
Through classic groves the wily wanton chase,
And logically urge the puzzling chase.

'Nancy the Bed-Maker'

The likely nature of the more extreme extra-curricular activities indulged in by William Pattison in Cambridge, which led to his tutor John Bell's disapproval, are perhaps best indicated by his poem, 'Nancy The Bed-Maker'.

'Twas once upon a summer's day,
As on my downy bed I lay:
All over in tedious sweat,
To ease my limbs, and cool the heat;
When pretty Nancy gently came,
Nancy the object of my flame!
So soft she looked, so sweet, so fair,
With such a winning, yielding air;
With such an easy comely pride,
She seemed a lovely, longing bride!
Obedient to her eyes' command,
I seized her warm consenting hand;
Upon the downy bed displayed,
The unmurmuring, panting, struggling maid.
There ravished, feasted on her charms,
Her heaving breast, her twining arms,
Her ivory neck, her roguish eyes,
Her slender waist, her taper thighs,
With magic beauties there between
Too soft; too dazzling to be seen.
Melting, I clasped them close to mine,
And in a moment grew divine!

Some Sidney men led such lives and went on to higher preferment in the church and influence in the public sphere. The Londoner John Garnett, son of a Yorkshire rector, came to Sidney as a pensioner in 1728 after a few years at St John's, became a fellow in 1730 and Lady Margaret preacher to the university. He went to Ireland in 1751 as chaplain to the Duke of Dorset and was made Bishop of Ferns in 1752 and of Clogher in 1758. Garnett was renowned by contemporaries as a highly cultivated, humane and kind man. Samuel Burdy wrote in 1792 of Garnett's 'great humility… This bishop, though he had but one eye, could discover, as I am told, men of merit, as well as some people with two eyes.' Garnett published a number of sermons as well as his highly original *Dissertation on the Book of Job* (1749), a copy of which he gave to 'Sydney College Library'. Dedicated to the university Chancellor and future prime minister, Thomas Hollis, Duke of Newcastle, it was described by Lord Morton as 'a very proper book for the ante-chamber of a prime minister'. Dwelling on the virtues of patience and fortitude, its main failing for many readers was that it was prolix 'to a degree which would have taxed all Job's patience', as the *Dictionary of National Biography* has it.

Joseph Greenhill, a near-contemporary of Garnett's, came to Sidney from Westminster School in 1723 and took his MA in 1731. The son of a Hertfordshire counsellor-at-law of Abbots Langley, and a relative of the local Combe family who had given land to the College in the early-17th century, he inherited some of his

John Garnett, Bishop of Clogher, by an unknown artist, 1752–1760

father's court-room skills. They may have helped him as an undergraduate when he was admonished in April 1726 for causing 'great disturbances…to Mr. Barnes…making very troublesome and needless noise in his Chamber and for his impudent behaviour and language'.

Although living quietly for 20 years in East Horsley in Surrey as a rector of two parishes, in the 1750s he decided to come out of the parochial life 'allotted by him to be spent in a Manner agreeable', provoked by the 'important situation of Public Affairs'. In a series of highly reactionary published essays and pamphlets he attacked a variety of developments, such as Pelham's Jewish Naturalisation Act (the so-called 'Jew Bill') of 1753, which was repealed after popular opposition in 1754; Lord Hardwicke's Marriage Act of the same year, which required parental consent, males to be at least 14 years old and females to be 12; and the spread of inoculation since Lady Mary Wortley Montagu had brought the practice to the West from Constantinople in 1721, and against which Greenhill published a sermon in 1756, *Inoculation a Presumptuous Practice Destructive to*

Man. Other targets for Greenhill's wrath were the Seven Years War of 1756 to 1763, when he argued against a standing army and Pitt's Militia Act of 1757; Quakers; and millenarianism. He claimed the millennium and the reign of Christ's saints on earth were yet to come.

Greenhill attacked fellow churchmen like the latitudinarian Bishop Benjamin Hoadly, the incarnation for conservatives of the complacent and bloated Low Church Whig; and the great Newtonian philosopher and liberal theologian Samuel Clarke, whose ideas had a profound effect on Enlightenment thought. Greenhill was a passionate conservative Anglican who wished the Church of England to strengthen its grip on social and political affairs and who believed it must be ready to act as the Church Militant at the end of days. He believed his efforts were largely ignored and ridiculed, and his frustration at the press's failure to support his causes led him to return to rural Surrey in the 1770s where he died in 1788, one year before the French Revolution.

'Beneficial to the Publick Interest': Samuel Taylor's Mathematical Lectureship

> It being in my Apprehension a Study very Usefull and beneficiall to the Publick Interest and National Good. Which sort of Study in the Time of my being a Student there, was, as farr as I did observe, much neglected.
> —Samuel Taylor's will, 1732

Samuel Taylor of Dudley, who had come to Sidney as an undergraduate in 1688, died in March 1732 during the early years of John Adams' mastership. In his will he left Sidney property and land worth £60 per annum in Staffordshire and Worcestershire. Taylor made it a condition that the College spend the income on the establishment of a fellowship in mathematics. The fellowship would support a 'person learn'd in the Mathematicks, who shall from time to time be thought fit and elected and chosen', and who would 'with great Application and Industry pursue his Study in all kinds of Mathematical Learning, Arts and Sciences'. The weekly lectures would be open to all students at Cambridge so 'that Mathematical Learning may there be taught, improved, encouraged and practised'. Taylor also stipulated that 'if any money should hereafter be raised out of the estate from any coal or other mine upon it, the produce be applied, first, in making good any deficiency in the rent of the said estate by working the said mines, and then to the maintenance and education of one or more such students of the College as shall principally apply themselves to the study of the Mathematics'.

The realisation of Taylor's bequest was complicated by the Sidney statutes, which insisted that 'the sole End and Design of ye Foundation is to breed up students in the Profession of Divinity, that they may be fitly qualify'd to take upon them ye Care of Souls'. A successful application was made to Chancery for leave to make such a fundamental change to the statutes, and the lawyer who saw the whole process through, Richard Woolfe of Lincoln's Inn, sent his bill for £102 5s 4d to Sidney in August 1740. He was paid in February 1743.

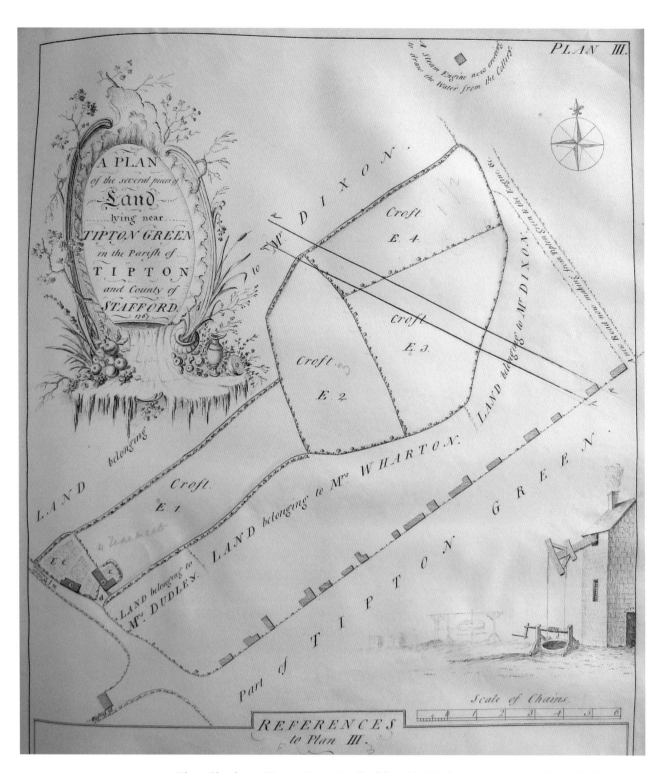

Plan of land near Tipton Green, Staffordshire (the Taylor estate), surveyed by John Snape, 1767

Sidney had seen Seth Ward and Gilbert Clerke pursue mathematics while under-graduates and fellows during the 17th century, but few other fellows were very interested in geometry and algebra. From the time of the publication of Isaac Newton's *Principia Mathematica* in 1687, however, mathematics began to grow in importance at an extraordinary rate in Cambridge. In 1748 the mathematics Tripos was founded, the only means for many decades thereafter by which an undergraduate might attain a BA with honours. Newton was virtually deified in Britain by the time he died in 1727, his tomb in Westminster Abbey referring to a 'mind almost divine'. Mathematics at Cambridge became part of a new theology in which the principles Newton had described were seen as the very image of God's creative intelligence. Newton's ideas became central to a new Whig vision of Britain as a providential world power. Taylor wanted Sidney to become part of this great historical movement, as Britain developed her naval prowess led by a superior mathematical understanding of the universe. An impoverished College, which at the time of the Young Pretender's Rebellion in 1745 could vote £100 towards George II for 'yᵉ service of his Majesty on occasion of the present unnatural rebellion', was an institution with the right patriotic credentials to receive such a bequest.

'Gelidus': John Colson, Lucasian Professor

> He has totally divested himself of all human sensations; he has neither eye for beauty, nor ear for complaint; he neither rejoices at the good fortune of his nearest friend, nor mourns for any publick or private calamity. Having once received a letter, and given it his servant to read, he was informed, that it was written by his brother, who, being ship-wrecked, had swam naked to land, and was destitute of necessaries in a foreign country. Naked and destitute! says Gelidus, reach down the last volume of meteorological observations, extract of an exact account of the wind, and note it carefully in the diary of the weather. —Samuel Johnson, 'Gelidus', *The Rambler*, 24, 1750

The first Sidney mathematical lecturer was John Colson, who was from Samuel Johnson's hometown of Lichfield, near Taylor's Dudley, where his father was vicar-choral at the cathedral. There seems to have been a close connection between Sidney and Colson through Lichfield, whose dean advised the College during the setting up of the new lectureship. Colson had gone to Christ Church, Oxford, in 1699, but left without taking a degree. A number of members of his family had been mathematicians associated with the Royal Society, some of whom had written on navigation, an area Colson was particularly involved with early in his career. His monograph on the resolution of cubic and quadratic equations was later appended to Newton's *Arithmetica Universalis* in 1732. In 1709 he was appointed master of the new mathematical school founded by Sir Joseph Williamson in Rochester, Kent, a post he held until 1740. This was intended to educate boys 'towards the Mathematicks and all Other Things which may fitt and encourage them for the Sea Service'. Colson became a fellow of the Royal Society in 1713 and vicar of Chalk, near Gravesend, in 1724, his theological interests evident in a co-translation of Dom Augustin Calmety's French etymological dictionary of the Bible.

Colson was made a fellow of Emmanuel College in 1728, but by 1737 was living in London where the young actor David Garrick boarded with him in order to receive instruction in 'the mathematics, philosophy and human learning'. Garrick came to Colson through Lichfield ecclesiastical connections, as did the young Samuel Johnson whom Colson tutored while Johnson was preparing to write his tragedy *Irene*. According to Mrs Thrale, Johnson based his cold philosophical character Gelidus (from the Latin for 'ice-cold') on Colson in *The Rambler* in 1750. Sidney had another member satirised at the time when the ecclesiastical lawyer Francis Topham (1729) was attacked in Laurence Sterne's *Tristram Shandy* (which began publication in 1759) as Didius, who had 'a particular turn for taking to pieces and new framing over again, all kinds of instruments to insert his legal whim-wham'.

Colson is best known for his translation from the Latin of Sir Isaac Newton's *The Method of Fluxions* (1736), to which he added a long commentary. Newton's theory of fluxions had been attacked by a number of major figures, including Leibnitz and Bishop Berkeley, and these criticisms caused outrage in a Cambridge for which Newton's infallibility was an item of faith. Any assault on Newton's supremacy was considered unpatriotic and furthermore a dangerous sign of failure to support the new latitudinarian Christian faith now widespread throughout the nation. Colson, however, was less fierce towards Newton's critics than some of his contemporaries.

John Colson, 1741, by John Wollaston. The Old Schools, Cambridge

When Colson was appointed Sidney's first Taylor Lecturer in 1739 he was also appointed Lucasian Professor of Mathematics, a post held previously by Isaac Barrow, Newton, Whiston and Nicholas Saunderson; later Lucasian Professors include Charles Babbage and Stephen Hawking. Colson's main contribution during his professorship was his work as a translator, making works in Latin, French and Italian available to English audiences. These included books on natural philosphy by Petrus van Musschenbroek and Abbé Nollet, and the Italian mathematician Donna Maria Agnesi's book on calculus, *Analytical Institutions* (1748), his draft title being 'The Plan of the Lady's System of Analyticks'. This was one of a number of 18th-century works by Sidney men aimed at the growing market for women's educational publications. Colson learned Italian late in life, and obviously not quite thoroughly enough. A mistranslation by him of Agnesi's 'versed sine' led to the curve known as 'the witch of Agnesi'. In Italian, the curve is called '*la versiera di Agnesi*', which means 'the curve of Agnesi'. Colson read this

of duty; so that it seemed as if alacrity of mind and sanguine thoughts were no contemptible preservatives from its fatal malignity.'

The steady decrease of his crew through scurvy outbreaks and the worn-out state of his remaining consorts forced Anson in the end to bring all survivors on board the *Centurion*. The ship rested at the island of Tinian and then arrived in Macau later in November 1742. It was at this point that Walter, who had become seriously ill, returned to England on an East India Company vessel. He was made MA at Sidney in 1744 and the following year was appointed chaplain of Portsmouth dockyard. He married in 1748 and in that year published the celebrated *A Voyage Round the World in the Years MDCCXL, I, 11, III, IV by George Anson Esq.* Six months after Walter left the *Centurion*, Anson captured the galleon *Nuestra Señora de Covadonga* off Cape Espíritu Santo, between Acapulco and Manila, a ship carrying over 1,300,000 pieces of eight. He sold the bullion to the Chinese at Macau and returned to England in 1744 a wealthy and famous man.

Richard Walter, c1750, by an unknown artist. Private collection

Thomas Carlyle later wrote that Walter's book, 'written in brief, perspicuous terms', was 'a real poem in its kind, or romance all fact, one of the pleasantest little books in the world's library at this time'. Walter's full authorship has been questioned and while he conceived the book, raised subscriptions and published it under his name, there was considerable editorial input from the mathematician George Robins as well as from Anson himself. Walter's wife Jane vigorously defended his authorship when it was later questioned after his death in 1785. However, whatever the intricacies of these issues, Walter was closely involved in both the voyage and the *Voyage*, an internationally popular classic of maritime literature.

CHAPTER 6

'Decency and Respect' 1746–1813

Mem. Ap:22, 1747. At a meeting of the Society in the College Parlor, viz: The Master, Mr. Allin, Mr. Barnes, Mr. Walter, Mr. Wood, Mr. Bell, the Master made complaint against Mr. Wood for writing & sending to him on or about the 14th Feb: last a false, scandalous, & abusive letter, directed To the Master of Sidney College; which Letter was produced & read before Mr. Wood, who did not deny his writing and sending the same.—Acta Collegii

WITH THE ELECTION in 1746 of Francis Sawyer Parris BD as master of Sidney, there began a remarkable renaissance in the College after a century of turmoil, financial insecurity and stagnation in many areas. Parris had come to Sidney from Huntingdonshire as a pensioner in 1721, and was elected a fellow in 1728. He was a scrupulous scholar, in the mould perhaps of Thomas Rymer, a very good administrator and financial organiser, and was clearly dedicated to the rejuvenation of the College he had been at for a quarter of a century. In 1744 he had already been given the responsibility to 'purchase out of hand £100 stock in yᵉ 3 per cent annuities for yᵉ use of yᵉ Treasury'. He was among those fellows who had objected to the then-master John Adams' use of College money in 1734 to make extensive and expensive repairs to the Lodge without consent, and who had passed an order that year that 'for the future the College shall not be liable above fifteen shillings each half year for work done within the Lodge without the consent of the Society'. The gossipy antiquarian William Cole's view that Parris 'had well-nigh ruined the College' is way off the mark.

Parris was Vice-Chancellor of the university in 1747–8 and in 1750 was appointed *Protobibliothecarius*, or principal librarian. He made a thorough survey of the College endowments, improved and extended the Sidney library, and elevated

The Resurrected Christ with attendant angels above King David, the Ark of the Covenant, Moses and Aaron and the Tables of the Law by Francis Hayman, engraved by Charles Grignion, frontispiece, Holy Bible, 1762, Bodleian Library, Oxford

Parris's 1762 edition of the Bible was printed for the University Press by Joseph Bentham. Only six copies of the folio edition survived a warehouse fire and now fetch in excess of £60,000

Sidney's profile within Cambridge, not only through important appointments but also by undertaking two major scholarly projects. The first was his work on the university's history in the 1730s, which George Dyer later hailed as the principal source of his own rather chaotic and opinionated effort of 1814. Dyer acknowledged the importance to him of 'two MS. Volumes, in quarto, entitled *An Index to Hare's Collections of the Charters and Privileges of the University, from the earliest time, together with a Collection of Statutes, Graces, Decrees of Heads, Interpretations of Statutes, and King's Letters, from the year 1570, when Elizabeth's Statutes were first given, to the middle of the last Century, made from the Vice-Chancellors' and Proctors' Books...*signed and written by F.S. Parris, 1735'.

Another, more significant, project was Parris's preparation of the Cambridge Standard Edition of the Bible, published in 1762. Parliament had passed a bill in 1653 to establish a new committee to revise the great 1611 Bible to which Sidney's Samuel Ward and James Montagu had contributed. Though this committee was appointed in 1657, the Restoration of 1660 had curtailed any further action. As translators and publishers of the text the two universities in a sense 'owned' the Bible, and it fell to them to standardise the text. This happened first at Cambridge, where Parris prepared a careful edition that regularised spelling and punctuation, corrected errors and emended the text to take into account translation mistakes. Oxford responded with a Standard Edition of 1769, which is essentially the text with which we are familiar.

Parris was a generous donor to Sidney's library and his books, which are still in the Muniment Room, make interesting reading for the light they cast on the intellectual range of a Cambridge don in the first half of the 18th century. They include a number of books on anatomy and medicine, among them William Oliver's *Practical Dissertation on Bath-waters*; various classical dictionaries and recent editions of classical texts such as Aristotle, Suetonius, Cicero and Lucan; Isaac Watts' *Logick*, Halifax's *Miscellanies*, Newton's *Optics* and Whiston's *Physico-theology*; and, with special Sidney relevance, John Gay's *Poems*, the work of the well-known cousin of the College's John Gay.

Parris enforced discipline on both undergraduates and fellows. In 1749, Shaw King, an Essex man, and William Dryman, son of an attorney and a Blundell's pupil, were admonished for causing 'great disturbances in the College', having been required previously to keep their chambers. Instead, they had 'appeared abroad, taken their names off the Buttery board, put off their gowns, and shown themselves so about the town...to the scandal of the College'. King is found at Oxford later that year, having migrated there soon after having been 'publickly sent away by the Master with the approbation of the Fellows'. There are no other references to disciplinary measures being taken during Parris's mastership, which may suggest he was respected by the students, though of course there were precious few of them at this time.

'Recantation & Submission'

Whether Parris had a sense of humour, as well as considerable scholarly and administrative skills, is open to question, though the College account of Parris's action against a fellow in 1747 clearly has an ironic overtone. That year he came down hard on a junior fellow, John Wood, for sending him a Valentine letter on 14 February, also of course the date of Sidney's foundation. Wood, a Blundell's boy who had come to Sidney in 1734, had been made a fellow in 1742, and at the time of his disgrace was one of only five fellows, including the aged Richard Allin and Sidney's former naval chaplain, Richard Walter. Wood was asked to make a public apology, 'promising for the future to carry myself towards the Master and others with more decency and respect; and I do consent that this my recantation & submission be publickly read in Chapple after evening service in my name & in my presence'. The College minutes show that, most magnanimously, 'the Master has consented at the particular request of Mr. Wood not to publish the above recantation in Chapple'.

'A Grand Apartment': The New Hall

> Sidneyans hardest dogs alive
> So very poorly do they thrive
> I have heard, their anxious cook Tom Sutton
> Say it cost him more in spits than mutton.
> —William Lee of Clare, 'Upon the Members of Sidney College',
> c1745 (A spit is a rod on which meat is roasted)

Undoubtedly Parris's greatest material contribution to the College was his re-modelling of the College Hall, turning a cavernous Elizabethan space into the elegant Rococo room still dined in today. This was a move intended both to repair a decaying part of the building, and to turn it into the kind of fashionable space other Colleges were creating at this time. It would attract students and, as we shall see, new fellows from beyond Sidney. The project was expensive and Sidney was still a poor college. Parris was successful in attracting some new money during his tenure: a £1,000 legacy in 1755 from the Londoner Sir John Frederick, who had gone to Sidney in 1695 as a fellow-commoner; and £800 for two exhibitions in 1753–54 from a former Wykehamist and scholar, William Barcroft, who matriculated in 1708 and was now the vicar of Kelvedon, Essex. Barcroft also gave Sidney £50 in 1753 'for glazing and beautifying the College Chappell'.

However, in order to undertake the work on the Hall, as well as on a badly deteriorating main drain, Parris was forced to suspend

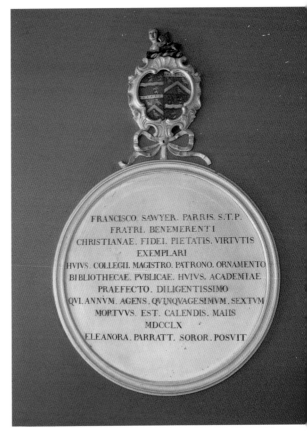

The monument to Francis Sawyer Parris in the antechapel, originally placed in the old Chapel by his sister, Eleanor Parratt, in 1760

The rococo ceiling of the bay window in the northeast corner of the Hall

four fellowships in the period 1746–49 'for the necessary reparation and decent refitting of the College Hall', and for a few years afterwards it seems that there may have only been three or four fellows in residence. In 1748 the minutes record that the fellowship consented to the suspensions, 'as there are none of our College of six years standing & fit to fill the said vacancys'. Parris took further financial steps to raise money by increasing chamber rents and undergraduate fees, and borrowing £400 from Corpus Christi and a Mr Mickelborough, 'interest and principal to be repaid again out of money arising from the Fellowships kept vacant'.

The Hall, with its new parlour and screens passage, was designed by the Caius fellow and amateur Palladian architect James Burrough, who built for a number of Cambridge colleges, including the chapel at Clare, the hall at Queens', and a new range at Peterhouse. Burrough's fee, paid in 1752, the year the work was completed, was £40. The result of his design and the fees of £1,129 for builders and craftsmen was an Italianate room measuring 30 by 59 feet, with a flat ceiling hiding the old six-bayed Elizabethan roof. This was achieved by removing the hammer-beams and pendant posts, and bolting a pair of beams one on each side of the hammer-beam ends. The new plaster cornice and decorated ceiling were then attached to this structure. The old roof can still be viewed from a small door at the top of the Master's Lodge and is a haunting reminder of the days of Cromwell. Another reminder of the old Hall is the bay window at the north-east corner, where James Montagu set the foundation stone, and the large rectangular window at the north end facing on to Cloister Court. Panelling removed from the old Hall and now in the Master's Lodge and in Hall Court are a final echo of those days.

The ceiling has main beams decorated with a cable pattern that divide the surface into nine sections with elaborate and painted flower designs. The main flower in the

The elaborate achievement above the doorway in the gallery of the Hall, probably carved by 'Mr Robinson', 1752. It shows Lady Frances' arms supported by the black bull of the Radcliffes and the porcupine of the Sidneys

The central panel of the Hall ceiling

centre is a hollow boss, which acted as a ventilation system and took the smoke from a central stove in the hall up through the roof. A music gallery, supported by two Roman doric columns, with a doorway now opening onto a grafittied wall, was used for both performance and as additional dining space. Above the doorway is a splendid coat of arms with the Sidney and Ratcliffe beasts, a bull and porcupine, adding a powerful flourish to the whole effect. This is probably the work of 'Mr. Robinson the Carver', who is mentioned in the accounts. The new Hall, complete with simple sage-green painted wood panelling, the painting done by one 'Ivers', and seating fixed along the main walls, was remarked upon by Edmund Carter in a 1753 history of Cambridge as 'a very spacious room…a grand apartment'.

Parris effected one other important change to Sidney's appearance, again requiring a fellowship to be suspended. This new feature welcomed a new generation of fellows and students who reinvigorated Sidney in the second half of the 18th century. The main gateway in the wall dividing Hall Court from the street, which we know only from Loggan's print, was replaced by a new classical entrance arch designed, again, by James Burrough. Though commissioned in 1749 it was only finished and paid for in 1762, after Parris's death. An observant visitor of the gate, now to be found at the north-east end of the Gardens fronting on to Jesus Lane, can make out an inscription on the upper face of the cornice: 'This job finished 1762'. As an old print shows, and the accounts attest, Parris also had poplars planted along the street front to form a green screen between Sidney and the outside world.

ABOVE: 'Sidney College', 1820, engraving
published by W Mason

LEFT: The Old Parlour today

The Lodge and the north side of Hall Court just before the Wyatville remodelling, 1822, watercolour by John Ireland

'Beyond this Sublunary World': Parris's Fellows and Students

> By Astronomy he was led in thought, far beyond this sublunary world of ours, and all its
> petty squabbles; and to suppose that those vast bodies he discerns above, must be peopled
> with their several gradations of inhabitants; and those inhabitants must be objects of the
> Divine favour, as much as Man.
> —Francis Wollaston, *The Secret History of a Private Man*, 1793

Parris made one further important contribution to Sidney's development, perhaps
the most important of all; he brought in a brilliant generation of students and, once
the finances had recovered sufficiently, elected some home-grown as well as imported
fellows.

Sidney was still a seminary for training Church of England priests, but a new
emphasis on scholarship, in new fields for Sidney, is indicated by the kinds of men
he brought to the College. There was a growing taste for classical, literary, musical,
artistic and scientific interests, which produced a distinctive kind of gentlemanly
scholar of the age. Ardent churchmanship seems to have been less attractive than
it had been for previous generations. John Cranwell (1743), a priest and translator
of Latin poems by Isaac Hawkins Browne and Marcus Hieronymus Vida, is a typical
figure. In 1748, Samuel Taylor Coleridge's adored father John, a vicar, teacher and
distinguished classical and Hebrew scholar, came to Sidney as a mature student from
Devon. Absent-minded, bookish, 'an Israelite without guile', as his famous son later
described him, John Coleridge symbolises in many ways a new breed of cultured,
gentle, priestly Englishman.

A similar character is Coleridge's exact contemporary and friend Philip Parsons,
who became a priest in Wye, Kent, and a teacher, later pioneering Sunday schools
in that county. Parsons was educated at Lavenham Grammar School, Suffolk, by
Thomas Smythies, a Sidney man, and went on to write books on the heat and light
of planets, such as *Astronomic Doubts* (1774), and on the monuments and stained
glass in east Kent and Suffolk. He was also a poet and humorist.

Sidney's tiny cadre of undergraduates performed exceptionally well in the Tripos
examinations under Parris. From 1748 these were dominated by the rigorous test-
ing of mathematical ability. Among distinguished performances were those of John
Cranwell, second Wrangler in 1748; William Byrch, fourth Wrangler in 1751; Robert
Ravald and William Nesfield, third Wranglers in, respectively, 1752 and 1754; and
George Wollaston, second Wrangler in 1758.

Wollaston, a close friend of the poet Thomas Gray, was grandson of William
Wollaston, the author of *The Religion of Nature Delineated*, who fostered an extraordinary family tradition of Sidney admissions. George, the son of Francis Wollaston
who had gone up to Sidney in 1712, also had three uncles and three brothers at
the College. All these men in turn sent sons to Sidney. His brother Charlton was
an eminent doctor, fellow of the Royal Society, and Harveian Orator at the Royal
College of Physicians, who died aged 40. George, himself an FRS, succeeded John
Lawson as Taylor Lecturer in 1760. He worked with John Jebb and Robert Thorpe

The Wollaston Dynasty

The Wollaston Family, by William Hogarth, 1730. New Walk Museum, Leicester (loan)

William Wollaston arrived at Sidney in 1674 and over the course of 150 years 13 Wollastons went to the College; many were distinguished scholars and scientists. This conversation piece by Hogarth shows a later William Wollaston in a fine Palladian room at his town house in St James's Square, surrounded by 15 members of the family and friends. William's third son Francis, who went to Sidney in 1712, and was elected a Fellow of the Royal Society in 1723, is the man standing and pointing behind his wife, the woman sitting on the right of the card table on the left. William's eldest son, Charlton, had died in 1729 and may be represented by the bust on the mantelpiece. William's second son, William, strangely is not in the picture. According to a pedigree printed by John Nichols in his four-volume history of Leicestershire (1795–1812), William Wollaston the elder married Elizabeth Fauquier, daughter of a 'Dr Fauquier of Sidney Coll'. There is no record of a Fauquier at the College then.

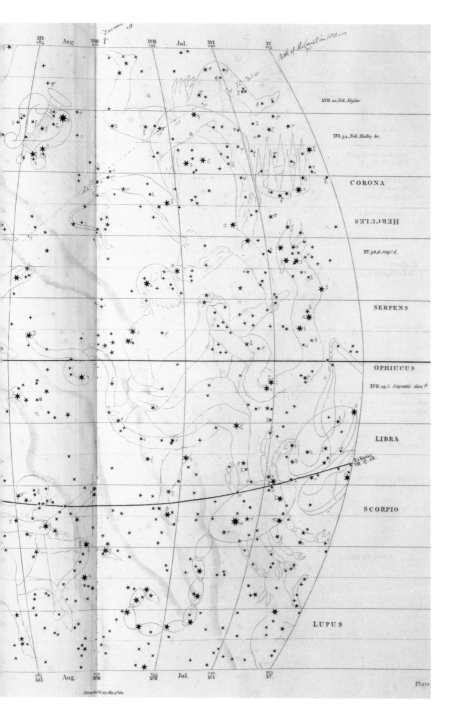

Plate from Francis Wollaston, A Portraiture of the Heavens, 1811. Museum of the History of Science, University of Oxford

of Peterhouse on an edition of Newton's *Excerpta Quaedam e Newtone Principiis* (1765), published the year of his marriage and therefore of departure from his Sidney fellowship. It became a standard work. George Wollaston later became a vicar and died in Richmond, Surrey, at the age of 87.

George's other eminent brother was the older Francis, who had gone up to Sidney in 1748. After training in law, which bothered his conscience, he became a priest in 1755, working in London, Essex, Norfolk and finally Chislehurst in Kent. He was earmarked for high preferment in the church but, expressing the views of many men of his century, 'never was ambitious of the parade attending an exalted station'. Francis, not untypically for a Sidney man of these times, was unorthodox in his religious views and could not subscribe to the Athanasian creed, which he never read to his congregations. He supported the 1772 bill in parliament designed to replace the obligation of university students to subscribe to the Thirty-Nine Articles with a declaration of faith. He wrote books and pamphlets against subscription that he sent to all bishops and MPs, though his efforts were unsuccessful; the bill was defeated by a heavy margin. Wollaston's reward for his defence of nonconformity was to be accused of Socinianism and to be ignored. *The Secret History of a Private Man* of 1793 is an account of Wollaston's intellectual and theological position.

Francis turned his interests to astronomy, to 'allow his thoughts to range without fear of giving offence' and 'without interference from those brethren of the cloth, who never have thought enough, to know what it is to doubt, or to have any feeling for those who do'. A Fellow of the Royal Society, like many Wollastons, he built a private observatory at Chislehurst equipped with a fine Peter Dolland triplet telescope, and described the spots and rings of Saturn in 1772. Wollaston also devised new scientific instruments. His *Astronomical Catalogue* of 1789 was used by William

Herschel, the great astronomer with whom he corresponded, while *Fasciculus Astronomicus* (1800) and *A Portraiture of the Heavens as they Appear to the Naked Eye* (1811) were major contributions to British astronomy.

'A good deal of residence': Parris's New Fellows

I can now venture to ask whether you would accept of a Fellowship of *Sidney*. The Fellowships require a good deal of residence, which possibly may not be disagreeable to you, who, if I am not mistaken, do not dislike an University life. Some knowledge of Hebrew is necessary; the rest of the examination is usually in Philosophy, Aristotle's Rhetoric, some part of the first six books in Homer, and Virgil's Georgics…

—Henry Hubbard, tutor at Emmanuel College, to his student Thomas Martyn, January 1758

Shortly before his death in May 1760 at the age of 56, Francis Sawyer Parris, who had seen his fellowship dwindle to a small rump during the 1750s, had sufficiently revived the College finances to be able to make six new appointments that changed the face

Gayton church, Northamptonshire, acquired as a Sidney living in 1765

of Sidney for the next half century. Given the small number of undergraduates, and thus a limited talent pool to draw on, it is not surprising that he went outside the College to recruit. While George Wollaston and Samuel Harness were Sidney men, the others were all 'migrants'. The elections, on 27 April 1758, of William Elliston from St John's, John Hey from St Catharine's, Owen Hughes from Jesus and Thomas Martyn from Emmanuel, were inspired moves. Soon afterwards Elliston was made steward and keeper of the chest and, in 1760, tutor; Hey was appointed praelector and Greek lecturer and, also in 1760, tutor; Hughes was made dean and ecclesiastical lecturer, and Harness and Wollaston were sublectores. These men took Sidney into a new era, one that seems a long way from that suggested by the last minute recorded under Parris:

'March. 24, 1757. Mem. At a meeting of the Society it was agreed unanimously to allow the Cook out of the Treasury or Coll: Stock one shilling each week towards the wages of a Skull in the Kitching'.

In 1760 Parris left books and £600 to Sidney in his will, £400 of the money going towards an advowson that, together with Sir Frederick Lewis's bequest, allowed Sidney to acquire the living at Gayton, Northamptonshire, in 1765. Parris had turned the College round. His successor, William Elliston, about whom we know comparatively little, was master for 47 years and did not let his predecessor down. The son of a poor Suffolk farmer, Elliston was only 26 when he took over, in the year of George III's accession; his youth, energy and intelligence were exactly what was needed. Sidney became a byword for civilised and convivial society, fuelled by tea-drinking and music, staffed by learned men in a wide range of subjects, by university professors, and by hardworking and talented undergraduates. With its new Hall and, a little later, new Chapel and newly landscaped gardens, it attracted musicians and writers; as we shall see, even Dr Johnson visited.

'Fifty different things in a minute': Thomas Twining

Friend of my heart! Whose pen, like magic wand
Has ev'ry mental treasure at command:
Wit, humour, learning, sense, all wait its motion,
And dance, like Merlin's Sprites, at its devotion.
What envy w^d thy partial love excite
Thy *Cheese* bestowing on a single *Mite*!
A gift, wch freely did thou but concede,
W^d foster worlds, & hungry myriads feed.
Did all mankind, like me, thy powers know,
And what delight thy talents can bestow
What wonder w^d thy partial love create
Among the learned, witty, wise, and great!
Thy genius gleams a pure & lambent flame
Free from the gross concupiscence of fame:
Though sedulous the public eye to shun,

Peeping through narrow apertures, its Sun
Prismatic tints emits with niggard hand
Would lighten worlds, if suffer'd to expand.
Blest with thy friendship, let its vivid rays
On me and mine continue still to blaze;
For where they penetrate, no sullen gloom
Can long subsist, were Erebus the room.
—Charles Burney, 'To the Revd Thos Twining', 1776

One of Parris's outstanding undergraduates was the Londoner Thomas Twining. His father was head of the great Twining tea company and Thomas was intended for the business. However, his lack of aptitude for that and his evident great talent for classical scholarship meant he was sent to Colchester Grammar School where he was taught by Palmer Smythies, a Sidney man, before entering Sidney as a pensioner in 1755 at the age of 20. He became a scholar the following year. He was made a fellow by Elliston in 1760 and, cushioned from economic worries by an inheritance in 1761, spent the rest of his life as a priest and classical and musical scholar. Married in 1764 to his boyhood sweetheart, Elizabeth, the daughter of Palmer Smythies, Twining became a country vicar at Fordham in Essex, and then rector at St Mary's-at-the-Wall, Colchester, where he died childless in 1804.

BELOW LEFT: *Thomas Twining (1734–1804), mezzotint by C Turner, 1805, after a portrait by J J Halls, 1799*

BELOW RIGHT: *Pair of candlesticks, Sheffield, 1788, given by Thomas Twining*

A gifted linguist, Twining was one of the most admired classicists of his generation; his translation with notes of Aristotle's *Treatise on Poetry* (1789) is still in print today. His friend, the Greek scholar Samuel Parr, who called Twining 'one of the best men that ever lived', considered the Aristotle 'unsurpassed by any translation in the English language'. The work included two dissertations on poetical and musical imitation, which were considered by contemporaries to have taken Aristotelian studies in aesthetics to a new level.

Twining was also one of the great English correspondents of the 18th century, his 'wit, sagacity, learning', as Samuel Parr wrote, evident on every page of more than 500 surviving letters. His letters were to scholars, priests and old Sidney friends such as John Hey, Charles Jenner and John Lettice, as well as to family members like his half-brother Richard and nephew Daniel. The topics covered range from Greek music and Chatterton's poems, to the French Revolution, fears of invasion and London society gossip. They also include drawings, poems and musical scores. Like Joseph Eyre (1733), the writer of sonatas, Twining's interest in music signals a change in Sidney's culture in the mid-18th century. Above all, it is in Twining's letters to Charles Burney, the great musicologist, that he displays his talent, humour and unique style. Burney's celebrated *A General History of Music* (1776–89) was deeply indebted to Twining's revisions and original contributions on ancient music, in which he had a special expertise. Some flavour of his energetic and engaging epistolary style is found in an excitable chatty letter to Burney of 1776, the year the first volume of the *General History* was published:

'There is something so solemn and frightful in this long silence that I can endure it no longer; I should not have patience so long if I had not been afraid of our letters meeting and jostling one another upon the road, for do you know that I have had the assurance to expect to hear from you every day for this fortnight past? But I can give no other reason than that I wished it: for I acknowledge with all humility that my last *barbouillage* was a sneaking return for your amusing *étrennes* – *marque au coin de l'aimable folie*. Pooh! As if you stood upon that ceremony! Pray excuse me – but I remember slumping all of a sudden into the slough of despond, and closing my letters in the dumps. I meet with these accidents now and then, but, thank God, I soon work myself out again. Chiaroscuro, pianoforte, light and shade, contrast, hill and dale, winter and summer – 'tis all very well and very pretty. And so let us talk of fifty different things in a minute. I long to know how you do, and what? Mr. Wegg and I begin now to look for your book. Ha! Well! Whereabouts have you whipt in all your straggling dogs of scripts? When do you present? – I'm out of breath…'

'Hideous Propensity': John Lettice and William Beckford

Mr. Hunter (who by the by is a very superior critic) and I have read together Aldrovandus and Og of Basan with great Delight…I shall to-day show them to several others of my Friends. The Master was unfortunately gone out of College before they came and will not return soon enough to read them, which mortifies me much; as I am sure he would have done it with particular pleasure. —John Lettice to William Beckford on his manuscript of *Memoirs of Extraordinary Painters*, in a letter of 1779

No less interesting than the tea-dealer's son was Twining's undergraduate friend and contemporary, the Reverend John Lettice, son of a Northampton rector, who was educated at Oakham and went to Sidney as a sizar in 1756. Lettice became a fellow in 1763, was later a tutor, and in 1764 won the prestigious Seatonian Prize with his poem 'The Conversion of St Paul'. The prize had been established by Thomas Seaton, a fellow of Clare, and from 1750 was awarded to the best poem submitted on a sacred subject. In the first three years it was won by the great poet Christopher Smart of Pembroke, and in 1763 by John Hey of Sidney. Lettice, Hey and, in 1767 and 1768, the novelist and fellow Charles Jenner, ensured Sidney was prominent among prize-winners in the 1760s. It was an appropriate sign of the new age at the College, bringing together religious faith and literary ambition.

Lettice, a keen poet since his first published undergraduate volume of six Cambridge-based love elegies in 1760, had a remarkable range of scholarly interests, from modern, classical and Nordic languages, to the nature of clerical rhetoric, to Wedgwood porcelain and classical archaeology.

In 1767, Lettice made a trip to Denmark where he acted as a tutor to the daughter of Sir Robert Gunning, the English envoy at Copenhagen. He travelled widely and began a translation of Ludwig Holberg's *Parallel Lives of Famous Ladies*. Lettice corresponded with Thomas Percy, the editor of the *Reliques of English Poetry* (1765), about Nordic and Icelandic literature. He also experienced the violent palace revolution in Denmark in 1772 during the reign of King Christian VII, and as a result returned to England. (This connection with the Danish Court presumably explains King Christian's visit to Sidney in 1768.) We find Lettice in 1772 at Charles Burney's London house, where he made a poor impression on his daughter Fanny, who found him 'really modest and gave his opinion with diffidence'.

It was at this point that Lettice came into contact with an extraordinary 10-year-old, William Beckford, who changed his new tutor's life dramatically and may rightly be considered an honorary Sidney student. Beckford's father, a sugar planter in Jamaica, had been Lord Mayor of London but died suddenly, leaving his son and heir a fantastically wealthy and indulged boy. Lettice lived with the precocious, mercurial and eccentric Beckford at Wimpole Street in London and at the family house at Fonthill in Wiltshire, receiving the generous sum of £350 as a stipend. The teaching day began at 7 a.m. with a ride in the park, followed by lessons in Greek and Latin, Bible studies, French, English, geography and arithmetic. Lunch and more riding

'Purple Radiance'

John Lettice, by an unknown artist. PCC of the parish of Beckley and Peasmarsh, Sussex

Behold! Th'illustrious convert now invades
The reign of Gentile darkness. See! Appall'd
Black superstition, with her baleful throng
Of self-bred fears, and unembodied forms
That haunt despair; the foul unholy train
Of molten idols and fantastic gods
Shrink at his presence, like the fleeting shade
Of sullen night, when first Hyperion's orb
Scatters its purple radiance o'er the skies.

—John Lettice, from 'The Conversion of St Paul', 1764

followed between 1 p.m. and 3.30 p.m., and then the pair returned to study until about 5.30 p.m. Lettice was free until supper at 9 p.m. when he joined adult members of the family and their guests for music and conversation. Lettice was in regular contact with Beckford's godfather, William Pitt, Earl of Chatham, and with Beckford's strict mother. He wrote elegant, evasive and soothing letters to both.

Rather than go to Oxford or Cambridge, Beckford's mother decided the best thing for William was to study law in Geneva, where he travelled with Lettice in 1777. Lettice greatly enjoyed the cosmopolitan city and the visits of Sidney friends such as Thomas Martyn, by then professor of botany at Cambridge, who stayed with his family in Geneva for several months. While Lettice became fascinated with the theological debates in the fashionable circles of Protestant Geneva, the 14-year-old William began to develop his passion for the romantically exotic in moonlit wanderings and spiritual communication. Among many tours in Switzerland and France, they visited Voltaire at his château at Ferney, their conversation perhaps turning to Sidney's Thomas Woolston, whom the great *philosophe* had admired half a century earlier. Lettice encouraged William's eccentric tastes and literary ambitions, and was an important influence on Beckford's seminal Gothic novel of decadence and cruelty, *Vathek* (1786).

Hall Court, 1822, aquatint published by W Mason

In 1778, Lettice and Beckford returned to England, and in 1779 set off on a tour of the country. They were arrested at Plymouth on suspicion of spying when Lettice took out a notebook to jot down ideas; visited various west-country sites such as Glastonbury; saw Boulton and Watt's new industrial works in Birmingham; and rode through the Peak District and Lakes. A sign of future problems was Lettice's difficulty in diverting Beckford's attentions away from his notorious 'sudden love', the 11-year-old William Courtenay, at Powderham Castle. Lettice later referred to Beckford's bisexuality as a 'hideous propensity'. It was not all adolescent passion, however, and Beckford showed his talent in his *Memoirs of Extraordinary Painters,* which Lettice saw through the press, having read passages to admiring Sidney fellows such as Christopher Hunter and John Hey in the College parlour.

This trip, however, was merely a prelude to the more ambitious, exhausting and exhilarating grand tour of the continent, undertaken from the spring of 1780. They left England via Margate at the time of the Gordon Riots and travelled through the Low Countries and Germany, across the Alps to Italy. In the company of the artist J R Cozens, Beckford and his 'bear-leader' Lettice visited all the major cities. They ended up at Sir William Hamilton's residence in Naples, where Lettice and his host were able to discuss Lettice and Martyn's recent major publication on the antiquities at Herculaneum, the site of the envoy's great passion. They returned to England in spring 1781.

Plate by Frederick P Nodder from Thomas Martyn, Flora Rustica *(London 1792–94)*

Beckford, for all his genius and capacity to follow set authors such as Locke and Hume, was not a serious scholar, and was bored by much of what he saw. He was desperate to get to Italy where his exotic longings for Mediterranean, often bi-sexual, romance might be satisfied. Beckford was inspired by contemporary literature such as Goethe's *Sorrows of Young Werther,* probably not a work Lettice would have recommended. As his correspondence shows, Lettice was a little out of his depth pastorally the further south the pair travelled, and was clearly hard pressed to contain his pupil's desires. His light-touch approach to discipline was in England's cultural favour, however. Perhaps this approach was appropriate for a man who had written a satirical pamphlet titled *A Council in the Moon* (1765), advocating that fellows be allowed to marry. Furthermore, the two men were close friends and later in life Beckford employed his ageing tutor to teach his own children. Lettice was presented to the Sidney living at Peasmarsh, Sussex, in 1785, where he lived until 1832, continuing his researches and writing and acting as a much-loved and caring parish priest.

'The Amusement of my Leisure Hours': Thomas Martyn

> Our Garden begins to flourish, shrubs and trees are already planted; plenty of seeds, both
> tender and hardy are sown; a stove is building; and Stone is preparing to raise the super-
> structure of the greenhouse on the foundation which was laid last year. All this, I hope,
> will increase the number of botanists among us. Indeed, we already begin to grow consid-
> erable, for I never had more than one companion before this spring, but now I have three;
> and expect soon to have three or more converts. —Thomas Martyn to Richard Pulteney
> on creating the first botanic garden in Cambridge, 1761

John Lettice's collaborator on a translation from the Italian of *The Antiquities of
Herculaneum* was Thomas Martyn, a pioneering botanist and connoisseur, and the son
of the Cambridge professor of botany, John Martyn. He had excelled at classics at his
father's college, Emmanuel, as an undergraduate, but not at mathematics, a shortcom-
ing he shared with Lettice and Twining. Martyn was a convert to the botanic taxon-
omy of the Swedish scientist Linnaeus by the time he arrived at Sidney in 1758 and
followed his father in being elected professor of botany in 1762, at the age of 26. His
Plantae Cantabrigienses, a systematically arranged catalogue of over 800 examples of
local flora with an appendix of many more further-flung species, was published the same
year; he followed this with a number of important botanic studies. In 1762, Martyn was
also appointed reader in botany under the terms of the Trinity vice-master Dr Richard
Walker's bequest of the five-acre Austin Friary site as Cambridge's first botanic garden.
His early lectures attracted many students, and for a number of years Martyn acted
as the garden's curator. In 1764 he published his lectures, which encouraged botanic

A Difficult Delivery

Martyn's project with Lettice to translate *The Antiquities of Herculaneum* ran into difficulties early on. Having acquired the multi-volume book for £50 and worked for five years on the translation, they were able to publish only the splendid 50-plate first volume in 1772 before the Neapolitan court objected and the publication ceased. That year, Martyn married Martha, sister of the Sidney master William Elliston. He left Sidney and became a priest, first in Cambridgeshire and Buckinghamshire, and then at Charlotte Chapel, Pimlico, London, which he had purchased. In 1798 he moved to Pertenhall Rectory in Bedfordshire where he died aged 89 in 1825, his professorship having been given Regius status in 1793.

Faun and bacchante, engraving by Peter Spenslowe Lamborn from The Antiquities of Herculaneum, *1772, by Thomas Martyn and John Lettice*

Etch'd by P.S. Lamborn from an original Drawing.

Dᴿ. SAMUEL JOHNSON.

Samuel Johnson, engraving by Peter Spenslowe Lamborn after a drawing by 'Mrs Martin', 1772

study of the new exotic flora that was returning to Britain from overseas and its importance to Britain's growth as a nation and centre of an empire.

Martyn wrote popular books for a female readership. His *Letters on the elements of Botany, Addressed to a Lady by…J.J. Rousseau. Translated into English* (1785) contained many more letters by Martyn than by the famous Swiss philosopher and ran to eight editions. It tactfully explained the 'sexual system of Linnaeus', and was followed in 1788 with a complementary volume of illustrations. Martyn was a dedicated lecturer in the fledgling discipline of botany at Cambridge for many years, but later found the subject losing popularity and turned his attention to other scholarly pursuits.

In Martyn, Sidney got more than a botanist, however, and in 1804 he wrote that 'Botany was rather the amusement of my leisure hours, than my serious pursuit'. He was also a keen systematiser of paintings and their locations, having travelled extensively in Britain and on the continent. In 1766 he published *The English Connoisseur*, a two-volume guide to Britain's greatest collections of art. It is interesting to note that Martyn's dislike of Dutch and Flemish painting and his preference for Italian art is the basis of Beckford's *Memoirs*, which Lettice read out to Sidney fellows in 1779.

There was much good-natured teasing too, with Thomas Twining giving Martyn 'many hours of rational pleasure and innocent cheerfulness' by 'lounging in my College rooms and read[ing] Linnaeus's works and question[ing] me much about them'. Twining wrote a playful piece on the apple-roaster in the new parlour in the style of Linnaeus:

MELOPTEUM *stanneum, monopum, versatile; seu Applé-ro-aster. Corpore versatili, circumtactili; fossulis stanneis, melo-decis, parallelis, intus distinctо: Cacumine fastigiato, suggrundiato; Latere uno pendulo, circumjectili, ambidextro, tinnitu crebro gaudenti; alteris fixis, bullatis. Habitat in Conclavi Combinatorio seu Combinatorio Collegii Sidney-Sussex in Academia Cantabrigiensi.*

The tin, one-footed, revolving apple roaster, or applé-ro-aster. It has a revolving body that can be touched on all sides and parallel tin grooves appropriate for apples. It has an inward distinction: it possesses a tapering, projecting peak; one side projects out and can be turned around in either direction with a constant, joyful ringing; the other sides are studded and fixed. It lives in the Combination Room of Sidney Sussex College in the University of Cambridge.

'Convivial Hilarity': Dr Johnson Comes to Sidney

Our distinguished visitor shone gloriously in his style of dissertation on a great variety of subjects. I recollect his condescending to as earnest a care of the animal as of the intellectual man, and after doing all the justice to my College bill of fare, and without neglecting the glass after dinner, he drank sixteen dishes of tea. I was idly curious enough to count them, from what I had heard remarked, and heard Levett (Johnson's physician) mention of his extraordinary devotion to the tea-pot. —John Lettice on Dr Johnson's visit to Sidney, 1765

In the middle of February, 1765, Samuel Johnson visited Sidney at the invitation of John Lettice. Johnson, an Oxford student, was driven to Cambridge by a young aristocratic friend, Topham Beauclerk, arriving at the Rose Inn on a Saturday evening. The following day he was entertained at a special party in Lettice's rooms, in the company of a small group of guests that included Baptist Noel Turner, Beauclerk, and the Regius Professor of Greek, Michael Lort. It seems fairly certain other Sidney fellows were present, including Thomas Martyn and John Hey. A drawing of Johnson by a 'Mrs Martin' was published in 1772 as an engraving by the Cambridge print maker P S Lamborn, who was the engraver the same year of a number of the plates in Martyn's and Lettice's *The Antiquities of Herculaneum*. It seems likely that 'Mrs Martin' was Thomas Martyn's sister Elizabeth, who was 27 in 1765. Lamborn made many prints of Cambridge buildings and highlights, including one of 'Oliver Cromwell's Head, from an Original in the Possession of Sidney College, Cambridge'. Later in his life, Lettice gave a brief account of the already legendary man's presence, noting in particular his tea-drinking habits. Johnson had come to the right College of course, given Thomas Twining's close connections.

The party went on in 'convivial hilarity' past sunrise, with Johnson, according to Turner, constantly in 'high glee', and the others seeking to 'elicit the sparks of genius by collision'. The conversation presumably included discussion of Cromwell, whom Johnson abhorred, as well as the mad poet Christopher Smart, whose editor and biographer was his cousin Christopher Hunter, a fellow of Sidney. Johnson was particularly fond of the unfortunate Smart, with whom he evidently identified. There was certainly discussion of the republican propagandist Thomas Hollis, a radical whom Johnson ridiculed, and who the following year presented Sidney with the portrait of Cromwell that Lamborn engraved.

Johnson seems to have stayed at Sidney, for he left the College on Monday morning in order to visit the great Shakespearean scholar Richard Farmer at Emmanuel, via a tour of the major Cambridge sites. He stayed at Trinity that night, enjoying another evening of excess, and left Cambridge on Tuesday morning. It was thought he might accept a fellowship at Cambridge at the time, and Sidney was probably high on his list. Johnson remained in correspondence with Lettice. When Lettice and Thomas Martyn began their collaboration on the Herculaneum project, Johnson warned them that the engravers would drive them 'mad'. At his death at Peasmarsh in 1832, the *Gentleman's Magazine* obituary described Lettice as the last survivor of the 'literary coterie of Dr. Johnson'.

'Good Sentiments': John Hey, Norrisian Professor

So I am now less perfect as a visible and audible object than I was; and yet Fanny Cooke is coming just now to drink tea and sup here. I am afraid my interest with the Ladies will decay apiece. —John Hey to his sister Rebecca about the loss of his wooden artificial tooth, 1776

John Hey, son of a Yorkshire drysalter, came to Sidney as a foundation fellow in April 1758, after a successful undergraduate career at St Catharine's where he was eighth

John Hey's teapot and stand, London, makers George Andrews (teapot) and John Crunch and Thomas Hannson (stand), 1788–89

Wrangler. Like his friend John Lettice a year later, Hey won the Seatonian Prize for poetry in 1763. His poem 'The Redemption' is a complex philosophical meditation on human and divine knowledge that runs to over 600 lines. It has a strong Newtonian and moral bias.

Hey's career was glittering in academic terms, though one unimpressed anonymous undergraduate refers in a satirical poem of 1774 to 'Black Hey of Sidney' at a disputation. In more than 20 years at Sidney Hey was tutor, dean, praelector and seneschal. His lectures on moral and political philosophy in the new Sidney Hall were attended by large numbers of students from across the university. These included William Pitt the Younger, who was an undergraduate at Pembroke, a college with which Sidney had many connections at the time. Hey was appointed the first Norrisian Professor of Divinity, a post he held from 1780 to 1795, and was a preacher at the Royal Chapel, Whitehall. His lectures were published in a number of editions well into the 19th century and his ideas, paradoxically, were an important influence on the High Church Oxford Movement in the 1830s. It is interesting to note that William Jones of Nayland, one of the great apologists for the High Church tradition, took an MA at Sidney in 1782.

As a theologian, Hey was a significant and popular figure until the later-19th century when his liberal views on matters such as the Trinity caused his reputation

Once more that adamantine tablet view;
The grand Redemption of degen'rate man
Is not a single, independent act,
But one great system; that perchance involv'd
In the one only greater God's high law
Pervading and supporting ev'ry part
Of the stupendous universe: to thee
Dark are this system's limits; nay the whole
To thee unknown, save some minuter spots
Display'd to shew the part thou hast to act
In the alarming scene.

—John Hey, from 'The Redemption', 1763

to decline. He can be seen as in some ways the intellectual descendant of John Gay in his utilitarian emphasis on moral reason and behaviour. His position was that of an apologist for the existing order in church and state, yet he called into question many traditional assumptions, in his attitude to the Articles for instance, often suggesting scepticism and a latitudinarian belief that all things were subject to historical conditions. Although his lectures, a beautifully written manuscript of which lies in the Muniment Room, dealt systematically with Christian doctrine, he considered more controversial areas were beyond debate: 'We do not know enough of the mysterious doctrines of religion to quarrel about them'. Hey saw Christianity, therefore, as a divine confirmation of a universal morality that could be discovered by reason and 'seems to make good provision for the generality of the *people*, considered in contra-distinction to the learned or philosophical'. He saw the church as an institution whose purpose was to ensure the good order of society rather than a mysterious body with divine sanction: 'The ends of religious society only require that such decency and regularity be maintained as is naturally productive of good sentiments; and therefore no member of a religious society need be absolutely compelled to observe its ordinances'. Such views led some to dispute his orthodoxy; attempts were made to prevent his lectures being published by the University Press, and when he was proposed for a bishopric he was denied it.

On a return to Sidney in 1793, Thomas Twining wrote to his brother: 'Not the worst part of my entertainment was my attendance upon two of Dr. Hey's Norrisian lectures in Sidney College Hall. Nothing could be more opposite to everything that is dull, heavy, tiresome, trite, etc. He has no paper or notes at all...His manner exactly the thing, with just enough of authority, without anything pompous or dogmatical. His audience were very attentive, and most of them took notes. The Professor stands at a small desk, and has a bench near him, on which are placed such books, Latin, English or Greek, as he has occasion to quote; and in the course of his lecture he takes them up and reads the passages. This relieves and makes a very pleasant variety.'

In political terms Hey was a moderate Whig of what was known as the 'intellectual party' at Cambridge, believing, like Locke, that the Glorious Revolution was a 'compact' between monarch and people. His view on Charles I and the contemporary French regime, for example, was that they made errors of judgement in 'keeping [their] subjects in subjection' to 'despotic tyranny'. Hey argued for a gradual and peaceful development in all human affairs. In matters of morality, he defined a virtuous action as one agreeable to God's will. That will might be defined as that which 'would promote the happiness of mankind'. His brother and correspondent Richard, also a Sidney fellow in the 1760s and 1770s, was a man of similar attitudes, and the author of influential essays on civil liberty as well as tracts against gambling and duelling. Richard Hey was a more thoroughly literary figure, writing a five-act tragedy that Thomas Twining told him had 'great merit', and a novel, *Edington*, which was published in 1796.

In his private life John Hey was sociable and devoted to polite culture, as were many of his colleagues at Sidney. Like his friend Thomas Twining, Hey was a gifted

OPPOSITE: *John Hey, by an unknown artist. First recorded in the master's inventory of 1807*

'One of the Commonest Creatures in London'

John Hey's failure to find a wife was not for want of trying, though he clearly had high standards. When Sir Charles Maynard married the ex-wife of a slave trader, the daughter of a Bond Street tailor, Hey agreed with Horace Walpole that she was 'one of the commonest creatures in London'. When Sir Charles began an affair with a Frenchwoman whom he kept at his other residence at Waltons in Essex, Hey described her as 'a low, vicious kind of woman'.

and learned musician and played in small concerts at Sidney and elsewhere. His letters to his sister Rebecca reveal a man open about his emotional life, describing his pursuit of various young ladies in the search for a wife he never found. His close relationship with a Sidney fellow-commoner of 1770, Sir Charles Maynard of Easton Lodge in Essex, was in part animated by a crush on his sister. Through her he met Fanny Cooke, whose reaction to the loss of his false tooth he so feared. When she married someone else, Hey described himself to Rebecca as 'desolate'. Through high society like that at Easton Lodge, where the house and gardens were a focus for fashionable life, he attended balls and dances, tea parties, and the Newmarket and Chelmsford races. The Maynards presented him to the rectory at Passenham near Stony Stratford, now part of Milton Keynes. John Hey retired to Marylebone, London at the end of his life, dying in St John's Wood where he was buried in St John's Chapel in 1815.

'The Liberty of a College Life': Work and Discipline Among Elliston's Men

> If any young person is disposed to abuse the liberty of a college life, there is hardly any kind of vice or folly that he has not in his power to practise, if he chooses it. It is a wide and common field: the gates all wide open and the fences (now I fear) almost all thrown down, and even while some of them remain standing, they were easily climbed over. A man must have the *murus aeneus* in his own breast; and so as much brass in your inside, and as little in your face, my dear, as you please. I think in college it used to be the fashion in my time to wear it chiefly upon the face…
> —Thomas Twining to his nephew Daniel, 1795

William Elliston's first decade, as we have seen, continued the transformation begun by Parris. The numbers of undergraduates remained small, as at many Cambridge colleges at this time, but the quality of the intake, matching that of the new generation of fellows, was very high. In the mathematics Tripos, our only consistent record of undergraduate academic achievement at Cambridge during the period, Elliston's students' performance generally matched their discipline. From 1765, when John Veryard Brutton and Julius Hutchinson were Senior and fourth Wranglers respectively, Sidney students were among the top 15 on a regular basis. In lists dominated by Trinity and St John's, the frequent appearance of the abbreviation '*Sid.*' in the lists stands out impressively as an indication of what a small institution can achieve.

Other students of a more literary kind were Christopher Hunter, the nephew, biographer and editor of the poet Christopher Smart, who went on to become a fellow; and Francis Newbery, the poet, classical translator, musician, keen sportsman

Insolence, Drunkenness and Indecency

Throughout his mastership, Elliston was obviously a strict disciplinarian, though he had his work cut out during a period of increasing wealth, leisure and free thinking among his various cohorts. Over more than 40 years, the punishments were few. Admonitions, suspensions or expulsions were given to Ashton Warner Byam, the future legal 'luminary of the Western World', for 'insolent behaviour to Mr. Hughes' in 1762; to Charles Belgrave, a scholar from Rutland and future priest, for 'being convicted of bringing a lewd woman into College… and detaining her all night' in 1766; to Craven Dodsworth, a man eventually rusticated for a whole year and later a Yorkshire vicar, for 'entertaining riotous company' in 1772; to Thomas de Lannoy, a migrant from Jesus and future priest, for 'drunkenness and for being concerned in a riot and in mischief done in the Town', in 1774; to John Barrell, a scholar from Norfolk, for consorting with a 'lewd woman' in 1781; to the cook, Matthew Palmer, for 'striking and bruising Charles Jackson the Porter' in 1784; and to Christopher Wilson, son of a canon at St Paul's, for 'going to Newmarket', on two occasions, in 1785. Also in 1785, Henry Rycroft, son of Sir Richard Rycroft, vicar at Penshurst, who inherited his father's title in 1816, was ordered to read out a composition in Chapel on the nature of his offence which was 'indecent behaviour in Chapel'. Sanctions were issued in 1796 to Thomas Land, a Blundell's educated migrant from Oxford, for 'using indecent language to the wife and servant of John Gilson', and Robert Ker 'for going into the shop of John Gilson, damaging the leather, calling his servant a whore and accusing her of having connexions with her master'; and in 1792 to Suffolk-born Edward Baynes, eighth Wrangler and future fellow, for 'disturbing and grossly ill-treating Falcon in the latter's room in company with Adams'.

and publisher, who migrated from Oxford in 1766. Newbery, a friend of Samuel Johnson, also inherited his father's patent medicine business and has the dubious distinction of having sold Oliver Goldsmith the fever powder that killed him in 1774.

'Picturesque Farming': Thomas Ruggles, Reformer and Bibliophile

> A necessary attention to the duties of a magistrate, together with compassion for the distress of my poor neighbours, particularly for those employed in daily labour on my estate, had occasioned me to visit at times, the sick cottager, and the miserable pauper in a parish work-house.
>
> —Thomas Ruggles, *The History of the Poor*, 1793–4

The kind of young man Elliston was seeking to encourage to join Sidney is well represented by Thomas Ruggles, son of a wealthy Essex wool manufacturer and cloth exporter. He came to Sidney from Lavenham Grammar School as a pensioner in 1763, perhaps inspired by the first book he owned as a 13-year-old boy, Richard Walter's *Voyage Round the World*. Ruggles became a barrister; in 1770 he was made a fellow of Sidney and later of the new Society of Antiquaries in London. A magistrate, High Sheriff and Deputy Lieutenant in Essex and Suffolk, he wrote two important books: *The Barrister, or, Strictures on the Education proper for the Bar* (1792), and *The History of the Poor, their Rights, Duties, and the Laws Respecting Them*, a two-volume work published in 1793–4. The first book proposed that all barristers should first take a law or arts degree at Oxford or Cambridge, to ensure the highest intellectual integrity and breadth of culture.

Ruggles's second book was a major contribution to contemporary debates on poverty. He deplored the appalling conditions in which many of the labouring classes lived and blamed their indolence and moral laxity mainly on easy access to the 'baneful and seducing habit of drinking strong liquors'. Enclosure, war and poor harvests had created a dangerous condition of deprivation and resentment among the rural poor. Ruggles, in patrician and rather complacent style, proposed that more reforming 'Houses of Industry' be established, replacing the old poor houses, and that men be set to hop-picking and women to spinning. He also believed that such institutions, which were far from popular with their inmates, were especially beneficial for children. He proposed the development of friendly societies to encourage saving. Ruggles was a close school friend of the great reformer Arthur Young, and his ideas

Pair of candlesticks, London, marks obscured, given by Thomas Ruggles, admitted as a pensioner in 1763, elected fellow in 1770

Spains Hall, Finchingfield, Essex, home of Thomas Ruggles

had such an impact on William Pitt that the prime minister sought Ruggles's advice on drafting his unsuccessful Poor Law Bill in 1796. Ruggles was also a writer on 'picturesque farming', the aesthetic improvement of the rural landscape, and produced many pieces for Young's *Annals of Agriculture*.

Ruggles was a great bibliophile. After inheriting Spains Hall near Finchingfield in Essex in 1784 he built a beautiful oak-panelled library there, which exists intact to this day. The fine curving shelves contain a range of books, lovingly inscribed, showing the tastes of a wealthy and successful late Georgian gentleman: *The Institutes of Justinian*; Ovid's *Art of Love*; works by Tacitus and Plutarch and Gibbon's *Decline and Fall of the Roman Empire*; the poems of Spenser, Milton, Thomson, Chatterton, Young, Byron and Burns; Johnson's *Lives of the Poets* and Boswell's *Life of Johnson*; a new 10-volume edition of Shakespeare; works by foreign authors such as Tasso, Bocaccio, Racine, Molière, Diderot and Montesquieu; various books on the peerage, including Dugdale and Debrett, and a number on heraldry, as well as general books on genealogy; histories by Hume, Smollett and Clarendon; and many volumes of the parliamentary *Annual Register*. Local history was a great passion: Ruggles had Philip Morant's great history of Essex, Morant having been awarded an MA at Sidney in 1729. There were also books on Manchester and Newcastle and picturesque tour literature on various parts of Britain. In addition to his childhood copy of Walter's *Voyage*, Ruggles had books by Captain Cook and James Bruce. His gardening books show the source of ideas for transforming the grounds at Spains Hall, volumes by Evelyn and Ray standing alongside more recent practical books on gardening. His scientific interests are shown by works on microscopes, botany, ornithology and chemistry. A lack of many theological books suggests Ruggles may have taken the extreme end of John Hey's thinking and moved to a near-agnostic morality in personal and social matters. He gave a copy of *The Life of Olaudah Equiano* (1790) to his son John.

'People of Every Nation': John Venn and the Clapham Sect

> A man will not despise his brother on account of the different shade of his complexion; he will not seek his destruction because he spoke in another language... People of every nation and kindred and tribe and tongue, will unite in one worship, will be animated with one spirit, will be actuated by one principle – and that, the principle of pure and universal love....
>
> ... There will be no sick to visit, no naked to clothe, no afflicted to relieve, no weak to succour, no faint to encourage, no corrupt to rebuke or profligate to reclaim.
> —John Venn, on the pros and cons of entering Heaven, from 'The Duty of Glorifying God,' in *Sermons*, vol. 1, 1819

Sidney became something of a stronghold of evangelical Christianity in the later 18th century, probably building on its strong Puritan and nonconformist traditions, and its politically and socially Whiggish, middle-class character. Of course, all fellows were Anglicans and most students remained within the church; for every nonconformist such as the Congregationalist convert and poet William Hurn of Woodbridge, there were many more orthodox members of the Church of England. However, the pull at Sidney to the evangelical tendency from the 1750s was very strong. William Elliston seems to have been powerfully inclined to the spiritual renewal called for by those dubbed at the time 'Enthusiasts'. Some indication of this is found in the award in 1790 of MA to one of the greatest evangelical leaders, Richard Cecil, the biographer of the abolitionist John Newton as well as an important writer on the visual arts. Henry Cox Mason (1781), who founded the Deaf and Dumb School in Bermondsey, and the lawyer, musician and scientific experimenter George Pattrick (1770), who became a leading evangelical preacher in London, are typical Sidney figures of this period.

The greatest Sidney evangelical, however, was John Venn. His two grandfathers had attended the College in the early part of the century and one, Richard Venn, became a prominent High Churchman who took great exception to his son Henry's conversion to evangelicalism in the 1750s. Henry became curate at Holy Trinity church in the wealthy village of Clapham, Surrey, in 1754 and became close friends with the merchant John Thornton. The Venns and Thorntons were the so-called 'angels' at the heart of what later became known as the Clapham Sect, one of the most influential sources of anti-slavery activity in Britain. These families were the founders of what Noel Annan famously called a British liberal 'intellectual aristocracy'. As John Venn's biographer Michael Hennell writes: 'Never have the members of one congregation so greatly influenced the history of their world. The effect of

REV.ᴰ JOHN VENN, A.M.

From an original Drawing by Mr SLATER, in Possession of the Family.

Engraved by E. Scriven, Historical Engraver to the Prince Regent & the Princess of Wales

London, Published Aug.ᵗ 8, 1813, by J. Slater N.º 17 Newman Street.

John Venn, by Joseph Slater, 1813, after an engraving by Edward Scriven. National Portrait Gallery, London

their prayers and actions not only profoundly altered the religious and social life of the country, it was also felt in Africa, in the West Indies, in India and in Australasia; in fact wherever freedom was given to slaves, wherever the ideal of trusteeship in colonial affairs was implemented, wherever the Gospel was preached by Chaplains of the East India Company, by missionaries of the Church Missionary Society or by the colporteurs [itinerant booksellers] of the British and Foreign Bible Society.'

John Venn was born in Clapham in 1759 but was brought up in Huddersfield where his father moved shortly afterwards to become a nationally famous preacher, drawing huge crowds to his church and to open air meetings. John was brought up in a highly devout atmosphere, a world of intense Bible-reading, prayer and strict moral observance. His father's reputation attracted many major Methodist and evangelical figures to Huddersfield, from Wesley and Whitefield to Newton and Romaine. Although Henry Venn moved to Yelling in Huntingdonshire in 1771, John went to Hipperholme Grammar School near Halifax, and then to school in Hull. Denied admission to Trinity because of his father's evangelical convictions, John entered Sidney in October 1777 on a scholarship and a grant from the Fishmongers' Company. Taught by the great Sidney theologian John Hey, Venn studied a wide range of subjects, enjoyed boating, and became friends with a group of fellow students at Sidney around whom he formed an evangelical religious society devoted to prayer and discussion. All were Wranglers or prize-winners, and included his cousin James Edward Gambier, from a Clapham family; the future Sidney fellows John and Robert Heslop, from Yorkshire; the scientist F J H Wollaston; and Henry William Coulthurst. Coulthurst, who was also educated at Hipperholme Grammar School, is particularly important with respect to the anti-slavery movement. His father was a merchant in Barbados. Coulthurst, who had witnessed the slave trade first-hand, came from St John's to Sidney as a fellow in 1781. He became the official Cambridge correspondent to Wilberforce's Abolition Society and was later vicar of Halifax Old Church where he preached on the occasion of Wilberforce's parliamentary election visit in 1806. Coulthurst was a friend of Charles Simeon of King's, who was a protégé of Henry Venn and later the most famous evangelical Cambridge preacher. Simeon was deeply influenced by his encounter with John Venn, 'a man after my own heart', and the two became close tea-drinking (no sugar allowed, of course) friends while undergraduates, devoted to earnest discussion and to a mission to convert their contemporaries. Simeon commented to Venn in a letter that Coulthurst 'grows, I cannot tell you, how big a Christian'.

Venn's father was impressed by the education his son was receiving at Sidney, though not by the behaviour of all his companions. He wrote to a friend that his son was 'obliged to be in the company of the sons of Belial, with whom he is engaged in keeping exercise in the public schools; because he would not get drunk with them, nor exceed the bounds of strict temperance, they abused him for a Methodist, saying none but Methodists believed there was a judgement to come or that there was any harm in whoring or drinking...and when he would leave them, they came drunk and broke in pieces the door of his room, but he was not in it....These are the young gentlemen who in two or three years' time, will be reading lectures on morality

from their pulpits.' We have already seen the kind of undergraduate Venn would have steered clear of: Thomas de Lannoy, John Barrell and other contemporaries. Another such young gentleman was Henry Wiglesworth. Later known as 'the bold rector of Slaidburn', in Yorkshire, Wiglesworth's addiction to hunting and alcohol made him the subject of a popular song.

Venn survived these outrageous assaults on his virtue, and even though he performed surprisingly poorly in the Tripos, after a decade as a charismatic and energetic vicar in Norfolk he became rector at the newly rebuilt Holy Trinity, Clapham in 1792, appointed by the trustees of the will of John Thornton. It is said that Charles Simeon encouraged another applicant to step down in favour of Venn, so convinced was he that his friend was the right man to become religious leader of the nascent Clapham Sect.

Venn was urged by Richard Cecil, the Sidney MA, to be cautious at first in his preaching to his congregation of nearly 1,500 souls, but another Clapham Sect figure, Venn's great friend William Wilberforce, advocated stronger fare. Wilberforce's view prevailed and Venn's first sermon, on 1 Corinthians 2:3 ('I was with you in weakness and in fear and in much trembling'), addressed the difficulties of Christian ministry. It set the tone for his preaching thereafter. 'We have to convey unpleasant things,' he said, 'to persuade to what is disagreeable; to effect not only a reformation in the conduct of men, and a regulation of their passions, but, what is of still higher difficulty, a change in their good opinion of themselves.'

J K Baldrey, Sidney Sussex College, *published by J Deighton, 1811. Private collection*

An engraving by S Sparrow showing the Master's Lodge from the Fellows' Garden. Fellows are bowling on their ancient green, in front of the small outbuilding abutting the Hall end, which was used to store the bowls and other equipment

Thomas Freeman, Satan at the Court of Chaos, 1784. Ackland Museum of Art, University of California at Chapel Hill

The Londoner Thomas Freeman came to Sidney in 1788 at the age of 31 and took an LLB in 1795. He had been a student at the Royal Academy where he had won a medal for drawing in 1779, the year William Blake became a student, and exhibited works in 1780 and 1784. Inspired by the work of Henry Fuseli, he painted various religious and literary subjects, including this large oil painting, drawn from Milton's Paradise Lost. Freeman was ordained in 1792 and became a rector in Leicestershire. He died in 1834

Venn soon won over the great and wealthy; the growing population of local poor was mainly absent, however. To change this he began catechising the local children and their parents at school on Sunday evenings, moving to the church when new lighting permitted. A local card club at the Plough Inn objected to this development, claiming that, like a Methodist, Venn would radicalise the poor; a meeting of the vestry, however, decided to support Venn. Over the next few years Venn developed a superb preaching, pastoral, educational and liturgical platform for encouraging evangelical virtue and compassion, which enabled the radical ideas of Clapham Sect members such as Wilberforce, Granville Sharp, Zachary Macaulay (whose brother Aulay, the writer, was at Sidney in 1780s), Hannah More, Thomas Clarkson, and others, to become dominant during the period of the French Wars.

When Venn founded the Society for Bettering the Condition of the Poor at Clapham in 1799, he pioneered a new form of local social services. In his extensive horseback travels around Britain and in his contributions to the influential *Christian Observer*, he helped to spread the word of social and religious reform nationally; as a founder and chairman of the Church Missionary Society, also in 1799, he was at the forefront of a worldwide campaign to abolish slavery and evangelise all continents. His school for young Africans in Clapham, his support of Catholic emancipation and women's rights, all reveal an extraordinarily progressive and visionary thinker.

Zimao the African: Weeden Butler and Slavery

> Should any one passage in the few following pages awaken either thine indignation or thy pity, cherish the sacred impulse; and humbly thank thy god, for bestowing upon thee the feelings of a MAN. —Weeden Butler, *Zimao the African*, 1800

A few miles across the river from Clapham, in Chelsea, lived another Sidney evangelical who fought against the slave trade. Weeden Butler was the son of Weeden Butler senior, a clergyman who preached at the fashionable Charlotte Chapel in Pimlico, purchased by Sidney's Thomas Martyn in 1784. The chapel, built by the Rev. William Dodd in 1766, was near Buckingham Palace and was later converted into a cinema and then a theatre. Weeden senior was also master of a school on Cheyne Walk where he educated his two sons, the other being the Sidney fellow and later headmaster of Harrow, George Butler. The elder Weeden was also a man of letters, a proponent of prison reform, and an outspoken campaigner against the slave trade.

Weeden Butler the younger entered Sidney in 1790 and took his MA in 1797. He became a priest and succeeded his father as afternoon lecturer at Charlotte Chapel, continuing the Sidney connection established by Thomas Martyn, whose own son, John King Martyn, was a Sidney mathematical lecturer and became a Moravian in 1823.

Butler was the author of poetry and translations and of the 70-page novella *Zimao, the African*, which was published in 1800, along with an appendix giving shocking details about the slave trade. This work is notable less for its literary quality than for its content and tone. The story concerns the lives of the African prince Zimao and his wife, the beautiful Benin princess Ellarhoe, who have been tricked into slavery and transported to Jamaica. Renamed John in captivity, the prince fights against his enslavement and leads a revolt under his Benin name, Zimao, meaning 'freedom'. Butler describes his majestic body and handsome features: 'The celebrated statues of Apollo and of Antinous possess not more regular features or more exact proportions. I was particularly struck with his noble and commanding aspect: I never saw a man who seemed so born to sovereignty. He was animated with the fierce glow of combat,

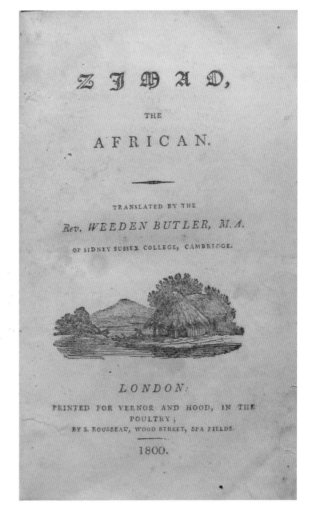

Weeden Butler, Zimao the African, *1800, title page*

and reeking from slaughter; but, when he accosted us, his eyes beamed mildness and benevolence.' The narrator's language expresses his righteous anger at the ignominy of such a man's condition under slavery: 'Oh! Shower down thy hottest indignation on the villains who blaspheme thy workmanship, and dare to debase black men to a level with the brutes.' Zimao's and Ellarhoe's love for one another sustains them during their harrowing journey across the Atlantic: 'Love triumphant, ecstatic love engrossed every sentiment.' Yet, after their arrival at Porto Bello, Ellarhoe is sold off and Zimao conceives his plan for revenge: 'I lolled up the insatiate tongue of slaughter…Mine eyeballs shot fire: my teeth gnashed with fury. I snarled. I found destruction.' The lovers are eventually reunited and Ellarhoe presents Zimao with their child. The father resolves: 'First-born of love! Thou shalt never, never become a slave.'

Butler's appendix makes it clear that the end is in sight for the dreadful trafficking of slaves and that those responsible will suffer eternal damnation: 'Retribution will come, when it will come. Let the wholesale dealers in blood, with their noble and ignoble abettors see to it. The voice of the blood of Abel crieth from the ground, and god heareth it.' One can almost hear Butler's voice echoing around the Charlotte Chapel, moving its fashionable congregation to action. Sidney's small but influential role in defeating slavery through word and deed, on the page and from the pulpit, is one the College continues to celebrate.

'A Complete System of Astronomy':
Samuel Vince, Bricklayer and Professor

One of John Venn's near-contemporaries was Robert Courbold Chilton, another product of the grammar school in Lavenham, Suffolk, who entered Sidney as a pensioner in 1781 and was soon made a scholar. He returned to Suffolk as a vicar and died there in 1816. He was the artist behind a satirical image of one of Sidney's most distinguished fellows of the later 18th century, Professor Samuel Vince. The aquatint engraving, published around 1784 when Chilton left Sidney, and called '*Helluones Librorum*', meaning 'book worms', shows the stern astronomer and mathematician reading in his bare candle-lit Sidney room; a celestial globe, a clock, other books, some prints on the wall, and a few pieces of plain furniture are all there is. The results of Vince's labours, his most famous work, *A Complete System of Astronomy* (1797–1808), was obviously to Chilton not quite as complete as Vince might like to think. Chilton was not among Sidney's Wranglers when he graduated.

Samuel Vince was also a Suffolk man, the son of a bricklayer and 13 years older than his student Chilton. He worked with his father laying bricks until, at the age of 12, a local priest noticed him sitting by his hod reading a book. The networks

An aquatint by F Jukes, with engraving by J K Baldrey, after Robert Chilton, Helluones Librorum, *c1784*

Chilton shows Samuel Vince reading in his rooms at Sidney, by the light of a shaded lamp, while on the floor his emaciated cat reads The Ladies' Diary

between parish priests and Cambridge worked in his favour and in 1771, following a lengthy secondary education, he entered Caius at the age of 21. He was Senior Wrangler in 1775 and then moved to Sidney as Taylor Lecturer.

Vince married in 1780 and attained a living in Norfolk, spending time in his parish and in Cambridge, where he was appointed Plumian Professor of Astronomy in 1796. Vince, who revived the flagging fortunes of the Plumian chair, supplemented his income by writing and lecturing, and wrote prolifically on religion, mathematics and astronomy. His textbooks ran into several editions and his importance was recognised in 1786 when he was elected FRS. At Cambridge and at the Royal Society, Vince gave lectures and papers on a wide variety of topics such as optics, magnetism, galvanism, progressive and rotary motion, the summation of infinite series, fluid rotation, fluxions, hydrostatics and gravitation. He realised that the old Newtonian 'physico-theology' needed reformulating, and wrote extensively on the relationship between gravity and God's providential working.

Like his Sidney colleagues and acquaintances H W Coulthurst, Thomas Martyn and F J H Wollaston, Vince was closely involved in the founding of the short-lived Cambridge Scientific Society for the Promotion of Philosophy and General Literature. The Society's closure in 1786 was indicative of the general lack of interest in many of the sciences at Cambridge at the time. Vince was also instrumental in getting a new university observatory built in Madingley in 1824, though he had died three years earlier in Kent in 1821. His years teaching at Sidney coincided with a remarkable sequence of results in the mathematical Tripos, with F J H Wollaston Senior Wrangler in 1783, along with Venn's friend Robert Heslop, who was fourth Wrangler and Senior Classical Medallist, and the misbehaving Nelson Rycroft, eighth Wrangler. John Holden was second Wrangler in 1784 and Joseph Watson third in 1785; Rowland Ingram was seventh Wrangler in 1786… and so on, impressively, into the 1790s when George Butler was Senior Wrangler in 1794.

ON THE ROTATION OF THE MOON.   229

True Time at Nuremberg	SM=	pSM=	Apparent long. of ☾	Appar. lat. of ☾	pM=	SpM=	Longitude of Manilius at ☾'s center
1748. D. H. M.	° '	° '	° ° '	' "	° '	° '	s ° '
April 11.11. 1	17.20	58.11	6. 0.35	4.16 s.	76.50	15. 4	0.15.39
—— 13. 9.30	15. 8	58.35	6.27.24	5.27-	76.52	13.14	1.10.39
May 11.10.56	15.29	60.40	7. 6.19	5.51-	76.48	13.50	1.20. 9
—— 16.16.11	13.26	28.45	9.22.14	2.31-	75.45	6.38	3.28.52
—— 17.15.56	14.23	20.49	10. 6.33	1.17-	75.18	5.14	4.11.37
June 5. 9.58	18. 2	62.16	6. 2.53	4.56-	76.59	16.20	0.19.13
—— 13.14. 0	14.18	25.48	10. 0.24	1.41-	75.29	6.23	4. 6.47
—— 14.12.50	15.12	16.47	10.14.43	0.25-	75. 3	4.30	4.19.13
July 2. 9.23	18. 2	61.56	5.28.25	4.54-	76.55	16.17	0.14.42
—— 4. 6.49	17.36	64.29	6.23.11	5.48-	76.57	16.16	1. 9.27
—— 5. 8. 4	17.23	64.49	7. 7.18	6. 8-	76.48	16. 7	1.23.25
—— 6. 8.34	16.20	62.37	7.21.34	5.57-	76.49	14.52	2. 6.26
—— 7. 9. 4	15.43	58.10	8. 6.15	5.30-	76.26	13.42	2.19.57
—— 8.10. 4	15. 8	52. 0	8.21.33	4.44-	76. 7	12.14	3. 3.47
—— 9.11.15	14.38	44.26	9. 7.12	3.38-	76. 2	10.30	3.17.42
—— 10.12. 5	14.34	34.40	9.22.50	2.19-	75.46	8.29	4. 1.19
—— 11.13.15	15.23	23.24	10. 8.37	0.51-	75. 4	6.16	4.14.53
—— 12.13. 5	16. 0	16.57	10.23.34	0.30N.	75.13	4.46	4.28.20
—— 15.13.35	19.38	2.14	0. 6.33	1.41-	74. 4	0.47	6. 7.24
Aug. 3. 7. 5	16.10	60.27	7.29.58	5.46 s.	76.31	14.25	2.14.23
—— 14.11.34	20.23	4.16	1.11. 2	4.25N.	74. 5	1.33	7.12.35
Nov. 1. 5.44	19.27	15.33	11.24.42	3. 4-	74.21	5.19	6. 0. 1
—— 2. 6.29	20.26	11.50	0. 9. 1	3.46-	73.51	4.16	6.13.17
Dec. 27. 4.47	20.54	7.19	0.14.44	4.21-	73.36	2.43	6.17.27
1749.	*	*	*	*	*	*	*
Jan. 28. 3.59	8.56	9.59	2.16. 0	3. 0-	74.22	3.21	8.19.21
Feb. 25.11.43	17.30	14.53	2.17.53	2-	75. 6	4.35	2. 28
March 4.11.42	14.46	54.26	5.22. 9	4.42 s.	76.53	12.17	0. 4.26

397. Let *QDV* reprefent the face of the moon next to the earth; *C* the center of the moon's difc; *QNX* the lunar equator, *P* it's pole; *DNW* the ecliptic referred to the moon's furface, or rather a circle paffing through it's center parallel to the ecliptic, and which extended to the heavens may be confidered as coinciding with it, *p* it's pole, which is not, as in the fun, in the outward circle *QDV*; *M* Manilius, through which draw the great circles *pMB*, *PML*; and let ♈ be the firft point of Aries feen from the moon's center; then *MB* is the latitude of Manilius, which is a variable quantity, and known.

Fig. 93.

Page from Samuel Vince, A Complete System of Astronomy, 1797–1808. Bodleian Library, Oxford

'According to His Own Taste': Elliston's New Chapel

The Chapel, & Library & Offices belonging to the Master's Lodge are in so ruinous a state that it is necessary to take down and rebuild the same. —*Acta Collegii*, 2 November, 1775

Sidney required further beautification to match its renewed academic status. In 1775 William Elliston decided to create a new Chapel to replace the ancient and now dilapidated one built by James Montagu in the 1590s. The antiquary William Cole recorded that 'the old Chapel was quite worn out, both in its Stone Work and Timbers, and was become dangerous. The wainscote was chiefly rotten.' This wainscote was the wood installed at James Montagu's expense in 1612. In order to afford this quite modest building work, Elliston had to suspend a fellowship in 1777 and took further action again in 1779 when three posts were suspended. He also used £670 from wood sales at the Cridling Park estate, £150 from degree and admission fees and sold £230 worth of stock.

Although George Dyer referred to Elliston's 'reviving the ancient character of the ecclesiastic, superintending and directing the building according to his own taste', in fact Elliston called in the well-known architect James Essex to draw up detailed plans. These plans also included the rebuilding of the Old Library, a room that survives to this day, though no longer used for its original purpose. Essex, a local builder and then architect and medieval antiquarian, had worked under his mentor James Burroughs on the new Sidney Hall and gateway some years before, and by the time

ABOVE: *James Essex's drawing of the new Chapel*

RIGHT: *Essex's Chapel, looking south, from* Pheon II, ii, *1923*

THE LIBRARY, SIDNEY SUSSEX COLLEGE, CAMBRIDGE

he was commissioned by Elliston was the pre-eminent architect in Cambridge. He had already built a small and now no longer existing summer house in the Fellows' Garden at Sidney, a small structure set against the north end of the Hall, in 1775, visible in images of the period.

The old Chapel was pulled down in July and August 1776, and on 1 October 'at half an hour after eleven' the foundation stone was laid by Essex in the south-east corner of the building, 'about 5 feet below the surface of the ground'. This was witnessed by the master bricklayer and a labourer alone, as the master and fellows were engaged in the College audit. The head of the stone, wrote Essex, 'which is 11 inches square, lies towards ye East, and projects 2 inches before the range of the wall. It has the date of the year, 1776, deep cut in figures 2 inches long; the length of the stone is 1 ft 2in, and on the lower surface this + is cut with a Chissel.' The work continued for some years; Essex only received his fee of £100 for 'superintendence of the New Building' in 1782. The slow pace was certainly the result of financial difficulties, yet another fellowship having been suspended in 1781.

Sidney thus acquired a new Chapel with an antechapel, following the old north-east-southwest axis, but adjusted in its new foundations to rectify an asymmetrical relationship to the rest of the College buildings, and extending behind the gable

The Old Library, postcard published by Walter Scott, c1950

At the far end are the box containing the Cretan skull seen by Charles I; a box containing a genealogical scroll printed in Paris in 1521, acquired by 1688; and the bust of Cromwell given by Thomas Martyn in 1801

of the Clerke range; a new library above the Chapel; a new kitchen and servants' offices; and a gallery for the master to enter from the Lodge. The floor was paved with flagstones, and deal was used as a cheap alternative to oak for the wainscotting. The plain white-brick west front of the new building, that is, the one facing Sidney Street, had a central portion with a pediment standing a little in advance of the main wall, a door flanked by classical pilasters and surmounted by a pediment, and above the whole a plain entablature. Six sash windows were arranged either side of the door, and above these seven on the upper floor.

'Pomposus': George Butler

> Old *Sidney* for ever. 20 June 1794…Imprimis, you are to congratulate me upon my final Election to the vacant Taylor Lectureship, an honour which Dr. Elliston notified to me a few days ago. He began his information as usual by desiring me to sit down in the Jobation Chair [a jobation is a scolding or reprimand]; then, putting aside a Book which he affected to hold in his Hand for the Purpose of Reading, he seemed, during a silent Interval, which I had not courage or Inclination to break, to envelope himself with his most impenetrable Gloom of Dignity, and at last he *oped his Mouth* and said: 'I suppose , Sir, you know the Reason of my sending for you'. 'No, Sir,' said I very innocently, imagining he alluded to my scaling the College Walls, a practice which I had of late very frequently adopted, and which I feared he might have discovered. At length, however, I found myself happily disappointed, and left him in Exultation… —George Butler, letter to John Browne

George Butler by W E Miller after ?Joseph Jacobs, given by his son, the Rev. Dr H Montagu Butler, master of Trinity, in 1894

George Butler was the second son of Weeden Butler of Chelsea. He entered Sidney with his brother Weeden in 1790 and both were elected scholars in 1791. He was a remarkable all-rounder, fluent in German, French and Italian, as well as a first-rate classical scholar and the pre-eminent mathematician of his year at Cambridge; he was Senior Wrangler in 1794. His remarkable notebook and drawings made during his attendance at William Farish's mechanical sciences lectures in the 1790s show his enormous appetite for all aspects of scientific knowledge.

In 1794 Butler was elected Taylor Lecturer and classical lecturer in 1797, describing to his friend John Browne, a future headmaster at Blundell's, the expenses of his hat and gown, and some of the impact of the French Wars on life at Sidney: 'Old Sidney is just now remarkably gay: our back Piece is in full Employ. 'Tis the Military Parade of our local Townsmen, who have united into a Body to learn their Soldier Duties under the Direction of some Professional Men. Every afternoon they are Exercised from 5 to 6, and very well indeed do they perform. Their uniform is a blue Coat lined and faced with White, red Cape and Cuffs, white Waistcoat and nankin Breeches.' Butler himself was one of those who joined the University Volunteer Corps in 1803, among six Sidney fellows and students, including his friend Browne.

Butler became fellow, praelector, dean and tutor at Sidney, and was also ordained before being appointed headmaster of Harrow School in succession to John Drury.

He had a true baptism by fire in his first few years at Harrow. Within weeks of his appointment Butler faced the anarchic fury of his new pupils, who had wanted

Presepio (Nativity), by Giambattista Pittoni, c1720

Sidney's altarpiece by the Venetian rococo painter Pittoni (1687–1767) was acquired by Thomas Martyn, the botanist and connoisseur, in 1783. Martyn negotiated for the picture through a well-known agent and diplomat John Strange, British Resident at Venice, at a price of 20 guineas, which Strange described as 'really a trifle'. Martyn was particularly keen on the painting's size, which was perfect for Sidney's Chapel and the space above the altar. Martyn's Puritan forebears at Sidney would certainly have been shocked by such sensuous Catholic imagery dominating the small, plain Chapel

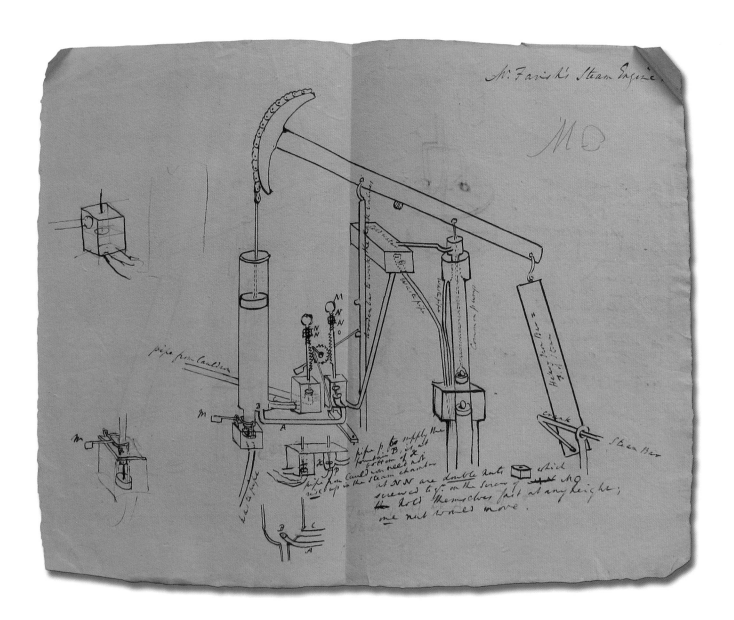

'Mr Farish's Steam Engine', from George Butler's notes on Farish's Lectures on Engineering and Manufacturing Processes, *1795*

another man appointed. Led by the future poet Lord Byron, the boys contemplated blowing Butler up and resisted all his efforts to instil discipline, rigorous examination and physical exercise. Butler deprived monitors such as Byron of their right to beat other boys, and banished the practice of blanket tossing, leading the fourth form to barricade themselves in, which Butler responded to in turn by expelling the ringleaders (though not Byron). Butler introduced writing and public speaking of Greek, Latin and English verse as well as science, French and Italian. In the midst of all this vigorous activity he allowed an enormous number of holidays to mark military victories, saints' days and political events. During his time there the Eton and Harrow cricket match was inaugurated, and the buildings were extended significantly. His later years were plagued by difficulties and he left Harrow in 1829 to take up the Sidney living at Gayton, Northamptonshire, where he died in 1853.

'One of the Most Favoured Children of Poverty': James Tate

> Cambridge, I am more and more persuaded, is a place of as much heart, soul and senti-
> ment – as any place on the whole face of the globe. The recollection of what I have
> known there delights and improves me. I am proud to avow that I honour and reverence,
> and as far as may be, without sorrow and in the enjoyment of pleasure, I regret the dear
> seat of Learning, Genius and Virtue. —James Tate, letter to George Butler, 1796

One of George Butler's closest friends at Sidney was James Tate, son of a North
Yorkshire maltster, who arrived at Sidney in 1790 after an education at Richmond
Grammar School under the master Anthony Temple, who had been at Sidney in
the 1740s. Tate worked as an amanuensis to a controversial local churchman, the
blind Francis Blackburne, and, through his exposure to Blackburne's library, the
young scholar acquired a wide knowledge and culture. Blackburne had refused to
take the Thirty-Nine Articles and, persuaded by Thomas Hollis, the political propagandist who had given Sidney its Cromwell portrait in 1766, and whose biography
Blackburne wrote, published his *Confessional* against orthodoxy in the same year.

Tate left Yorkshire for Cambridge on a 'cold and frosty' evening, and upon arrival
was examined by Christopher Hunter 'on Thursday night after chapel in Quintilian,
Homer and Demosthenes'. The life of a sizar, even
one such as Tate, who had support from a few
patrons as well as a promise of £20 from Elliston,
was financially hard. He was given accommodation at the top of 'the middle staircase in the back
court' (H staircase in Chapel Court) in a room
that was once occupied by his mentor Temple,
where he recorded the narrow bed was 'breadth
3ft length 6ft 3ins'. Tate wrote to his mother about
the heating and washing arrangements: 'Coals
with you are much better and much cheaper,
than with us. However, I keep a warm little fire,
and, I assure you, my cloaths are very well dried,
before I put them on. Our washerwomen are very
well paid and she, that washes for me, is a very
clean neat looking woman. Though I think you
wash better in Yorkshire.' In his second year his
father died, and one of his touching notes reads:
'At College to eat no breakfast or supper three
times a week to save for my mother'.

Tate faced no social stigma at Sidney, which
he found very friendly. One of the fellows, Joseph
Watson, seeing that Tate's gown was old and
shabby, purchased him a new one and offered help
and advice any time he might need it. Late in his

*James Tate by H W
Pickersgill, 1833*

life Tate wrote: 'The Master and Fellows of Sidney (I sometimes wonder why, knowing my academic idleness as I do) were exceeding kind to me…during my whole life; in so much that I consider myself one of the most favoured children of poverty that ever lived.' He formed a close friendship with his tutor, the future Sidney master Edward Pearson, and also with George and Weeden Butler and their friend John Browne, who became Blundell's headmaster. Along with the young fellow Rowland Ingram, future headmaster of Giggleswick School in Yorkshire, and a few others, they formed Sidney's first debating society, the Speculative Society.

Tate became a Sidney fellow and the College librarian and, after being ordained, earned extra money by private tutoring at Sidney and preaching in Cambridgeshire villages. On one occasion, he recalled, he was given a horse to travel to a local church and the creature set off at an alarming pace down Jesus Lane, 'worse than a gallop to John Gilpin'. He dismounted and walked the rest of the way, also returning by foot. He wrote at length in his letters of his compassion for his congregations: 'It hurts me much to reflect that the village peasants whose toil is the severest and the least social or cheerful in many cases, should yet be the worst recompensed for perhaps the most trying exercises of muscular strength. "Meat, Sir", said a poor man (probably meaning food) whose spirits even the Sunday had not relaxed in cheerfulness, and into whose house in a village near Cambridge, I took an opportunity to make a hasty visit, "Meat, Sir, is all we can think of getting with our wages, and scarcely that – decent clothes we cannot expect, and it is not our fault if we go in rags".' Even when he described, in a long letter to his friend Mrs Ottley, a visit to London in 1792 that took in dinners, clubs, shopping, picture galleries and book dealers, he referred to 'a poor lad' who 'uttered a petition' to him and that Tate had 'ventured to engage him', and on his later return to the area, 'dismissed him with two shillings, which he had well earned by a long trudge'.

Tate achieved his great ambition early: in 1797 he was appointed headmaster of his old school at Richmond, in succession to Anthony Temple. He made it one of the leading classical schools of the day and his pupils were known as 'Tate's Invincibles', 13 of them alone becoming fellows of Trinity. He banished corporal punishment and encouraged hard work and physical exercise, in particular long walks in the Dales. Most of his own publications were school textbooks, especially for students of ancient Greek. He also published a major attempt to arrange Horace's books in chronological order, *Horace Restitutus*, in 1832. The great writer and conversationalist Sydney Smith met Tate by chance on a coach trip and wrote to a friend afterwards that he had met a 'man dripping with Greek'. Tate died in 1843 and was buried near Nelson's tomb in St Paul's Cathedral.

'New-Fangled Rules'

Byron later regretted his behaviour towards Butler with whom he subsequently developed a good friendship. However, his satirical piece of juvenilia, 'On a Change of Masters at a Great Public School'(1805), attacking Sidney's golden boy as the intruding 'Pomposus' at Harrow, is still amusing:

Of narrow brain, yet of a narrower soul,
Pomposus holds you in his harsh controul;
Pomposus, by no social virtue sway'd,
With florid jargon, and with vain parade;
With noisy nonsense, and new-fangled rules,
(Such as were ne'r enforc'd in schools.)
Mistaking pedantry for learning's laws,
He governs, sanction'd but by self-applause…

Drawn by R.B.Harraden.

Etchd by Eliz.ᵗ Byrne.

'The Hour of Difficulty and Danger': Sidney and the French Revolution

Sidney Sussex College, by Richard Bankes Harraden, from Cantabrigia Depicta, *1811, etching by Elizabeth Byrne*

> It is very easy for a man of a warm and great genius, like Mr. Burke, to declaim virulently against the outrages of the swinish multitude in this country or elsewhere. But a wise man would investigate the causes, political or moral, which have influenced the temper and character of the commonalty for the worse, and a good man would avail himself of the reports of those investigations to cut off the tendency to outrage or sedition by giving a check to the operation of its distant cause. —James Tate to Mrs Ottley, 12 June 1793

James Tate evidently imbibed strong Whig beliefs during his work with Francis Blackburne. He later supported Catholic emancipation, which debarred him from preferment under the Tory regime and until the Whigs returned to power in 1830, when Lord Grey appointed him canon of St Paul's. Cambridge in the late-18th and early-19th centuries was a predominantly conservative university, and even though many undergraduates and some fellows at colleges such as Trinity and Jesus were radical in their political and religious views, they were often treated harshly by the university's governing powers. Sidney men reflected a variety of attitudes towards the great events.

Older men such as John Lettice and Thomas Twining were sympathetic during the first years of the Revolution, but soon asserted their loyalty to Britain, and expressed their horror at the events of 1792 and 1793 and their commitment to the defence of the realm. Lettice referred to the French as 'ferociously bent on mischief, plunder and destruction', and in 1803 drew up elaborate published plans for 'the safe removal of inhabitants, not military, from towns and villages of the coast of Great Britain and Ireland in the case of threatened invasion'. These were so highly regarded that they formed the basis for plans in 1940 in the event of a German invasion. Lettice also published a translation of his friend Isaac Hawkins Browne's popular Latin poem '*De Animi Immortalitate*' ('The Immortality of the Soul') in 1795 with a long commentary and notes, which in particular addressed a female readership on the political dangers of radical and atheistic ideas:

'For I am ambitious of having many readers of that Sex, being entirely persuaded, that were the grovelling principles of Materialism, and of the Mortality of the Soul, once to become prevalent among the Ladies of this Country, as they have for some time been among the Female Citizens of a neighbouring people, there would want little else, at this alarming Crisis, than that universal Depravation, which such a circumstance would certainly, and quickly, produce, to shake the Constitution of Great Britain to their very foundations…'

Twining's correspondence is full of commentary on the French Revolution and ensuing wars. In 1791 he believed Burke had gone too far in 'his abuse and contempt of the National Assembly', but by the following year he wrote that while he had wished the Revolution well, 'this despotism of his majesty the people – I cannot endure it'. He denied the necessity of war when it broke out in 1793, and sided with Fox on the issue. He continued to dread the war and in 1803, on a trip back to Cambridge, was alarmed to hear the town was especially vulnerable to invasion.

H W Coulthurst was an evangelical opponent of slavery but also a loyal supporter of Pitt and the established order in the 1790s. He was a fierce denigrator of what he called 'Jacobinical criticism'. He had clashed with the controversial Jesus radical William Frend in 1789, the year of the French Revolution, over the latter's support for John Edward's grace against subscription, and as the Revolution developed and Britain went to war against France he became an evermore strident defender of traditional views of church and state. His sermon, 'The Evils of Disobedience and Luxury', preached before the university in 1796, by which time he was vicar of Halifax, used Ecclesiastes 10:20 as its text: 'Curse not the king, no not in thy thought; and curse not the rich in thy bedchamber; for a bird of the air shall carry the voice, and that which hath wings shall tell the matter'. Referring to David Hume as a 'metaphysician' who was 'pleased to exalt Politics to the Dignity of Science', Coulthurst warned his university colleagues to stand firm at a moment of apocalyptic decision:

'The Hour of Difficulty and Danger is now come. – We, the Clergy of the Established Church, "are fallen upon evil Days, and upon evil Tongues". – Infidelity and Irreligion reign triumphant. – The Name of God and the Word of God are openly insulted and despised – and every knee must now bow down – at what? – at the Name of the Holy, blessed and glorious Reason – I speak not of those inhuman Monsters, who by their abominable Usurpation have deluged the wide-extended Plains of France with Blood…I speak of our Enemies at Home. – Their Outcry is

most vehemently directed against us. – "Delenda est Ecclesia!" – We are destined to be the first Victims…'

Coulthurst's remedy for these evils was a 'strict Conformity to the Doctrines and Disciplines' of the Church of England. 'We may in general assert that he is the best Subject who is the best Christian.' Behind the views of the radicals and dissenters lay the curse of 'luxury'. By means of luxury 'the pestilential Tenets of Anarchy… gather strength and prevail; the sinews of Government are enervated, and a certain effeminate Languor, or rather a deadly Stupefaction pervades all the lower Branches of the executive Department'. In turn, this submission to luxury stems from an ultimate cause, 'the Corruption and Depravity of Man'.

James Tate took a different view. He was remembered by a friend as 'Metaphysical Tate of Sidney', a reference to his interest in Coulthurst's much-loathed writers Locke and Priestley. Tate had declared himself, in a letter to one of his Yorkshire patrons in 1793, as 'as near to the great Charles Fox in my opinions on almost all the leading traits of policy in England and the larger theatre of European actions, as can be expected from one who wishes to preserve his thoughts…independent

Ridgway porcelain plate, 1815, showing the Master's Lodge from the Fellows' Garden, based on the Baldrey print of 1811 (see page 209). Private collection

and uncontaminated with the prejudices of party and the narrowness of systems'. Tate was concerned about the growing jingoism of the 1790s and wrote: 'I could not bear to witness in silence the growing habit of exultation at successes in war, a habit which bids fair to confirm the unnatural – I had almost said the impious – idea of natural enmity betwixt nations…'

However, he was no extremist, and although he admired the French Constitution of 1791 he was horrified by the Terror. While his future friend William Frend was sensationally expelled from Cambridge in 1793 for proposing peace with the new post-Terror French regime, Tate was more cautious: 'I cannot but feel myself painfully concerned for the discredit which may accrue to the cause of freedom…from the ferocious and brutal vehemence with which some seem to pursue it…I mean not to derogate from the general merit of the French Revolution. My exaltation at that event arose from the contrast of that degrading despotism which it supplanted.' Tate would not have concurred with Coulthurst's view that it is 'a dreadful Thing for the multitude to be deluded with the Idea that there is sometimes in themselves', though he feared an 'ignorant and irreligious mob, under the direction of a few bad men'. His view was well expressed in a letter of 1794: 'I will not disavow that the arguments of those who contested the necessity, the justice, and the holiness of this war [i.e. against France] carried conviction in my mind.' Tate's failure to get the Fishmongers' Fellowship was not only due to the Fishmongers' strong Calvinist position, but also to whispers in Cambridge that he was a Jacobin.

'A Deranged State of Mind': Robert Luke and William Elliston

I do account it my bounden duty, and service, unto the Almighty Jah, my creator, to avow myself as one authorised, and required, to invite the disconsolate of all the earth to the Standard of the Son of God; that they should become the followers of me, as I am of him. —Robert Luke, *The Avowal of the Secession of the late Rev. R. Luke B.D. and Fellow of Sidney Sussex College, Cambridge, Now considering himself, and desiring to be considered only in the light of an English layman*, 1804

William Elliston, as in almost all matters, remains a mysterious figure as far as the politics of the Revolutionary and Napoleonic period in Cambridge are concerned. One imagines that while he had liberal views, he was completely loyal to the church and state and would not have welcomed Jacobin sentiments among his fellowship and students. The legal writers Samuel March Phillips (1797), who was a highly influential permanent under-secretary for home affairs during the Chartist era, and Jabez Henry (1803), an anti-slavery writer and pioneer in international law, were perhaps the kind of students he would have been particularly satisfied with during his last years.

One curious episode, which casts an uncertain light on Elliston during this time, concerns a fellow, John Luke, son of an Exeter merchant who had gone to Sidney from Eton as a pensioner in 1786. A correspondence between the two men is preserved in the Muniment Room and tells a tale of spiritual conversion, secession and insanity.

Following a sermon he preached before the university in November 1800, Luke resigned his fellowship in autumn 1801. The sermon, on 'The Afflictions of England, a Warning from God', which he said was influenced by 'the signs of the times', was intended to prescribe 'the very principal of all the means which my Countrymen may be enabled to employ, whether for the re-establishment of the health of the kingdom, for the promotion of the peace of the whole world, or for the attainment of higher degrees of social happiness than ever yet have been enjoyed upon the earth'. The text Luke preached upon was Psalm 127, 'Except the Lord Build the House, their Labour is but lost that built it; except the Lord keep the City, the Watchman waketh but in vain'. Luke saw the war of the time as divine retribution and warned against the ultimate worldly punishment, 'the blotting out of the very name of a country from under heaven'. He bewailed the 'numerous and very grievous offences of this disordered country, as they pass in contemplation before my mind, and disquiet and depress my spirit'. In urging that 'obedience to the laws both of the Church and State be more seriously considered' he had moved appreciably away from a strongly orthodox sermon of 1794 on 'The Defence of the Constitution in Church and State', based on the Epistle of St Peter, 11:17, 'Love the Brotherhood: Fear God: Honor the King'. Now he was proposing 'unity among Christians' and desiring that 'no subject of earthly governors neglect the duty of subjection to the King of all Kings'.

These views would have had for many a whiff of sedition about them. In what exact circumstances Luke resigned his fellowship is not known, yet clearly he had had an intense spiritual awakening and was among the earliest of those nonconformist seceders from the Church of England, many of whom were based in the west country, and who caused alarm in official quarters. In 1804, living in Exeter, Luke published *The Avowal of Secession* in which he announced that 'having been born again, having been born a Christian, and not without the affections of Christianity, I belong also a native subject to a Kingdom not of this World; the Kingdom of Israel'. He gave the opinion that the Church of Rome was a 'sanctuary more safe than the Church of England', and that he was duty-bound to spread the word by all means, in particular through pamphlets. In a follow-up 'Link', Luke asked for people to support him by buying his pamphlets so that he might both minister to them spiritually and not starve. In this Link he explained that he would pray not only for England but for all countries 'under Heaven, rulers, and, ruled, Head, and Feet, together; the religious establishments of the Earth'.

Luke was aware of the impression he was giving to his readers, who 'not without grounds to conclude that mysteriousness about my disposition, and manners, since secession from the Church of England, and during the alarms of invasion by France, may have occasioned a distrust of my attachment to the peace of my native country'. The 'mysteriousness' refers to what was clearly a severe mental breakdown, evidence for which survives in his bizarre correspondence with Elliston. Luke sent Elliston notice of his *Avowal* in February 1804, and in August wrote asking for money. 'Think not, Sir, let me intreat you, that I regret, in the least, because of poverty, the step which I have taken, in secession, my persuasion being that all are safe...A small sum, gift, or, loan, which might take, but, a trifle, allow me to suppose, Sir, out of your

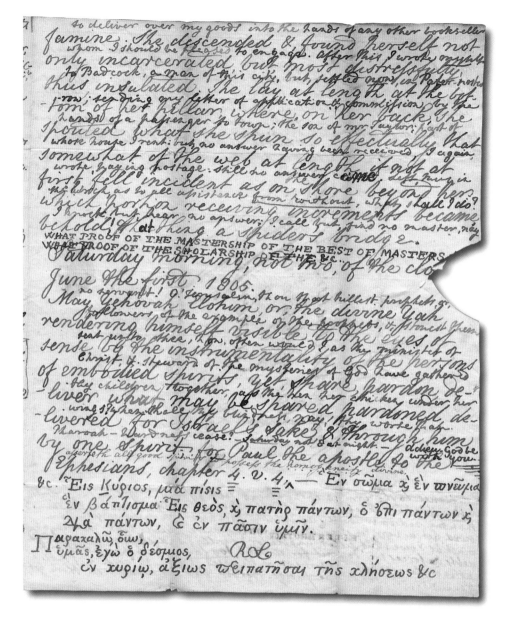

Letter from Robert Luke to William Elliston, 1805, showing the bizarre style of address Elliston received from the former Sidney fellow after his secession from the Church of England

purse.' Elliston's reply apologised for his delay in getting back: 'My only difficulty has been to ascertain what was to be understood by a small sum or trifle'. He enclosed a draft for £15 that could be drawn on Twining's bank, and received a reply that must have alerted him to Luke's state of mind. He could not, said Luke, accept the cheque as it was made out to the 'Reverend Robert Luke', a title he had rejected 'to renounce the pretensions of my-former-self….I dare not, as I value the safety of my-present-self, encourage the continuation of that title…As the Revd. R. Luke, behold! I am no more; being dead and gone; gone, off, as if I had never trodden on the stage of human life; yet, as being the present Mr. R. Luke, the same being the late Revd. or, he who was lately the Revd. R. Luke B.D. etc, etc, etc, behold! I live.'

In his reply Elliston suggested that Luke simply draw his pen 'across the offensive word', to which the seceder sent further responses asking the master to make out a new cheque, at one point writing in large letters: '*Be an honest man, Bob*', and wondering what he was to make of Elliston's 'mysteriousness'. He describes himself as a physician 'much more able depend upon it to cure the disorders of a beloved Master than even the renowned Dr. Willis [Francis Willis, a contemporary physician, famous for treating George III's madness]….Oh! dear, what can the matter be? Are you dilemmaed, or reluctant on some other account; dissatisfied with yourself or disgusted with me, because not capable of administering smooth recipes, where rough ones best consult the state of the receptions, whose palate may be somewhat out of order, either as fungous, tender, or as callous, hard…Give me leave to proceed *as if by your bedside*. You cannot unless not yourself, I mean, unless not, now, what once, at any time, in the days of former years, in the days of old, unless not, now, what, Olim, you appeared to me to be, unless not, now, Dr. Elliston.' Elliston sent him a new draft and wrote to Thomas Twining's family bank a note saying the original one was unsatisfactory to Luke, 'from some unnecessary scruples, arising probably from a deranged state of mind'. One wonders if Luke knew a fellow Devonian, Edward Spry, described as a 'doctor in philosophy and medicine' when a mature student at Sidney in the 1770s. Spry was a well-known Plymouth experimental physician who was a freemason, cabalist and musician, who reputedly lived on one gooseberry a day during summer months.

Further letters from Luke during 1805, the year of Trafalgar, become increasingly bizarre in their language and calligraphy, using Greek and Hebrew and yet still asking for money to deal with 'my extreme of poverty'. A handbill in 1806 announced a series of evening lectures Luke was to give at the 'Hotel-Assembly-Room' in Exeter on 'the structure of the English language', with front seats costing three shillings and back seats one shilling. Elliston, who presumably had no intention of attending the talks, replied to Luke's query as to whether he should ask the masters of Cambridge colleges if he could deliver such lectures and whether he could wear his MA gown, that the first matter was unnecessary but that to wear 'Academical habit' would be inappropriate. Elliston then wondered if the new undertaking would really appeal to the inhabitants of Exeter, 'not that I object to the subject or doubt your ability'.

Luke disappears into obscurity after this, Sidney paying his brother his annual emoluments in order, it seems, to have him looked after. A few letters to local newspapers show him continuing to act as a nonconformist proselytiser, and an advertisement in 1808 announced, in the interests of world peace, a Greek translation of 'Rule Britannia' along with a new verse encouraging a universalism among all peoples. Robert Luke was living with his nephew John in Exeter when he died in 1844, the senior fellow at Sidney, his resignation of 1800 unrecognised by the College.

CHAPTER 7

'Wanted – a Few Freshmen' 1813–1843

So huzza for all Tutors and Lectures
And for our able promoters of knowledge,
And the rest of our learned protectors,
Not forgetting the Cooks of the College.
And long may a Tutor be found
To explain Dr. Gall's lucubrations,
And his humbugging system profound
Of prancing and proud botherations.

— Edward Smedley, fellow 1812–16, 'On E D Clarke'

WILLIAM ELLISTON'S DEATH in 1807, in the midst of the war against France, ended an era and ushered in a period of difficult change. Three masters followed Elliston in quick succession before William Chafy took over in 1813. Sidney's fellowship in 1807 was not as strong as it had been a few years before. George Butler had taken over at Harrow in 1805 and could not easily consider such a quick return to Cambridge. Thomas Hosking, a migrant from Peterhouse, and William Chafy, were the only current fellows keen to be considered. Edward Pearson, a former fellow and now vicar at the Sidney living of Rempstone in Nottinghamshire, declined an invitation to apply by those opposed to Hosking and Chafy.

Out of the past appeared Professor F J H Wollaston, son of the astronomer Francis who had been a Sidney undergraduate in the 1780s, Senior Wrangler, Smith's prizeman, Taylor Lecturer and, from 1785, a fellow at Trinity Hall. A Fellow of the Royal Society, he had been made Jacksonian Professor in 1792, lecturing on chemistry and

OPPOSITE: *View of Sidney from the south, steel engraving by Ebenezer Challis, published by R Backhouse, 1845*

Two Sidney Organists

Sidney had two important west-country organists in the early 19th century. Joseph Kemp, the Bristol Cathedral organist, took his MusB in 1808 and his MusD in 1809 with an anthem, 'The Crucifixion'. Kemp went on to become a popular composer and a major exponent of musical education for children.

Edward Hodges was born to a nonconformist father in Bristol and became an organist and composer there at Clifton and St Nicholas's churches. He took a MusD at Sidney in 1825, and wrote widely on music. Unable to get a cathedral post because of his dissenting background, Hodges travelled with his family to America in 1838 and was appointed organist at St John's Episcopal church and then, in 1846, to the newly opened Trinity Church, Wall Street. The organ there was built to his specifications. He composed psalms, hymns and other religious music, continued to write, and had an enormous impact on American church music. Hodges died in Bristol in 1863.

Trinity Church, Wall Street, by John Forsyth, 1847. Museum of the City of New York

'experimental philosophy'. In 1794, he became vicar at South Weald, Essex, where a fine marble plaque with a profile portrait still hangs on the wall. The rather macabre inscription reads:

> 'He Went To Bed
> In Perfect Health 11th October 1823, And Was Found
> A Corpse
> On Sunday Morning
> Reader Reflect.'

Wollaston was a highly distinguished man and his supporters, such as George Butler, had hoped that this, along with his family and academic connections with the College, would avoid the statutory problems that in fact arose. He was confident, too, apparently having ordered the pruning of fruit trees in the Master's Garden in advance of the election, at least according to Henry Gunning, the chief Cambridge gossip of the period. Following the election in February 1807, which Wollaston won by a good margin, Chafy, who had only received one vote, immediately objected that Wollaston had never been a fellow at Sidney, nor at Trinity, and was therefore ineligible. He appealed to the Visitor, Captain Sir John Shelley-Sidney, father of the first Lord De L'Isle and Dudley. The Visitor was also being approached by Trinity, which had a claim on the mastership in default of a Sidney candidate. Sir John declared the election void and ordered a new election from among former fellows. Edward Pearson agreed to stand this time and was elected in January 1808.

'Orthodox Churchman': Edward Pearson

It is not unusual with us, at Sidney, to admit by proxy. —William Elliston to Henry
Hankey, Rector of East Bergholt, on admitting Pearson on his recommendation, 1778

Edward Pearson, son of a Norwich wool-stapler, was noted by the rector at East
Bergholt, Suffolk, as an exceptionally bright pupil at Ipswich Grammar School, and
entered Sidney as a sizar in 1778. Pearson was a favourite of William Elliston and John
Hey, who appointed him his curate at Passenham in 1781. A Norrisian prize-winner
for an essay on the goodness of God, and author of a piece in the *Gentleman's Magazine*
arguing against the number of capital offences in Britain, Pearson had become a fellow
and tutor in 1788. During his time at Rempstone from 1797, when he was married,
he became a noted preacher and a strongly orthodox religious controversialist who
wrote against secession from the established church. He opposed lay preaching and
favoured a ritualistic revival. Pearson gave sermons intended to persuade dissenters and Catholics in his area to reconcile themselves to the Church of England. In
1807 he was made Warburtonian Lecturer at Lincoln's Inn. Like Wollaston, Edward
Pearson was a man of considerable distinction and a fitting successor to Elliston.

Pearson's position as a staunch defender of Anglicanism is clear from his writings
against the doctrinal errors he observed in the moral philosophy of William Paley,

BELOW LEFT: *Monument
to F J H Wollaston, South
Weald church, Essex 1823*

BELOW RIGHT: *Edward
Pearson, engraving by
W C Edwards, after a
drawing by W M Bennett,
1808*

the most influential Cambridge theologian of his day, and a writer much admired by Thomas Twining. A more serious attack was levelled against evangelical church-men, whose Calvinism he found to contain 'certain gloomy, harsh and revolting doctrines'. He attacked John Venn's friend Charles Simeon, the leading evangelical of the time, for the use of the term 'evangelical', which 'by arrogating so much to yourselves, was directly calculated to derogate from the just claims of others'. In his articles for the magazine *Orthodox Churchman* he wrote against David Hume's refuta-tion of miracles.

Pearson moved in elevated political circles, and was a close friend and advisor to the Tory, anti-Catholic prime minister, Spencer Perceval, who had come into office in 1807. Perceval, who was assassinated in 1812, strongly supported Pearson's proposal for a 'ritual professorship in divinity' at Cambridge, although nothing came of the proposal in the face of university indifference. A Vice-Chancellor, noted theo-logian, committed parish priest and defender of the faith, Pearson died suddenly in 1811, aged 55, of an apoplectic fit suffered while walking in his garden at Rempstone. Sidney was thrown back into confusion.

'A Wretched Pale, Unhealthy Object': John Davie DD

> Mr. Smedley desired me to tell you that this Vice Chancellor was a year and half ago, a healthy hale country curate. High College living and the change from an active to seden-tary life have brought him suddenly to this sad pass.
> —Maria Edgeworth to her half-brother, C Sneyd Edgeworth, on meeting John Davie, May 1813

Pearson's successor was not William Chafy, as some had expected. Chafy was on a driving tour through the Lake District and the north of England with the Sidney fellow William Gee, and was not expecting a mastership election. Hearing about the death of Pearson while in Liverpool, he returned in great haste to Cambridge in late August, a few days too late to enter the competition. The successful candidate was the 34-year-old fellow, John Davie, a Suffolk farmer's son who had gone to Sidney as a sizar in 1794.

Davie was described in a letter the Anglo-Irish novelist Maria Edgeworth wrote to her half-brother about a visit to Sidney in May 1813 to meet Edward Smedley, a newly appointed fellow from Trinity who went on to win the Seatonian prize no less than four times: 'Thursday we went to breakfast with Mr. Smedley. It had been a dreadfully rainy night, but luckily the rain ceased in the morning, on purpose for us. In Sidney College we found your friend Mr. Smedley in neat cheerful rooms, with orange fringed curtains, pretty drawings, and prints – a breakfast table as neatly and plentifully prepared as you would have had it for his friends – Coffee, tea, tongue, cold beef, exquisite bread and many *inches* of butter...Mr. Smedley made us feel at home at once, Mrs. E made tea – I coffee...'

After touring the grander colleges, the party returned to Sidney where Maria's father gently chastised Professor Samuel Vince for not having acknowledged his ideas about carriage springs in an essay in the *Cyclopedia*. Edgeworth continues: 'After having recruited our strength with sandwiches, and by talking, and laughing, we set out again to the Vice chancellor Davie's, to see a famous picture of Oliver Cromwell. As we knocked at his Vice-Chancellorship's door Mr. Smedley said to me, "Now Miss E if you would but settle in Cambridge! Here is our Vice-Chancellor a batchelor...*do* consider about it."

'We went upstairs – found the Vice Chancellor's room empty; had leisure before he appeared to examine the fine picture of Cromwell, in which there is more the expression of greatness of mind and determination, than the usual character of Presbyterian hypocrisy. This portrait seems to say *"Take away that bauble"* not *"I am seeking the lord – (that is looking for the corkscrew)."*

'The Vice chancellor entered – and such a wretched pale, unhealthy object I have seldom beheld! He seemed crippled, and writhing with rheumatic pains, and scarcely able to walk. After a few minutes had passed, Mr. Smedley came round to me, and whispered "Have you made up your mind?" "Yes – quite – thank you." Saw the vice Chancellor's fine apartments and the Chapel – He poor man shivering (as well he might) with the cold; My father comforted him by suggesting that the whole building, and the eating hall, could be warmed with hot cockles for £50 – made our curtsies – bows and thanks and walked off.'

Then there were none: Davie lasted less than six months and died in October 1813, aged 36, leaving the way clear for William Chafy.

Edward Smedley. Engraving by W Holl after a miniature, frontispiece to Poems by the late Rev. Edward Smedley, A.M, *1837*

'Such a Scene of Perjury': Frederick Kendall, Arsonist

I suppose you know he has published minutes of the trial of that Mr. Kendal [*sic*] who was accused of having set fire to Sidney-College and who, though *brought off* by the talents of Garrow on the trial, was so generally thought to be guilty and to have escaped only by a quirk of law, that he has been expelled the University. —Maria Edgeworth, letter to her half-brother C Sneyd Edgeworth about Edward Smedley's minutes of the trial of Frederick Kendall, May 1813

Maria Edgeworth's reference to fires at Sidney concerns an extraordinary series of attempts to burn down the College in 1812 and 1813. The first fire was discovered late one night in April 1812 in an uninhabited room when, 'by prompt exertion', Gunning writes, 'the flames were extinguished'. In its wake Sidney offered £200 and the university £300 for information leading to a conviction. The Prince Regent even offered a free pardon to any accomplice who came forward. Nothing was forthcoming. The arsonist struck again in May when an attic was set on fire in the Clerke range of Chapel Court. This time it was serious; £500-worth of damage was caused and the fire was stopped just short of a loft full of tar and pitch. Nothing further happened until late January 1813, when rooms in both the north wing of Hall Court and in the Clerke range were found ablaze.

The suspect was Frederick Kendall BA, a Yorkshireman and 'heir to a considerable fortune', who had migrated from Trinity in 1810. Kendall had apparently spent the evening of 29 January going about Sidney cursing his tutors and many others for his failure to gain honours in his BA, and had been seen by the porter, William Parkinson, coming down the staircase from one of the fires. Kendall lied when confronted in his room that night, saying he had been in bed during the critical period. It seemed an open-and-shut case.

Kendall's family (his father was a notable rear-admiral), acquired the services of the solicitor-general, Sir William Garrow, to defend him. The trial was a national sensation, as accounts in the *Times* and other papers attest. The *London Packet* reported on 22 March 1813: 'Before the Solicitor-General had finished the cross-examination of Paterson [sic] the watchman, such a scene of perjury was displayed that Mr. Kendall was immediately acquitted.' According to the *Cambridge Chronicle*, not only Kendall's friends but the jury itself rushed up to congratulate the young defendant.

Cambridge Lent Assizes may have acquitted Kendall but Sidney, under John Davie, sent him down 'in consequence of the events which have lately taken place'. Smedley published anonymously his own account of the trial, giving Sidney's position, correcting various errors, and pointing out that Parkinson the night porter was 'an artless and illiterate man…(who) could not even read the posters seeking the arrest'. There is still a mystery to be explained, however: a few days after the trial a fifth fire was started at Sidney. This was reported only in the *Times* and the *Gentleman's Magazine*. If Kendall was still in Cambridge, that might explain it; if not, we might need to look for a different culprit for the fires.

Kendall reappears only three years later, in 1816, as the anonymous author of *A Descriptive Catalogue of the Mineral and Fossil Organic Remains of Scarborough and Vicinity*. The book's anonymity was no doubt due to Kendall's recent notoriety. It is a pioneering piece of geological work drawing on the 'catastrophist' ideas of the famous geologist William Buckland. Kendall's knowledge of the palaeontological literature, according to a recent scholar, was 'phenomenal', and he must have been working on the catalogue while at Cambridge. His Sidney tutor was Josiah Rowles Buckland, a noted mathematician, who was related to William Buckland; William's father Charles had been at Sidney in the late 1760s. Charles and William Buckland

Pensioner   Fellow Com.nr

SIDNEY SUSSEX COLLEGE.

Sidney academical dress, early 19th century

OPPOSITE: *William Chafy, by an unknown artist, c1813*

had both been at Blundell's School, reinforcing these close Sidney links. Kendall later became a vicar at Riccall in Yorkshire, married and had two sons and, ironically, became a magistrate in the East Riding.

'Horror and Beauty': William Chafy and his Travels

> Thy choice has been th'enlighten'd mind,
> The lib'ral heart, and soul combin'd, –
> And to reward thee, Heav'n
> Thy hospitable wish to aid,
> Together with the lovely maid
> A splendid dow'r had giv'n!
> —Charles Shrubsole Bonnett to his tutor William Chafy on his election as master, October 1813

William Chafy's was the most controversial mastership in Sidney's history, if we exclude the short tenure of Joshua Basset. He was the eldest son of a former Sidney Fishmongers' Fellow who had become a minor canon at Canterbury Cathedral and who sent his boy to the King's School. From there William went to Corpus Christi as a sizar in 1796, and then migrated to Sidney where a near contemporary of his was the unfortunate John Davie. The number of undergraduates at this time was very small, around 25 in total. Chafy was elected a fellow in 1801, and as we have seen was a contender for the mastership in 1807, and then successful in October 1813.

Chafy was academically ordinary and this aspect of his career is marked by only two published sermons, one on the invasion scare of 1803 and the other at the time of George IV's coronation in 1820. However, Chafy was a cultivated man who travelled widely and had a great interest in architecture and the visual arts. Some of his diary accounts of his tours through the Lake District, the Peaks and Scotland in 1811, and later of the West Country, Wales, the Channel Islands and Germany, demonstrate an enormous energy and curiosity. His language is conventional for the time, dwelling on 'the awfulness with which the mind is struck', the 'horror and beauty' and sublimity, on encountering mountains and certain buildings. Yet he had a good eye for the newly fashionable Gothic architecture; when he visited Fingal's Cave he noted 'the fine Gothic Arch' formed by natural forces, and wrote knowledgeably about the great English cathedrals. It seems likely that his early trips helped inspire the changes he made to Sidney's buildings during the 1820s.

Chafy also visited fast-growing industrial cities such as Manchester and Liverpool, and popular sites such as Arkwright's Mill. He was a high-ranking freemason, a chaplain-in-ordinary to four monarchs, a fellow of the Royal Horticultural Society and a prize-winning cultivator of grapes, cucumbers and peaches. Chafy was made a fellow of the Zoological Society of London at the suggestion of his friend Francis Henson, and was a strong and active supporter of the plans for new botanic gardens in Cambridge. It was Chafy who asked for designs from the architect Edward Lapidge in 1826 that were the basis for the new layout, which was realised in the 1840s.

Chafy married Mary Westwood of Chatteris shortly after his election and the couple produced a much-loved son, William Westwood, who was sent to Eton and went on to be a Sidney undergraduate in 1833, famous as 'Sidney's Pride' for his great height and build and his passion for fox hunting. Anthony Trollope wrote that he rode after William Westwood 'as a mark' to test his own prowess, and proposed: 'If he would give him an honourable mention in his threatened Hunting Memoirs, he in return would introduce him in a domestic scene in one of his novels.' William Westwood's 'promise of brilliance', a family historian wrote, 'practically went to the dogs' at Cambridge. He travelled widely in Britain with his father and in the 1830s undertook a lengthy voyage to India and China, his correspondence with the master showing that he was being encouraged throughout to 'remember your classical authors'. In 1837 William Westwood was given rooms in the Lodge, along with three hunting horses, a hack and the use of a phaeton. His wife and children lived there with him in the early years of their marriage.

'Loudly and Vehemently': Chafy, 'Tory of Tories'

The iron dart of persecution, envenomed with the poison of malice, ceases not to wound and lacerate those amongst us who are most eminent for piety and virtue. —William Chafy, A Sermon Preached at the Parish Church of Gillingham…, 1803

William Chafy, in the robes of a doctor in divinity, engraved by J Agar after a drawing by Thomas Uwins, from Ackermann's History of the University of Cambridge, *1815*

Chafy was renowned as a 'Tory of the Tories' and his election emphatically signalled the end of Sidney's long identification with the Whigs. In 1813 he was among the fellows who recorded in the College minutes that 'whereas it is understood that a Club called the Wig Club is established within the College contrary to all academic Discipline and propriety, it was agreed…that the Society's Disapprobation of all such Meetings be strongly expressed'. Chafy was later responsible for reviving 'The Family Over the Water', a Jacobite club whose members hosted dinners at which long clay pipes were smoked. He objected strongly to Catholic emancipation, and in 1825 presented an address to the Duke of York praising him for his resistance to the measure, which was finally passed in 1829. This was also the occasion when Chafy was the victim of a hoax carried on through the letters page of the *Cambridge Courier*. A gently inflammatory letter was published purporting to be from the Sidney master dissociating the heads of colleges from the corporation of Cambridge over the matter. Two letters were then received by the *Courier* three days later, one from the real Chafy, one not, but both denying authorship of the first letter. The editor chose the wrong one as authentic, causing Chafy to react furiously when it was printed alongside his own, which was dismissed as a forgery. Chafy's tendency to stand on his dignity was perhaps in part due to the fact that, although born in the Archbishop's Palace, he was a sizar at

Corpus who liked to remind people that he was 'descended from an ancient and respectable family in the county of Dorset'.

In 1814 Chafy spoke out against the Chancellor of the university, William, Duke of Gloucester, over his handling of the slavery question. An address to both houses of parliament, sanctioned by the Chancellor, regretting that ministers had not been firm enough on abolition in their negotiations with foreign powers, was to be laid before the Senate at the beginning of commencement week. Chafy, the Vice-Chancellor, was a supporter of the Earl of Liverpool's new administration and, as Gunning recorded, 'objected to the Address *in toto* in the most violent terms…He spoke so loudly and so vehemently, that the parishioners…crowded together in order to learn the cause of this uproar. His Royal Highness at length broke up the meeting without replying otherwise than by merely observing that the language and the tone of the Vice-Chancellor were very unsuitable to the place and the occasion.'

Chafy was not to be deterred. Even though most of the Senate and his colleagues at Sidney were in favour of Gloucester's address, he went back to the Senate with a compliant Sidney fellow, Francis Henson, and voted against it. When the great general Blucher arrived at the Senate House that day to receive an honorary degree, he unexpectedly found himself participating in a vote. The following day Chafy left the Senate House without bowing to the Chancellor and was asked to see him at Trinity Lodge at three o'clock. After waiting three quarters of an hour the Duke learned that Chafy had gone for a ride and was unlikely to return soon.

Chafy's belligerence and rudeness were legendary by the time of his death in 1843. It is no surprise to find that he was not a supporter of William Cobbett, the great social and political reformer. In his *Rural Rides*, Cobbett records a journey to Cambridge during Chafy's second vice-chancellorship, in March 1830, just after the Catholic Emancipation Act was passed: 'We got into Cambridge, about noon, with the intention of my giving a little common sense in this seat of pretended learning. I naturally expected that these pretenders would be eager to see me expose what they would deem my want of learning. Just the contrary; for the Vice-Chancellor, having the jurisdiction of the whole place, play-house and all, as far as related to matters of this sort, refused to let me lecture either at the play-house, or any where else. Intelligence of this had been sent me to Ely; but it arrived after I came away.'

'Music and Revelry at Sidney Gardens': Chafy's Hospitality

> The Sun is sinking on the couch of Night,
> And with his milder eye beholds the scene
> Adorn'd, ye stately groves! With liveliest green,
> And with his lustre brighter makes the bright!
> —William Pulling (1809), 'Written in the College Walks of Cambridge', 1840

Although Gunning considered Chafy a 'covetous' man in his business dealings, he also acknowledged that socially he was extremely generous. His lavish entertainments in the Lodge and gardens at Sidney were as celebrated as his outbursts in the

Senate House. Following his appointment to a second term as Vice-Chancellor, he organised a party for members of the Senate and revived what in recent years had been a failing annual event by the lure of his remarkable wine cellar, which reputedly stood at 600 dozen bottles.

Gunning recalled a huge party in 1835: 'Chafy's entertainments were always on a costly scale; and I believe nothing pleased him better than to provide the most choice wines that could be procured, and to see them freely taken. I can well remember that at the Installation of the Marquis of Camden in 1835, he gave a sumptuous breakfast in Sidney Gardens. Many amongst his guests were obliged to dine with the Vice-Chancellor at Jesus College. On returning from this dinner between eleven and twelve o'clock, we heard the sound of music and revelry at Sidney Gardens. Several of us…agreed to go in by way of finish. We found in a large marquee Dr. Chafy and

A Rustic Seat

Engraving of Sidney gardens and the Master's Lodge, by John Le Keux, from Memorials of Cambridge, 1841

Sidney's gardens have always been greatly admired and bear witness to hundreds of years of history. They were the site of many grand entertainments during William Chafy's mastership. In 1833 the *Cambridge Chronicle* reported that the remaining stem of an old pear tree supposedly planted by Cromwell had been cut down, leaving four dead stems still visible. The *Chronicle* wrote, 'It is intended to erect a rustic seat within the area which they embrace'.

many distinguished guests who had been enjoying his good fare. There were even at that late hour the remains of a splendid dessert upon the table, and about two hundred persons were dancing or walking about the garden. I used frequently to hear about Chafy's boast, with much apparent satisfaction, of the quantity of champagne and other expensive wines that were consumed on that occasion.'

It is no wonder that Chafy suffered extremely painful attacks of gout, his diaries showing that these started as early as 1819. By the winter of 1836 he complained of gout, fog, damp, snow, and 'rheumatic pains all over me'. These attacks did not make him a relaxed master. When two men he encountered in Hall Court in 1834 refused to identify themselves to him he had the College gates locked. He stuck his tongue out at them, shouted in a 'loud and imperious' tone, and ordered a constable to arrest them, only to discover that one was a solicitor who brought a suit of false imprisonment against Chafy. Lord Chief Justice Denham found in favour of the two men to the tune of £25 each. That Chafy reputedly twice kicked down a neighbouring wall of which he did not approve, seems entirely in keeping with his approach to most things.

'A Very Whited Sepulchre': Wyattville's Transformation of Sidney

Unfortunately, the style chosen was 'Elizabethan Gothic', – to be indulgently viewed now in the light of other days… —Rev. W K W Chafy, *Gesta Chaforum*, 1910

We have seen that while Frederick Kendall was attempting to burn down Sidney in 1812 and 1813, he was also undertaking significant research into the minerals and fossils of Yorkshire. Much of the impetus for such study at the time came not only from intellectual curiosity but also from attempts to discover coal and other useful minerals. It is interesting, therefore, that from the proceeds of leasing mineral-rich lands the College largely financed an architectural transformation of Sidney that was, in its own way, almost as drastic as the outcome Kendall was intending.

At the November 1813 audit, the fellowship agreed to lease part of the Dudley estate to raise money for further scholarships and the purchase of more advowsons; Sidney had very few livings to offer fellows compared with most other colleges. Dudley was the land bequeathed by Samuel Taylor nearly a century earlier to support a mathematical lectureship. Taylor had anticipated the value of his estates increasing due to the rich seams of coal beneath it, in which case he desired any income should go towards mathematical scholarships only. The College therefore had to wait some years to get two acts of parliament passed to allow for the money raised to be used for other purposes. The act of 1818 had the mines vested in trustees. It allowed the College to spend up to £100 on mathematical books and scientific instruments and up to £4,000 on what became the mathematical library in the 1820s. A further act in 1823 permitted Sidney to spend another £4,500 on providing rooms for the new Taylor scholars.

The acts also allowed Sidney to divert the money towards building works, rather than to purchase livings. Thus the heavy focus on mathematics at Cambridge during

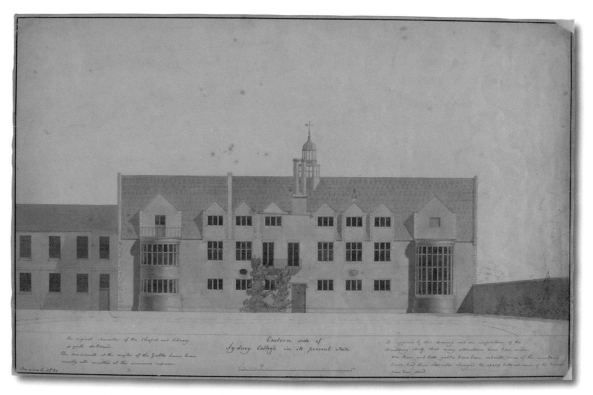

Drawing of the eastern front of the College by Wyatville before remodelling, 1821

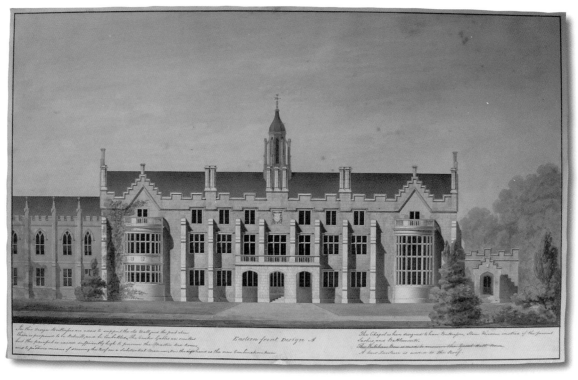

Drawing of the eastern front of the College by Wyatville to show how it would look after remodelling, 1821

the period, the requirements of Taylor's will and, above all, Chafy's architectural ambitions, were satisfied by the outcome of the two acts. In the event, the building works of the 1820s and 1830s cost about £14,000, of which £8,500 came from the Taylor monies. The outstanding sum was supplied by vacating fellowships, reducing dividends, selling stock, borrowing from the College treasury, and by Chafy's personal generosity.

Chafy was motivated by a desire to improve Sidney's appearance, by a need for new accommodation for an expanding number of students since the end of the Napoleonic Wars, and by a simple urge for self-aggrandisement. Such schemes were common in Cambridge in the 1820s and 1830s, where some form of Gothic style was prevalent for new college building; Corpus Christi, St John's and King's are notable examples. Chafy turned to the fashionable Jeffry Wyatt (from 1824, by royal authority, 'Wyatville'), who was renowned for his reworking of old buildings in a rather picturesque and romantic way entirely in keeping with the taste that made Sir Walter Scott's novels so popular. The two men became friendly, and in 1821 Sidney took Wyatville's son, the short-lived architectural artist George Geoffrey, as a fellow-commoner.

Wyatville drew up three alternative proposals that included a survey of the existing fabric and some beautiful drawings produced by his office. Chafy eventually decided to go for a more radical, and more expensive, option; the alternative would have preserved far more of the ancient appearance of the building. The result met with mixed reactions at the time, followed by a near universal opprobrium brutally summarised in Nikolaus Pevsner's authoritative judgement: 'There is no getting away from the fact that Sidney Sussex College is architecturally the least attractive of the old colleges in the universities.'

At the time of Wyatville's alterations, however, there was none of the high regard for old red brick that we take for granted today. Chafy would have concurred with Richard Harraden's opinion of 1809, that Sidney's brick was 'so gloomy, that no correctness of form or distribution of parts can counteract its impression', and with John Storer's of 1835, that before Wyatville Sidney was a 'misshapen and unsightly house'. The novelist Samuel Philip's description of Sidney as a 'very whited sepulchre' in 1844 expresses a view that grew in strength as the 19th century wore on, but was not universal at the time. By the end of the century most photos of Sidney show it was an opinion held by the College, the extraordinary shaggy appearance created by vast growths of ivy being, for most students, the classic Sidney look for many years.

Wyatville had also suggested a classically styled 'museum' in the garden, with a portico facing onto Jesus Lane alongside some new residential properties; a grand carriage drive from the northeast corner of the garden to the Master's Lodge; and a covered arcade along the Sidney Street side of the two courts as 'a promenade for the use of the Students'. Expense and taste prevented these from being built, though it might be imagined that Chafy, who later remodelled the gardens in the form they largely take today, was sorely tempted by the carriage way.

What Sidney got in terms of additional space, mainly achieved during two phases of building in 1822–23 and 1831, were an expanded Master's Lodge, a Mathematical

Library, a new Combination Room, and additional student accommodation, mainly in the roofs of the three ranges. The new accommodation was fitted out to high modern standards and considerably enhanced the comfort of the inhabitants, especially that of the master. In particular, the student rooms were lighter and had many more modern conveniences. Along with this expansion, a considerable amount of structural repair was undertaken, most of which is now hidden, and included the strengthening of the walls of the Master's Lodge and Hall, which were badly impaired by the weight of the old roof, and new roofs tiled with fashionable grey Welsh slate.

The most striking feature of Wyatville's work is undoubtedly the new gate tower above the entrance porch, with its Gothic ribbed vaulting and carved heads and bosses, allowing access into either of the front courts and replacing the classical gate from the time of Parris and Elliston, which is now in the far northeast corner of the garden. Begun in 1831, the tower, built from stone like the new front of the Master's Lodge, dominates narrow, curving Sidney Street and makes a powerful impression. In spite of this strong vertical emphasis, however, the tower, like all of the work done by Wyatville, is decoratively restrained, even austere. The crow-stepped gables and drip-moulds are in no sense fanciful, even though they were not part of Sidney's original buildings. This was typical of the architect's aesthetic, to be found in his greatest project, Windsor Castle, as well as at smaller country houses such as Golden Grove in Carmarthen. He regarded this look, in describing his work at Longleat, Wiltshire, as 'in the manner of the days of Queen Elizabeth'. Even the refaced and newly-porched Chapel, paid for by Chafy, was restrained, though far more 'Gothic' than the 'Old English' look achieved elsewhere at Sidney. Mrs Chafy, who died in

Watercolour by Wyatville's office of the projected remodelling of the College, viewed from the north side of the Fellows' Garden

Cambridge, Sidney Sussex College.

1831, was buried in the new Chapel as Wyatville's remodelling of the College was being completed.

'A Bad One and a Sham': Thackeray and Henry Matthew

Chafy wanted Sidney to take more wealthy students and fewer poor ones in order to change its political and social culture; the income was useful, too. Names in the College register such as Zachariah Shrapnel Warren, Poyntz Seymour Stewart, Gostwick Prideaux, Vicesimus Knox Child, Martin Cramp Tolputt and Horatio Folliot Nelson, evoke a whole period we have come to know through the works of writers such as William Makepeace Thackeray. Men such as the priest, novelist and co-founder of the Athenaeum, Henry Stebbing (1819), and the soldier, priest and author of the verse tragedy *Attila* (1832), Richard McDonald Caunter (1820) are minor figures, but possessed the flair Chafy no doubt admired.

There was a fair degree of misbehaviour during a period when Sidney was not among the 'working' colleges. The statistics for Tripos examinations in mathematics, however misleading and limited in scope, are still the best guide to Sidney's relative academic status until Chafy's death in 1843. Bearing in mind the huge expansion of some colleges and Sidney's usually very small population, and also taking into

The Master's Lodge, postcard, c1890. Private collection

This Frith's postcard shows the Lodge just before the erection of Cloister Court; thus the tower of St John's chapel can be seen in the distance

account the increasing numbers of students submitting to examination, it is apparent that Sidney's performance declined during much of Chafy's mastership. During the 30 years Chafy was master there were 19 Wranglers. This was during a period when the Wrangler list had expanded from about 10 to 15 in Elliston's years, to between about 30 and 45. Elliston's small cadres of students produced 24 Wranglers over 47 years. Chafy, of course, had been much preoccupied with a major building project and university matters during his first 15 years. It seems that when the main phase of building was completed in the early 1830s things began to improve markedly. Thirteen of the Wranglers came after 1830 and paved the way for the improvements and changes of the 1850s and later. Only one of Chafy's students, Perry Nursey in 1822–3, was awarded the wooden spoon for being last among the 'junior optimes'.

Discipline at Chafy's Sidney was probably lax. Although the records are scant for this period, the College minutes record punishments for Joseph Veal in 1821 for 'drunkenness and riotous behaviour'; for Charles Thomas Carpenter in 1825, 'for gross immoral conduct, repeatedly committed, with a female servant of the College'; for William Gattey and John Roe, for 'bringing two lewd women into College'; and for Thomas Artemidorus Russell 'for entertaining…riotous and disorderly company'.

'Little Sidney'

See they advance from every College door;
With waving caps and flowing gowns outpour;
These are the Tufts of Trinity, and these
The Sons of Queens and all that bunch of Caius.
Saint John's sends forth a bacchanalian train,
Corpus peeps forth and skelters back again,
And little Sidney issues all she can,
Her force concentred in a single man.
    —Rev. P V Savile, 'The Snobiad', 1835 – a poem about a battle between town and gown

Savile's poem exaggerates Sidney's size; in fact, as well as the master and fellows, there were 19 undergraduates in total in 1835. Nevertheless, it was a very small college, which, under Chafy, took great pride in the clubability and social standing of its students. It had been much larger in 1815 when *The New Cambridge Guide* put the total population at 74; Trinity had 876. Sidney was larger than only three other colleges. In 1829 Thackeray, in the undergraduate magazine *The Snob*, published a witty advert: 'Sidney Sussex College. Wanted – a few freshmen. Apply at the Butteries where the smallest contributions will be thankfully received.'

One of Thackeray's greatest works, the semi-autobiographical *Pendennis* (1849–50), features Sidney prominently and produced one of the novelist's most memorable characters, Bloundell-Bloundell, based on a notoriously dissolute Sidney undergraduate, Henry Matthew. Matthew was described to Thackeray at the time by Edward Fitzgerald as a 'bad one and a sham'. In *Pendennis*, Arthur Pendennis goes from the significantly named Grey Friars school to the University of Oxbridge, where he enters St Boniface College. Although Thackeray himself went to Trinity, which features in the novel as St George's College, Pendennis arrives at a college with many obvious features in common with Sidney: it is the smallest college in the university, a 'petty hermitage' compared with St George's; 'the best families of certain counties' have time out of mind sent their sons there; it has an old wainscotted hall where, among the portraits, is one of 'Dr Blogg, the late master, and friend of Doctor Johnson, who visited him at St Boniface'. St Boniface is a Devonian saint, which fits well with the 'Bloundell' references.

Pendennis is shocked by the behaviour of many undergraduates in chapel, but, says the narrator, 'these circumstances, it must be remembered, took place some years back, when William the Fourth was king. Young men are much better behaved now, and besides, St Boniface was rather a fast college.'

Pendennis's friendship with Horace Bloundell-Bloundell fictionalises the real relationship Thackeray had with Henry Matthew, the son of a Somerset vicar and a pupil at Blundell's, who had gone up to Balliol, Oxford in 1825. From there, by way of St John's and Trinity, Cambridge, he arrived at Sidney as a pensioner in 1828. He was part of a relatively large intake of 18 young men. In 1830 Matthew was elected president of the Union, following Sidney's Edward Duncan Rhodes, who had been president in 1820, an honour one imagines would have greatly gratified Chafy since the Union, only founded in 1815, was dominated by Trinity and St John's.

Thackeray describes Bloundell-Bloundell, the son of an old Suffolk family of Bloundell-Bloundell Hall, as coming to St Boniface's via Camford University and one or two Oxbridge colleges 'who had refused to receive him'. Bloundell-Bloundell is worldly, cynical and decadent and his fellow undergraduates are all in awe of him. Pen's father warns his son against 'the most popular man in the university', regarding him as 'a most ineligible young man…a low man…there is the unmistakable look of slang and bad habits about' him. 'He frequents low gambling houses and billiard-hells, sir – he haunts third-rate clubs – I know he does. I know by his style…Did you not remark the quantity of rings and jewellery he wore? That person has Scamp written on his countenance…'

The naïve Pen does not heed these words and allows Bloundell-Bloundell and his fast set to tempt him away from study. The 'moral tone' of St Boniface is lowered and the students become 'unruly, and almost ungentleman-like, soon after Mr. Bloundell's arrival'. Pen begins to play dice, drink champagne and deceive his tutor, Mr Buck, into believing he is working hard. Bloundell-Bloundell and Pen travel to London where they go to Bloundell-Bloundell's military club and hang out with 'gallant young fellows'. Inevitably these escapades lead Pen into debt. He is fleeced by cardsharpers introduced to him by Bloundell-Bloundell. He goes down after being 'pluck't' (i.e. having failed) in his third year examinations. Thackeray himself left Trinity after two years, having experienced precisely the same setbacks as his novel's hero under the influence of Henry Matthew. Bloundell-Bloundell reappears in other shorter writings by Thackeray, both by that name and in other guises.

Henry Matthew got his BA from Sidney in 1832, was ordained in 1837, entered a loveless marriage with a 'vulgar wife', and for a while tried to make a living as a poet and writer in London. He was a correspondent of Charles Darwin, with whom he

'Pen's Staircase – 2', by William Makepeace Thackeray from Pendennis *(1848–50)*

This image, from chapter 20 of Thackeray's novel, alludes to the matter of 'a few little bills', the arrival of some of Pen's creditors outside his room at St Boniface and the beginning of his downfall. By now Pen's 'university debts were large… He was as gloomy as a death's-head at parties.' The disgrace is complete when Pen is 'plucked' (failed) in his final examinations

was good friends at Cambridge and to whom he wrote long letters about his financial difficulties. In 1849 Matthew was visited by Thackeray, who found 'an old man in a room smelling of brandy and water at 5 o'clock at Islington', having suffered for many years from paralysis of the legs. As a vicar at Eversholt, Bedfordshire, he was so infirm that he needed hoisting into his pulpit. He died in Brighton aged 54, as the *Gentleman's Magazine* put it in 1861, 'after 20 years of patient suffering'.

'Sidney – that's the College!' Samuel Phillips and *Caleb Stukely*

Thus informed, I set out for the Vice-Chancellor's residence. He was the master of a small college, situated in one of the principal streets of Cambridge. In my time, it was an old and picturesque building, and looked grave and comely; snugly protected as it was by its long brick wall and row of lofty poplar trees. That wall and those poplar trees have since been razed: the edifice has been plastered over, and stands with its immodest glare of pretension, a very whited sepulchre. —Samuel Phillips, *Caleb Stukely*, 1844

Auguste Charles Pugin, Hall of Sidney College, engraving by D Havell for Ackermann's History of Cambridge, *1815. Private collection*

Ackermann's volume was one of the most popular books on Cambridge in the 19th century. The old stone floor is visible and the benches along the walls are still in place

Not all Sidney men were from conventionally privileged backgrounds. If Bloundell-Bloundell was the archetypal Regency rake of the kind with whom Sidney was identified by many during Chafy's mastership, then the author of *Caleb Stukely* was an altogether different Sidney man. Samuel Phillips was the son of a Jewish lamp dealer in London. He was a talented child actor and appeared in an act of *Richard III* at Covent Garden at the age of 14. He studied at the new University of London and at Göttingen before entering Sidney as a pensioner in 1836, intending to take orders in the Church of England. He resided for only one term, due to money problems following his father's death. Like another Jewish and Conservative novelist, the prime minister Benjamin Disraeli, Phillips had converted to Anglicanism because Jews were not allowed to enter Oxford and Cambridge at this time. This he did through the help of Sir Moses Montefiore and the Duke of Sussex. He took over his father's business, which failed, and began to earn a living as a writer. Suffering from consumption, he nevertheless spent the next two decades working as a highly successful journalist, owning and editing the *John Bull* newspaper.

He was a severe and conservative critic of art and literature, disliking the Pre-Raphaelites and considering the main theme of Harriet Beecher Stowe's *Uncle Tom's Cabin* as the violation of property rights. Thackeray claimed that a vicious review by Phillips of *Henry Esmond* in 1852 'absolutely stopped' sales of the book. Phillips was by now literary editor of the *Times*, and was appointed literary director of the Crystal Palace in 1853, for which he wrote a guide. He also founded a society for promoting archaeological excavations in Assyria, before dying, like Henry Matthew, in Brighton, where he had gone for his health.

Phillips's novel *Caleb Stukely* was published in 1844. It tells the story of a young man's journey into adulthood in a narrative that has much in common with Thackeray's *Pendennis*. Indeed, given the similarities in plot and characters, and Phillips's harsh reviews of Thackeray's books, it may be that *Pendennis* was a response to *Caleb Stukely*. Set in the late-18th and early-19th centuries, the story takes the young Caleb up to Cambridge in a coach, which he shares with a motley cast of characters, including an 'Israelitish gentleman', the dirty and dark-skinned Mr Solomon Levy, and a dubious but attractive young gentleman called Mr James Temple. When Caleb tells the latter he is going to Trinity, Temple replies:

THE GRAVE OF ELLEN FAIRMAN.

Frontispiece by William Connell to Caleb Stukely, *by Samuel Phillips, 1844. Private collection*

'Ah, low – shocking low; Trinity is going down very fast. The market is over-stocked, as they say in the city. They have sent out a good young man or two, who, I should guess, have bitten all the *paters* in existence; for they have been mad about Trinity ever since – No, that won't do at all. You must migrate to Sidney – that's the college! Nobody goes there. Select and gentlemanly. Nothing snobbish. Men are friends and brothers – quite a little family.'

Ignoring this advice, Caleb nevertheless ends up at Sidney one day soon after his encounter, duped by Temple into believing he is invited to breakfast by the Vice-Chancellor. Ordered to appear 'in full dress', Caleb arrives at the Master's Lodge:

'I rang gently at the lodge gate, and modestly placed my card in the hand of the well-dressed domestic who opened it. He retired for a quarter of an hour, and then returned, desiring me to follow him up-stairs. During his absence, I had not failed to notice the painful silence that extended through the place. It was not the delicious quiet that I had experienced on the orchard-ground the day before. No, that was the silence of nature and life, cheerful and exhilarating. This was oppressive – the cold and earthy stillness of the tomb. A cough echoed through the house again – once a door slammed, and there rung through the dwelling a long and hideous rever-beration. We passed into a spacious and well-filled library, then through a noble room with polished oaken floors. This looked upon a beautiful and extensive lawn. Shadows of massive floating clouds skimmed the green surface as I softly trod the room, and deepened the sombreness that pervaded the scholastic habitation. Beyond was the drawing-room, an apartment of good dimensions, and literally crowded with costly furniture. Here the lackey stopped, and drawing to the fireplace a bulky chair, capacious enough for four, he begged me to be seated, and then took his leave.

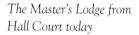

The Master's Lodge from Hall Court today

The Chapel front today

'As it seemed to be the fashion in this establishment to proceed with as little hurry and fatigue as possible, I had ample time afforded me to observe the various sumptuous articles by which I was surrounded; but my curiosity was particularly excited by a small curtain which hung at the far end of the room, evidently concealing something that was held too sacred for the vulgar eye. For some time I fought against my desire, but, unable at length to resist the temptation. I withdrew the curtain, and discovered, not what I had expected to find, the form and feature of some ladye love, but a portrait by Vandyke, painted in all the boldness and truth of that great master, and bearing beneath it the following inscription, "Oliver Cromwell, Protector of England".

'The thunder of another door permitted me only to glance at the portrait and to replace the curtain. The drawing-room opened, and in an invalid's chair, wheeled into my presence by the aforementioned lackey, entered the Vice-chancellor.

'He was a fine man, tall, sinewy, and robust-looking; his chest was broad and manly, his voice strong and sonorous, his face very florid, and his hair white as the purified particles of snow.'

This is obviously Chafy – a reference to 'this infernal gout', as well as the physical description and the lavish furnishings in the refurbished Lodge, are unmistakable. The Vice-Chancellor asks Caleb a few questions that reveal Caleb has been gulled. The old man continues: 'And now, before you go, take a word of advice. If you don't

improve very rapidly, this is likely to be not the last occasion of your being duped. You must be a man, sir – think, act, and feel like a man – oh – oh, this cursed gout.' Hearing from the master a full account of how a sober life and pious study had raised him to the heights of academic achievement, Caleb recalls a very different description of the Vice-Chancellor from his gyp at Trinity who said he remembered 'Chafy' as a young man 50 years before and as a 'mortal wild one'.

OPPOSITE: *The Tower today*

'In No High Repute': Chafy's Fellowship

> How else can we account for my Friend's Extraordinary desire to become a member of Sidney College?... A college, be it remembered, at that time in no high repute – whose external appearance, too, though decent, was inferior to that of many other colleges.
> —James Rickards, *A True Account of Certain Passages in the Life of the Revd. William Broderick* (formerly Ick), 1878

Chafy inherited from Elliston and his immediate successors a number of ageing professorial fellows such as Samuel Vince and Thomas Martyn, and from a younger generation men such as Charles George Renouard, Thomas Mitchell and Edward Smedley. They were all considerable scholars. Renouard was an undergraduate migrant from Trinity in 1800 and became a fellow in 1804. A remarkable linguist and classicist, he served as chaplain to the British embassy at Constantinople and to the factory at Smyrna, where he identified a Hittite figure on a rock at Nymphaion as the Pharaoh Sesostris described by Herodotus. In 1815 he was appointed Lord Almoner's Professor of Arabic, and in 1821 was presented to the Sidney living at Swanscombe, Kent, where he died in 1867. His correspondence with the great European orientalists and geographers of his day maintained the cosmopolitan learnedness of Twining's and Lettice's era. Another classicist, Thomas Mitchell, just missed having Chafy as his master, coming from Pembroke in 1810 as a fellow but being required to resign in 1812 for refusing to take holy orders. This was a great loss to Sidney, as Mitchell went on to become a notable translator of Aristophanes and editor of other Greek texts, as well as a close friend of Byron and Leigh Hunt.

Chafy's own appointments were in the main undistinguished academically. Following improvements to the provision for Taylor exhibitions, and the making of the new mathematical library in the 1820s, he brought in John Hind, a second Wrangler from St John's, and James William Lucas Heaviside, a second Wrangler from Trinity, thus perhaps confirming the opinion of the American student Charles Astor Bristed in the 1840s that small colleges such as Sidney were full of fellows and students from larger colleges who were not quite the very best. Heaviside, a friend of Henry 'Bloundell' Matthew and Charles Darwin, had migrated to Sidney in his second year and became professor of mathematics at Haileybury College. Hind's textbooks went into many editions.

One eccentric fellow who might also have found his way into a Thackeray novel was William Richard Ick, son of a slave overseer in Antigua, who apparently came to Sidney in bizarre circumstances in 1837 at the age of 22, not long after

William Richard (Broder-) Ick, by an unknown artist. Private collection

Samuel Phillips had left. A colleague at Sidney, the fellow James Rickards, later wrote in 1878 *A True Account of Certain Passages* in Ick's life. According to Rickards' satirically and fictionally nuanced tale, Ick's surname was originally Brodrick but an ancestor, having had his legacy reduced from £8,000 to £5,000, shortened it proportionately. William Ick was in the navy for six years before arriving in Cambridge by coach at the Eagle Inn. In the morning he asked a waiter how he could be admitted to Cambridge and, after some misunderstanding, realised he must apply to a particular college. Rickards gives an account of a dream Ick had on his second night in Cambridge. He was 'pacing a city of the dead', looking up to see 'hideous, diabolical heads' all around him before coming to 'the hated corner'. He meets a lady 'attired in Elizabethan costume' who 'seems to lean for sup-port on an ivory-headed cane, and is accompanied by one of the tiniest dogs ever seen'. The lady tells Ick, 'Banish thy sorrow, good youth; thou must come with me to my home, for to thee, and to such as thee, my door shall ever be open'. They walk through the streets 'till they came to a stately mansion, built in the form of the letter "E"' and within which there is a 'fair hall' where they drink 'audit ale'.

The next day Ick walked into the town and looked for 'the old Lady's Mansion'. He came to Sidney, and thinking, 'Ah! I know this place', asked who owned it, to which question he received the reply, 'Dr. Chafy'. He entered Sidney's new porch and talked to a third-year undergraduate, William Towler Kingsley, who introduced him to James Heaviside, the College tutor who was 'curiously learned in all matters pertaining to the culinary art'. Heaviside told Kingsley to turn Ick away as 'our college…has got into bad repute by admitting all kinds of men indiscrim-inately'. The narrator says that though many have prophetic dreams few people today 'have the moral courage to declare them…' Ick bucked the trend and was admit-ted to Sidney. Ick, who changed his name back to Brodrick shortly before Rickards wrote his *True Account*, was a Wrangler in 1841 and went on to become dean, tutor and mathematics lecturer, and was eventually presented to the living at Peasmarsh, something the *True Account* says was anticipated in the dream by Lady Frances offer-ing Ick a 'mash of peas' to eat in hall. Ick died in Weymouth in 1897.

'A Supernatural Visitation': The Sidney Haunting of 1841

The inhabitants of Sidney Sussex College Lodge have lately been alarmed by a super-natural visitation of a very awful description. The following are, as far as we can learn, the circumstances of this extraordinary affair… —*Cambridge Advertiser*, 9 August 1841

It seems appropriate that Ick's dream occurred when it did. Chafy, as described by Phillips, was a frightening old man consumed by gout, 'living in the cold and earthy stillness of the tomb'; the ancient brick of the College had been recently covered in stucco and thus existed in a kind of living deadness; and the popular imagination was fascinated by the Gothic novel, whether Scott's historical tales or the darker imaginings of Thomas Love Peacock. The recent accession of Queen Victoria had also ushered in an age increasingly obsessed with paranormal activity.

On Friday 6 August 1841, very near the end of Chafy's mastership, 'about the dread hour of midnight', according to a new local paper, the *Cambridge Advertiser*, the nursery maids looking after the children of William Westwood Chafy and Annette his wife, Alice Dunford, aged 40, and Eleanor Stern, aged 20, were going to bed when they heard 'several strange and mysterious noises' on the top floor. These noises then ceased and the nursery door 'was slowly opened, and a figure of tall and unnatural proportions presented itself before the horror-struck maids. The appearance had a head white and ghastly, long legs, also white, but the body was distinguished only by a dim outline – The body was a shadow – it was a thing of head and legs; the affrighted maids rushed shrieking from the room – the lodge was aroused – the police was called in, but no trace of the apparition was visible,

Mrs Annette Chafy, née Kyle, first wife of William Westwood Chafy (1833), with her children Mary Anne Elizabeth (b. 1840) and William Kyle Westwood (b. 1841), by an unknown artist

unless a curious odour which perfumed the apartment might be considered so'. Two magistrates made a 'precognition' the following morning, and although the story got into the *Times*, nothing more seems to have disturbed the echoing spaces of the Lodge. The official report noted that doors and windows in the Lodge were locked from the inside, there were no signs of forced entry and all the other occupants had convincing proof that they were asleep at the time. As the *Cambridge Advertiser* put it, 'the affair remains shrouded in mystery'. The older, more staid *Cambridge Chronicle* had not deigned to report the incident at all. Sidney's next publicised supernatural occurrence came in the late-1960s, when an eerie floating head supposedly haunted a staircase in Chapel Court, shortly before it was gutted for renovation.

CHAPTER 8

'Gentlemen Who Also Climb' 1843–1918

'Go travel round the town, my friend, whichever way you please,
From Downing up to Trinity, from Peterhouse to Caius;
Then seek a little college just beside a busy street,
It's name is Sidney Sussex, and you'll find it Bad to Beat.'

—E H Griffiths, chorus to 'A Song of Sidney Sussex', 1900

WILLIAM CHAFY DIED in 1843 leaving Sidney £1,000 towards new livings and books for the library. He had been a devoted and generous master, but his legacy also included a diminution of the College's academic reputation and buildings structurally more sound but aesthetically dubious.

Robert Phelps, Chafy's successor, came to Sidney just as Cambridge began a half-century of profound change of a kind not seen since the period before the College's foundation. With the Prince Consort's election as Chancellor in 1847, the political and administrative domination of Trinity's great master William Whewell, and the influence of Henry Sidgwick's reforming zeal, the university began a lengthy process of self-analysis and transformation, responding to the great social changes of industrialisation, urbanisation, scientific discovery and political reform. The new universities of London and Durham, along with the growing power of German higher education, and the perceived superiority of the Scottish universities, gave urgency to the impetus for reform at Cambridge. Between 1851 and 1905 new subjects were examined in the Tripos in addition to mathematics and classics: moral sciences, natural sciences, law, history, oriental languages, medieval and modern languages, mechanical sciences and economics. Many more undergraduates took honours degrees in 1900 than

OPPOSITE: *Cloister Court from the gardens on the east side. Above the bay window of the Senior Combination Room are the figures, from left to right, of Sir John Harington, Lady Frances Sidney and Bishop James Montagu*

had done in 1850; to some extent, these undergraduates were drawn from a broader social spectrum and in any event were far more numerous.

The growth of properly housed and administered faculties, greatly improved examination systems and a restructured teaching regime took power away from the colleges. In particular, the sciences grew rapidly. The Cavendish Laboratory and the new museums are the architectural symbols of this growth, while Darwin's growing reputation indicates the challenge to the university's religious traditions and the development of a secular and more specialised intellectual ideology.

As well as looking at university governance and curricula, a royal commission began a lengthy process of inquiry into college statutes, privileges, finances and awards. These inquiries met with great resistance, not least from Robert Phelps. The university's privileges with regard to licensing, trading, punishment of prostitutes, and so on, were largely dissolved, and as a result the town's interests became a more powerful factor in Cambridge life. In 1871 a bill was passed removing the age-old religious restrictions and by 1882, when all their statutes had been rewritten, the colleges had changed markedly in character, not least because the celibacy laws were abolished. Fellows could now marry and remain in Cambridge colleges, many of them moving into the growing number of newly built detached houses in the suburbs. Fellows were no longer churchmen, but rather 'dons', a modern professional group who played a central role in British society throughout much of the 20th century. With the growth in student numbers, many undergraduates were now forced to live in lodgings. Most significantly, with the foundation of Girton in 1869 and Newnham in 1871, women changed the social as well as intellectual landscape of Cambridge, though absurdly they were not given full academic parity until 1948.

OPPOSITE: *Robert Phelps, by A E Emslie, 1890*

'*Phelps, when he was ageing, used to be taken round country lanes in his landau. He was passing through Willingham and was attracted by the village. He asked his companion its name. His companion replied, "You should know, Master, because you are its Rector." He was in fact Rector of Willingham from 1848–90, but is only known to have taken two services there, both of them funerals, to which no doubt a fee was attached.'*
—*Thomas Knox-Shaw, Reminiscences, 1972*

'A Besieged Fort': Robert Phelps and University Reform

> It is not as a politician that his friends will remember him, but rather as the eager fisherman, who when long past three score and ten, would still recount with glee how he caught his first salmon in the River Blackwater below Lismore; as the artist whose works filled all the walls of his charming old house and overflowed into many portfolios; or as the musician whose clarinet might be heard in the court below for many a happy year.
> —*Cambridge Review*, volume xi, 1890

Robert Phelps is remembered in the history of Cambridge not as a fisherman, artist or musician, but as a controversialist on behalf of a beleaguered university 'old guard'; as a later Sidney master, Thomas Knox-Shaw, called him, no doubt with great exaggeration, 'a complete tyrant'. Phelps, fifth Wrangler in 1833, came from Trinity to Sidney as Taylor Lecturer in 1836, and was made a fellow in 1838 at the age of 30. His brother was the famous Shakespearean actor Samuel Phelps. He took on many private pupils in mathematics, as was the custom at the time, and also wrote a standard textbook on optics, making him academically a great contrast with Chafy. The son of a naval outfitter in Devonport, Phelps was made a tutor in 1840 and was the outstanding candidate for the mastership three years later. In that year he had joined the High Church Cambridge Camden Society, founded in 1839, which sought a revival of the ecclesiology and architecture of the pre-Reformation period. This was a significant step for Sidney's future religious trajectory, transforming a strongly Calvinistic and evangelical college into one identified with Anglo-Catholicism by the turn of the century.

Phelps later earned himself a reputation as the most reactionary head of any Cambridge college. His religious views are evident in his passionate defence of the *status quo* in respect of proposed changes to the Church of Ireland. However, in the 1840s and 1850s he was a committed reformer. As Vice-Chancellor in 1848 he was close to the Prince Consort in seeking to broaden the scope of the education on offer at Cambridge, and was responsible in large part for gaining the support of the other college heads and the Senate. Phelps was happy to introduce a wide range of reforms, and it was largely his objections to what he saw, quite correctly, as the erosion of the colleges' power that brought him into conflict with the royal commissioners in the 1870s. Phelps wanted the colleges to remain in control of teaching and the university to focus on examining. When it was proposed that the colleges' funds be partly diverted to setting up independent faculties and laboratories, he refused to comply with the commission's request that each college provide a return of their revenue, and revealed a split with most of his fellows over the matter. In 1874 the commission's report announced: 'We regret to state that Sidney Sussex College, Cambridge, failed to give the required information. The Fellows of the college indeed expressed their willingness that the information should be given, but as the Master discharges the duties of Bursar, and has the college account books in his custody, the Fellows had not the means which would enable them to make the necessary returns'.

In fact, Phelps's intransigence was a gesture of principle rather than secrecy, for he independently published a full set of Sidney's accounts. In 1879, he was still

An Essex Living

William Lewes Pugh Garnons came from Wivenhoe, Essex, to Sidney in 1810. He was a fellow throughout Chafy's mastership and was a botanist and entomologist of some distinction who was elected a fellow of the Linnaean Society. Garnons was also a mathematician and appointed Barnaby Lecturer at Cambridge in 1833. In 1846, when he was senior fellow, he presented Sidney with the advowson of the vicarage of the tiny Essex church at Ulting, which sits in an idyllic setting by the River Chelmer. It is a 13th-century building with a small wooden spire added in 1873. There had been a chapel dedicated to the Virgin Mary before the Reformation when the site was a place of pilgrimage.

Ulting church, Essex

Hall Court, in The Railway Traveller's Walk Through Cambridge, *c1885*

Great Taste

The railway came to Cambridge in 1845. Sidney was poorly served by the station architects as its crest is hidden around the corner of the main façade. However, the College was included in all the main guide books, special mention usually given to the Hall, gardens and Cromwell. The guide book, from which this illustration is reproduced, gave the opinion that it had been 'faced with cement in the last forty years' and that the College previously had been a 'gloomy, irregular pile', repeating the views of early-19th century commentators. The writer also observed that 'the Master's Lodge is one of the most pleasant in the University' and the grounds 'laid out with great taste'.

fulminating against the proposals, and wrote to the commission making 'a personal protest and remonstrance in reference to the amount of contribution proposed to be levied from this College, as intimated in the recently issued "Draft of Proposed Statutes". I make no reference at present to the general scheme of the draft. I will only observe that its effect on almost all parties here can only be likened to that of an explosive shell thrown into a besieged fort in close proximity to the powder magazine.'

Phelps's defiance was in vain; the new measures enacted in the 1882 Act changed many old assumptions for ever. Masters and fellows, who might be from any college in Oxford or Cambridge, were no longer required to be in holy orders, nor need they study for a divinity degree. Of Sidney's 24 scholars, 12 were to be funded through the scholarship fund and the others from the Taylor estate. Taylor Scholars were to be proficient in mathematics or natural sciences, some of the others in theology, and there were to be college lecturers in mathematics, natural sciences, theology and classics. Phelps's reign thus coincided with the Cambridge move to sciences, while at the same time he pursued a strong rearguard action in favour of the College's historic role as a place not only of education but also of religion.

'England's Oldest Rector': W T Kingsley, Scientist and Artist

The man who embodies the transformation of Sidney during Phelps's mastership is William Towler Kingsley, a St John's sizar from Northumberland, who migrated to Sidney in 1836. The son of an army pay-officer who was at Waterloo when William was born in 1815, Kingsley was polymathic: a priest, scientist, inventor, artist, engraver and photographer. His distant cousin Charles Kingsley (whose father Charles had

ABOVE: *W T Kingsley,
1902, drawing by Lionel
Fawkes*

BELOW: *Photograph of
Chapel Court by Henry
Fox Talbot, c1843. The
Fox Talbot Collection,
British Library, London*

*One of very few
photographs of Cambridge
colleges by Fox Talbot,
taken from a position
where Sainsbury's is
now. It shows Sidney a
decade after the Wyatville
remodelling was completed.
There is no passage through
to the Garden Court area,
no clock, and the Chapel
is faced with stucco rather
than the stone that replaced
it in the 1950s.*

taken an LLB at Sidney in 1816), the famous novelist and Regius Professor
of Modern History, was a near contemporary at Magdalene, then known
as a 'fast' college. W T Kingsley was also an inspiring teacher and, as well
as Taylor Lecturer, was made tutor in 1843, nurturing much of the talent
that came to Sidney in the 1840s and 1850s. His friends included John
Ruskin and J M W Turner, and his artistic abilities provided him with
work for many years as an army examiner in technical drawing. He found
training his army students difficult because, he claimed, their vision had
been too distorted by the conventional picturesque vision of landscape to
make accurate drawings. Kingsley acquired a number of Turner's watercolours, and during a conversation with the painter, Turner made his famous
remark: 'I know of no genius but the genius of hard work'. Ruskin got
Kingsley to review the Turner watercolours exhibition at the Fine Art
Society in 1878. Many years earlier, in 1839, he took his mother to meet
Turner and she became obsessed by *Snowstorm*, now at Tate Britain, telling her son that she had experienced precisely the same thing off the coast
of Holland. When he told Turner this later, the artist was unimpressed and
gave another famous response: 'I got the sailors to lash me to the mast to
observe it. I was lashed for four hours, and I did not expect to escape; but
I felt bound to record it if I did. But no one had any business to like the
picture.'

Kingsley exhibited his photographs at the Paris International Exhibition in 1855,
and may have been the link that brought the photographic pioneer William Fox
Talbot to Sidney in 1843, when he took a photograph of Chapel Court from the
buildings now occupied by Sainsbury's.

Kingsley's scientific interests led him to become a university lecturer in natural
science, a fledgling Tripos subject that commenced in 1851. The Cambridge professor
of chemistry, George Downing Liveing, met Kingsley at the scientific 'Ray Club' – a

Sidney in Sydney

Among the originators of Sidney's modern scientific success during Kingsley's tutorship was William Scott, a Blundell's scholar who was third Wrangler in 1848, was made a fellow in the same year, and Taylor Lecturer in 1850, the year he was ordained. Following his marriage in 1851, he became a private mathematics coach in Cambridge and wrote an important textbook on plane co-ordinate geometry. In 1856 he accepted the position of colonial astronomer in New South Wales. After his arrival in Sydney, Scott supervised the building of the new observatory at Dawes Point, secured the appointment of an observatory board and instituted meteorological records at new weather stations throughout the colony. He was thus the founding director of the Sydney Observatory. In 1861 he acquired an equatorial telescope along with many other pieces of modern equipment, and also established a magnetic survey of New South Wales.

Before resigning due to ill health in 1862, Scott had also begun a process of encouraging astronomical interest in the region, involving himself with the scientific culture around him and the new and flourishing societies it produced. Later Scott became warden of St Paul's College at the University of Sydney where there is a superb stained-glass image of Lady Frances holding a model of Sidney, installed in 1859 by Clayton and Bell. Unlike his mentor Kingsley, Scott began to doubt revealed religion and lectured widely on the relation between science and faith.

Lady Frances Sidney, from the Cambridge Window (east wall) of the Great Hall. University of Sydney

Cambridge club founded in 1837, chiefly with the aim of holding discussions about botanical and zoological matters – in 1850, and later said he was 'the most remarkable man I ever knew'. From 1859, as a priest at the Sidney living of South Kilvington, North Yorkshire, he was an ardent horticulturalist, botanist, zoologist and fisherman. A gifted carver and carpenter, he built his own boats, and also produced many oak carvings for the church decorated with animal, bird and plant forms. Kingsley even built a large and elaborate old-style organ. Like his students Robert Machray and Charles Gutch, he was a committed teacher of his congregation, encouraging a wide range of interests reflecting his own enthusiasms. Kingsley died in 1916 at the age of 101, long known as 'England's oldest rector'.

The exercise ground in Pentonville Prison, 1880, by Thomas Pelham Dale from Life and Letters of Thomas Pelham Dale, *1894*

'A Prisoner for Conscience Sake': Thomas Pelham Dale, Ritualist

> Yesterday evening, at a meeting called by the members and undergraduates of the University of Cambridge who sympathise with Mr. Dale in his resistance to the Court, members were elected to attend the St. James's-hall meeting, and resolutions were carried unanimously of sympathy with the prisoner (who was formerly fellow of Sidney Sussex College)... —*The Times*, 18 November 1880

Under Phelps, who was elected master at the age of only 35, Sidney revived its academic and religious reputation. His High Church sympathies are evident in the careers of many of his fellows and undergraduates, men such as George Theodosius Boughton Kingdon, from Cornwall, who took Anglo-Catholic ritual to New Zealand in the 1850s; his namesake Samuel Kingdon, a fellow from 1839, who joined the Cambridge Camden Society in 1841; William Pinero Burn, who migrated from Oxford in 1844; and James O'Brien of Dublin (the last two became Catholic converts).

Thomas Pelham Dale came to Sidney in 1841, via the newly founded Anglican King's College, London, and was 25th Wrangler in 1845. His private tutor at Cambridge was the celebrated mathematician the Reverend John William Colenso of St John's, later a controversial bishop of Natal. Dale was the son of the dean of Rochester, a sacramentalist but otherwise an evangelical churchman, and during his time at King's was also apprenticed as an engineer. At Sidney he was among the 'reading set' and enjoyed the novels of Dickens, whom he later frequently quoted in his sermons. He was a Sidney fellow before getting married in 1848, by which time he had entered the church. He was a priest in a number of London parishes, the librarian at Sion College, and a keen scientific experimenter. In particular he studied spectrometry and the relationship between temperature and refraction in materials.

Inspired by the Oxford Movement and the revival of Anglican sisterhoods, Dale founded the North London Deaconesses' Institution in King's Cross in 1861, a residential society of ladies undertaking charitable work with the urban poor. He left over a matter of principle in 1868, by which time his liturgy had become more ritualist. In 1873 he began to use eucharistic vestments at Christmas. His parishioners, at St Vedast, Foster Lane, in the City of London, objected to his style, and in 1876 the churchwardens complained about him under Disraeli's new Public Worship Regulation Act. The Church Association brought a prosecution against Dale, who was prevented from preaching. In 1876 he joined the Society of the Holy Cross, an Anglo-Catholic organisation, and returned to his practices in 1878, only to face another prosecution. This led to his imprisonment in October 1880 in Holloway prison.

Dale drew much support across England and the case provoked national debate, which eventually led to a rejection of Disraeli's act. The Church of England Working Men's Society leaflet denounced those who had made him a 'prisoner for conscience sake' and demanded 'FAIR PLAY FOR ALL. An Englishman's Motto'. Dale was released on Christmas Eve, having been treated with great kindness, Lord Justice James giving his opinion that the technical flaw in the writ leading to his release was as trivial as the offences for which he had been incarcerated. Dale's release was followed by presentation to a Lincolnshire rectory, where he studied religious subjects and Hebrew, and scientific topics such as optics, electricity, chemistry and magnetism. Like Kingsley, he was a keen watercolour artist, a friend of John Ruskin since childhood, and a disciple of Turner's painting. He died in 1892 aged 71.

'Ragged and Dirty': Charles Gutch and the Poor of Marylebone

> I have noticed that the number of lads who come to school with shock heads of hair, out at elbows and knees, and with holes in their shoes, is on the increase. It is, therefore, necessary to remind all parents that St. Cyprian's is not a ragged school and that we cannot take in any children who are ragged and dirty. No one in this quarter need send out children unwashed, uncombed, with clothes buttonless, all tattered and torn. —Charles Gutch to parents of the St Cyprian Schools

Charles Gutch migrated to Sidney from St John's in 1842. Like his friend Dale, he was a 'reading man', and was 19th Wrangler and a prizeman in classics and divinity. He was a fellow of Sidney from 1845 until his death in 1896. Gutch was a pious and austere man, his colleague Canon Charles Betham later remembered: 'In the Lent Term of 1845 at his suggestion, as well for discipline as for instruction, we bound ourselves to meet for Divinity studies quite early, before morning Chapel (7.30)...a Spartan arrangement to get our private readings over before that time, on wintry

St Cyprian's mission church, London c1870

Perhaps appropriately, given Sherlock Holmes's supposed Sidney connections, Gutch's little chapel was built in two houses backing on to one another between Park Street and Park Lane, and in turn backing on to 221B (Upper) Baker Street. Joined by a coal shed and designed by G E Street, the great Victorian ecclesiastical architect, it opened in 1866 and was in use for 30 years

mornings.' In 1859, Gutch became curate of the newly built High Church All Saints', Margaret Street, just north of Oxford Street, London. Like Dale, he was committed to creating a sacramental, doctrinally Catholic and socially progressive form of worship. He spent two years negotiating the creation of a new parish and church in the Marylebone area, then very poor and crowded. Gutch opened a temporary chapel in two houses backing on to one another in 1866; his friend, the architect G E Street, designed the conversion.

Gutch named the church after St Cyprian, a saint he chose for his 'tender loving care for his people'. The simple chapel, with its stable

acting as a vestry and choir in 'that miserable part of Marylebone' just north of the Marylebone Road, served as the centre of Gutch's ministry. He created a sisterhood to administer charity and St Cyprian schools, which taught across an unusually wide range of subjects. He also founded an orphanage, guilds for local working men and women, a Youth's Institute, a Home for the Aged Poor, and a house of mercy for unmarried mothers, called 'Bethesda'. In all his many educational activities Gutch insisted on the centrality of the fourth 'r'– religion.

Gutch's small improvised church could seat 180 people and local demand meant that it was soon overcrowded. The local landowner, Lord Portman, who disliked Gutch's High Church principles, persistently refused to sell him land to build a new church. It was only after Gutch's death in 1896 that funds could be raised to build the church of which he had dreamed. The beautiful and ornate Ninian Comper building, which opened in 1904, is one of the great landmarks of Anglo-Catholic architecture in London. Its first priest was the Sidney-educated ex-banker George Frederick Forbes, who presided there until 1921. One of Gutch's former curates, the missionary John Rickards, opened a tiny ramshackle church in Kimberley, South Africa called St Cyprian's, thus extending his influence into the empire.

'A Grave Duty': Robert Machray, Missionary Archbishop

> A grave duty lies upon us to do what we can for the evangelisation of the natives of this land, many of whom still are worshipping they know not what. May we rise to feel that in giving to such a work we are not coldly meeting a duty, but laying hold of a privilege, and discharging not the least important part of our worship and service to God. —Robert Machray, a pastoral letter, 1886

Robert Machray, Archbishop of Rupert's Land, by W S Sutton

In the early 1850s, three remarkable men arrived at Sidney and became life-long friends: Robert Machray, John Clough Williams-Ellis and John Rundle Cornish.

Machray, brought up as a Presbyterian, came to Sidney from King's College, Aberdeen in 1851. He joined the Church of England and was a strong but moderate evangelical throughout his life. At Cambridge he was affected by constant financial difficulties, but his academic ability ensured him the support of the College, especially through the care of his tutor, William Towler Kingsley. His set of rooms on the second floor in Hall Court was the setting for meetings of the Dudleian Society, which he founded with fellow undergraduates to discuss sermons delivered by the members. Machray was popular, though he had no great interest in the sports clubs that, by 1850, were becoming a central part of many students' lives. Williams-Ellis recalled the one occasion when Machray was persuaded to cox a boat practising on the flooded Midsummer Common in 1852: 'The sight of that tall, thin figure in full academical costume steering a racing four was overpowering! Had the boats been like the present riggers, we must all

*Sidney boat crew,
1867–68*

*Standing 3rd from left is
Edmund Phelps, son of the
master, who was No. 6
in the winning Cambridge
boats in the 1870 and
1871 Boat Races. The
Sidney boat was unusually
successful at this time*

have been upset by laughing.' Machray later enjoyed mountaineering holidays in Switzerland, an activity, as we shall see, very popular with the new breed of 'muscular Christians', with its scientific, physical and spiritual dimensions.

Machray was 34th Wrangler in January 1855, a disappointment to many in Sidney, but he competed successfully to gain a fellowship. He was made dean in 1858 and was closely involved in the discipline of students, ensuring in particular their attendance at chapel. He was also a curate at Newton in Cambridgeshire where he started a night school, and from 1862 was vicar of Madingley. Of the night school in Newton, Williams-Ellis wrote: 'The school was well attended. There were youths of all ages, and there would be old ploughmen with their heads almost on the desks, holding their pens like pitchforks, and admiring the huge pothooks that they laboriously and slowly formed. I need scarcely add that Machray was so greatly loved by rich and poor that his very name has ever since been held in the deepest reverence and affection.'

In 1865 Machray was appointed bishop of Rupert's Land in Canada and joined the ranks of many Sidney men in the 19th century who found a life of service in the furthest parts of the empire. The first on record to visit Canada is James Rudd, who went to William Henry Town in 1804 as a missionary. Machray's diocese covered two million square miles and had a small but rapidly growing population. His clergy, centred on the tiny trading hamlet of Fort Garry (now Winnipeg), in the Red River Settlement, numbered only 18. Without benefit of a railway system for many years, Machray set about building up his diocese, visiting remote Indian missions, reviving St John's Theological College, founding a boys' school and becoming chancellor of the new University of Manitoba in 1877. He faced innumerable difficulties, including the

*Robert Flett, photographed
in 1874, wearing a
Blackfoot chief's suit now
in the British Museum,
London*

Cornish Bishop

John Rundle Cornish came to Sidney from Bideford Grammar School in Devon in 1855 and was 14th Wrangler in 1859. He was dean and Taylor lecturer at Sidney until 1868 when he became a priest in Truro, Cornwall. He was appointed Bishop of St Germans, Suffragan of the Bishop of Truro, in 1905. He was a close friend of John Clough Williams-Ellis and Robert Machray with whom he preached in Cambridgeshire villages and conducted early scientific experiments in a makeshift laboratory in Chapel Court.

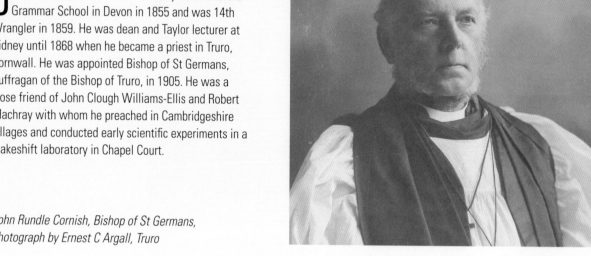

John Rundle Cornish, Bishop of St Germans, photograph by Ernest C Argall, Truro

devastation of crops by locusts and the Metis rebellions in 1869 and 1885 in north-west Canada, during which his moderating intervention prevented serious bloodshed. During the rebellion he communicated with the colonial secretary through a Sidney fellow using a cipher based on the College Latin grace uttered before meals.

Machray's great achievements were recognised when he was made Archbishop of Rupert's Land and Primate of all Canada. Sidney awarded him an honorary fellowship. Machray sent a number of young men to Sidney from his schools, including William Robert Flett from St John's College, who arrived in Cambridge as a sizar in 1876 and whose Native Canadian ancestry is evident in the photograph of him in the warrior's suit of a Blackfoot chief, two years before he went to Sidney. It is made of deerskins with, appropriately, a breast plate of porcupine quills and an extensive ermine fringe. While at Sidney, Flett gave the suit to the British Museum where it is now in the Department of Africa, Oceania and the Americas.

Machray's nephew, Robert, entered Sidney in 1879 and also was a churchman in Canada. Due to ill health, however, he became a writer and was the author of many Edwardian crime thrillers, such as *The Ambassador's Glove* (1904), a biography of his uncle and the great survey of bohemian London, *The Nightside of London* (1902), with illustrations by Tom Browne.

'Some Simple Experiments': Sidney's First Laboratory

We used occasionally to try some simple experiments. Once in Bishop St German's rooms we started an experiment, a fine india rubber was carrying hydrogen to our experimental retort. We suddenly discovered that the tube was on fire and the fire stealing up to the explosive mixture. We used to accuse Machray of rushing into Cornish's bedroom and bolting the door – this was possibly unjust – we I think dived under the table as the safest place waiting in agony for the coming explosion to blow the College to atoms. Finding nothing happened, we naturally accused each other of abject cowardice. —John Clough Williams-Ellis, unpublished memoirs

Machray's close friend at Sidney, John Clough Williams-Ellis, was a vicar's son from Llanaelhaiarn in Caernarvonshire, who entered as a pensioner in 1852. He was a brilliant student and in 1856 was third Wrangler, a feat that earned him a fellowship. In 1877 he was presented to the Sidney living at Gayton in Northamptonshire. Williams-Ellis's tutor was William Towler Kingsley, who encouraged him in his scientific interests. Williams-Ellis became Taylor Lecturer and in 1859 was appointed tutor in succession to his mentor. His friend John Rundle Cornish, a mathematician, scientist and later bishop of St German's, recalled that as undergraduates he and Williams-Ellis took up, 'I fear somewhat superficially, many subjects, attending the Professors' lectures on Chemistry, Geology, Anatomy, Mechanism and some others'.

John Clough Williams-Ellis, c1895

Ellis helped rejuvenate Sidney's academic reputation, building up a fine library of scientific books, offering courses in natural sciences, changing some Taylor scholarships to others focused on science and creating awards for work on chemistry, electricity and general physics. In 1862 Sidney was the only college offering natural science awards. In 1863, a Sidney student, F B Allison, gained a first in the natural sciences Tripos, the first of many top degrees over the following decades. By the mid-1870s Sidney was offering inter-collegiate teaching in the natural sciences with Trinity and St John's.

A Working-Class Astronomer

Joseph Hough was born in Leeds in 1837 and left school early to work as an apprentice at Fairbairn's Engineering Works. He attended evening classes at Leeds Mechanics' Institute and also became fascinated by astronomy. In 1859 he was appointed astronomer to the second Lord Wrottesley, a past president of the Royal Society and Royal Astronomical Society, and ran his observatory and library at Codsall Wood near Wolverhampton until his employer's death in 1867. He entered Sidney as a scholar in 1869 aged 32 and later became headmaster of Burnley Grammar School. In retirement he lived near the Wrottesley Observatory and devoted himself to teaching the poor.

Watercolour of the Wrottesley Observatory. Royal Astronomical Society

In 1860, Williams-Ellis managed to persuade Phelps 'to allow me to make a chemical laboratory at Sidney, the only other College laboratory being at St John's'. As the College minutes record: 'Also agreed that a room be assigned for a Taylor Chemical Laboratory to be fitted up with all requisite fixtures and apparatus, the rent of the room and all expenses connected with it to be defrayed out of the Taylor Fund.' The laboratory was in some ground floor rooms on H staircase in Chapel Court, close to the latrines near the end of the Chapel, 'but as the complaint of fumes was made in rooms above, possibly to disguise the fear of explosions, the Sidney Laboratory was moved to a separate building'.

'A New Era in Mountain Climbing': Sidney and the Alpine Club

> Some few days before I left Cambridge, in July, 1857, proposing to make an eight week's tour in Switzerland with my friend, Mr. Ellis of Sidney College, a laugh was raised at my expense, by the suggestion of a facetious friend that I might distinguish myself by an ascent of the Finsteraar Horn. —J F Hardy, 'Ascent of the Finsteraar Horn', in *Peaks, Passes and Glaciers: A Series of Excursions by Members of the Alpine Club*, edited by John Ball, 1859

Peaks, Passes and Glaciers, 1859, *frontispiece. Bodleian Library, Oxford*

John Clough Williams-Ellis was one of those remarkable Victorian polymaths whose energy and intelligence today seem almost superhuman. His personality and intellect drew a generation of outstanding students to Sidney, and ensured the College survived the reforms of the 1860s and 1870s not only intact but thriving. He was awarded a silver medal by the Royal Humane Society in 1855 for saving the student Peter Clarke's life 'in circumstances of exceptional danger' at a lock on the Cam; he was deeply involved with the Cambridge University Volunteers; and later, in semi-retirement at Glasfryn in his native Wales, was a leading figure in agricultural reform who managed to learn Esperanto and Italian, and to write poetry. He acquired a great deal of land around the family home of Plas Brondanw, Glasfryn, where his son Sir Clough Williams-Ellis built the extraordinary village of Portmeirion, setting for *The Prisoner* TV fantasy series in the late 1960s.

Williams-Ellis was a talented sportsman and rowed for Sidney as well as playing football, cricket, rackets, fives, tennis and skating. It was possibly at his request that Sidney built a fives court in 1857. Above all, Williams-Ellis is remembered for his taking part in the first British ascent of the Finsteraarhorn in 1857, and the subsequent founding of the Alpine Club during the 'golden age' of British mountaineering. Williams-Ellis and the Sidney Fishmongers' Fellow and mountaineering enthusiast, John Frederic Hardy, went on a holiday to Switzerland in the summer of that year. In August, in the Bear Hotel in Grindelwald, they met by appointment the mountaineer E S

Wine Cellars

The Sidney wine cellars, looking south. As the plaque shows, the cellars were built in 1871. They were constructed in the extensive cellars forming the foundations of the Grey Friars that reached under Hall Court. J F Hardy, the mountaineering fellow, was then the steward. An unconventional form of entertainment for one evening's dinner guests at Sidney was the roasting of a donkey's leg. It seems he chose a young rather than old animal, and the dish was not as tasty as it might have been.

HAE CELLAE VINARIAE SUBTER COENACULO
COLLEGII POSITAE
ANNO MDCCCLXXI CONSTRUCTAE SUNT
ROBERTO PHELPS *MAGISTRO*
JOHANNE FREDERICO HARDY
SENESCHALLO

Kennedy of Trinity, along with two other Cambridge dons, who had decided earlier to attempt the very difficult ascent of the 4,274 metre Finsteraarhorn, the highest mountain in the Bernese Alps. Williams-Ellis and Hardy accompanied them, along with five guides. Hardy's account of the ascent in *Peaks, Passes and Glaciers* is one of the classics of early mountaineering literature, stylish, amusing, exciting and informative.

Loaded with wine, brandy and a cornucopia of food, the party set off on a two-day journey towards and then up the dangerous and rugged mountain via the Aeggischhorn, the Marjeln See, the 15-mile long Aletsch Glacier, and the rocky base of the Faulberg, where they camped the first night. Setting off at 2.30 the following morning, they reached the base of the Finsteraarhorn. 'For the next two hours', wrote Hardy, 'we are climbing up a wall of rock which seems almost vertical. Now hand over hand; now getting well into a corner, and bringing our backs into play after the fashion of chimney-sweeps; now coming to some awkward place, where the tallest man must go first, for his arms alone are long enough to feel the way, and choosing some safe ledge, must stretch down thence a helping hand to his shorter brethren, who occasionally, too, are thankful for a shove behind; now, completely baffled by some monstrous crag, we are driven to take to the hard snow at the side, and ascend by sharp, short zig-zags, which without the confidence-inspiring rope, are not altogether pleasant; then back again to the rocks, and holding on like grim death, or taking advantage of some small – very small – plateau for a moment's delay, while we wipe the steaming sweat from our faces…'

At 9.15 a.m. they reached the terrifying knife-like edge called the Strahlgrat with its spectacular views of the Finsteraarhorn glacier. The arête commenced, so narrow and dangerous that if one man fell he would drag all the others down with him. At the summit the patriotic Tory Hardy, hat in hand, led a triumphant chorus of cheers and a rendition of 'God Save the Queen'. 'The noble old anthem fills our English hearts with happy thoughts of home and fatherland, and of the bright eyes that will sparkle, and the warm hearts that will rejoice at our success.' The 12 men sat down to enjoy their brandy and the 300-mile panorama around them. Williams-Ellis's family still owns his alpenstock with the names of his fellow mountaineers engraved on it.

It was following this ascent that an Alpine Club, 'for gentlemen who also climb', was founded. Williams-Ellis didn't join, but Hardy, later known as 'King of the Riffel' after his exploits in the Austrian Alps, was a founding member of the Cambridge-dominated club, and only resigned a year before his death in 1888. Hardy was a typical example of what *Fraser's Magazine*, writing of the Alpine Club in 1859, called 'that rambling, scrambling, exercise-loving disposition' of the Englishman.

Life Among the Zulus: George Holditch Mason

> I seem to behold a chaos of confusion in the present condition of South Africa; which nothing but Christianity can correct. —George Holditch Mason, *Zululand: A Mission Tour in South Africa*, 1862

Under the influence of Kingsley and Williams-Ellis, adventure and exploration were part of the wider culture at Victorian Sidney. One student even travelled to Natal on what must be one of the greatest gap-year escapades in undergraduate history, going there as a participant in the largely unsuccessful 'Byrne Scheme' in 1850. Joseph Byrne was a promoter of colonisation in Africa, who in 1849–51 advertised a new life for Britons on the 100,000 acres of land in Natal he had bought and divided into 1,000 plots. George Holditch Mason, son of the headmaster of the Perse School, Cambridge, entered Sidney in 1852 after his extraordinary epic journey, which he wrote about in *Life Among the Zulus* in 1855, the year John Colenso, Thomas Pelham Dale's private tutor, published his *Ten Weeks in Natal*.

'It was the first of March. Ah! Well do I remember – as though it were but yesterday – how I took my seat in my snug room at Cambridge upon that morning, while yet the grey twilight only sufficed to show the neighbouring housetops whitened by a passing snowstorm...When I looked back, and thought of the days and nights spent on that row of musty books, and considered how little had been accomplished, compared with what still remained to be "got up" within the next three eventful years; when I surveyed the dread "Littlego" [preliminary examination] and "Tripos", with all their attendant horrors; I fancied myself already "plucked" [failed], or "gulphed" [given an ordinary degree but listed], or "spoon" [awarded the 'wooden spoon' for being the last on the list]; but never thought of substituting Caffre clicks for Grecian accents, or Caffre picks for pens and paper.'

Mason describes in great detail the seasickness, drunkenness, violence, and extraordinary range of Dickensian characters on the long boat journey from Liverpool to Durban, before telling the story of his encounter with native Africans and their language and customs, the different social classes of the colonists and their religious practices, the Boers, the wildlife, the landscape and much other fascinating detail. Following a long and eventful journey inland, he finally arrived at Byrne Town, near Beulah in the Vley, where their land, or 'erf', was situated. Mason evokes the energy and optimism of the emigrants who engage in 'trading, building, cattle-jobbing, and in fact any thing but cultivating the soil', and the generosity of the Caffre Christian converts. The towns were full of shops, houses, hotels, workshops and canteens, all dominated by a central market: 'Dogs, Hottentots, untidy women, neglected children, laughing Caffres, cooking utensils, bedding, and smouldering fires, lined the broad open streets, or occupied the vacant and deserted erven of the expatriate Boers.' Once he had settled, Mason built his thatched brick house while living in a tent and cultivating an oat crop. The Byrne scheme was largely crooked, backed up by corrupt colonial officials. Like many others, Mason was forced to look for work in the local town before returning home to start his Sidney career. 'Oh! trigonometry! I wish you anywhere but at the Umlaas', he exclaimed, on receiving from Cambridge a manuscript treatise on spherical trigonometry.

Mason entered Sidney as a sizar in 1852 and, following his three years study there, was ordained. Rather than go into the poor districts of London and other great English cities, as many Sidney men did in the 19th century, he returned to Natal as a missionary in the late 1850s, where the former Cambridge mathematics

Watercolour of a view from Toncaati verandah, from Zululand, by G H Mason, 1862. Cambridge University Library

don John Colenso was the controversial and liberal bishop. Colenso, unlike Mason, believed Zulu polygamy should be tolerated. Such conciliatory attitudes towards the indigenous people, and his unorthodox views on biblical interpretation, led to his prosecution by the church authorities. Mason's *Zululand*, published in 1862, certainly expresses a deep sympathy with the 'Caffres'. He admired them as a 'noble race' whom he compared favourably with most Englishmen on account of an 'often vastly superior mind', muscular development and indomitable courage. In Mason's opinion, many of their social problems, such as drunkenness, pilfering and unemployment, were the result of a pernicious European influence. However, he was adamantly opposed to the encouragement of the 'abomination' of polygamy, as he was to witchcraft, and felt that as Christians and civilised people the multiple wives of the tribal chiefs, 'our suffering sisters', should be shown great mercy. Firm and just British rule and the spread of Christianity, Mason believed, would be the only route to progress: 'Then Africa will possess sons capable of steering a course worthy of a country enjoying so large a share of natural capabilities and resources'. While travelling around preaching, teaching elementary subjects and communicating with the Zulus, he constantly reminded them of the truth of 'the Resurrection, future Judgement and Man's redemption', and that Englishmen were once semi-naked savages without religion or Christianity.

Mason mostly met with a friendly and positive response, especially when rewards were offered for remembering the Creed or hoeing the soil efficiently. He was delighted when the local people demanded '*Caffoola foonah insonda*' ('Caffres want their hymns'). The conclusion of *Zululand*, that 'the English have become "Angels"

Gentleman Usher to Queen Victoria

Cuthbert Larking matriculated at Sidney in 1860 and went on to become a well-known courtier and a soldier in the British army. He was a Bey in the Egyptian Service, Gentleman Usher to Queen Victoria and King Edward VII and equerry to the Duke of Connaught. He married Lady Adela Maria Hare, daughter of the 2nd Earl of Listowel, in 1864 shortly after leaving Sidney. This cartoon by the famous 'Ape' was published shortly after his appointment as Gentleman Usher to Queen Victoria.

Cartoon of Cuthbert H Larking by 'Ape' (Carlo Pellegrini), Vanity Fair, *August 1888*

The Largest Organ in the World

In the wake of the organists Joseph Kemp and Edward Hodges, it is appropriate that Sidney produced one of the greatest ever organ makers. Arthur George Hill entered Sidney from Westminster School in 1876 as a pensioner. He became the head of the family firm William Hill and Sons, founded in 1829, and of Norman and Beard Ltd, both organ manufacturers and operating as Hill, Norman and Beard until 1973. Hill was a designer of many huge and elaborately decorated organs, especially for cathedrals, including this remarkable one in the Centennial Hall in Sydney Town Hall, which was built in 1890 and is the largest mechanical pipe organ in the world. Hill also wrote books on the history of music and organs.

Organ, Town Hall, Sydney, Australia

(messengers) for good or evil, to every nation under heaven', strikes an ironic note today. Mason returned to England, worked as a curate in parishes across Britain and published a number of essays on religious topics. He died in Kent in 1893. A spiritual successor to Mason was George Tobias, born in South Africa and sent to Sidney as a scholar in 1903. He fought on the Western Front, acted as a chaplain, was wounded twice and awarded the MC. He became Bishop of Damaraland and translated John Bunyan's *The Pilgrim's Progress* into Kwanyama.

'Exquisite Troll of Genius': Bob Stevenson, Bohemian

> He doubles like the serpent, changes and flashes like the shaken kaleidoscope, transmigrates bodily into the view of others, and so, in the twinkling of an eye and with a heady rapture, turns questions inside out and flings them empty before you on the ground, like a triumphant conjuror. —Robert Louis Stevenson on his cousin R A M Stevenson

Sidney, under Kingsley and Williams-Ellis in particular, fostered individual and often eccentric talent beyond mathematics, science and religion. As well as encouraging sports, these two inspirational figures made the arts an important focus. In 1858, Sidney allowed the weekly use of the Hall for the new Fitzwilliam Musical

Society founded by the King's Chaplain Arthur Beard; in 1861 Sidney contributed £50 towards the restoration of Lady Frances' monument in Westminster Abbey; in the same year the Hall was completely redecorated and central heating installed; in 1865, the College lent a number of its paintings to the Earl of Derby's exhibition of 'National Portraits'; and in 1866 it initiated the frequent use of the College gardens by the Horticultural Society for flower shows.

John Ruskin stayed overnight at Sidney in 1858 as Kingsley's guest, following his inaugural lecture for the opening of the new Cambridge School of Art, which was then housed in Sidney Street; Thomas Holwell Cole, who came to Sidney in 1845, co-founded the eminently Victorian-sounding Hastings School of Science and Art in 1875; Arthur Temperley, who matriculated in 1871, became, like Kingsley, a priest and wood-carver, his work still extant at Willingham church in Lincolnshire; Arthur George Hill, who entered in 1876, became head of the London firm of organ-builders responsible for building the biggest organ in the world at Sydney Town Hall, an extraordinary construction, the ornate case designed by Hill himself.

R A M Stevenson (centre) with his cousin, Robert Louis (left), and 'Enfield the painter', c1870s. Princeton University Library

The most talented of Sidney's artistic students, however, was Robert Louis Stevenson's cousin Robert Alan Mowbray Stevenson, or 'Bob' as he was known to friends. He was the son of an eminent Scottish lighthouse engineer from the great Stevenson dynasty of engineers, and went to Sidney as a pensioner in 1866. He was an outstanding sportsman, excelling at gymnastics, athletics and canoeing. A natural bohemian type, he discovered at Sidney that engineering was not going to be his vocation, and instead developed his interest in painting and the history of art. During his Cambridge vacations he visited the artists' colonies at Fontainebleau near Paris, and at Barbizon, developing a great enthusiasm for the painting of Jean-Baptiste Camille Corot.

After taking his BA, without honours, in 1871, Stevenson returned to live in Edinburgh, where he studied painting at the art school. He moved to Paris where he enrolled at the atelier of the great portraitist Carolus-Duran. Stevenson then moved to the cosmopolitan village of Barbizon, and painted landscapes that he exhibited at the Royal Academy. His lack of material success as a painter, his marriage in 1881, and the encouragement of the poet and editor W E Henley, led him to take up art criticism, which proved to be his real forte. He became an advocate of modern French painting, including the Impressionists, in journals such as the

The Ear

William Dalby, son of a Leicestershire surgeon, entered Sidney in 1860, the same year as the Gentleman Usher Cuthbert Larking. He became one of the most distinguished otologists (a specialist in diseases and injuries of the ear) in Victorian England, based at St George's Hospital in London. He was knighted in 1886 and was president of the Medical Society in 1894–5. A keen player of whist, he is characterised by 'Ape' as 'The Ear' in this cartoon.

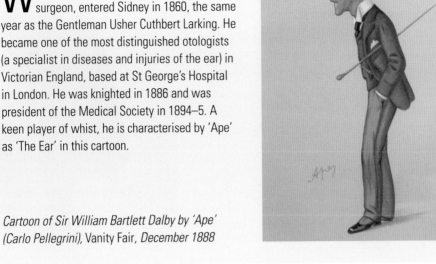

Cartoon of Sir William Bartlett Dalby by 'Ape' (Carlo Pellegrini), Vanity Fair, *December 1888*

Saturday Review and the *Magazine of Art*. He also wrote books on Rubens, Raeburn and Velázquez. This last book, published in 1895, was his masterpiece, presenting Velázquez as the first Impressionist; it became a bible for art students. The art critic D S MacColl said that it was 'the most substantial contribution to the theory and defence of painting since John Ruskin's *Modern Painters*'. With its flowing and original prose, Stevenson's criticism was concerned with the subtle integrity of the concept of style. He had no time for English literary or moral traditions, but sought instead to convey a comprehensive way of seeing that was inseparable from the flexibility of the artist's techniques: 'Breadth of view was Velázquez's most admirable possession; by it he made composition, modelling, and style the slaves of his impressions. This breadth of view led him to vary his manner of painting according to the sentiment of his impressions, so that you will find in his work no pattern of brushwork, no settled degree of intimacy in the modelling, no constantly equal force of realisation in edges and, in short, no fixed habits or methods of expression.'

Stevenson taught painting to Cambridge undergraduates in 1882, and was professor of fine art at University College, Liverpool from 1889 to 1893, a post he resigned because he felt too constrained by the provincial gossip, genteel conformity and naïve do-gooding tendencies of most of those around him. His extraordinary character and conversation were noted by all who came into contact with him; he naturally appeared in many memoirs and other writings of the period. H G Wells based the conversational style, but not the views, of the artist Ewart in *Tono-Bungay* (1909) on him, explaining later that Stevenson, unlike the socialist Ewart, was 'all on the side of aesthetic concentration and letting the rest go hang. He could not imagine what the Fabians were up to. They were not real in his universe.'

'A Most Select Speaker'

Charles Stubbs, the son of a Liverpool spice-merchant, entered Sidney in 1864 as a pensioner. He was a Tripos prizewinner and became DD in 1894 when he was also appointed Dean of Ely. In 1906 he was appointed Bishop of Truro, shortly before this cartoon appeared with the title 'A Most Select Speaker'. Stubbs is best known as the author of many Christian Socialist books, including *Village Politics* (1878), *Christ and Economics* (1883), *The Land and the Labourers* (1890), and *International Morality* (1893). He also wrote a history of Cambridge (1905) that gives Sidney especially sympathetic attention.

Cartoon of Charles William Stubbs by 'Spy' (Leslie Ward), Vanity Fair, *February 1907*

It is in his relationship with his cousin Robert Louis that Stevenson's character becomes most clearly visible. They had been friends since childhood, and the whimsical Bob's impact on his younger cousin was considerable. As young men in Edinburgh in the early 1870s the pair were members of the 'Liberty, Justice and Reverence Club', formed to 'disregard everything our parents taught us'. Robert Louis's father was so shocked by Bob's opinions that in a bid to prevent his son from becoming an atheist he made him swear that religion would not be discussed. Robert Louis described Bob in his autobiography: 'He had the most indefatigable, feverish mind I have ever known; he had acquired a smattering of almost every knowledge and art; he would surprise you by his playing, his painting, his writing, his criticism, his knowledge of philosophy, and above all, by a sort of vague, disconnected and totally inexplicable erudition.' The writer Edmund Gosse, author of *Father and Son*, called Bob that 'exquisite troll of genius'. Robert Louis's friends were often concerned that Bob was leading him astray, yet the most important effect he had was to liberate Robert Louis's imagination. The theme of the story 'The Suicide Club' in *New Arabian Nights*, dedicated to him, was Bob's idea, along with a number of other brilliant conceits. Robert Louis also featured versions of Bob in his writings – 'The Man Who Sold Cream Tarts' in *New Arabian Nights*, Somerset in 'The Dynamiter', and Prince Otto in the eponymous political romance, are largely modelled on Bob. Arethusa, in *An Inland Voyage*, a record of a celebrated canoeing trip in France, and Spring Heel'd Jack in the essay 'Talk and Talkers', are directly based on him. Bob Stevenson died of heart disease aged 53 in 1900.

The Sidney Laboratories: F H Neville and E H Griffiths

During the period 1875–90, under the dynamic tutorship of Charles Smith, son of a Huntingdon cobbler who was third Wrangler in 1868, Sidney had excellent results in the mathematics Tripos: S R Wilson was fifth in 1877; J Edwards was fourth and J A Martin 10th in 1878; S H Haslam was 11th in 1879; F W Stokes was eighth in 1881; S R Loney was third, R H Pigott was fifth and H C Robson sixth in 1882; G W Kuchler was ninth in 1883; A Anderson was sixth in 1884; A G Cracknell was sixth in 1888. A number of these men went on to become fellows, and helped sustain Sidney's results well into the 20th century. In lists dominated by the far larger colleges, it was a very good record, and answered those who earlier in the century had wondered, 'what is Sidney Sussex for?'

As well as excellent Tripos performances in maths, Sidney excelled in many of the newer subjects, with a string of firsts in law and natural sciences. However, it was in the sciences that Sidney created a real powerhouse among students and fellows. Much of the focus of Sidney science was on the experimentation and teaching possible in the laboratories built along the Sidney Street wall in what was then the Fellows' Garden, where bike sheds now stand. These were built some time before the mid-1870s, and remained on the site until their closure in 1908, by which time the university was able to provide larger premises elsewhere for work in physics and chemistry. Sidney's eminence in science, alongside St John's and Caius, was one

Interior of the main laboratory building, c1908

Francis Henry Neville,
c1890

reason that Dorothy L Sayers proposed that Sherlock Holmes had been an undergraduate there in the 1870s.

The most famous research in the laboratories was undertaken by their manager, F H Neville, 15th Wrangler in 1871, later fellow and Taylor Lecturer in natural sciences, and C T Heycock of King's. Their work in physical metallurgy, centred on measuring the boiling and freezing points of alloys such as gold and cadmium in tin, was published between 1884 and 1914. It is still important today and has had a great impact on a number of modern developments, for instance, in computing technology. Neville and Heycock were helped by E H Griffiths, the son of a Welsh priest, who came to Sidney via Owens College, Manchester in 1870. After taking a pass degree, he formed a successful coaching partnership with Heycock, introduced him to Neville, and went on to develop the platinum resistance thermometers that allowed Neville's and Heycock's measurements to be taken to new levels of accuracy. Griffiths became a fellow in 1897, by which time he had published a number of his own very important articles on metals and temperature. Griffiths was closely connected with the Cambridge Scientific Instruments Company, founded in 1877, and then under the control of Horace Darwin, ninth child of Charles. Griffiths designed thermometers for the company and became a shareholder in 1895. Neville and Heycock were regular customers. Griffiths was also a very loyal Sidneian, a sportsman and the author of 'A Song of Sidney Sussex' (1900), composed for the popular smoking parties of the time.

Neville and Heycock at first experimented with x-rays, but settled on the examination of polished and etched surfaces by reflected light microscopy, and undertook analysis using photomicrography. Their most significant work was delivered to the Royal Society as the Bakerian Lecture in 1903, the study of copper-tin alloys, the foundation of modern research into phase equilibria and microstructure in alloys. Where Heycock was the gifted experimenter, Neville was the theorist, a modest man who became a convert to Rome and thus Sidney's first Catholic fellow. He was in contact with many of the world's leading scientists and mathematicians, a brilliant linguist, a keen historian and had a great interest in 'metaphysical' questions, joining the new Society for Psychical Research in the early 1880s.

When Neville resigned his Taylor Lectureship in 1908 and retired to Letchworth, the laboratory was closed and the apparatus given to the university. Sadly, over-exuberant student revelry following the very successful May Bumps in 1910 destroyed much paperwork, books and photographic negatives, in a huge bonfire in the new Cloister Court. While Sidney seemed unperturbed by this revival of its incendiarist tradition, Heycock refused to teach Sidney students for a number of years afterwards.

Interior of the annex to the laboratory building, c1908

'Wonderful Optical Phenomena': C T R Wilson and the Cloud Chamber

> The whole of my scientific work undoubtedly developed from the experiments I was led to make by what I saw during my fortnight on Ben Nevis. —C T R Wilson 'Reminiscences of my early years,' *Notes and Records of the Royal Society*, 1959–60

The most famous student trained in the Sidney laboratory was the physicist Charles Thomson Rees Wilson, or 'C T R', a sheep farmer's son from Midlothian who, like Griffiths, arrived at the College by way of Owens College, Manchester. Wilson took a double first in natural sciences in 1892, and worked in the laboratory as an under-graduate to supplement his income, assisting Neville and Heycock in work on thal-lium alloys. Following a spell of school teaching, he returned to Cambridge in 1894, just before J J Thomson discovered the electron in 1897. In September 1894, Wilson had spent a few weeks in the now ruined Ben Nevis observatory, where he had an almost visionary experience of what is known as the 'Brocken Spectre' during a period studying cloud formation. He later wrote: 'The wonderful optical phenomena sown when the sun shone on the clouds surrounding the hill-top, and especially the coloured rings surrounding the sun (coronas) or surrounding the shadow cast by the

The Cloud Chamber

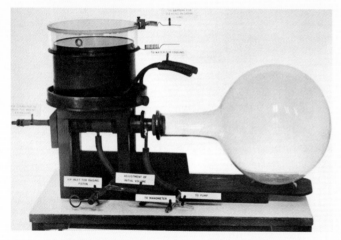

A cloud, or 'Wilson', chamber

One of the first photographs (right) to show the tracks of subatomic particles in a cloud chamber. It was taken by the cloud chamber's inventor, Sidney physicist C T R Wilson, at the Cavendish Laboratory in Cambridge in 1911. The tracks are due to alpha particles emitted by a small amount of radium on the top of a metal tongue inserted into the cloud chamber. As an electrically charged particle moves through the water vapour in a cloud chamber, it ionises the gas and water drops condense on the ions, thus producing a track of droplets where the particle has passed. In 1927 Wilson was awarded the Nobel Prize for physics for his invention.

hill-top observer on mist and clouds (glories), greatly excited my interest and made me wish to imitate them in the laboratory.' Returning to Ben Nevis in 1895 he was caught in a severe storm and witnessed the extraordinary and sublime electrical forces released.

In 1896–7 Wilson held the Clerk Maxwell scholarship at the Cavendish laboratory where he conducted a groundbreaking sequence of experiments that established the key features of the condensation of water droplets from a supersaturated dust-free gas. Trained by Neville and Griffiths, he had become an expert glassblower and created a number of 'cloud chambers', also known as 'Wilson Chambers', which allowed him to study the formation of clouds and rain in controlled laboratory conditions. At a certain point in the dust-free chamber the cooled rain clouds became fog, and Wilson examined the effect of irradiating this with x-rays and ultra-violet light. He concluded that at a certain level of supersaturation, water would condense on any charged nuclei in the chamber. A cloud chamber consists essentially of a closed container filled with a supersaturated vapour, such as water in air. When ionising radiation passes through the vapour, it leaves a trail of charged particles or ions that serve as condensation centres for the vapour. The path of the radiation is thus indicated by tracks of tiny liquid droplets in the supersaturated vapour. The photographs Wilson was able to take of these previously invisible forces were published in 1911 and 1912 and were of an astonishing magical quality.

C T R Wilson, by Sir James Gunn, 1936

The ramifications of Wilson's work were immense and transformed experimental physics. In 1899 J J Thomson used a Wilson chamber to determine the number of electrons from the number of water droplets that condensed out, enabling him to confirm the tiny mass of the electron. Ernest Rutherford later said the cloud chamber was the most original apparatus in the history of physics. The device allowed the discovery of the positive electron, the cosmic ray shower phenomenon, the u-meson, charged and neutral v-particles, and the negative cascade hyperon. In the practical world, Wilson's chamber paved the way for understanding the nature of cosmic rays and the development of nuclear technology.

A Sidney fellow and FRS from 1900, Wilson became Jacksonian Professor of Natural Philosophy and continued to teach in the Cavendish Laboratory. His lecturing style was notoriously difficult to follow. Around 1930, one Sidney physicist, J G Wilson, remembered attending his lectures on condensation on nuclei: 'His greatest admirers dare not describe his conventional lecturing manner as anything but quite dreadful: his quiet voice was directed to the blackboard, he wrote very faintly and moved in front of what he had written as he went on. In his left hand was a duster, and when his writing did emerge from behind him it was instantly rubbed out. But the matter was priceless, and very much more distinguished people than I, for example Patrick Blackett and Cecil Powell, would recall these lectures with enthusiasm.'

Wilson was awarded the Nobel Prize for physics with A H Compton in 1927 for his work on the cloud chamber. He was a quiet and modest man, who never lost his love for Scotland, where he died in 1959.

Pterodactyls and Meteors: the Birth of Sidney Geology

These old flying animals sleep through geological ages, not without honour, for the study of their story has illuminated the mode of origin of animals which survive them, and in cleaving the rocks to display their bones we have opened a new page of the book of life.
—H G Seeley, *Dragons of the Air*, 1901

Another young student in the Sidney laboratory was the geologist William George ('Bones') Fearnsides, son of a Yorkshire grocer who went to Sidney as a scholar in 1897 and took a double first in natural sciences in 1900. He became a fellow of Sidney in 1904, having already contributed a significant insight by geological analogy for Neville and Heycock's work for the Bakerian Lecture in 1903. While continuing to work on alloys, he became the leading authority on the Lower Palaeozoic rocks of Wales and was made professor of geology at Sheffield in 1913. He produced the first structural map of the coalfields of Yorkshire. In the First World War Fearnsides researched alternative energy sources such as non-phosphoric iron ores. In 1939 he discovered the Eakring oilfield in Nottinghamshire, and during the Second World War he worked extensively on coal production and water supply.

Geology was in many ways the most Victorian of natural sciences, posing religious and philosophical questions while being, quite literally, down-to-earth. Fearnsides was part of a new but soon-to-be great tradition of Sidney geology, which had its origins in the arsonist Kendall's work in the early-19th century and in the arrival of Harry Govier Seeley in 1859. A near contemporary of undergraduates such as Charles Smith and Bob Stevenson, Seeley was typical in background, intelligence, and later career, of many Sidney students who arrived during the period dominated by Kingsley and Williams-Ellis. Son of a bankrupt London bookseller and scientific experimenter, he became an apprentice piano-maker, and was briefly a law student. He studied English and maths at the Working Men's College in the late 1850s, where

Dimorphodon macronyx (*common name: pterosaur*) *by* Miss E B Seeley, *from* H G Seeley Dragons of the Air: An Account of Extinct Flying Reptiles, *1901.* The London Library

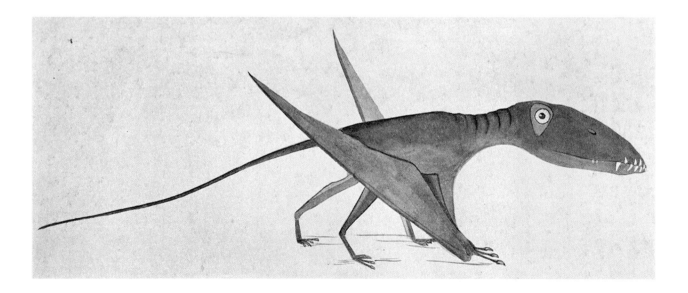

he was secretary to the college museum. From this unorthodox background Seeley entered Sidney in 1863 as an early student in natural sciences, and soon became an assistant at the Woodwardian Museum to one of the founders of British Geology, the anti-Darwinian friend of Darwin, Adam Sedgwick. He arranged the collection, catalogued fossils, lectured, and conducted field studies of the flying reptile remains in the Cambridge greensand. He suffered a nervous breakdown, failed to take a degree, and migrated to St John's in 1868. He is famous for his anti-evolutionist and platonic theory of morphology, and in particular his study of pterodactyls, popularised in his *Dragons of the Air* in 1901. Seeley became professor of geography and geology at Queen's College, London in 1876 and of geology and mineralogy at King's College, London in 1896. He was a strong advocate of the expansion of higher education, especially for women, and wrote and lectured widely to promote geological understanding.

Between Seeley and Fearnsides, a number of Sidney undergraduates became major international figures in geology. William Whitehead Watts, a music teacher's son from Shropshire, came to Sidney as a scholar from St Chad's School, Denstone, in 1878. He took a double first in natural sciences in 1881, was elected a Sidney fellow in 1888 and worked as one of the new breed of university extension lecturers and as an assistant professor of geology at Oxford before becoming petrographer to the British Geological Survey in 1891. Renowned for his amusing 'Watticisms', Watts was an inspired professor and teacher at the Royal School of Mines in London, soon to be part of Imperial College, introducing innovative subjects such as oil technology and mining geology. A gregarious man committed to the widening of educational opportunities, Watts was an active member of many committees and organisations dedicated to education and geology. At his death in 1947 it was recognised that no man had had a greater influence on British geology in his lifetime.

A few years after Watts, the mineralogist Leonard James Spencer came to Sidney in 1889 as a scholar from Bradford Technical College and the Royal College of Science in Dublin. He took a double first in natural sciences in 1893 and was awarded the Harkness scholarship for geology. He worked on the mineral collection at the British Museum and described eight new non-silicate minerals, including miersite and tarbuttite. He led a career of worldwide scholarly acclaim, travelling extensively and extending his interests to the study of meteorites, his training under Neville and Heycock allowing him to reach some important conclusions about the formation of meteorite craters.

William Whitehead Watts, c1885

Herbert Henry Thomas, from Devon, went to Sidney as an exhibitioner in 1894 and like Spencer took a double first in natural sciences and was awarded a Harkness scholarship in 1898. He went to Balliol College, Oxford, to begin a prize-winning study of the detrital minerals of new red sandstone in his native southwest England, revealing the palaeogeography of the Triassic period. Like Watts, Thomas was appointed to the British Geological Survey in 1901, and worked on Welsh petrology, Scottish vulcanology and petrological archaeology. He worked for the government in the First World War, like Fearnsides and many Sidney geologists, preparing reports on mineral resources and advising on other matters, such as the possible uses of the piezo-electric properties of quartz for submarine detection. In the 1920s Thomas worked in the Western Isles of Scotland and most famously at Stonehenge, where he identified the 'bluestones' there as coming from the Preseli Mountains in Pembrokeshire. A talented artist who provided drawings to accompany his books and papers, Thomas also wrote a long prize-winning poem about Stonehenge in 1925, contrasting new technology with the ancient monument:

'Above,
Secure across the skies men move,
Splendidly proving their conquest there,
Yet is this ring forlorn and bare
Not less a conquest great and rare.'

Voyage of the *Discovery*: H T Ferrar and Scott of the Antarctic

The scenery is lovely, but we have seen very little more than the Southern Cross expedition. I have done about two and a half month's sledging, but sledge pulling is very unscientific work and as revolting to a wet-bob [rower] as rolling a cricket pitch would be to him. Dogs are the things down here. We had about twenty, the size of mastiffs and the build of fox terriers. Three of them can pull a fortnight's gear (tent, jars and food) for three men. —Hartley Travers Ferrar, Oundle School magazine, July 1903

H H Thomas, like all geologists, travelled widely, including a trip to Iceland in 1902. The year before that, however, Hartley Travers Ferrar, a Sidney student from Oundle School, joined one of the most famous exploration trips of all time. Born in Ireland and brought up in South Africa, Ferrar was a typical young man of his period and class, a school prefect, captain of the Oundle boat club, football club, gymnasium and of the school, before going up to Sidney in 1898, the year after Fearnsides, to study natural sciences. He was appointed geologist to Captain Scott's first voyage to Antarctica in *Discovery* in July 1901. He quickly prepared himself and impressed Scott by his diligent and intelligent response to the challenge. Sir Clements Markham of the Royal Geographical Society chose Ferrar as a capable but 'very young, unfledged, and rather lazy' scientist who might, he believed, be 'made into a man' by the voyage.

Throughout the hastily planned but nearly three-year journey of exploration, Ferrar lived in a cabin in the bow of the ship that also functioned as a laboratory,

which he filled with geological specimens. His researches identified a category of hard stones that included basalts and dolerites, now known as the Ferrar supergroup, and his work cast much light on the geological structure of the Antarctic region. In October 1902 the great Ferrar glacier was named in his honour.

In February 1902 Ferrar accompanied Ernest Shackleton on a sledge party, and in June was adrift on an ice floe from which he and his group were rescued only with the greatest difficulty. Ferrar wrote to the new Sidney *Annual* in 1903 about the severe blizzard conditions, scurvy outbreaks and temperatures ranging between –32 and –62 degrees Fahrenheit: 'My poor nose has been having a very rough time…However, for the last three weeks I have wrapped it in cotton wool and cold cream!' He also described hunting seals, penguins and skua gulls, the sad and frequent deaths of the dogs, and the heartening concert parties and drama productions that took place on board the ship. In the Antarctic summer of 1903 Ferrar accompanied Scott to the high plateau of Victoria Land, and on that journey discovered rock samples containing fossilised plants, which proved the Antarctic had once had a warm climate. His geological surveys provided a considerable appendix to Scott's account of the voyage, published in 1905.

Ferrar returned to New Zealand on *Discovery* in 1904, from a remarkable if flawed voyage with the often bullying Scott. He later worked for the Egyptian geological survey in the eastern desert, served in Palestine during the First World War, and became assistant director of the Geological Survey of New Zealand, where he died in 1932.

H T Ferrar (third from right) in the wardroom on RRS Discovery. Scott Polar Research Institute

The wardroom was the venue for formal dinners where officers and scientists ate from Royal Doulton china and with engraved silver cutlery. Every Tuesday after dinner a debate was held on a scientific or topical subject

Mapping the Oil

Victor Charles Illing was the son of an army officer in India and entered Sidney as a scholar in 1909. Influenced by the Sidney geologist W G Fearnsides, Illing won the Harkness scholarship in 1912 and studied the trilobite fossils in Cambrian rocks in Warwickshire. He became a demonstrator in petroleum technology at Imperial College, London and worked for various oil companies around the world conducting major international surveys. Illing believed strongly in combining academic and practical work. He was elected a Fellow of the Royal Society in 1945.

V C Illing in 1912, his final year at Sidney

The Hall, c1913

This postcard was sent to his little brother 'K' on 14 November 1913 by Clarence Bailey (1913), a natural sciences student from Bromley, Kent. It explains that this is where the students dine 'at least five nights a week: there are four or five courses. The paintings you see are very valuable'. Bailey served in the war, took his degree in 1920 and later became a teacher

'A Rising College': Sidney Grows, 1890–1914

McCOMAS. Democracy, Crampton! – modern democracy!
WAITER. No, sir, not democracy: only education, sir.
Scholarships, sir. Cambridge Local, sir. Sidney Sussex College, sir.
Stone ginger, miss? Right, miss. Very good thing for him, sir: he
never had any turn for real work, sir.
VALENTINE. Which of us dare give that man an order again!
—George Bernard Shaw, *You Never Can Tell*, 1897. Walter the waiter, whose favourite
phrase gives the play its title, explains his son's background to social superiors

During Charles Smith's mastership, Sidney began to shape itself more clearly into the institution we know today. The building of Cloister Court in 1890–1, a project resisted by Robert Phelps, reflected the need for new accommodation as numbers rose: in 1843 there were nine admissions; in 1873, when the old tradition of entering the College register in Latin was abandoned, there were 11; in 1893 there were 20; and in 1913 there were 39. However, although the first issue of the first College magazine, *Pheon*, in 1894 proudly proclaimed 'we are a rising College', Sidney was among the smallest colleges in Cambridge, as it remains today. By comparison, in 1890 Clare had about 60 freshmen, Caius about 70, and Trinity 200. Sidney was still resolutely a 'reading college', and in addition to its impressive results in the Tripos, in 1908 a *Cambridge Review* survey showed that it had the second highest number of honours degrees to matriculations since 1850, and the highest between 1902 and 1908. Certainly the academic achievements of the late-Victorian and Edwardian periods were very considerable. Between 1898 and 1907, for instance, Sidney attained 54 firsts; similar-sized colleges, such as Magdalene (eight), Corpus (five), and St Catharine's (one), were not in the same league.

Charles Smith, by his son W Hammond Smith (1904)

More students now lived in licensed lodgings, fellows no longer had to be celibate, and the traditional clerical atmosphere changed to something more modern and secular. The abolition of fines for failure to attend Chapel in 1867 was a significant step, as was the appointment of the first College chaplain, Charles Thomas Whitmell, in 1889.

The Sidney intake in 1873 was distinctly middle-class. Boys came from schools such as Blundells, Sherborne and Bedford Grammar; their fathers' professions were typically in the church, medicine and farming. Geographically, the students hailed from across the country, including Wales, Scotland and Northern Ireland. In 1893, following a similar geographical spread, the schools included Blundell's, as ever, St Paul's, and Loughborough Grammar, and the fathers were still vicars and doctors, but now there were more businessmen and civil servants. The influence of the empire can be seen in the presence of boys from India and elsewhere, most having been to school in England. In 1894

Postcard of Sidney, dated 23 October 1914. One of the classic Frith's series showing the College at its most shaggily ivy-clad. By 1900 Sidney Street was Cambridge's most fashionable shopping street

Mamilal Doshi and his brother Tribhowandas Manekchand were among the first Indians at Sidney. From that time on many men native to the Indian subcontinent matriculated: Don Albert Kekulawal, a merchant's son from Colombo, in 1907, and Chandra Sinha Gaekwad from Baroda, in 1911, are typical examples. Gurunath Bewoor, who came to Sidney from Deccan College, Poona in 1909, was the first Indian appointed as director-general of the Indian Posts and Telegraphs Department, an appointment he held for seven years from 1934 to 1941. He was knighted for his services and appeared on an Indian stamp in 1989.

There were a fair number of Jewish boys, too, usually from London: Alfred Raphael Wolbrom, a wool merchant's son, in 1907; Isidore Montague Gluckstein, in 1909; and Benny Lockspeiser, a diamond setter's son, in 1910. Gluckstein ran the family business for many years during its hey-day, the famous J Lyon's catering empire with its Corner Houses and 'nippy' waitresses; Lockspeiser was knighted in recognition of a remarkable career as a scientist and administrator.

In the period 1900–14, along with the sons of vicars, civil servants, lawyers and doctors, we find those of many accountants, teachers, some missionaries, various manufacturers, a tea planter, a Welsh mining engineer, a Bradford wool merchant, a colliery cashier, a tug owner from North Shields, an East End baker, a Norfolk blacksmith, the curator of the Raffles natural history museum in Singapore and a Russian landowner. It was a fascinating mix of young men.

Discipline among students seems to have been good, with only rare admonitions appearing in the College minutes, and only a few fathers receiving letters about their sons' fighting, drinking and whoring. Something of a public school atmosphere can be found in this minute of 26 February 1877: 'Two undergraduates, Henry and Williams, having on Saturday evening, the 24th inst. just after Hall, had a disgraceful and ungentlemanly brawl in the Court – in which the terms 'Liar' and 'Blackguard' were interchanged and blows resorted to by Henry…' The unfortunate Albert Alexis Henry was sent down temporarily, but later became a priest. His adversary, Alfred Williams, son of a civil engineer from Brixton, became a barrister and judge and died of typhoid in Montreux in 1904.

All manner of sports clubs and academic, musical and social societies proliferated, with famous names such as the Porcupines, the Cromwell Club, the Lunaticks, the Confraternitas Historica and the Banjo Club established. *Pheon* first appeared in June 1894, and the following year, testifying to the revival of the Chapel in College life, it announced that 'a regularly organised choir is to be raised…The Hymns and Chants will be in harmony instead of in unison…and Tallis's responses will be sung'. The college cat became a major character in *Pheon* in the 1890s, accused of all kinds of misdeeds: 'An anti-feline

Indian postage stamp showing Gurunath Bewoor, 1989. Private collection

The Cromwells, c1910, taken in what is now the Knox-Shaw Room in Cloister Court

society is being formed', it announced in 1896. *Pheon* was superseded by the College *Annual* in 1903, but returned in 1922. All this, along with events such as May Balls and smoking concerts from the 1890s, further helped to define a strong sense of collegial identity among the increasing numbers of students.

The College minutes became longer, more detailed and regularised, and, following the Cambridge reforms enacted in 1882, an annual College meeting was established. The roles of fellows became more specialised, both academically and within

Sidney May Ball, 1894, photograph by Stearn & Sons

The novelist John Cowper Powys, a student at Corpus Christi and friend of the Sidney undergraduate W E Lutyens (1892) can be seen sitting second from the left in the first seated row. Fourth from the left is the master, Charles Smith

Aerial view of Cleethorpes taken in 1996

Street names in the town read like an index to this book and include: Basset, Blundell, Bramhall, Combe, Craven, Cromwell, Dugard, Fuller, Hardy, Harington, Hey, L'Estrange, May, Minshull, Montagu, Phelps, Sidney, Sussex, Ward, Weekes and Wollaston

College administration; the role of bursar independent of the master, for instance, was established. The fellowship remained very small, however, never rising above 10. By comparison, Clare had 18 in 1880, Caius 29, King's 43 and Trinity 56. Only the fellowships at Downing, Magdalene and St Catharine's were smaller than Sidney's.

The Sidney Fellowship, 1897

21st June 1897

E.H Griffiths,   H.C Robson,   A.H. McNeile,   G.A Weekes,

R.H.D Mayall,   F.H. Neville,   G.M. Edwards,

J.W. Hicks,   C. Smith,   H. Marshall Ward,   R. Machray,
(Bp. of Bloemfontein)   (Master)   (Prof. of Botany)   (Abp. of Rupertsland)

Three hundred and one years on from the foundation, the first group photograph of the master and fellows shows that Sidney still comprised just 10 fellows and a master, along with a relatively small number of undergraduates and no post-graduates. Scientists (Griffiths, Neville and Ward) and mathematicians (Smith, Robson, Edwards and Mayall), now outnumber the churchmen (McNeile, Weekes, Hicks and Machray).

The Sidney gardener, W Baily, and assistant, with a useful-looking new mowing machine, in front of the Master's Lodge, c1865

Sidney's growth was matched by that of the town of Cleethorpes, much of the land of which had belonged to the College since it was purchased in 1616. Until the second half of the 19th century it had provided around 15 per cent of Sidney's income through agricultural rents; by 1914 that percentage had risen to nearly 60 per cent, in spite of the agrarian depression that affected all Oxbridge colleges' incomes. The reason for this huge improvement was that the growth of Grimsby as a port had created a demand for housing for local workers and businessmen in the north of the area, now known as 'New Cleethorpes'; and, since the late-18th century, the southern area of the estate around Oole, Itterby and Thrunscoe had become popular as a seaside resort. Following a Sidney Sussex College Estate Act of 1853, and the arrival of the railway in 1863, Sidney-leased land became far more valuable. Through a variety of shrewd commercial (and often generously paternalistic) development, Sidney, supported by the local council, leased land on 99-year leases and reaped enormous profits. By 1914 Cleethorpes had expanded to a remarkable extent: Sidney owned land on which were built residential properties, commercial sites, churches, a park, recreation grounds, cottage homes, council offices and a cemetery. A map of Cleethorpes today shows how deeply Sidney influenced the character of the town: almost every street name is connected with the College, perhaps the most famous instance being Blundell Park, the home of Grimsby Town Football Club.

Alongside the usual focus on such estate management, academic awards and building works, other matters dealt with at meetings included the selling of land to railway companies; the donation of money to the new All Saints church in Jesus Lane in 1859, the Zoological Museum in 1868, and the Woodwardian Museum in 1871; the creation of a new role of head waiter (to be paid £60 a year) and the reorganisation of the kitchen and catering; the purchase of a new mowing machine for the two gardeners; and construction of an iron staircase on the garden side of the Master's Lodge in 1866. In 1869, the cook of 40 years standing, George Wilson, retired and was succeeded by Charles Barber on a salary of £100 a year. His duties included hiring all cooks and servants, and serving all dinners, which that year were one shilling and eight pence. Although he could run a private business, he was not allowed to make a profit from College meals. A sign of new times in 1907 was the conversion of the old stables into a larder for the kitchen, and the replacement of the blacksmith's shop by a greenhouse for the improved gardens.

Roll of the Confraternitas Historica, illuminated by Morton and Newey, Birmingham, 1910. The date under the crest suggests basic historical skills still needed improvement

Cloister Court

Cloister Court today, showing the view perhaps most loved by members of Sidney, with the building erected in 1890–91 to the left, the Hall and north side of Hall Court, looking on to the croquet lawn. Cloister Court, inside and out, is a fine example of neo-Jacobean architecture, designed by the great Victorian architect J L Pearson. It perfectly complements the old Elizabethan red brick visible since Wyatville's stucco was removed about 1930. The inset shows a 1914 postcard of the Pearson building.

Cambridge, Sidney Sussex College, New Court.

'The Master': Frank Lee Woodward, Buddhist

> What a lot of rubbish, this talk of Frank becoming a Buddhist; there *ought* to be a law to make everyone Church of England! —F L Woodward's sister on hearing of his conversion, c1900

Whereas H T Ferrar had gone out into the physical world to study it, others went abroad to travel inwards. Sidney missionaries went to countries such as Africa and India to spread Christianity among people they regarded as heathens. By the early-20th century, however, there were new possibilities.

Frank Lee Woodward, the third son of an impoverished Norfolk parson, went to Sidney from Christ's Hospital as a pensioner in 1890. He considered himself of 'Puritan stock' and was always proud to have gone to Cromwell's college; he considered Cromwell the greatest of Englishmen. Woodward earned a Lovett exhibition in 1892 intended for the sons of graduate clergymen expected to take holy orders. He was by no means an especially gifted scholar when he entered Sidney, and like many found more satisfaction in rugby, rowing and athletics. However, he was awarded the classics prize as well as a prize for a Latin essay in 1891, and was a keen member of the debating society. He was Chapel organist throughout his time at Sidney, perhaps playing on the harmonium that was hired in the 1890s for musical services. Woodward's sense of fun can be seen in his playing of passages from Gilbert and Sullivan as slow-paced voluntaries on this notoriously deficient instrument.

Woodward took a lower second in classics in 1893 and, rather than entering the church, as his father expected, he became a school teacher. He taught at various

F L Woodward by K L Sumathipala, 1921. Mahinda College, Sri Lanka

ous grammar and minor public schools before becoming vice-principal at Stamford in 1898, where his educational philosophy was that pupils should 'learn to learn' rather than be crammed. Woodward was a fairly typical late Victorian in his admiration for Tennyson, Plato and especially for the Stoic philosophy of Marcus Aurelius, a late-19th-century fashion that stressed reason, moderation and removal from passion as well as service and manliness. Marcus Aurelius, whom he later characterised as a Bodhisattva, led Woodward's thinking beyond western traditions. Stamford was an active theosophical centre and Woodward joined the Theosophical Society in 1901, developing a belief in reincarnation and above all in the teachings of the Buddha. He believed the Society was a preparation for the coming of the Buddha and the reconciliation of the world's religious and political conflicts.

Through his correspondence with the Society's president, Colonel H S Olcott, Woodward was appointed principal of the Mahinda Buddhist College in Galle, southwest Ceylon (Sri Lanka), where he arrived in August 1903. In rejecting both Christianity and the dominance of science, Woodward had turned his back on the foundations of the education offered at Sidney.

Like Harrow's George Butler, Westminster's John Rae, and many other Sidneians, Woodward was a legendary head of school. He was a strict disciplinarian and a charming eccentric who gave his pupils Shakespearean nicknames. Through his efforts and personal financial contribution he expanded Mahinda College so that it had to move. Calling himself 'Wanapala', Woodward devised a logo and school flag, designed new buildings, built a science laboratory and made *dharma* (Buddhist doctrine) and the Sinhalese language central to the curriculum. A strong believer in the integrity of Ceylon's national identity and self-determination, he was closely involved in the founding of the nation's first university. Woodward also sent a number of his pupils at Mahinda to Sidney, men such as Mohamed Cassius Ismail, a jeweller's son, who matriculated in 1908. He hoped these young men would return to their native country to form a progressive elite. In his western guise, though, Woodward was a conservative, an anti-Catholic and opposed trade unions.

By 1919, Woodward had achieved all he could at Mahinda College. He had grown impatient with many aspects of Sinhalese society, and looked for a quiet and remote location where he could meditate and undertake the translations of the Buddhist scriptures that he had begun for the Pali Text Society. Through a friendship with a colonial businessman in Ceylon, he chose a site at Rowella, on the river Tamar near Launceston in Tasmania, 'the poor man's England', where he lived as a recluse until his death in 1952. He bought a simple bungalow, 'Bhatkawa', in a deserted orchard, living the poor and austere life of a vegetarian, yoga-practising mystic. He translated Buddhist texts from the original Pali on palm leaves, and created a massive concordance of them with a former Stamford pupil who called him 'the Master'. The Buddhist judge Christmas Humphreys called Woodward's popular *Some Sayings of the Buddha*, reprinted many times from 1925, 'the finest anthology of the Pali canon ever produced'. Woodward, who would often wear a paper bag for a shirt, made astrological charts for locals and practised 'astral projection'. Yet the rather suburban location at Rowella was also where he hung school and Sidney sports team photographs on the wall, diligently recorded the scores of the old boys' rugby team, and looked after an army of cats. In 1932 he wrote a book called *Francis Bacon and the Cypher Story*, an eccentric contribution to the theory that Francis Bacon wrote Shakespeare's plays. His ashes were scattered on a rose bed in a neighbour's garden in 1952.

'The Oaten Incident': Subhas Chandra Bose and a Sidney 'Racialist'

And of course, the basic idea was so absurd, that I thought of my students as barbarians, students with whom I spent hours on the cricket field, and whom I in many cases made my friends. It was just too silly. But everything is grist to the mill of the political agitator.
—E F Oaten, *My Memories of India*, 1984

Little did I then realise the inner significance of the tragic events of 1916. My Principal had expelled me, but he had made my future career. —Subhas Chandra Bose, *An Indian Pilgrim: An Unfinished Autobiography*, 1937/1997

*Subhas Chandra Bose
shakes hands with Hitler,
1 June 1942, in East
Prussia, Germany*

Frank Lee Woodward had a largely untroubled relationship with admiring cohorts of Sinhalese students at Mahinda College. Not all Sidney men working as teachers in the empire had such a happy time, however, and one of them inspired one of the most famous anti-imperial political careers in 20th-century history. Edward Farley Oaten, a pupil of Tonbridge School, went up to Sidney in 1903 and took a first-class degree in classics in 1906. In 1907 he took an LLB, wrote two books on Anglo-Indian subjects, and was then appointed a professor of history at Presidency College, part of the University of Calcutta. He had a remarkable time in India, and later recounted many adventures and encounters. He recalled one incident on Woollar Lake in Kashmir that has a particularly Sidney touch: 'On the occasion I had had difficulty in resisting the invitations of the boatman to utilise the services of a woman he knew was available. Fortunately my Puritan upbringing and the knowledge that syphilis was rife in Kashmir came to the rescue.'

Among a number of increasingly rebellious Indian students was Subhas Chandra Bose, often called Netaji, whose violent encounter with his English professor has gone down in the history of the Indian Nationalist movement as a seminal moment.

Two main accounts of the notorious 'Oaten Incident' in early 1916 have come down to us, one from the point of view of Bose and his supporters, and one from Oaten himself. In fact there were two incidents, which have been conflated as one. In the first, in January, Oaten gave a talk in which he drew a parallel between the Hellenisation of the Middle East by the Greeks after Alexander the Great, and the Anglicisation of India and the introduction of English among the educated. According to Oaten, 'it was a perfectly fair and natural comparison' seized upon by a 'handful of "bad hats"'. His opponents maintained that it revealed 'racial prejudice on the part of an arrogant Englishman'.

The second incident, in February, caused a strike among students. Under college rules, they were not allowed to walk in the corridors during lectures, and when some did so very noisily, Oaten came out from his classroom with his arms outstretched and stopped them from going further. Oaten claims there was no contact between him and any student. Many believed, however, that he had raised his hand, and about 10 students attacked him later that day; 'Oatenisation' became a term used by students at the time to describe assaulting a teacher. As a result of the attack, Bose, considered by the authorities to be a very clever but dangerous 19-year-old and a likely ring-leader, was expelled from Presidency College. The principal was dismissed for failing to maintain discipline at the college. Bose later said that this incident gave him the 'character' that spurred him on to become a legendary and highly controversial leader of the Indian Independence Movement against the British Raj.

After a spell at Cambridge and a briefer one in the Indian civil service in the early 1920s, Bose entered politics. He was often in conflict with Gandhi over the issue of non-violence, and resigned from the Indian National Congress to form his own more radical party, the All India Forward Bloc. He was imprisoned 11 times by the British authorities, and in 1939 fled from India to Germany via Russia seeking an alliance with Hitler and Mussolini against Britain. He then went to Japan and helped to create the Indian National Army from Indian prisoners of war and southeast Asian plantation workers, leading them against British forces. He is believed to have died in a plane crash over Taiwan in August 1945.

During the Great War, Oaten served with the 11th King Edward's Own Lancers (Probyn's Horse) on the Northwest Frontier, then as a high-ranking administrator in the Indian education system, and returned to England in 1928, where he became a barrister and judge. His memoirs show that although a loyal imperialist he also supported the essential aims of Bose; in 1967, six years before his death, he wrote a poem comparing the young rebel with the Greek hero Icarus:

'Let me recall but this,
That while as yet the Raj that once you
    Challenged in your land,
Was mighty, Icarus-like,
Your courage planned to meet the skies,
And storm in battle set
The ramparts of high Heaven.'

'Obscure Geometry': Arthur Romney Green, Designer

This mould of cross-wise plank and timber wrought
    By wind and wave – unletter'd age-long thought
And dauntless toil in conquest of the sea!
    Well may I ask, And which most wonderful,
    The elemental, means the perfect hull,
The script of its obscure geometry?
—Arthur Romney Green, 'The Sailing Ship'

Photographic cabinet by A R Green, 1924–39. Victoria and Albert Museum, London

Another Edwardian idealist and nonconformist was the socialist designer, poet and theorist, Arthur Romney Green, son of a London barrister, who went up to Sidney as an exhibitioner in 1891 from a Quaker boarding school in Devon. He did not excel in his subject, mathematics, and his life at Sidney was dominated by sports, women and wide reading. He rowed in the College eight and won the maiden sculls in his first term, later recalling that 'in a small college if you row and play rugby you must sometimes row a trial eight race in the morning and play a football match in the afternoon, with an intervening lunch of beefsteak and champagne – such was the prescription. And so the time passed merrily away.'

'Keeping a Term': Edwardian Reminiscences from Thomas Knox-Shaw

Thomas Knox-Shaw, a London oculist's son, came to Sidney from Blundell's in 1905 to read mathematics. He remembered taking the 'Previous Examination' as a diminutive choirboy and dining in Hall with Charles Smith, the fellows and his father.

'In my undergraduate days the word "keep" was frequently used. If one was going to tea on a Sunday with Mrs Weekes [the master's wife], one would ask one's friends if they were "keeping a Kate next Sunday". If one wanted to know where a friend had rooms in College or digs, one went to the Porter's Lodge and asked where he kept. One went to Whitechapel [the old bath house] to keep a forth. I do not know what they looked like, as I had a wc at the top of K and did not have to go there. The word has survived in "keeping a term".

'When I went up in 1905 I was in A1, New Court; now K1, Cloister Court. The bedmakers in those days had a very hard life. They both had to come at six o'clock in the morning to light the fires and to remove the baths if the bath had been in the sitting room because the bedroom was too small. They were the ordinary, round, little saucer baths. The bedmakers had to go later to the buttery to draw commons which were three inches of butter and a loaf of bread. Any commons which were left over from the previous day was the bedder's perquisite. I used to see them leaving College with their bags packed, sometimes with quite unused loaves of bread and all the other things left over.

'I always used to have breakfast in my room. One of the assistants from the local grocers used to come round for orders for those groceries which were wanted, such as porridge, jam and marmalade, apples and so on, and they used to be delivered the same morning…You could get a sixpenny breakfast from the College kitchens or a more elaborate shilling breakfast. The only meal served in Hall was dinner and, looking towards the high table from the left, the freshmen's table, the middle, second year table, and the one on the far right was the third year table. The BAs dined in the gallery. There were only, I think, 10 fellows and 75 undergraduates and graduates in residence…

'When I was an undergraduate, education was not given the status of a charity. It was made so in one of Lloyd George's budgets. Scholars and exhibitioners therefore paid income tax on the value of their awards. There was a

Thomas Knox-Shaw, by Sir James Gunn, 1949

personal allowance but unfortunately I did not record it in my account book. I think it was £150 or £160 pa. Tax was paid on the average income for the previous three years. My scholarships were as follows:

Open major scholarship £80 for four years
Blundell exhibition £60 for three years
Huish exhibition £50 for four years

'The numbers in the College were so small that it was only possible to have one boat in the May and Lent races. The club tried but failed to get a second boat on. I rowed bow in the first boat. Our coach was a Jesus rowing blue. He was then in his fourth year and had not even taken the Previous Examination. That was possible when Fairbairn of Jesus was the famous rowing coach.

'Funerals. If any undergraduate was sent down he went to the station in a hansom cab, with a large piece of black material tied on the whip. His friends followed in any horse-drawn vehicle they could hire.

'In my fourth year I had to go to lodgings in Chesterton Road, but only for one term because the freshman in K4 New Court was noisy and disturbed G M Edwards [fellow and first historian in Sidney] in K3. He rolled stone ginger-beer bottles down the stone staircase to see how far they would go before they broke. His final episode was to toboggan down the staircase in his round tin saucer bath. He was sent out of College and I was put in his rooms.'

Green took a third in 1894, and trained as a teacher before, like George Hilditch Mason nearly half a century earlier, working among the Zulus in Natal. In South Africa he wrote poetry, designed furniture and built boats. Shortly after the outbreak of the Boer War, Green returned to England and set up a workshop at Bosham in the harbour at Chichester. Self-trained, he turned to mathematics as the source of many of his designs, using angles, curves and a variety of other geometrical shapes as his inspiration for some remarkably original designs. Though he was academically mediocre at Sidney, his training in maths underpinned most of his creative and theoretical work.

Green moved to Haslemere, Surrey in 1903, where he set up a larger workshop. By this time he was under the influence of the Arts and Crafts movement. Green became an internationally exhibited designer and furniture-maker before the First World War. He also set up a local Independent Labour Party above the workshop, attended by the great socialists William Beveridge and R H Tawney. Green lectured at the Fabian Society in 1908 against the utilitarian socialism espoused by Ramsay MacDonald, and argued for the centrality of art and creativity in any future utopia.

In 1909 Green ran away with his dentist's wife, leaving his own wife with their only child. As a result, even the Senior Art Workers' Guild refused to accept him as a member when he was proposed. The couple moved to the Arts and Crafts community at Hammersmith, London, where Green met Harold Monro, whose poetry bookshop he furnished in 1913, the sculptor and designer Eric Gill, and the painter Augustus John. In 1919 he moved to Christchurch (then in Hampshire) and remained there for the rest of his life. His workshop produced an enormous range of furniture and other objects, and Green continued to make boats. He wrote and lectured widely on art, craft, and social and economic matters, his arguments frequently supported by mathematical concepts and equations. During the 1930s, when his workshop was faring badly, he worked for the Rural Industries Bureau, travelling the country teaching unemployed men. He died following a road accident in 1945 and therefore did not witness the growth of his reputation and the acquisition of some of his pieces by the Victoria and Albert Museum.

Riots in Wisbech: Horace Dimock and the National Insurance Act

> It was an awesome and impressive sight. A scene not easy to describe, but never to be forgotten. There were screams from frightened women. Men shouted and commenced running but the Police were on them. The noise increased to a roar, people rolled over like ninepins and the dull sickening thud of the truncheons could be distinctly heard as they found rest on the backs of the men. —Eyewitness report of the Wisbech Riots, 1913

We have seen that increasingly lawyers and doctors sent their sons to Sidney. This was a general development by which the new professional classes began to dominate the intake and ethos at Oxford and Cambridge. Law was introduced as a Tripos subject in 1858 and medicine was part of the natural sciences Tripos. From around

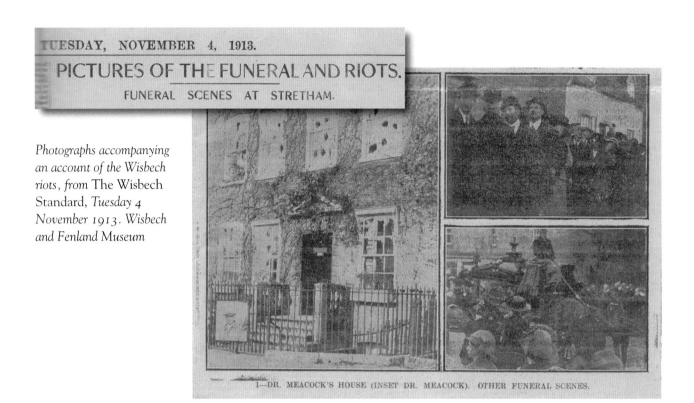

Photographs accompanying
an account of the Wisbech
riots, from The Wisbech
Standard, *Tuesday 4
November 1913. Wisbech
and Fenland Museum*

1860, when William Bartlett Dalby, later an eminent ear specialist and president of the Medical Society, entered Sidney, the College produced many doctors and major figures in the medical profession. They include the fellow Arthur Wanklyn, Charles Powell White the cancer specialist, the radiologist Alfred Charles Jordan, the medical lawyer and psychoanalyst William Alfred Brend, and the president of the British Medical Association, Frederick George Thomson.

Perhaps the most fascinating, and tragic, medical student is Horace Dimock, a local boy who entered Sidney as a pensioner in 1899. Subsequently trained at St Thomas', and a specialist in anaesthetics, he became a house surgeon at Addenbrooke's hospital, and eventually a general practitioner in Wisbech, Cambridgeshire in 1911. This was the year of the National Insurance Act, which required 12 million workers earning less than £160 a year to pay into a scheme providing protection against sickness and unemployment. The Act marked the beginnings of the welfare state, which expanded rapidly after 1945. At the time, private GPs worked in affluent areas and the free medical care due to workers was usually provided by less well-paid 'panel doctors'.

Few private doctors were prepared to do such work, and in Wisbech Horace Dimock was drafted in as a panel doctor to deal with the greatly increased workload. As a local man and a principled servant of his patients, Dimock was hugely popular with the poorer sections of Wisbech, but caused resentment among most of the other doctors. Dimock's relationship with his fellow doctors deteriorated and in October 1913 some locals, mistakenly thinking it would help, sent poison pen letters and postcards to many of Dimock's adversaries in a hand similar to his own. One recipient, the wealthy Dr H C Meacock, called the police and Dimock was arrested and sent before the magistrates. Remanded on bail on a charge of criminal libel, he appealed to the Medical Defence Society, only to discover that they were acting on behalf of the other doctors. On 27 October, tired, depressed, and in a seemingly impossible situation, Dimock returned home to nearby Stretham. He was found dead the next morning; he had taken a huge overdose of morphine and veronal.

On 30 October, after the news of Dimock's suicide had broken, a large mob gathered in Wisbech, charged towards Dr Meacock's house by the river and threw bricks and stones through his windows. Meacock's wife fainted. The situation became very dangerous, as the chanting crowd grew to over 6,000 and the police had to call in reinforcements. With the rising violence apparently getting out of control, the mayor of Wisbech read the Riot Act, and the police moved in with truncheons and dispersed the crowd. It was a local incident with national repercussions, and became the focus of much debate in the newspapers and in parliament as unrest continued in Wisbech for several days.

Death in the Laboratory

George Mines, son of an HM Inspector of Schools, entered Sidney as an exhibitioner in 1904. A brilliant physiologist, Mines was elected a fellow in 1909 and married the poet Marjorie Rolfe, a member of Rupert Brooke's circle. He travelled widely to conduct his research on the heart. In 1914 he was offered the professorship of physiology at McGill University in Canada where he conducted original and highly complex experiments in electrophysiology on frog and tortoise cardiac muscle. Mines was discovered unconscious in his laboratory on 7 November 1914 and died in hospital aged 28. The cause of his death is still a mystery though it is thought he may have been a victim of self-experimentation, something in which he was known to be very interested. Mines's pioneering work is still considered important today.

George Ralph Mines, c1909

'The Spiritual Atmosphere of Devotion': Sidney's New Chapel

The beauty of this building is quiet, yet absorbing; it is solemn, yet it represents the joyous freedom of the Renaissance with cherubs and clusters of carving alive and dancing, all held in check by the vertical lines of the piers. Nor does the oak carving in its detail lack dignity; each separate part of it the architect has designed with exacting care, in strict relationship with its surroundings. —The Architectural Review, March 1924

Detail of carving by Herbert Read of Exeter, Chapel window

Detail of marble and bronze altar

John Wale Hicks, later Bishop of Bloemfontein, had entered Sidney in 1866, took a first in natural sciences and became a fellow, dean, a fully trained doctor and author of books on both inorganic chemistry and theology. He had realised during Phelps's time that the new 1882 statutes would affect the future religious life of the College very seriously, by taking away the requirement that the master and fellows be ordained. He moved successfully that the Chapel be put under the authority of a dean or chaplain and not the governing body. This allowed successors to develop Sidney's churchmanship in a direction quite radical among Oxford and Cambridge colleges, and a rather strange one for a college with Sidney's traditions. Among these successors was the future master G A Weekes, a fellow since 1894, chaplain from 1893 to 1895, an army chaplain in the Boer War and then dean; and Thomas Knox-Shaw who, except for his service in the army during the First World War, lived in Sidney from 1905 until 1957, and attended matins, communion and evensong every day. Such fellows, who also included E J Passant and B T D Smith, shaped the College's character in the early decades of the 20th century.

Smith, who had come to Sidney in 1918 via Jesus, Westcott House and St John's, and who was dean from 1919, was especially active in encouraging the Anglo-Catholic tendency at Sidney. He collaborated with Eric Milner-White of King's in 1920 to produce *Cambridge Offices and Orisons*, an anthology of medieval liturgies, and wrote *A Little Guide to Eucharistic Worship* in the same year, in which he appealed for a 'spiritual atmosphere in devotion'. Throughout the 1920s he contributed to the regular Anglo-Catholic congresses.

Smith, Knox-Shaw and Milner-White, with advice from the older A H McNeile, had been founders of the Oratory of the Good Shepherd in 1913, an important confraternity of priests and laymen in Cambridge that later adopted the Mission to Fruitpickers at Wisbech. The declaration of intention of the Oratory was made in the new Sidney Chapel, partially completed in 1913, and the daily mass was held there for the first few months. Weekes was a president of the Sanctae Trinitatis Confraternitas, comprising Cambridge fellows and students devoted to supporting Catholic services. When J W Reynolds set up Sidney's Confraternitas Historica in 1910, he was in part making a humorous reference to the STC and, in the constitution and ceremonies, to the terminology of the late-medieval Catholic church.

Opposite: *The Chapel today, looking south towards the altar*

ABOVE: *Statue of St George, with the arms of Archbishop Machray below*

BELOW: *Serpent coiled round the Tree of Knowledge, detail of arch to Lady Chapel*

The camaraderie of these devout fellows, their shared aesthetic interests and theological convictions, brought incense and elaborate vestments, bells, statues of saints, the worship of Mary, private confession, plainsong, prayers for the dead, the English Missal, and a host of other forms of worship that would have appalled most of their predecessors. Many Sidney fellows believed that in ever more secular times such features might attract undergraduates who could just as easily be drawn to the new philosophies of, for instance, Nietzsche, theosophy, the Bloomsbury thinker G E Moore, and a number of other secular and scientific ideologies. Theirs was the same Anglo-Catholic impulse that was found earlier in J W Shorthouse's historical novel *John Inglesant* (1888), J W Reynolds's favourite book.

In 1896, J L Pearson, the architect of New (Cloister) Court and a highly regarded ecclesiastical architect in his own right, was asked by the College to draw up plans for a new neo-Gothic Chapel to run along the northern wall of Cloister Court. These proved unaffordable, and instead by 1911 the decision had been taken to transform the old Chapel, the funding to come from past and present members, three-quarters of it from the fellows. The architect chosen, T H Lyon of Corpus Christi, was an Anglo-Catholic and later the director of design in the university's School of Architecture.

The old Chapel, built by James Essex in the 1770s, was very small at 20 by 30 feet, and about the same size as the one at Trinity Hall. It had a stone flagged floor and deal wainscotting, a panel with pillars for the Pittoni painting above the altar at the south end, and a gallery at the north end for the master and his family to enter from the Lodge through the library. Lyons kept the shell of Essex's building, but lengthened it considerably to 90 feet by extending the Chapel southwards. The dividing line between the old space and new is at the point where the readers' stalls are placed. The floor rises from there by a number of steps towards the altar.

A memorial chapel, the present Lady Chapel, was added to the west side of the building next to the sanctuary. From Wyatville's building, Lyons altered the last upper window to the south and the last but one on the ground floor to the north. The old bell, bought from Pembroke Hall in 1707 and recast in 1739, was retained until 1930 when it was replaced with a new one.

Although the structural work was finished in 1912, the preparation and installation of the elaborate internal fittings was delayed by a financial shortfall and the outbreak of war. Freshmen of 1919 later recalled the old painted deal stalls in the old (north) end and the workmen's benches in the south end. That year, with further fund-raising underway, it was decided to complete the work as a memorial to the men who had fallen in the Great War and to inscribe a roll of honour in the antechapel.

The builders on the project were Coulson and Son of Cambridge, the marble floor was laid by T Jenkins of Torquay, the panelling and oak work were executed by Herbert Read of Exeter, and the large carved figures were by Nathaniel Hitch. When the work was completed in 1923 the building was dedicated by the Archbishop of York, Cosmo Gordon Lang, on 21 October.

The antechapel now contains wall memorials to the dead of the two world wars and to three masters, Parris, Elliston and Chafy, and to an obscure undergraduate who died in College in 1836, Robert Field of Ipswich. Phelps's brass memorial is on the floor in front of the Second World War memorial. Memorials of other masters and fellows can be found inside the Chapel. As with windows in the Old Library above it, the antechapel windows now have inset panels created from the Franciscan glass found during the 1958 excavations by Sidney's Peter Salway. The presence of Oliver Cromwell's head buried somewhere nearby is marked by a tablet installed in 1960.

Commemoration of the living from the Roman Canon on a panel near the altar

The interior of the Chapel is remarkable for its long barrel-vaulted space, ornate free neo-Wren style, and Grinling Gibbons-inspired carving. The view down the Chapel is dominated by the marble and bronze altar and by the Pittoni painting. The floor is paved with different coloured marbles – soft grey, black, white and medium dark green, with two pieces of Arizona in front of the readers' stalls and one square of yellow Sienna in front of the altar. The walls are panelled in oak up to a height of 19 feet.

The complex symbolism of the Chapel's wood-work was explained by B T D Smith in two issues of *Pheon* in 1923. Above the picture at the altar end stands the pelican in her piety and below are the instruments of the Passion. The circular panels over the arches leading to the Lady Chapel refer to the sacrament of the altar: the gift of manna to the Israelites, the feeding of the multitude, the striking of the rock by Moses, and the piercing of Christ's side. The arch over the Lady Chapel entrance portrays the serpent coiled round the tree of knowledge at one end and, at the other, the serpent slain. The figures on the bosses beneath the cornice represent, on the east side, the four evangelists and the angel of the Gospel and, on the west side, across the sanctuary, the five authors of the New Testament epistles. The sanctuary windows

honour the Passion and blessed sacrament. The curving plaster ribs in the ceiling portray subjects from the 'Benedicite' entwined in a riband inscribed 'Laus Deo': peacocks, fishes, children, and the beasts and cattle of the field.

The spandrels above the readers' stalls carry peacocks symbolising the Resurrection.

The wooden figure of St Francis preaching to the birds to the right of the altar, carved by Nathaniel Hitch, was given in memory of J W Reynolds, the fellow who died in the Great War in 1915; he was a great enthusiast for Sidney's 'patron saint'. In the gallery above the Chapel entrance there is a statue of St George dedicated to Archbishop Robert Machray.

The Chapel windows commemorate the early benefactors of the College: James Montagu, Sir Francis Clerke, Peter Blundell, Sir John Harington and the Earl of Kent, the Montagu family, Sir John Hart and Sir John Brereton. The Lady Chapel windows include an annunciation given by the Sanctae Trinitas Confraternitas, and a memorial to G M Edwards, author of the first history of Sidney and a benefactor of the Chapel. On the pillars in the Lady Chapel entrance are the arms of Archbishop Hicks, and on the floor beneath the windows, a slab commemorating Charles Smith, master when the Chapel work was begun.

Rhun and Porius: W E Lutyens and J C Powys

> 'Porius and Rhun had been suckled at the same breast, the breast of the beautiful Alarch daughter of Iddawc, but *that* wouldn't make them alike! They both had the blood of Iddawc the Apostate – but *that* wouldn't make them alike!
> 'Why were they so alike? Morfydd might well indeed have asked herself that disturbing question. She might well have wondered whether she would not sooner have been sister to them both rather than bride of either!'
> —J C Powys, *Porius*, 1951

The priest and poet William Enderby Lutyens, brother of the architect Sir Edwin Lutyens, met the novelist John Cowper Powys at Sherborne School in 1887 and they became firm friends. Lutyens was the more scholarly of the two, helping Powys with his homework and advising him on classical and Hebrew references throughout his career. In 1892 they both went up to Cambridge, Lutyens to Sidney and Powys to Corpus Christi. Lutyens was a remarkable athlete who won the mile against Oxford four years in succession, held a number of athletics records, and was president of the Athletics Club. In 1895 he won the Cambridge versus Yale mile race on the Cambridge athletics team tour of America.

The two men remained good friends at Cambridge and Powys attended the Sidney May Ball in 1894 for which Lutyens was the secretary. Through Powys, Lutyens met the future Sidney Chapel architect T H Lyon, who was also at Corpus and clearly in love with Powys. In 1895 Lutyens went to the Anglo-Catholic clergy training school, now Westcott House, around the corner from Sidney, where the assistant principal later was B T D Smith. In 1914 Lutyens was appointed vicar of St Luke's,

Gillingham, Kent, a parish mainly populated by Chatham dockworkers. In 1918 he joined the Oratory of the Good Shepherd, an order with which Sidney had very close connections, and which provided him with curates as assistants in his large parish, including the future theologian Alec Vidler. With the advice of his brother, he gave the church an ornate Anglo-Catholic interior. Lutyens was an enormously prolific writer of poetry, plays and sermons, most dedicated to the children of his working-class parishioners, and composed with a simplicity aimed at the young imagination reminiscent of William Blake. His *Thor's Stone*, a re-telling of a Norse legend, and *Balder the Beautiful*, have echoes of Powys's *A Glastonbury Romance* (1932). Lutyens was a devoted priest, but also a man of powerful physical appetites and pagan interests, who ended a life of celibacy in 1942 to marry Muriel Chapman at the age of 70.

When Powys married his first wife, T H Lyon's sister Margaret, in 1896, Lutyens officiated at the ceremony. The Powys's only son, Middleton, was born in 1901, following the clinical 'deflowering' of Margaret in hospital, so great was Powys's horror of 'taking a virgin'. The marriage was an unhappy one, and Powys seems to have believed that Lutyens might be the natural father of Middleton.

Powys's finest novel, *Porius*, is set in the year AD 499. The scene is a Roman fort in north Wales, and the title character is a son of the reigning prince. The Saxons and their forest-people allies are advancing on Edeyrnion in a desperate attempt to save the remnants of their matriarchate. Arthur has sent ahead the magicians Merlin, Neneue and Medrawd, to help the beleaguered Porius. Begun in 1942, it is a mythological but also highly personal novel concerned with the early years of Powys's first marriage. Powys appears as two characters, Porius himself and the god-like Myrddin Wilt. He based the fleet-footed foster-brother of Porius, Rhun, who has broken his vows of chastity, on the athletic Lutyens. It is Rhun whom the matriarchal forest people would prefer as leader, and Porius's wife Morfydd, based on Margaret Lyon, is in love with Rhun. However, Porius is triumphant. Like Powys in real life, he wonders throughout the book about the paternity of his son. Margaret died in 1947, Lutyens in 1950, the year before *Porius* was published, Lyon in 1953 and Powys in 1963.

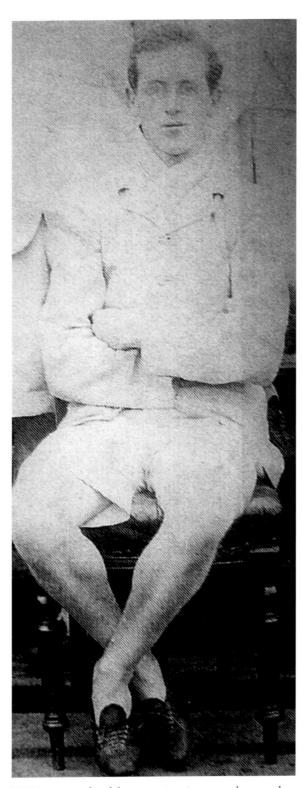

W E Lutyens, detail from a university team photograph c1895. Lutyens attended Commemoration Dinners at Sidney throughout his life

'I Would Not See Him Again': Sidney and the Great War

On one particularly fine evening, after we had lain down, we all jumped up: it was too
beautiful: a moonlight night – and we were too full of the joy of life to sleep: we adjourned
to the Fellows' garden, Reynolds leading the way, in a particularly gorgeous dressing-gown.
We ran about the grass after each other. Then, J.K.S., throwing a sheet over my head, ran
round the lawn, pulling me after him – making ghostly noises; for after the Tripos, at the
end of the summer term, several of us had had candlelight readings of Provost James'
incomparable Ghost Stories. Reynolds shrieked with boyish laughter. We were simply
young and happy. His pupils had done him no small credit at the close of the year: we were
at Cambridge: there was never going to be any war. As far as concerns S.S., I think that
this moonlight scene in the Fellows' garden may be taken as the last of Cambridge before
the war – 'In the Last Age'. —Euan Donaldson (1912), 'Personal Reminiscences of John
William Reynolds, M A' (typescript), 1918

When war broke out in August 1914, Sidney was in the middle of the idyllic long
vacation term recalled by the rather misty-eyed grammar school boy Euan Donaldson,
a vicar's son from Leicester. By October 1919, as a new cohort entered the College,
the bare facts were as follows: about 400 Sidney men had served in the war, of whom
six were current or future fellows. Most men had been undergraduates after 1900 and
many after 1910, but a few had been at Sidney much earlier and served in training

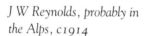

*J W Reynolds, probably in
the Alps, c1914*

1916
J·E·R·ROSIER
G·SHANKSTER
A·M·REES
B·S·HOLMES
H·S·P·BLAIR
O·C·RAYNER
1917
G·C·EWEN
F·C·KING
T·P·WATSON
N·GAWAN TAYLOR
O·B·G·JOHNSON
W·H·SMITH
N·B·DICK
W·A·BELL
D·G·ROUQUETTE
1918
J·S·HALL
H·P·B·GOUGH
D·N·GARSTIN
G·FYSON
W·D·WARD
V·T·PEMBERTON
C·S·EMBREY
J·S·ROBINSON
W·O·R·KING
1919
R·R·R·FLETCHER
REQUIESCANT IN PACE

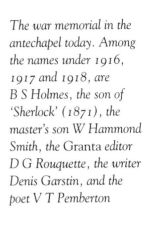

The war memorial in the antechapel today. Among the names under 1916, 1917 and 1918, are B S Holmes, the son of 'Sherlock' (1871), the master's son W Hammond Smith, the Granta editor D G Rouquette, the writer Denis Garstin, and the poet V T Pemberton

Part of a scroll drawing of P M Neighbour leaving Cambridge for the front, 1916

capacities. About 250 had served in the army or land forces, mainly on the Western Front; 30 in the RAF; 10 in the Navy and around 10 in research and other roles. Nearly 60 men had served in the various medical corps and eight had been chaplains. Fifty-eight Sidney men had died, mainly in action, and 50 of those we have records for (those in the Cambridge University *War List* of 1921) had been wounded, some more than once. A very young casualty was the future anthropologist William Armstrong who lost a leg in action at Ypres in 1915; he was 19.

The first man to die, fighting on the Magadi River in September 1914, was S F Edmonds, who had come to Sidney in 1898 and was a trooper with the East Africa Mounted Rifles; the last was R R R Fletcher, who had matriculated in 1905, and died of dysentery contracted on active service in October 1919. Two men died in 1914; 12 in 1915; 19 in 1916; 12 in 1917; nine in 1918; and one in 1919. In 2007 another name was added to the memorial: Arthur Herder (1902), a Newfoundlander who was killed in Cambrai in 1917, whose family recently discovered the oversight. Of those Sidney men in the 1921 list, about 40 had been awarded the Military Cross and five had been taken prisoner. Many others received awards including OBEs, MBEs, DSOs, and so on.

At the end of 1916 the master, Charles Smith, died at the age of 72. A few months later, in April 1917, his third son, William Hammond Smith, was killed in action at Athies near Arras when a shell splinter entered his head. The younger Smith, who had been at Blundell's, had graduated in classics in 1905 and then gone on to study painting at the Royal Academy and the Slade at the same time as artists such as Matthew Smith and Paul Nash. He was a talented portrait painter, and Sidney still owns two of his portraits, one of his father, and the other of the natural sciences fellow, F H Neville. In 1914 he applied for a commission through the Cambridge

University OTC and was gazetted to a temporary commission in the Royal Field Artillery. He was promoted to major and twice mentioned in dispatches.

A scroll with a pen drawing on it shows Philip Morgan Neighbour, a businessman's son who came to Sidney in 1912 from Henley School to read medicine, departing for service as a captain in the RAMC in June 1916. He is led out in a procession by Cambridge proctors and bulldogs, along with 'Queen Alexandria's [sic] Nurses', the CUOTC, the VAD, mournful lady admirers, grateful patients and 'college servants with impedimenta'. At the College gate lies a pile of unpaid bills. Neighbour survived the war to become a highly successful GP in Wiltshire and his surgery is reconstructed in the museum at Salisbury. Neighbour's fellow Sidney medics John Maitland Stonehouse (1897) and W O R King (1906) were less fortunate: Stonehouse survived pneumonia and the Chinese Revolution before 1914, but was killed by a shell splinter at the Somme in 1916, and King, who was researching into dysentery, died of the disease in the spring of 1919.

Many College servants served in the war, including the head porter J Hiscock, who was a regimental sergeant-major with the Suffolk Regiment and the RAF; William Maltby, the fellows' butler, who served as a gunner in the Royal Garrison Artillery on the Italian front; and A Hunt, a lance-corporal in the Hussars.

Of course, Sidney's undergraduate population dwindled sharply during the war; many men who had been given places were sent on military duty before they could come into residence. A typical annual intake was about 10 students. With fellows on active service and, from 1916, the master's position vacant, the great majority

R A McCance taking off from HMS Indomitable

McCance recalled in 1972, 'taking off from the platform laid on the guns. We had not reached flying speed by the end of the platform, so the wheels [were] lower than the platform they [had] just left'

of residents in College were young men training with the Signallers School, the Garrison Officer Cadets, and the School of Adjutants, all of whom were billeted at Sidney and who received their training in its rooms and grounds. About 1,000 men passed through Sidney during the war, including, according to the tutor G A Weekes, a brigadier who lived with his parrot on B staircase.

Three of the 1914 Sidney fellowship saw active service, including the recently elected Trinity classicist Reginald Hackforth, who had arrived from the University of Manchester in 1912 and was a private in the London Regiment of the Artists' Rifles. John William Reynolds, who had been rusticated from Marlborough, was a brilliant and inspiring teacher. He had come to Sidney from Trinity in 1909 as the first history fellow, and had founded the Confraternitas Historica in 1910. He was commissioned as a 2nd lieutenant, 4th (Hallamshire) Battalion, York and Lancaster Regiment. Thomas Knox-Shaw remembers how he and Reynolds as young fellows had shared a large set of rooms in Cloister Court. They tidied up a rather scruffy College, changing ashtrays, giving silver cigarette boxes, reforming the kitchen, and so on. Knox-Shaw, by then a lieutenant in the Sherwood Foresters, remembered the last time he saw Reynolds:

'In July (1915), my battalion was resting after a period of duty in the trenches. I walked over to see Reynolds. Poor man, he was miserable, hating the War. As I walked away I turned round, having a premonition I would not see him again. Within three weeks he was shot through the head by a sniper.' Reynolds was killed in action near Ypres and is buried in the Talana Farm Cemetery, Boezinge.

Knox-Shaw had been in the university OTC since its foundation in 1909 and became regimental sergeant-major of the Signal Company, running the telephone section and, from 1912, was a 2nd lieutenant in charge of the wireless section. An alternator was made in the university engineering laboratory, fixed up to a receiving device and aerial powered by a man on a bicycle, allowing Morse code messages to be picked up from 10 miles away. Knox-Shaw had a wireless receiving set in his Cloister Court rooms and could receive signals from the Eiffel Tower. In December 1914 he was sent to the 2nd South Lancashire Regiment at Kemmel where, he said, the liquid mud stank of dead bodies, his captain was evacuated with trench foot, the machine-gun officer was shot by a sniper, and he himself had a mastoid abscess. 'I drenched a handkerchief with pus, held in position by my balaclava woollen helmet.'

After recovery in England, Knox-Shaw returned to Poperinghe in Flanders to discover the 1st Battalion had been wiped out. In March 1918, he was sent to Staff School in Cambridge. Charles Smith, the master, had died in 1916 and had not yet been replaced, and so Knox-Shaw, feeling 'in my bones that the War would not go on much longer', persuaded the fellows to elect G A Weekes as master, B T D Smith as dean, and the scientist C R A Thacker as college lecturer in natural sciences. He was overwhelmed to be back at Sidney. 'I did not want to see France or Belgium again and certainly not visit Germany. That resolution I have kept', he wrote at the end of his life.

Future fellows who fought in the war included the nutritionist R A McCance, who went up to Sidney in 1919. He was a pilot in the Royal Naval Air Force from

1917, having applied as a schoolboy for a commission in 1916. Trained at Chigwell, Essex on single-seater Camels, he flew two-seater observation aircraft from the battle cruiser HMS *Indomitable*, based at Scapa Flow. As his own photographs show, the crude take-off provision, in the days of proto-aircraft carriers, was a precarious platform laid along the ship's 12-inch gun barrels.

The future bursar, A H 'Davvy' Davenport, the brains behind the major building projects of the 1920s and 1930s, suffered combat wounds and was awarded an MC as a major in the Royal Engineers; the scientist J A Carroll, Sidney's first research fellow in 1922, worked at the Royal Aircraft Establishment.

'Leave Not Death Behind': Sidney War Writers

You see by day a ragged field, pitted with shell-holes, in each of which there is always a bully-beef tin. The grass is lank and untidy, where it has been allowed to grow. There are some bodies lying stiffly about, the skin dark brown from exposure, and the clothes rotten. There is a look of a refuse heap about the field. Even the barbed wire, mended and strengthened in the darkness, helps the impression of disuse. Beyond this No-Man's-Land you see a low line of sand-bags — coloured sand-bags. And that is all. —Denis Garstin, *The Shilling Soldiers*, 1918

'Optimism' by Alfred Ratcliffe

At last there'll dawn the last of the long year,
Of the long year that seemed to dream no end,
Whose every dawn but turned the world more drear,
And slew some hope, or led away some friend.
Or be you dark, or buffeting, or blind,
We care not, day, but leave not death behind.

The hours that feed on war go heavy-hearted,
Death is no fare wherewith to make hearts fain.
Oh, we are sick to find that they who started
With glamour in their eyes came not again.
O day, be long and heavy if you will,
But on our hopes set not a bitter heel.

For tiny hopes like tiny flowers of Spring
Will come, though death and ruin hold the land,
Though storms may roar they may not break the wing
Of the earthed lark whose song is ever bland.
Fell year unpitiful, slow days of scorn,
Your kind shall die, and sweeter days be born.

This poignant wartime photograph shows four sombre figures in Cloister Court in 1916, the year of the Somme. They include Euan Donaldson, who later eulogised his teacher and hero, J W Reynolds, killed at the front the year before; M V Hardy; H F Green; and G A Weekes, who succeeded Charles Smith as master in 1918. Smith died in November 1916, a few months before his son, the artist William Hammond (1904), was killed at the front in 1917.

Denis Garstin, the model for this image for the 'Skipper's Guide' book reviews in Granta. *His sister Alethea Garstin (1894–1978) made the woodcut image in 1912, clearly indebted to the style of the great Edwardian artist William Nicholson*

Among students at Sidney before 1915, the wartime fatalities included many men considered to be of exceptional promise in the arts. One was the editor of *Granta* in 1912, Denis Garstin, son of the well-known Newlyn School Impressionist painter Norman Garstin. He was a Blundell's scholar who was killed in Russia in August 1918 at the age of 28, shortly after undertaking what he had described as a 'quiet little expedition' conducted alone during the 'Onega Expedition' against the Bolsheviks near Archangel. He was awarded both British and Russian military honours before and after his death.

At Sidney, Garstin had been secretary of the debating society and took a 'special examination' in 'classics and military subjects'. His portrait, by his sister, was the image heading the *Granta* book review section, 'Skipper's Guide'. He was a prolific journalist with *Punch* and other journals after Cambridge. A Russophile who had written *Friendly Russia* (1915), a book of essays with an introduction by H G Wells praising his 'lucidity, humour and wisdom', Garstin was attached to the British Embassy at St Petersburg and then Moscow from 1916. He had previously served in France with a machine-gun corps, and his experiences there produced his book, the minor masterpiece *The Shilling Soldiers*, which was published after his death in 1918 with a glowing preface by Hugh Walpole.

Two other Sidney writers were budding poets. The Yorkshireman Alfred Victor Ratcliffe, who had entered Sidney in 1907 and gone on to train at the Inner Temple, was a friend of Rupert Brooke and had published two volumes of poetry by 1913. Serving as a lieutenant in the 10th West Yorkshire Regiment (Prince of Wales's Own), he was killed fighting on the first day of the Battle of the Somme, 1 July 1916, the same day as W Hall, a lieutenant in the South Staffordshire Regiment, who had joined up before he entered Sidney, and S T Martin, a lieutenant in the Royal Inniskilling Fusiliers who had come to Sidney in 1909 to read classics. Ratcliffe was part of the disastrous attack at Fricourt that Siegfried Sassoon watched from the Bois Français trenches, and his battalion suffered the highest number of casualties of any battalion at the Battle of the Somme. He was buried in the Fricourt New Military Cemetry, where his parents placed a private memorial in front of his gravestone. A fellow officer had written to his mother after the Somme: 'Your son's work was very highly thought of by his company officer, who also lost his life in the fight, and "Ratters", as we called him, was very popular with everyone. His senior officer having been killed early on, your son was commanding the company at the time of his death.'

Ratcliffe had been engaged to Pauline Clough, sister of the poet Dorothy Una Clough, with whom he had had a brief affair before she married his brother Charles in 1915. The foursome had met on holiday on the Isle of Wight. Ratcliffe's poem 'Optimism' was included in George Herbert Clarke's *A Treasury of War Poetry* in 1917, alongside poems by Rupert Brooke, Robert Frost and John Masefield.

The other Sidney poet, Vivian Telfer Pemberton, was a major in the Royal Garrison Artillery when he was killed in October 1918 at Bélicourt to the south of Cambrai, only a month before the end of the war. He was awarded the MC and his poems were published posthumously in 1919 in *Reflections in Verse*. Pemberton had come to Sidney from Cheltenham College in 1913 to read mathematics and had got a first in part one of the Tripos in 1914 before enlisting. His bittersweet war poetry is full of references to the mathematical skills required of the gunner:

> When you're passing Ginchy Corner and the Hun
>   begins to strafe,
> And you want to throw yourself down in the mud,
> But you daren't because you know that the tele-
>   phonists would laugh,
> So you can but hope the next will be a dud,
> When you get to your O.P. and find you've worked
>   your factors wrong,
> And you're well within the hundred per cent zone,
> Have you never felt that feeling when your whole
>   Soul seems to long
> For home, a dog, a wife to call your own.
> —From 'War Meditations'

The Mandarins: Sidney's Early Civil Servants

The Great War saw the rise to prominence of a number of Sidney-educated civilian and military civil servants, a new professional bureaucratic breed who had grown in importance since the civil service reforms of the mid-19th century following the Northcote-Trevelyan Report of 1854 and the setting up of the Civil Service Commission the following year. Many of these men became attracted to socialist politics and used their wartime experience to inform post-war policy. For such men the catastrophe of the war had created an urgent new political imperative.

Arthur Lewis Dixon, son of a Swindon Wesleyan minister, went up to Sidney in 1899 and was ninth Wrangler in 1902. He joined the Home Office and transformed and integrated the police and fire services. During the war he drew up a mutual assistance scheme between fire brigades following the first Zeppelin raids. In 1919 he set about reforming the police force, which had gone on strike at the end of the war, acting as secretary to Lord Desborough's review committee and masterminding two reports that completely modernised the police force. He had a great interest in scientific and technological matters, developed early radio links within the police, and established forensic science laboratories and training programmes for detectives. Dixon also took over the fire brigades division of the Home Office in 1932 and,

Sir Frederick Brundrett, 1965. National Portrait Gallery, London

seeing the next war as posing a particular threat from incendiary bombs, he re-equipped and retrained the firemen so that when in 1940 Britain faced exactly the threat he had forecast, they were able to respond effectively. Herbert Morrison called this achievement 'one of the quickest administrative revolutions that ever took place'. Dixon, a reclusive bachelor who lived in hotels and who was an ardent Christian and teetotaller, was also highly popular with all those who worked with him. He was knighted in 1941 and died in 1969.

Edward Frank Wise, son of a Bury St Edmunds fishmonger, went up to Sidney in 1903 to study mathematics and natural sciences. At the start of the First World War he was appointed secretary to the Anglo-Russian supplies committee of the War Office. He was then made principal assistant secretary to the Ministry of Food in 1917, and in 1919 was one of the British representatives on the Inter-Allied Supreme Economic Council, which worked on wartime rationing and post-war food supply. Wise's distinguished career in the civil service ended in 1923 when he became an economic advisor on foreign trade to the Russian co-operative movement in the 1920s. Wise had been a committed member of the Independent

Molecules and Mustard Gas

The distinguished chemist William Pope came to Sidney from the University of Manchester as Professor of Chemistry in 1908, having already been elected a Fellow of the Royal Society in 1902. His most important work was in stereochemistry, which is concerned with the relative spatial arrangement of molecules within atoms. During the First World War Pope acted as a consultant for the Board of Invention and Research and worked on the preparation of photographic sensitisers and on the production of mustard gas. For his war services he was knighted and went on to establish chemistry at Cambridge, the three chairs which replaced his own indicating his great influence. He died unmarried in 1939.

Sir William Jackson Pope

Labour Party since before 1914, and supported the use of wartime planning in socialist agricultural economies and the supply of basic commodities. He wrote books on the supply and prices of imported goods, and his *The Russian Co-Operative Movement* of 1926 was a highly sympathetic account of its subject. He opposed the Labour Party's monetary policy, believing that the City and Bank of England were institutionally biased against socialist policy, and advocated the nationalisation of the latter. In the early 1930s, Wise helped to create a new moderate Socialist League of which he was chairman before his sudden death from heart failure in 1933.

Sir Frederick Brundrett, son of a Welsh steel works secretary in Ebbw Vale, went up in 1913 and was a Wrangler in 1916, (Wranglers were no longer ranked after 1909) after which he joined the wireless branch of the RNVR as a lieutenant, working on underwater communications with submarines and playing a leading role in developing short-wave radio transmission. A superb administrator and pragmatist, he joined the scientific staff at the Admiralty in 1919 and was appointed to the Royal Naval Signal School. During the Second World War he was principal scientific officer for the Royal Naval Scientific Service, assistant director of scientific research, and chief of the service in 1946, when he was made CB. In 1954 he became head of the Atomic Energy Research Establishment, where he co-ordinated scientific research and its application to military equipment. In the same year he was elected an honorary fellow of Sidney, having already been awarded KBE. He died in 1974.

CHAPTER 9

'Action and Reaction'
1918–1945

'… these degenerate times in which we live, when not only an ever-expanding Historical section necessary, but even the study of Economics has necessitated, some provision being made for its misguided devotees.'

—James Passant on developing the Sidney library, *Pheon*, II, i, 1922

WHEREAS IN OCTOBER 1918 only eight students arrived at Sidney, by October 1919 the College had admitted 126, including men who had been awarded places before or during the war but who had been called up; men who had fought in the war and been offered places after it; boys straight from school; and British, Commonwealth and US military personnel on short courses. The mix of ages and experiences made for an extraordinary and also a crowded life, 18-year-old boys from comfortable boarding schools rubbing shoulders with war veterans. In October 1920, 189 students came into residence, most of whom lived in lodging houses. The College needed to transform itself once again to meet the many challenges of post-war Britain.

While undergraduate numbers grew markedly, Sidney's fellowship remained small over the 20 years between the wars. In 1919, in addition to the newly appointed master, G A Weekes, there were only 13, including two honorary fellows, and in 1939, when Weekes was still master, there were 17. Two of these were men appointed in the 19th century (R H Mayall and the senior fellow, H C Robson).

There was great continuity at Sidney. The younger fellows in 1919, such as Knox-Shaw, Hackforth, Smith and Passant, who typically took on the key roles of tutor and dean, were still at Sidney in 1939. However, by the outbreak of World War Two, a newer generation had come to the College, usually drawn from the undergraduate

OPPOSITE: *Sussex Street in 1938, not long after its redevelopment by the College*

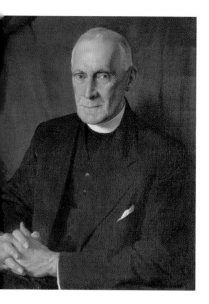

George Arthur Weekes, by
Sir James Gunn, 1941

body, including the anatomist Howard Green; the physicists J A Ratcliffe and P I Dee; the engineer R H Angus; from Trinity, the mathematician Gordon Welchman; and from Christ's, via Corpus Christi, the economist E A G Robinson.

Perhaps surprisingly, in 1926 Sidney was, in terms of gross taxable income, the fifth wealthiest college in Cambridge, with an income calculated at £17,096. This compares with Trinity's £68,577 at the top of the table and, at the bottom, Magdalene's £5,372. Colleges in roughly the same financial league with Sidney included Christ's, Clare and Jesus. It was therefore possible for the College to undertake some much-needed improvements. Throughout the 1920s and 1930s, Sidney sought to improve and extend its buildings. Some projects were minor but significantly enhanced the College's facilities and appearance. A new bathhouse designed by T H Lyon (a structure known as 'Whitechapel' to generations of students) was built in 1920 on part of the site now occupied by the Mong Building. It provided two showers and seven latrines, hardly a generous provision. T H Lyon redecorated the Hall in 1923, removing the grime and soot from the ceiling, painting the woodwork in a deep blue, and covering the walls with aluminium leaf, thus creating a striking if controversial Futurist look.

The old and often ruinous medieval clunch wall, running from Cloister Court along Jesus Lane and down to the end of the garden by the 18th-century gate, was demolished at the College's expense to widen Jesus Lane. A new one in red brick replaced it, also paid for by Sidney. The old brick can be seen along northern parts of the wall dividing the garden from the houses in Malcolm Street. The two Victorian Eton fives courts were demolished at the same time and replaced by a squash and fives court.

In the early 1920s the new dean, B T D Smith, a dedicated and self-taught horticulturalist, created a large rock garden along the Jesus Lane wall that nurtured over

Fellows, 20 June 1923.
Standing, left to right:
E J Passant; B T D
Smith; C R A Thacker; R
Hackforth; T Knox-Shaw.
Sitting, left to right: A H
McNevile, R H D Mayall,
Lord deLisle and Dudley
(the Visitor); G A Weekes
(Master), H C Robson,
Sir William Jackson Pope,
C T R Wilson.
G M Edwards and
A H Davenport were
absent

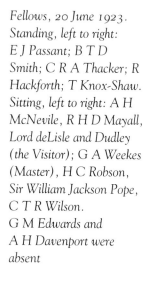

*The rock garden,
oil painting by Keith
Henderson*

350 species of high alpine plants, continuing Sidney's mountaineering tendencies from the 1850s. *Pheon* in 1923 referred also to six 'timid goldfish' in a small pool. The Westmoreland rock was delivered by rail and much of it survives today by the greenhouse. Smith also appointed a head gardener, Jim Blades, who assisted him in his work. An unfortunate victim of the storms in January 1935 was a sycamore from 1607–8, which had been planted by James Montagu along the King's Ditch, half way down the Fellows' Garden.

New bike sheds were built along the Sidney Street wall on the site of the old laboratories, and a new junior combination room was opened in 1927 in two sets of rooms at the foot of G and H staircases. In 1930 the geologist W G Fearnsides presented a new bell for the Chapel, replacing the old 18th-century one with a B flat bell made by the same founders, the world-famous John Taylor of Loughborough, who are still in business today. Structural work on A staircase in 1931 had required the removal of the Wyatville stucco; thereafter, all the stucco facing on to Cloister Court was removed, exposing a fair section of the much-mourned old Elizabethan brickwork. In 1931, Chapel Court was paved with York flags and a surround of cobbles to match Hall Court.

Two major building projects allowed Sidney to expand its student numbers considerably. T H Lyon, who had designed the Chapel, was asked to draw up plans for a large new block in the Master's Garden, which was opened in 1923. This was the first new building since Cloister Court in 1890–1, and provided 36 sets of spacious rooms for undergraduates and one fellow. It was a plain modern classical building in style, built with pale plum-coloured brick and stone facings in an L-shape. Built on four floors, it broke with the traditional staircase arrangement by introducing a central staircase and corridors. The kitchen and bathroom facilities were a considerable improvement on previous provision elsewhere, although electric fires were only introduced as late as 1931.

77087 Sidney Sussex College, CAMBRIDGE

Copyright
Frith's

ABOVE: *A Frith's postcard of the newly built Garden Court, 1925*

RIGHT: *The lawn tennis team 1924: R W Spencer, C J Baker, L F Roberts (Captain), J C Skinner, A Bisalyaputra, F R E Mendis. Photograph by Stearn & Sons*

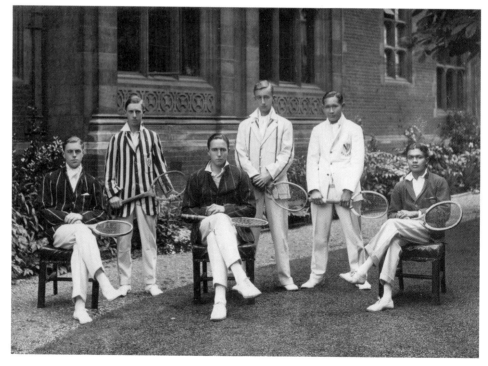

The College owned the decrepit buildings on its side of Sussex Street and bought those on the other side in the late 1920s in anticipation of a new development. During the 1930s Sidney completely remodelled the southern side of its site, first building the Sussex Street arcade of shops running round into Sidney Street and Hobson Street (1930–32). It was designed by the major London practice of E R Barrow, specialists in town centre building. Nikolaus Pevsner described the whole red-brick neo-Wren ensemble in 1954 as the finest piece of urban planning in 20th-century Cambridge. It probably still holds that distinction half a century later. The whole street was demolished and the first part of the project, on the south side, created shops, offices, apartments and basements above and below a terrace supported by a colonnaded arcade and approached by stone steps at either end. Eight luxuriously finished and centrally heated two-bedroom flats for fellows were created, and Sussex House had lifts installed.

The South Court development facing the arcade, completed in 1937, was also built with a red brick, chiming with Garden Court, the southern end of the east side of the Chapel and the rest of Sussex Street. On the College side a rusticated stone wall supports a terrace from which the staircases ascend. To the east a Muniment Room was provided to house the College treasures, manuscripts and rare books; since the 1920s many books had been stored in the roof of Garden Court. This new facility freed up the Old Library for undergraduate use only. As with Garden Court, initial excavations for South Court had revealed old bones, waste, cooking utensils and other remains of the Grey Friars and Sidney's early years. A number of these remains are now stored in the Muniment Room.

Sidney's Dartmoor Ghost

T H Lyon, the architect of Sidney's new Chapel and of Garden Court, owned a house at Middlecott on Dartmoor. The architect Gordon Pringle, who was at Sidney in the early 1920s, sent this photograph to the master David Thomson in 1959 of the 'ghost of Sir Roger de Bovey' seen on a reading party to Middlecott in 1922. From left to right are the Sidney dean B T D Smith, Tuckerman, Beamish and Thomas Henry Lyon (all of Corpus). On the right, in profile, is Frank Maurice Culverwell (1919). The ghost of Sir Roger de Bovey is Charles Wilfrid Giles, as he was known then (known as Scott-Giles from 1928). Pringle, presumably the photographer, was responsible for the military hospitals erected in North Africa in the Second World War.

'The Unsung Hero of Cambridge Economics': Sir Austin Robinson

'No economist is more dangerous than the pure theorist without practical experience and instinctive understanding of the real world that he is attempting to analyse, seeking precision in a world of imprecision, in a world he does not understand.'
—Austin Robinson, 'My apprenticeship as an economist', 1992

Economics, a Tripos that had begun in 1905, was a relatively new subject at Cambridge in the 1920s, and not necessarily the first choice for those who went on to careers as economists. Sir Roy Allen, who entered Sidney in 1924, was a Wrangler in 1927 before turning to economics as a research student. He achieved great eminence at the London School of Economics as a statistician.

In 1931, however, Sidney appointed its first fellow in economics, Edward Austin Gossage Robinson, a churchman's son who had gone to Christ's as a scholar in 1919, after having piloted flying boats with the Royal Naval Air Service during the war. Although his subject was classics, Austin Robinson's military experience had persuaded him that further wars must be prevented. Influenced by hearing John Maynard Keynes's lectures on 'The Economic Consequences of the Peace' in the early 1920s, he decided to switch to economics. He soon became a charismatic figure at Cambridge and, after research at Corpus, tutoring the Maharajah of Gwalior and lecturing for the new economics faculty, Robinson moved to Sidney where he remained until his death in 1993. A devout Christian, he was no doubt attracted by Sidney's particular blend of quiet scholarship, scientific enquiry, unpretentious pragmatism and religious devotion. His reputation no doubt attracted the exiled Jewish political philosopher Leo Strauss to Sidney as visiting fellow in 1936.

Austin Robinson, 1931

Robinson's work was profoundly important in the development of economic thought, especially during the 1930s and 1940s. He was the *eminence grise* of his faculty, tirelessly administering and smoothing relations between factions. Robinson's co-editing of the 30 volumes of his friend and colleague Keynes's writings ensured the survival of the latter's work during a period of great controversy and polarisation in economics. He was part of the so-called 'Cambridge Circus' who worked with Keynes on *The General Theory* of 1936. One of his pupils, Joan Maurice, became his wife, and as Joan Robinson was one of the greatest British economists of the 20th century. Two of Robinson's books, *The Structure of Competitive Industry* (1931) and *Monopoly* (1941), are still regarded as classics. The first emphasised the need, beyond technical competence, for management skills, industrial relations and competitive behaviour in any theory of the firm. Of the second, Robinson wrote in his introduction: '[This book] is intended to be…a tin-opener to open the tin of knowledge. But there is nothing so useless as a tin-opener, unless it is a tin without a tin-opener.'

Throughout his career Robinson argued against the impersonal macro-economics that left free markets to themselves and ignored the social and human aspects of industry. Equally, he was impatient of the Marxist theories, to which his wife was far more sympathetic, which ignored particularity and history. Robinson was a humane, subtle and kindly man who wanted to make a difference to people's lives, not live in an ivory tower. From his work in Africa during the 1930s until his final years, Robinson was a pragmatic advisor to many developing economies around the world, focusing in particular on energy policy. He worked hard to extend Britain's commitment to improving the incomes and welfare systems in developing countries.

During the Second World War Robinson worked in the Cabinet Office, Ministry of Production, and Board of Trade. Sir Stafford Cripps attempted on a few occasions to entice Robinson into the civil service after the war, but the quiet academic decided he was not 'tough enough' to undertake such work. In fact he was a hugely energetic and effective administrator, working on two major economic surveys in the immediate post-war period, editing journals, and acting as secretary and president to the International Economic Association. Elected a fellow of the British Academy in 1955 and knighted in 1975, Robinson was, in the words of G C Harcourt, 'the unsung hero of Cambridge economics'. His memorial service took place in his beloved Sidney's Chapel in 1993.

'Straight from Golder's Green Academy': Sidney Inter-War Undergraduates

Between the wars the typical annual Sidney undergraduate intake was 50, almost all of whom were housed in rooms in College. The majority of second- and third-year students were in lodgings, a number in nearby streets such as Malcolm Street, Wray's Court and Parkside, but also some further away in Hertford Street, Maid's Causeway and elsewhere.

Sidney, still a notably middle-class college, took up to six students from Blundell's each year, and usually two from Oakham. There were virtually no men from the most famous public schools like Eton, Winchester and Westminster, although Harrow sent boys regularly. The public school cohort was drawn from schools such as Marlborough, Tonbridge, Rugby, Uppingham and Oundle, as well as some of the smaller ones such as Felsted and Sutton Valence. Grammar schools were major providers of fresh talent: Coatham, Bromsgrove, Wolverhampton, Manchester, Sir George Monoux and various King Edward VI institutions appear frequently in the admissions register. There were still a number of men coming from abroad, Geelong Grammar in Australia, for instance, sending no fewer than three freshers in 1926. The number from schools that would in all likelihood have guaranteed their being barred from membership of the Pitt Club was also fairly significant: the Mathematical School, Rochester, Manchester College of Technology and Battersea Grammar are typical examples. When the statistician Sir Roy Allen, son of a fishing-tackle shop owner, applied to Trinity from the Royal Grammar School, Worcester in 1924 he was told that, clever as he was, they did not really take his sort and he was directed to Sidney. *Pheon* had a spoof review of a novel called *Fred at Sidney* in 1922, which referred to the hero arriving 'straight from Golder's Green Academy'.

The major subjects were mathematics, natural sciences and history. There were also substantial numbers of classics, mechanical sciences and languages students. Medicine continued its growth since the end of the previous century: Leslie Witts, Sir Michael Stoker, the psychiatrist Y P Meng and the man later known as 'Britain's Dr Spock', Hugh Jolly, were among the outstanding students. Most other subjects produced small numbers. The results these men achieved were impressive in the days when firsts were few and far between, a lower second perfectly respectable, and a third a common result across the university. There were many Tripos prizes, especially in the sciences. In 1921, out of 70 candidates, 18 attained firsts, and all 10 mathematicians were Wranglers. In 1935, by no means an exceptional year, 17 Tripos prizes were awarded. These included a first for Otto Smail, the future history fellow, a first in natural sciences for the electrochemist and future fellow John Agar, and a Wranglership for one of Sidney's renowned Bletchley Park contingent, A L Yoxall. Of the Tripos examinations taken that year, over 20 per cent resulted in firsts and 50 per cent in seconds.

'Apt and Ready to Pierce': The Return of *Pheon*

When approaching Sidney one is immediately struck by the magnificence of its architectural features. The beautiful examples of Pseudo-Gothic archery and the delicate Early Norman Bradley tracework combine to form one of the noblest piles that Sidney Street can boast. —Thomas Wrott (MA Borstal), 'An Architectural Tour of Sidney Sussex', *Pheon*, 1, i, 1922

Tipperary Tim, with jockey W P Dutton up, returning to weigh in at Aintree, Liverpool after winning the Grand National in 1928

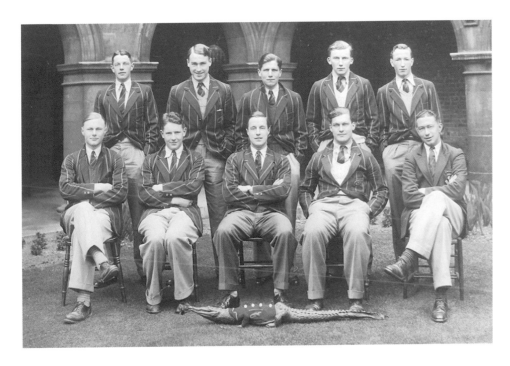

Pheon was revived in 1922, having folded after the *Annual* began to be published in 1903. It gives a wonderful insight into College life and student interests and attitudes during the 1920s and 1930s. Besides the various efforts at poetry and short stories, much of it was devoted to College history, sometimes as parody, with articles on the College portraits, its heraldry, great men, memoirs by old members reaching back to the 1850s and material from the Muniment Room. With enthusiastic young members of the Confraternitas Historica, such as the future College historian and herald Wilfred Scott-Giles, a prime mover of the *Pheon* renaissance, this was hardly surprising. Since the 1890s there had been growing interest and pride in the College's past and this was magnified by the growing presence of serious historians at Sidney between the wars.

Sport was a central feature of *Pheon*, with team news and results, humorous written and drawn sketches of particular characters, and cartoons appearing in every issue. Though Sidney was rarely very successful at team level, producing some outstanding individual talents, there were many great moments on the way, such as the punishing defeat of Magdalene 98–0 at rugby in 1922, and the lawyer W P 'Billy' Dutton's extraordinary victory at the Grand National in 1928 on Tipperary Tim, 'the most sensational win of all time'. This triumph, won by a prizewinning classicist who had graduated in 1925, must be counted as Sidney's greatest and most unlikely ever. The Boat Club, which celebrated its centenary in 1937 and represented the senior sport in the university, generally had the best news to report, although any encounter with St John's formidable Lady Margaret Boat Club, or with Pembroke or Jesus, was likely to produce a stoic tale of brave defeat.

The fellows, who contributed to and vetted *Pheon*, were given playful profiles and feature in the undergraduate imagination in a way suggesting near hero-worship. In 1929 *Pheon* published 'A Sidney Alphabet':

Mrs Catherine Weekes, who inspired the expression 'Keeping a Kate' (see page 302) and died in 1940. Pheon VIII, ii, March 1929

'D stands for our Dons the best ever seen,
With Mayall, Smith, Ratcliffe, Passant, Hackforth and Green.'

'W' was for the Master, Weekes, of course, who…

'…reigns in his office supreme,
And produces those curt little notes by the ream.'

In the main, the fellows were seen as wise and avuncular public school housemasters, which in some senses they were. B T D Smith's capture of over 3,000 slugs in the gardens got a special mention in 1924, and Hilaire Belloc's overnight stay in the College was reported as a celebrity triumph reflecting well on the fellowship. When the master conducted the first provincial transatlantic telephone conversation in 1927 with President Lowell of Harvard, it was a moment of genuine pride for a college so dedicated to the new technologies. A photo of Mrs Weekes strikes an unusual feminine note in a bastion of male bonding, the other women referred to in this era being usually anonymous staff or those seen in May Ball photographs. Photos, anecdotes and other material about the College staff, especially porters, bedmakers and kitchen staff, are regularly featured, suggesting a friendly, tight-knit community. Encouraged it would seem by the master and fellows, such efforts included 'The College Servants' Song' in 1922, a notably funny piece, and 'The Woes of the Waiter', a poem laced with sympathy.

Action and Reaction

The Cromwells staged a three-act play in 1921 called 'Action and Reaction: A What-Not in 3 Knots' with music by the Roundhead Orchestra. Alexander McCance, in drag on the far left, played Euthymol a 'Girthamite', and Howard Green, third from the right, played Sir Galahad Glaxo. The costumes seem extraordinarily Dadaistic even today. The three scenes were a 'Palaeolithic Lecture Room', 'Girtham College AD1100', and 'A Room in Sidney Sussex AD??'. In 1920 C W Scott-Giles and J A Carroll had organised a highly contentious poll canvassing undergraduate opinion about a Senate vote on a proposal to give women full rights in the university. Sidney's voting was hardly feminist, only 34 voting for the proposal and 110 against.

The various College societies were given considerable space. The debating society flourished; in 1922 a motion 'That this House would welcome the Nationalisation of the Universities of Oxford and Cambridge' was narrowly defeated. The art club (succeeded by the Argonauts, who had Sir Arthur Quiller-Couch to speak in the 1920s) had lectures by Scott-Giles on Dante, and a lecture by T H Lyon. The Cromwells, founded in 1892, sported a distinctive blazer and had become mainly a drinking society, like the Ironsides, and often caused the dean considerable disciplinary bother. The Alchemists, founded in 1919, encouraged scientific interests alongside the required drinking and singing. The Hypocrits, with their mascot, Hubert the stuffed crocodile, performed the same role for medical students. The growth of musical activity in the Chapel is recorded, with regular announcements for concerts of music across the historical range from Gibbons to Debussy.

Politics features throughout, with articles on Fascism, the League of Nations, the General Strike, and the political turmoil of the 1930s. A 'League of Nations Tea Party' in James Passant's rooms, and the 'translation' of C H P D Hindley 'from leading the Fascisti in Cambridge to lecturing in the Ohio State University on the History of Education', all suggest the often light-hearted attitude of most undergraduates. In the late-1930s a new editorial group quoted Auden and Isherwood extensively and struck a more earnest note, but by then student activities were under the growing cloud of impending war.

'Sharks and Hostile Natives'

*P*heon carried an occasional melancholy note that disrupted the general tone of arcadian innocence, such as the death in 1932 of Maltby, the fellows' butler, and the murder in Venezuela of Edward Schneider, son of a fire station clerk from Cambridge, who entered in 1919 after war service to read engineering. Schneider was working with the 'Anglo-Saxon Petroleum Company', and had been sending frequent letters to *Pheon* about his experiences of 'alligators, mosquitoes, sharks and hostile natives in the bush'. He was stabbed by 'a native with whom he had had some misunderstanding'.

The Garden Court Mystery of 1931: Accident…or Murder?

> You will find that every parent whose son is coming to Cambridge next October, will fight shy of Sydney [sic] Sussex. We do not intend to see our sons settled in a College which allows a crime so vicious to settle down into oblivion. —'An Old Varsity Man' from Gloucester, to the master, G A Weekes, 14 April, 1931

One College event did not make it into *Pheon*. Early on Monday 23 February, Francis John Charles Ellis, a first year archaeology and anthropology student from Rhodesia whose father had recently died, was found dead on the floor of his sitting room in room 23 on the second floor in Garden Court by his bedmaker, Reuben Flack. The long-serving Flack later told the coroner's court that in his view archaeology and anthropology were 'rather unusual pursuits'. As *The Times* reported, Ellis's 'hands were tied together behind his back with handkerchiefs, his ankles were similarly bound with handkerchiefs and khaki puttees, and other handkerchiefs, apparently his own property, tied over his mouth and nostrils'. Electric flex also bound his legs and a leather strap was fastened to the handkerchiefs around his arms. There was no evidence of a struggle and he appeared to have been dead since about midnight. One Sidney undergraduate, the future tropical physiologist William Ladell, claimed that he had passed Ellis's room at about 11 p.m. and heard heavy breathing behind the closed doors. The doors had been found open by the bedmaker.

CAMBRIDGE DAILY NEW

CAMBRIDGE COLLEGE MYSTERY

Inquest This Afternoon

THE LATEST THEORIES

Sir Bernard Spilsbury

LAST NIGHT'S VISIT

Scotland Yard Activities

THE inquest on Mr. Francis John Ellis, the 19-year-old Freshman who was found dead in his rooms at Sidney Sussex College under mysterious circumstances yesterday morning, was opened at five o'clock this evening.

The hearing, which was held in the Police Court, yielded only formal evidence of identification.

The Borough Coroner (Mr. G. A. Wootten) then adjourned the inquiry until March 4th, when it is expected 12 or 14 witnesses will be called.

Sir Bernard Spilsbury, the eminent pathologist, who has been called in to assist the investigation, will give evidence at a later stage in the inquiry.

Police efforts to discover a solution to the mystery continued to-day, and a number of possibilities were investigated, though seemingly with little result.

[Photo]
Our picture shows the wing of Sidney Sussex College containing the room (second down an extreme right) in which the tragedy occurred.

[" Cambridge Daily News."

A careful record has been made of the way in which the knots were tied, and a police officer has endeavoured to secure himself in the manner in which Ellis was tied.

The room was carefully searched for finger-prints, and certain articles were taken away to be subjected to more minute examination.

NEW LINE OF INQUIRY

Later in the morning the Scotland Yard detectives, together with the Chief Constable (Mr. R. J. Pearson) returned to the college.

They had, it is understood, some communication with the dead man's tutor.

The examination of the rooms was continued, and detailed photographs taken of the room in which he was found and its

THE INQUEST

Evidence of the Mother

"NO LOVE AFFAIR"

Happy Life in Cambridge

BEDS

Dama Cou

Fire broke o Castle, the resid twelve miles no It is one of t Bedfordshire.

It has been Alston family f contains valuabl In recent year occupied, its own family, Mr. Row 80 years old an having moved h iage of Odell, of The estate go and he discove after 10 a.m.

The villagers fighting party, cope with the sent for the Be When the brig wing of the ca country mansion alight, but as a available the fi spreading.

Soon after definitely under practically out the castle was h Among those fire was Mr. Ab

COMPE L

Settlem Thi

The Viceroy t stance of his tal eight Round T who are assistin They unanimo of compromise o Round Table Co Mr. Gandhi h authority to en the Viceroy to e a Congress Worki It is consider compromise cont ly before the en Mr. Gandhi w to see the Vice TROOPS IN R

Five columns Hensada distric break occurred sign of the trou DEATH S

The High Cou of Hari Kishen, nate Sir Geoffr Governor of Pu tence. The Gov police inspector CONSERVATI

An article about the death of F J C Ellis, from the Cambridge Daily News, *24 February, 1931. The photograph identifies the room in Garden Court where Ellis died*

The local police were called in by the master, who then brought in chief inspector Helby from Scotland Yard, who in turn called for the celebrated forensic pathologist Sir Bernard Spilsbury, who had worked on the Crippen and many other high-profile cases. Spilsbury examined the body and removed certain organs. The dean, B T D Smith, told the press that the case was a mystery as Ellis, in spite of his grief over his father, was a happy and popular boy enjoying his studies.

The coroner's inquiry began on 24 February, with a jury and about 12 witnesses, including Spilsbury. They heard from Ellis's mother that her son's time at Sidney had been 'the happiest period of his whole life', and that his letters 'were full of the kind way his tutor and professors' treated him. He was young for his age and 'extraordinarily shy with girls', and this precluded, she believed, the possibility that he had been disturbed by some romantic attachment. Ellis's uncle, the Rev. F R Dickinson, said he and the mother had tried to replicate the knots on themselves and had found it impossible. He wondered whether it was a prank undertaken with some other students that had gone wrong. Ellis seems to have had no interest in conjuring, and was not a member of the university magicians' society, the Pentacle Club. The following day he was buried at Mill Road cemetery, and a service was held in the Chapel at Sidney, presided over by Weekes.

The following week, when 400 applicants applied for 16 places in court, hoping for a murder verdict, a letter was read out from a fellow pupil of Ellis's at Gresham's School. He claimed that Ellis was once found in a similar position at the school, so tightly bound that he needed to be released by friends, and that this was a practice popular with his year who would tie themselves up as a dare. Spilsbury then gave expert evidence about how, although difficult to imagine, an accidental death was in his opinion entirely possible and indeed likely. On 4 March the court decided that death was accidental and caused by asphyxia.

That was not the end of the matter. The popular press pursued the 'University Riddle' for all it was worth, and stoked up popular feeling against Sidney and the university. Weekes received a number of letters from members of the public criticising the College, offering advice, and suggesting other possible explanations. Ellis's mother had received a letter after the inquest claiming to be from three students who said Ellis's 'sneering' at sports had led them to punish him by tying him up and leaving him in his room. Mrs Ellis said her son enjoyed sports very much; and Weekes had to write to one irate correspondent, who had referred to a 'suspicion of blood-guiltiness', to inform him that the letter from the three students was 'a palpable hoax'.

There were more unusual letters. P Collen Fox of Somerset offered to 'give you the name of such a man who has this rare gift', and that 'all I know is that he lives in Weston-super-Mare…', and in another letter that 'it is a matter of national importance that Our Universities should turn out fine characters…'. Ada E Chappell, 'a pioneer Plunket Nurse of New Zealand', asked Weekes if 'you know about the wonderful machine which Abrams of "Abrams Reactions" invented, which registers the vibrations of the individual from his handwriting'. In August *The Harbinger of Light*, a spiritualist magazine based in Melbourne, Australia, published a piece by the South African psychic T A R Purchas that had appeared in the *Rand Daily Mail* of 4 May. This was sent to Weekes by an anonymous Bournemouth correspondent. Purchas claimed to have met a friend of Ellis's recently deceased father and had thus taken a special interest in the case. Purchas's 'direct-voice spirit communications' on 24 March revealed that Ellis died from suffocation as the result of a practical joke, the student himself, heard gasping through a medium's voice, describing the incident and eventually seeing the whole scene after losing consciousness 'from a great height – like a stage'.

As late as 1937 *John Bull* published a long piece claiming the inquest disguised an establishment cover-up. By then Weekes may have felt the dreadful events of 1931 were a faint memory for most parents sending sons to Sidney.

'Mac': R A McCance and the Science of Nutrition

Raise your teacup this morning to Professor McCance. He has succeeded where public demand and the Daily Express both failed. For years this paper sought to restore the white loaf…But the gentlemen in Whitehall thought they knew best. They said that the dreary grey national loaf was better for us. Professor McCance is the man who exploded this nonsense…Parents are perfectly capable of choosing good food for themselves and their children. Professor McCance has shown that the gentlemen in Whitehall can only be trusted with baby rats. —Chapman Pincher, *Daily Express*, July 1949

When Robert Alexander McCance came out of the RNAS in 1919 wanting to study agriculture, he came to Sidney and studied natural sciences and physiology under C R A Thacker, whom he found 'most inspiring'. As an undergraduate he was a keen member of the Cromwell Club, a vigorous dancer with Girtonians and others at the 'Vingt-et-Un' club, and grew fond of Fred Maltby, the fellows' butler, with whom he would sing 'Galloping Major' at musical sessions during the long vacation. Although taken ill just before his finals, McCance was allowed to take his exams in Knox-Shaw's rooms in Cloister Court and, although he took a second, was awarded

R A McCance

a scholarship. He married Molly MacGregor immediately and the two lived over a heel-bar opposite Sidney where Sainsbury's is now.

In 1922, abandoning the desire to become a farmer in his native Ireland as a result of the political climate there, McCance studied biochemistry and, after taking a PhD in 1926, went to King's College Hospital, London, to study medicine. He became interested in diabetes and its link to carbohydrates, analysing over 100 plant-derived foods for their carbohydrate values. As head of the biochemistry laboratory at King's, McCance made groundbreaking studies in the effects of salt deficiency. In 1933 he met Elsie Widdowson in the basement kitchens where he went to collect food samples, and the two established a 60-year working partnership that transformed the science of nutrition. In 1940, they published *The Chemical Composition of Food*, which became the international standard for computing dietary needs.

In 1938, McCance and Widdowson had moved their research to Cambridge, where McCance became a Sidney fellow, working in a laboratory at Addenbrooke's. They began to test the body's limits as preparation for proposals on wartime diets. On one occasion McCance hyperventilated to the point of collapse, providing evidence that saved many lives in North Africa. On another occasion he lived on a very low-fat and high-carbohydrate diet for three months, before cycling 200 miles to the Lake District over two and a half days in blizzard conditions, then walking 36

Design for a Brain

William Ross Ashby entered Sidney from the Edinburgh Academy in 1921. He became a psychiatrist and was one of the founding fathers of cybernetics, the study of the structure of regulatory systems, working both in England and the USA. Ashby developed inventions and ideas such as the 'Homeostat' machine, the law of requisite variety, the principle of self-organisation and many others. His books *Design for a Brain* (1952) and *Introduction to Cybernetics* (1956) remain standard textbooks. Ashby's writing style is characterised by its clarity and pithiness: 'The brain has no gimmick, just five billion years of research and development'; 'The educated brain is the wreckage left after the experiences of training'; 'Every skilled dramatist understands the inexorable logic of the emotion.'

W R Ashby in his prizewinning 'Thinking Cap', on board SS Maasdam *travelling to New York, 1960*

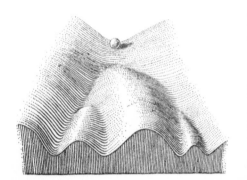

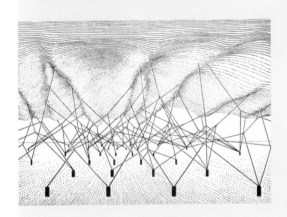

Strategy of the Genes

Conrad Hal Waddington, the son of a Quaker tea-planter, entered Sidney as a scholar in 1923. He took a double first in geology but his interest soon moved to evolutionary biology under the influence of Gregory Bateson. A fellow at Christ's from 1934 until 1942, Waddington was among the first in Britain to relate embryology to the new science of genetics. After service with RAF Coastal Command on operational research against U-boats, in 1947 he was appointed professor of genetics at Edinburgh where he created one of the largest departments in that subject in the world. A philosopher with a special interest in modern art (he was a friend of artists such as Henry Moore and architects such as Walter Gropius), his book *Beyond Appearance* (1969) concerned the links between art and science. Waddington, a keen morris dancer and jazz enthusiast, died in 1975.

C H Waddington The Strategy of the Genes: A Discussion of Some Aspects of Theoretical Biology, *1957. Lady Margaret Hall Library, Oxford*
These two images seek to make clear aspects of what Waddington called the 'epigenetic landscape'. The upper plate shows a ball, representing part of an egg, as it is about to follow its particular genetic development; the lower plate shows the complex system of interactions underlying the landscape

Governor of the Punjab

Dada Chintappa Pavate came to Sidney from Karnatak College, Dharwar in 1924. He was a Wrangler and research scholar and returned to India where he was a professor of mathematics at Hindu University, Benares, a leading university administrator at Karnatak University and, from 1967 to 1973, Governor of Punjab. Pavate's two sons also attended Sidney. When he died in 1979 the Karnatak campus was named after him. Since 2000 Sidney has welcomed three Pavate Fellows a year, a scheme initiated by friends and admirers to bring Indian students to Cambridge for three months.

Blood in Spain

The South Africa-born Reginald Saxton, standing on the right in this photograph, went to Sidney in 1929 where he came into contact with communist ideas and developed strong anti-fascist beliefs. He trained at Bart's Hospital and became a specialist in blood transfusion. In 1936 he volunteered to join the Spanish Medical Aid Committee and joined the 35th Medical Division Unit. At the Battle of Jarama in February 1937 10,000 Republican soldiers died and Saxton set up hospital as an advance party in Villarejo de Salvanés. He later recalled: 'We had at that time no transfusion syringes and no satisfactory needles. I collected, however, two sets of instruments to enable me to dissect a vein and insert a cannula [a thin tube]. The blood was poured into a funnel and led by a rubber tube to a cannula.' Saxton's most famous patient was Julian Bell, son of the Bloomsbury artist Vanessa Bell. His remarkable bravery was recognised 60 years later when Saxton was made an honorary Spanish citizen. He became a GP in Brighton and died in 2004.

miles up and down hills in one day, wearing a heavy rucksack. His conclusion, that such deprivation would lead to no serious loss of fitness, provided an important basis for government planning. The discovery during this experiment that adding calcium to bread flour would supplement the loss of milk through rationing, was enforced by law and remained a statutory requirement for bread-making for many years. During the war McCance, who worked for the Admiralty, established that drinking no water was better than drinking seawater, and that boiled sweets could avert dehydration. He also developed seasickness pills, and designed a new form of covered inflatable life raft that saved many sailors from death by exposure.

After the war, as first professor of experimental medicine, McCance, following work on the poor nutrition of post-war Germany, continued his nutritional research across a wide area and became particularly concerned with the physiology of new-born children and the harmful effects of manufactured milk formulae on their kidney development. In the late 1960s he worked in Uganda as head of the Medical Research Council's Infantile Malnutrition Research Unit. He was thus the founding father of a new area of neo-natal science and the first president of the Neo-Natal Society, which still holds an annual McCance lecture. After retirement, McCance, who loved walking and cycling, lived in Cambridge, a dedicated and eccentric member of the Sidney community, famous for his huge intake of vegetables at meals in hall. After his death in 1993 'Mac''s memorial service was held in the Chapel and his ashes buried by the apple tree in the Fellows' Garden.

'London's Yellowest Press': Sidney's New Journalists

'Nay! one, Jake Owen, fills me with distress,
Pens moral themes for Londoner's Yellowest Press.'
—James Passant as 'Clio' in 'A Masque of Vice and Virtue', *Pheon*, IX, ii, 1932

Wray's Court by R C Genlloud, from By-Ways in Old Cambridge, 1933

Many Sidney students lived at numbers 4 and 5 Wray's Court, opposite the College front gate, in the 1930s and 1940s. Number 5, home of 'Mrs Cooper', included the talented cellist Theodore Mathieson (1932) who was later a famous missionary in Calcutta and set up the Mathieson Trust and Musical School to encourage musical development among poor Indian boys. Mathieson was inspired in his vocation by the Sidney chaplain Hugh 'Juno' Maycock

Weekes was keen to keep Sidney out of the newspapers' spotlights in 1931. During the 1920s and 1930s, however, Sidney, whose last great journalist had been Sir Roger L'Estrange in the 17th century, produced three of Britain's greatest 20th-century newspaper editors.

Sir Gordon Newton, son of a north London plate glass manufacturer, entered Sidney from Blundell's as a scholar in 1926, the year of the General Strike, to read economics. He gained a running blue and left in 1929 to enter the family business. This collapsed in 1930, leaving the family bankrupt, and Newton bought a motor accessory business, which also failed. He entered journalism in 1935 with the *Financial News* and then fought with the Honourable Artillery Company during the Second World War. After the war, Newton joined the *Financial Times* and was made editor in 1949. He transformed a specialist city journal with a circulation of 60,000 into the world-famous pink broadsheet read by over 200,000 that we know today, extending its coverage to include the arts and making it the leading opinion-former in its field. A lean, chain-

smoking, bespectacled and quiet 'Mr Pooter' figure with absolutely no pretensions and much loved by his staff, Newton chose Oxbridge graduates, almost always male, as trainees and expected them to learn on the job. These included Samuel Brittan, Jock Bruce-Gardyne, Nigel Lawson and William Rees-Mogg. Newton was knighted by Harold Wilson in 1966.

In 1927, the year after Newton entered Sidney, Frank Owen, a regular contributor to *Pheon*, arrived from Monmouth School, the son of a Welsh innkeeper in Hereford. He won a rugby blue, was a prodigious drinker, and took a first in history, specialising in military history. After entering local journalism, he was the Liberal candidate for Hereford in 1929 and won the election, identifying himself then and subsequently with Lloyd George's radical liberalism. He was a friend of Aneurin Bevan and in 1931 rejected the National Government, leading to disaster at the polls. As he wrote later: 'The wise, far-seeing, independent electors of my native Hereford sent me to Westminster, and two years later, the lousy bastards kicked me out.' Owen returned to journalism and worked for Lord Beaverbrook's *Daily Express* and then, as editor from 1938 to 1941, the *Evening Standard*. He had taken a strong stand against appeasement throughout the 1930s, and in 1939 led a deputation of editors to their proprietor, Beaverbrook, to insist he change his stance on Hitler and support Churchill's line. By the time of the 1940 blitz, Owen had turned an unremarkable London paper into the campaigning voice of wartime London. In 1940 he wrote *Guilty Men*, under the pseudonym 'Cato', with Michael Foot and Peter Howard. It aimed at shaming Chamberlain and the appeasers, and helped put Churchill firmly in power. It was a huge and legendary success. Owen continued his pioneering journalism throughout the war, often under the pseudonym 'Thomas Rainsboro', a Leveller captain in Cromwell's army, demanding a second front and criticising aspects of Churchill's policy. He was an expert in military history, a friend of Wavell, Liddell-Hart and Mountbatten, and used these connections extremely effectively to support his arguments. He joined Mountbatten in Burma as editor of the forces newspaper there, and with him helped to forge the British military campaign. After the war Owen was not the force he had been, editing the *Daily Mail* for a few years and writing a number of books, including a biography of his hero and friend, Lloyd George. He died in 1979.

Michael Curtis followed Owen in his unwavering support for the radical wing of the Liberal Party and his brave stands on matters of principle. A dentist's son from Cambridge, he entered Sidney from St Lawrence College, Ramsgate in 1939 to read economics under Austin Robinson. He served in the army during the war, suffering severe wounds in Tunisia in 1943, and returned to Sidney to complete his degree in 1945. He joined the *News Chronicle* in 1946 and became its highly innovative editor in 1954. He had some of the finest journalists ever brought together

News Chronicle,
3 November 1956

Ambrose Reeves at a press conference with Dr Martin Luther King Jr, 27 July 1957

in one office in James Cameron, Geoffrey Cox, Ian Mackay, Ritchie Calder, A J Cummings, Geoffrey Goodman, and the great cartoonist 'Vicky'. Curtis made various far-sighted suggestions to its conservative-minded proprietor, Laurence Cadbury, to halt its long-term decline, all of which were rejected. However, it is for his stand against Eden's government over the Suez Crisis in 1956, despite Eden's pressure on him to fall into line, that Curtis is best known. The result, after one of the most dramatic confrontations between government and press in British history, was disastrous for the paper's circulation. Realising that Cadbury was anyway intending to sell up to Lord Rothermere, Curtis resigned in 1957 and went on to work for the Aga Khan, setting up the mogul's East African media empire, the Nation Media Group, supporting Kenyan nationalism, and vastly expanding operations. He introduced technical innovations in newspaper printing well in advance of those in Europe, and used his power to promote political change in Africa into the 1970s. Curtis died in the Cotswolds in 1994.

'The Beloved Country': Ambrose Reeves, John Collins and South Africa

Ever since George Holditch Mason travelled to 'Zulu-Land' in 1850, Sidney has had a close involvement with all matters African, symbolised by Archbishop Desmond Tutu's honorary fellowship, awarded in 1999. The anti-apartheid lawyer John Dugard, who discovered 17th-century Sidney connections when he came to the College in the 1960s, is another strong link. Two Sidney churchmen in particular made a significant impression on African affairs in the 1950s and 1960s.

Ambrose Reeves, a Norwich chemist's son, was educated at Great Yarmouth School, served in the army during the war and entered Sidney in 1921 to read history and moral science. The cox of one of Sidney's boats, Reeves was a small and frail man, not a 'hearty' type, and he became involved in Christian socialist groups

John Collins (right) on the second CND march from Aldermaston to London, 1959

at Cambridge. Inspired by Sidney's Anglo-Catholic traditions, he trained for the priesthood at Mirfield, and during the 1930s and 1940s was a rector in Fife, and then a vicar in working-class districts in Liverpool. A key figure in mediating the dockers' strike in 1945, Reeves was appointed Bishop of Johannesburg in 1949. His diocese was, like Liverpool, a poor industrial area, including the Rand gold mines. He took a strong stand against apartheid and the pass laws, and was alone among South African bishops in opposing the oppressive Bantu Education Act by seeking to establish his own educational centres. His home was a focus for extremist attacks, and his support for a radical Afrikaans trades union newspaper brought him opposition from the National Party and suspicion from the Church of England.

By the mid-1950s Reeves was collaborating with his fellow Sidneian Canon John Collins in anti-apartheid activities, and with Collins established a fund to support Nelson Mandela and other African National Congress leaders during the treason trial of 1956. When the Sharpesville massacre took place in 1960 in his own diocese, killing 69 people and wounding many more, Reeves decided to leave for London to inform the rest of the world. It was a brave but unwise move. He alienated possible conservative support in South Africa, took himself away from the country he was hoping to influence, embarrassed the Church of England and damaged his own career. A hero among black Africans, and one of the leaders of white opposition to apartheid, he died as a vicar in Lewes, Sussex in 1972.

Reeve's friend John Collins, a master builder's son from Kent, entered Sidney from Cranbrook School as a scholar in 1924 to read mathematics. He graduated with a first in theology in 1927 and entered the church before returning to Sidney in 1929 as chaplain. He became a follower and friend of the excommunicated French liberal Catholic theologian Albert Loisy, moving rapidly from the conservative position in which he had been brought up, both religiously and politically, and joining the Labour Party. Collins was vice-principal of Westcott House in the 1930s before being elected dean of Oriel College, Oxford. He was a chaplain at an RAF training base during the Second World War, and organised a group of Christian socialists, which brought him into conflict with his senior officers. Following the war he convened a public meeting in Oxford that led to the formation of Christian Action. Collins's appointment by Clement Attlee in 1948 as a canon at St Paul's allowed him to continue his work in London, through sermons and meetings. St Paul's was opposed to the appointment and some events he organised, such as his invitation to the South African Alan Paton, author of *Cry, the Beloved Country* (1948), to preach at the church, caused great controversy.

Collins was thrust into the public limelight and became a worldwide spokesman for action by Christians in the areas of international freedom, justice and peace, arguing against capital punishment at home and, as we have seen, acting against apartheid in South Africa as president of the International Defence and Aid Fund, which led to many other such groups being formed around the world. The considerable money IDAF sent to South Africa contributed significantly to saving the life of Nelson Mandela and other activists. In 1958 Collins was a founder, with Bertrand Russell, of the Campaign for Nuclear Disarmament. He marched to Aldermaston, and acted as secretary for CND. By the time of his death in London in 1982 he was recognised as one of the leaders of a new socially and politically engaged wing within the Church of England.

'Confraternitas Historica': David Thomson and the Rise of Sidney History

The College of Thomas Fuller, Thomas May, Thomas Rymer and Philip Morant might be expected to have produced some major historians in the 20th century. J W Reynolds had re-founded historical studies before the First World War, firsts were regular in the Tripos, and the Confraternitas Historica was Sidney's most thriving society. Reynolds produced at least one major historian in the Tudor specialist Professor C H Williams, who entered Sidney in 1914. Reynolds's successor James Passant, who, like B T D Smith, lost his faith in the 1930s, was a fine teacher with a subtle mind and a charming personality, but until the early 1930s Sidney had not really produced the major professional historians to match its remarkable young mathematicians and scientists. A significant exception is Wilfred Scott-Giles, herald, devoted long-term member of the 'Confrat' and author of the second history of the College, who died in 1982.

In 1932 *Pheon* published 'A Masque of Vice and Virtue' by S W White, to celebrate the occasion of the Confrat's 21st birthday, in the style of a Jacobean masque suitable to Sidney's history. The historical muse Clio was played by Passant who, among other references, slights the historian Herbert Butterfield of Peterhouse, author of *The Whig Interpretation of History*. Other characters include a 'Virtuous Student' and a 'Wicked Student', a 'Pantheon' of the 'Virtuous', including Rymer and Fuller, and of 'Repentants', Oliver Cromwell and the ever-present Wilfred Scott-Giles, who played himself. Cromwell was played by a second-year undergraduate, David Thomson.

Thomson, who was born in Edinburgh, went to Sir George Monoux Grammar School in Walthamstow before entering Sidney in 1931. He took a double first with distinction, and went on to undertake research on political parties in 18th-century Britain. He was a research fellow at Sidney from 1938, and succeeded his teacher Passant as history fellow in 1945. During the war he worked for the BBC and the Ministry of Information, and wrote his first book, *The Democratic Ideal in France* (1944), highlighting his continuous and influential interest in French history. After the war his output as teacher and author was enormous: he wrote the two most historically recent volumes in the Pelican History of England, and the

David Thomson in his study, Q3, Garden Court, with a student, 1950s

massive and authoritative survey *Europe Since Napoleon* in 1957, along with a world history since 1914 and a book of historical theory, *The Aims of History* (1970). In this last, following the lead given to him by Passant, he stressed the need for history to engage with ideas of the state and with contemporary issues, and to inform the decisions of politicians. For Thomson, a regular contributor to newspapers and widely read journals, and a pioneer of TV historical broadcasting, 'history is the best liberal education a student can have in the modern world'. Thomson, a lifelong enthusiast of the Workers' Educational Association as well as of the grammar school system he felt he had benefited from, was an active member of the Cambridge history faculty throughout his career and, above all, a devoted member of Sidney. He succeeded 'Tommy' Knox-Shaw as master in 1957 and, until his death in 1970, was a prime mover in pushing Sidney into facing the new challenges of the late-20th century.

Fellow Sidney historians with Thomson during the 1930s included Otto Smail, the crusades expert and future fellow, and Asa Briggs, Sidney's most famous 20th-century historian and now an honorary fellow of Sidney. Thomson and Smail nurtured a remarkable generation of historians after the war, including Hugh Tinker, Derek Beales, Peter Salway, Royston Lambert, Tim Blanning, Tony Badger, John Brewer and John Styles. The legacy continues strongly today.

'The Turning Point of the War': J A Ratcliffe, P I Dee and Radar

> Whenever I am out of the lab. and Skinner has to do this he forgets to turn off the water before pulling off the cooling pipes with the result that I am standing all day in about ½" depth of water, and the water on the bench is about equally deep but has its surface relieved somewhat by floating cig-ends, tea leaves, banana skins, etc. However, we have managed to get quite a lot of power out of it and light a Pea Lamp nearly a foot away.
> —P I Dee, diary entry for 13 June 1940, while working on the klystrons used to generate and amplify microwaves

P I Dee in his study at TRE, Malvern, in 1942

With C T R Wilson as a fellow, some remarkable physicists came to Sidney between the wars. John Ratcliffe, the son of a Lancashire quarry owner, came to Sidney as a scholar from Giggleswick School in North Yorkshire in 1921. He took a first in both parts of the natural sciences Tripos, and in 1924 began research on radio wave propagation under Edward Appleton, then professor of physics at King's College, London, assisting in the experiments that established the existence of the ionosphere. Ratcliffe was made a university demonstrator in the Cavendish Laboratory, and later became a reader, inspiring generations of students with his lectures and lucid writing. One of his students at Sidney, the cosmic ray specialist J G Wilson, who entered the College in 1929 from Hartlepool Secondary School, and was later Cavendish Professor at Leeds, recalled his teaching style: 'In college supervisions he focused one's mind on what was becoming important in the development of physics...the relation of magnetic force and induction, the dimensions of electrons in nuclei..., the wave-particle duality...and the relation of Dirac's theory of electrons with physical reality. We talked about the development of the wave-mechanical description from the Bohr model of the hydrogen atom... He was often full of recent data and thoughts about the transmission of radio waves in the ionosphere (his specialism) and finally he persuaded me...to go to J J Thomson's lecture course.' Other students of Ratcliffe's were the pioneer of radio astronomy in Australia, J L Pawsey; J P Henry, the aerospace researcher, the first man to subject himself in a partial pressure suit of his own design, to rarefield atmospheres; the astronomer Donald Blackwell; and the radio astronomer R N Bracewell.

A senior staff meeting at Durnford House, a school at Worth Matravers taken over by the TRE management in 1940. J A Ratcliffe is seated on the left

Ratcliffe was head of the radio ionosphere research group at the Cavendish and experimented with radio waves, seeking to find how they were reflected back from the ionised regions of the upper atmosphere and how those regions were formed. In 1939 Ratcliffe joined the Air Ministry's Telecommunications Research Establishment (TRE) at Dundee, working on new equipment called CHL (Chain Home Low) for detecting low-flying aircraft. Then, at Petersham in Surrey, he organised the Anti-Aircraft Radio School, which trained scientists to keep anti-aircraft radars working on the gun sites around cities, in particular those of London. He returned to the TRE in 1941 and headed the large new Development Services section, which was concerned with taking new and untested equipment and making it work in the field. This involved designing, testing and installing equipment in aircraft, writing clear manuals for RAF personnel, and living with squadrons while they adapted to their use.

After the war, Ratcliffe returned to the Cavendish, taking with him from TRE a brilliant young researcher, Martin Ryle, the future Astronomer Royal and Nobel Prize winner, who, although he later became a fellow at Trinity, was a registered research student and member of Sidney until his death in 1984. Ratcliffe encouraged Ryle to follow up recent discoveries about radio emission from the sun using techniques developed in his wartime radar work. Ryle headed a new group of radio astronomers, while Ratcliffe continued as leader of the radio ionosphere team. As the pioneer of ionospheric physics, Ratcliffe was elected FRS in 1951 and was made CB in 1965.

A hard-working and talented administrator, Ratcliffe in 1960 became director of radio research in the Department of Scientific and Industrial Research, and director of the Radio Research Station at Slough. He was closely involved in the early use of satellites for studying the upper atmosphere. Ratcliffe died in Cambridge in 1987.

Philip Ivor Dee, a schoolmaster's son from near Stroud, went up to Sidney as a scholar from Marling School in 1922. Like Ratcliffe, he took a double first in natural sciences and went on to conduct research at the Cavendish. Greatly admired by Lord Rutherford, Dee was Stokes Student at Pembroke for three years and began research under C T R Wilson on cloud chambers in the early 1930s. He was a masterful technician with the chambers and proved the absence of significant interaction of neutrons and electrons. He moved on to look at the transmutation of atoms by bombardment with accelerated ions, in particular the two modes of reactions between deuterons to yield tritium and protons or helium-3 and neutrons. In the later 1930s he became deputy to Lord Rutherford for the construction of electrostatic accelerators.

In 1940, Dee joined Ratcliffe at the TRE 'radar university' at Worth Matravers, and was a superintendent for virtually all the work on the generation of energy sources for radar equipment. His young team of physicists developed new microwave radar for aircraft interception (AI), anti-surface vessel (ASV) and H2S (blind bombing). Dee was fascinated by the possibilities of an airborne cavity magnetron and in 1941 tested its use in a Bristol Blenheim aircraft that was able to pick up towns and other locations clearly. Dee's team photographed the images from the cathode ray tube of the equipment as proof the system could work. His superintendent A P Rowe exclaimed, 'This is the turning point of the war.' The following summer Dee was part of a delegation to Downing Street that was informed by Churchill that he wanted 200 of the new centimetre navigational sets (H2S) within a few months. With GEC, Dee pushed through the production on time so that night bombing could proceed from January 1943.

Dee, a charismatic and infectiously energetic man, was not only a brilliant scientist but an excellent manager and diplomat, able to bring politicians, military officers and other scientists together to focus on a particular project. He was made FRS in 1941 and later left Sidney to become a professor at Glasgow, where he created a world-renowned department. Dee worked on the establishment of CERN at Geneva where the great particle accelerators were developed. He died in Glasgow in 1983.

Ratcliffe and Dee, like Welchman at Bletchley Park, drew on their talented students during the war, men who went on to major achievements in peacetime. Not all were physicists, however. Tom Kilburn, a prize-winning mathematician, was recruited into TRE in 1942 straight from Sidney. After the war he was a pioneer in computing technology at the University of Manchester and devised the world's

Two large wooden aerial towers for Chain Home Low (CHL) radar on A-site at Renscombe Farm, Worth Matravers, c1941

J A Ratcliffe managed the development of the CHL radar system, three aerials for which can be seen to the left in the middle distance.

'Onuna-Ekwulu Ora'

Since William Armstrong's work on the shell money system of Rossel Island in the 1920s, Sidney has produced some major figures in anthropology. The doyen of African archaeological and anthropological studies, Charles Thurstan Shaw, went up as a Blundell's scholar in 1933. His earliest work, on the Bosumpra Cave at Abetifi, Ghana, was an instant classic. Thurstan Shaw, a passionate advocate of African nationalism, was a prime mover in establishing archaeology as a discipline in African universities: in Nigeria he has the honorific 'Onuna-Ekwulu Ora'. He became a professor at Cambridge, a fellow of the British Academy, and was awarded the CBE. Yet Thurstan Shaw was a conscientious objector during the Second World War and as recently as 2000, in his mid-80s, was arrested during anti-war demonstrations at the Faslane nuclear submarine base in Scotland. He has been an honorary fellow at Sidney, the college his father entered a century earlier, since 1994.

Charles Thurstan Shaw, image from Pheon, *XV, iii, June 1936*

first stored-programme computer, the Small Scale Experimental Machine, in 1948. John Flavell Coales came to Sidney as a scholar in 1926 and studied maths and physics under J A Ratcliffe. He worked for the Admiralty at the HM Signal School, Portsmouth, and during the 1930s was put in charge of a research team working on the transmission and reception of decimetre radio waves, with application to radar. He decided on the 50 cm wavelength used so successfully by most gunnery sets in British ships during the war. After the war Coales worked in the computer industry before returning to the engineering department in Cambridge in 1953 to lead a research team in advanced automatic control systems. During the 1960s he worked with Sidney's robotics expert John Billingsley on innovative model-based predictive control. Coales became one of the most influential R&D entrepreneurs in British universities. Among many honours, he was elected to a personal chair at Cambridge and Fellow of the Royal Society.

'The Birth of the Atomic Era': Sidney's Nuclear Physicists

One of Ratcliffe's contemporaries at Sidney in 1921 was Cecil Frank Powell, a gun-smith's son from Tonbridge, Kent, who entered Sidney as a scholar from Sir Andrew Judd's Commercial School, and took a double first in physics in 1925. He was a research student with C T R Wilson at the Cavendish Laboratory, working on the improvement of cloud chambers, before moving to the University of Bristol, where he spent the rest of his career. He was a fellow of the Royal Society and, in 1950, was awarded the Nobel Prize. His interests were seismology and nuclear physics, and he is best known for producing a powerful proton beam with a generator that he built at Bristol. With a new cloud chamber and improved microscopes, emulsions and processing techniques, Powell, aided by his all-female team of scanners, was able to

C F Powell (centre) and his assistants at Bristol University prepare a research project to send a huge balloon into the stratosphere to collect data on subatomic particles, 21 November 1950

produce precise images of cosmic rays never seen before. He was, like Dee, a leading figure in the foundation of CERN in Geneva.

As a communist for much of his life, Powell was an object of suspicion to many in authority, but his political position moderated after the war and he was a key figure in the discussions that led to the 'Russell-Einstein Declaration' in 1955, urging world co-operation in controlling nuclear proliferation. Powell was one of the 11 signatories of the manifesto, which included the sentence: 'Remember your humanity, and forget the rest.'

Philip Moon, a ship's mate's son from Lewisham, entered Sidney from Leyton Grammar School as a scholar in natural sciences in 1925. He graduated in 1928, and investigated the interaction of positive ions with metal surfaces at a range of temperatures and low ion energies. From Cambridge he went to Imperial College, London, to work on neutrons, and the conclusions of this work were taken up by Niels Bohr, the great Danish physicist, to propose his 'compound nucleus' theory. At the outbreak of the war, while at Birmingham University with the Australian physicist Mark Oliphant, Moon joined the Admiralty to work on microwave transmitters for radar. In 1940 Moon, a member of the MAUD Committee, which took decisions on Britain's development of nuclear capability, joined the 'Tube Alloys' directorate

Sidney and the Atomic Bomb

The Trinity Test (below) was the first test of an implosion-design plutonium device (i.e. an atomic bomb) and took place at Alamogordo, New Mexico, on 16 July 1945. It was equivalent to the explosion of about 20 kilotons of TNT.

THE BRITISH MISSION

INVITES YOU TO A PARTY IN CELEBRATION OF

THE BIRTH OF THE ATOMIC ERA

FULLER LODGE

SATURDAY, 22ND SEPTEMBER, 1945

DANCING. ENTERTAINMENT.
PRECEDED BY SUPPER AT 8 P. M.

Mr & Mrs C. Critchfield

R.S.V.P. TO MRS. W. F. MOON
ROOM A-211 (EXTENSION 250)

Philip Moon, shown in a security photograph for Los Alamos. His wife is the respondent for the rather alarming invitation to a party at the Los Alamos laboratory to celebrate 'The Birth of the Atomic Era' on 22 September 1945, about six weeks after the bombing of Hiroshima and Nagasaki on 6 and 9 August respectively. Los Alamos National Laboratory

Philip Moon

that was developing Britain's military and civil uses of nuclear technology at the Cavendish and at Rhydmwyn in Wales. He was joined by another Sidney physicist, Anthony French, who had entered the College in 1942. Moon and French were transferred to Los Alamos in 1944 as British delegates to the Manhattan Project, and worked on the site preparation and instrumentation for recording the first atomic test, witnessing the Trinity test in the desert at Alamogordo in July 1945. After the war, Moon was appointed professor at Birmingham, in preference to the favourite, C F Powell, whose politics made him unacceptable.

'Stringent Security Precautions': Sidney and the Second World War

> So, we have parted with a large proportion of our teaching staff: in fact a larger proportion than any other College. —G A Weekes to C T R Wilson, 1 November 1939

Another long vacation, another world war; history caught up with Sidney again in September 1939. By the end of the academic year, seven fellows were on important national service, many undergraduates had joined up, and numbers entering in October 1941 were down from the usual 50 to 28. 'Communal eating' of breakfast and lunch as well as supper in Hall, the norm today, began in 1940 as a result of rationing. The cold supper supplied in rooms on Sundays was the only reminder of the ancient privileges of the pre-war period. Sidney continued to do well in the Tripos in spite of the conditions, with 11 Tripos prizes awarded, including a history prize for Asa Briggs, who was soon to be recruited to the code-breaking efforts at Bletchley Park. As the war continued, increasing numbers of students based at Sidney were cadets doing special courses. Old boys, many of whom had fought in the First World War, took senior positions in administrative, planning and intelligence areas. The titles awarded before, during and after the war to Sir Frederick Brundrett, Sir Ben Lockspeiser, Sir Clifford Jarrett, Sir J W Crofton, Sir Frank Ewart Smith, and the Sidney library benefactor, Sir Richard Powell, suggest their eminence.

Sidney's *Annual* over the last few decades has carried many obituaries and wartime memories by former members, and this section can only touch on a small fraction of their remarkable content: Brigadier P S Leeper's work on the logistical aspects of the North Africa, Italian and Normandy invasions, for which he helped design and construct the crucial Mulberry harbours; the recollections of surgeon Christopher Parish, later a fellow and keeper of Sidney's muniments, of his life as a field surgeon at Salerno and Anzio and his five-hour conversation with, and blessing by, Pope Pius XII in the Vatican; Charles Brereton's experiences as a machine-gun instructor and his severe injury after D-Day, which left him hospitalised for a year; D F Stephenson's letter from Holland in December 1945 to his history teacher, David Thomson, about differing French, Belgian and Dutch attitudes to the allies, Monty's 'conceit' and the laying on of girls, dinner and theatre by a Belgian woman for him and three colleagues ('a perfect way of learning French in six easy lessons!'); the engineer Hugh Reeves's work at 'Station IX', the SOE research centre, where he invented the Welrod silenced pistol and the Sleeve gun used by the SAS; the civil engineer Sir William Gordon Harris's work for the Admiralty; and the lawyer Sir Hugh Park's work with the SOE for whom he debriefed the famous allied herione Odette Sansom.

The *Annual* obituary pages recorded the first fatality: 2nd Lieutenant H C Secretan, aged 24, killed in action during the Dunkirk evacuation, 23 May 1940. By the end of the war, 70 Sidney men had lost their lives in action, along with one member of staff, Frederick Maltby, the son of the late fellows' butler, who died in a Japanese prison camp in September 1944. In 1941, when there were 31 freshmen, there were notices in the *Annual* of seven men killed or missing. The *Annual* also proudly announced the many military and other awards made to men on active service and to those, such as Austin Robinson and Gordon Welchman, who had been awarded OBEs for special contributions to the war effort. The *Annual* recorded in 1943 that an earlier report of one member's death had been inaccurate and that he was in fact alive and well. In 1944 a member of staff, able seaman Joseph Coleman, on board the submarine HMS *Shark*, had lost an arm when it was sunk, but had been repatriated by the Germans and was in good health. The last Sidney death was squadron leader M R Hill, killed in action in Norway on 12 March 1945.

The sports clubs struggled to raise crews and teams during the war, often having to amalgamate with other colleges to provide enough men to compete. The swimming team was forced to swim in the Cam when a coal shortage closed the Cambridge indoor pool. The musical society was reduced mainly to playing gramophone records in the chaplain's room. The war brought some unusual people to College: on Founder's Day on 14 February in 1943, King Peter II of Yugoslavia was in the Chapel and heard a sermon followed by a lecture by archpriest Dr Z Ristanovic and dinner in the Lodge.

Throughout the war, Garden Court and Cloister Court, with the exceptions of the rooms of Knox-Shaw (then Sidney's first vice-master in 1944) and the dean, were occupied by the Eastern Division of the Ministry of Labour and National Service. The *Annual* was able to announce in October 1945 that lecture room L in Cloister Court 'under stringent security precautions' had been used to house 'the all-important "National Register"'. Sidney's gardens had been the site of undergraduate ARP activity under the direction of Knox-Shaw. A trailer-pump and a sunken pond used as a static water supply, along with a first aid post in the master's garage, were housed in the Master's Garden. A blast wall was also built around the Porter's Lodge. Sidney took one slight 'hit', at 3 a.m. on 28 July 1942, when 'our bomb', as the *Annual* had it, bounced off the Jesus Lane wall, killing a passer-by and shattering some windows in College.

'Enigma': Gordon Welchman, John Herivel and Hut 6

> One evening early in the second term [January 1940] I was in my rooms in College when there was a knock at the door, and in came Welchman himself. After a few civilities – he was evidently pushed for time – he told me that he was doing very important war work at Bletchley, and would I like to come there and help him. It did not take me very long to make up my mind...
>
> —John Herivel, *Herivelismus and the German Military Enigma*, 2008

The Hut 6 machine room at Bletchley Park

We have already seen how Sidney's physicists J A Ratcliffe and P I Dee, through their work at what was known as 'radar university', and others in nuclear warfare, such as Philip Moon, made major contributions to the war effort. The most famous Sidney intellectual wartime input, however, came at the Government Code and Cypher School (GCCS) at the Victorian mansion at Bletchley Park near Milton Keynes. James Passant, working for the Admiralty, was there in the early days before moving on to run the Austrian and German sections of the Foreign Office research department. After the war, he prepared indictments of Nazi war criminals for the trials at Nuremberg. Through Passant, a number of historians, including Asa Briggs and Paul Coles, were recruited to Bletchley.

Gordon Welchman, c1930

A Sidney colleague of Passant's at Bletchley was Gordon Welchman, Sidney's young maths fellow who had been taught at Marlborough by Alan Robson, a Sidney Wrangler before the First World War. Recruited by the head of GCCS, Alastair Denniston, and joining other Cambridge figures such as Dilly Knox, Stuart Milner-Barry, John Jeffreys and Alan Turing, Welchman played the major role in building up Hut 6 in late 1939 to work on breaking the Luftwaffe and Wehrmacht 'Enigma' codes. Welchman was a brilliant mathematician and one of the key progenitors of the famous

Front cover illustration drawn by Susan Herivel for Herivelismus and the German Military Enigma, *by John Herivel, 2008*

electromechanical 'bombe' machines used to process Enigma traffic. However, unlike many of his colleagues, he was also a born leader and organiser who could work very quickly and effectively. Where Knox, for instance, could be temperamental, a poor communicator and disorganised, Welchman, understanding that no amount of brain-power could make up for proper organisation, set about creating a system that could gather information and disseminate it in the utmost secrecy. Thus, although he made two major early theoretical breakthroughs in deciphering Enigma, he realised above all that he needed a major expansion of staff and facilities, and that cyptographers, processors and military chiefs needed to be co-ordinated to the highest degree under a total policy system. This he achieved by sheer force of intellect and great personal charm.

Welchman rapidly recruited many Cambridge mathematicians into Hut 6, including four of his best Sidney mathematics students: John Manistry, another student of Robson's at Marlborough, David Rees and the future head of MI5 Howard Smith, in December 1939, and John Herivel, Edward Dudley-Smith, another Marlburian, and Malcolm Chamberlain, in February 1940. The historians Asa Briggs and Paul Coles arrived in 1943. Briggs recalls that David Thomson described Coles as 'the most outstandingly brilliant student I have ever taught'. In 1941 A L Yoxall, a PhD student, was recruited into the nearby Hut 8 by Welchman, where he devised a naval code-breaking method known as 'Yoxallismus'.

Of these young men, however, it was John Herivel, a maths scholar from Belfast who had gone up to Sidney in 1937, who made the most dramatic breakthrough with his own system, 'Herivelismus'. Billeted alone in a terraced house near the park, Herivel, struck by how few breakthroughs were being made, spent most evenings, perhaps as any undergraduate might, pondering Enigma in front of his fire: 'Then suddenly one night something very strange happened; I may have dozed off before the fire – a dangerous thing to do as I often smoked a pipe and might have burnt a hole in my landlady's carpet or worse – and perhaps I woke up with a start and the faint trace of a vanishing dream in my head. Whatever it was, I was left with a distinct picture – imagined of course – in my mind's eye, of a *German Enigma operator*.' That this dream was, according to Herivel, around St Valentine's Day, is a fine Sidneian coincidence.

The consequences of this lucid dream were far-reaching. Herivel began to imagine a German Enigma operator setting up his machine each day. He wondered, if the operator were lazy, bored or in a hurry, what short cuts he might take in his normally strict routine. Coming up with some thoughts about what might happen, Herivel told Welchman about his ideas and the latter told him to go away and look for clusters in early messages from each day. Using a 'Herivel Square', Herivel and others worked assiduously every day until the Blitzkreig of May 1940 following the 'Herivel tip'. Suddenly some operators forgot themselves and started to make exactly the kinds of error Herivel had predicted. David Rees is credited with having spotted the first significant cluster of errors, and Herivel remembers arriving at a shocked Hut 6 at 4 p.m. around 10 May (although others remember it as 22 May), to be met by Welchman just as the 'break' was occurring. Welchman memorably said to his student, 'Herivel, this will not be forgotten'. From then on the Allies had a priceless access to Nazi coded communication, until the 'bombes' Turing and Welchman had been working on came into use months later. It has been said that without Welchman and Herivel the war might have proceeded very differently and lasted three years longer.

Welchman moved to America after the war, worked in US military communications for many years and wrote his account of Hut 6 in 1984 in which, indeed, Herivel was not forgotten: 'If Herivel had not been recruited in January 1940, who would have thought of the Herivel tip, without which we would have been defeated in May 1940 – unable to maintain continuity until the bombes began to arrive many months later? Let there be no misconceptions about this last point. Loss of continuity would, at all stages, have been very serious, if not disastrous.' John Herivel, whom Welchman introduced to Churchill during the war, became a lecturer at Queen's University, Belfast, and was later a visiting fellow of All Soul's College, Oxford, having turned his attention to the history and philosophy of science.

Baling Out: Tom Hughes, Spitfire Pilot

Tom Hughes sitting astride his Spitfire, Malta, 1943

> Two Sicilians appeared by magic. How could they tell whether I was German, American or British? At least they knew I was not Italian. They took me to a little shack near by and I was introduced to a tiny, ancient, shrivelled woman who must have been their grandmother. They gave me a glass of wonderful red wine and soon I was as cheerful as they were. —Tom Hughes on bailing out over Sicily, 1943

Many Sidney men flew in the RAF during the Second World War. Wing Commander F J A Chase was awarded the DFC and was an offical 'ace'. Denzil Biggane was killed flying his Lancaster over Munich in December 1942. There were also a number of senior air force figures such as Edward Addison, who had flown in the RFC and RAF during the First World War before going up to Sidney in 1918. He re-entered the RAF in 1921, became a specialist in electrical engineering, and was made an air vice-marshall. He set up the new 100 (BS) Group of Bomber Command in 1943, tasked with jamming enemy radar and communications systems from the air. Charles Betts flew in Coastal Command, was part of the Fort Halstead team working on the British atomic weapon and went on to a distinguised career in the RAF as a research and development specialist.

The pilot Tom Hughes was born in Rugby and attended the public school there until 1940, when he joined the RAF Volunteer Reserve and trained as a flying instructor. He was sent to Gibraltar in 1942, air-tested new Spitfires, and flew them over to North Africa. He was then posted to 72 Squadron in Algeria in January 1943. During a dogfight in March his Spitfire's engine failed and he was forced to crash land in the desert just before dusk. He walked through the night back to his squadron at Souk el Khemis, following the North Star and taking water from local Arabs. By dusk the following day he had made it back. Following the Germans' defeat in Tunisia in May, Hughes's squadron operated from an enemy aerodrome and flew abandoned Messerschmidt 109s as well as Spitfires, moving to Hal Far in Malta in June. During the invasion of Sicily, Hughes was involved in various air fights with German and Italian aircraft, and was then moved to Pachino on the east coast of Sicily. Among various adventures, he was forced to bail out of an Me109 while test-flying at night. In August, while flying a Spitfire IX as commander of 'A' Flight, Hughes was shot down by machine-gun fire north of Monte Cassino. He was captured and his burns treated by the Germans before he was moved to Germany, where he was exchanged for German prisoners. Travelling by train via Switzerland to Marseilles he arrived by boat in Liverpool before the end of the war in 1945. He was awarded the international Caterpillar Club badge, given to those who have saved their lives by parachute. In 1946, Hughes went up to Sidney, one of many to arrive after war service. He read mechanical sciences before entering a career as an engineer with AEI, Hotpoint and other major companies.

Das Theatermädel: Jock Hamilton-Baillie, Leading Lady and Serial Escaper

John (Jock) Hamilton-Baillie was born in Carlisle in 1919 and educated at Clifton and the Royal Military Academy, Woolwich, where he passed out top of his intake. He was commissioned into the Royal Engineers and had a place to read mechanical sciences at Sidney in October 1939. However, with the outbreak of war, he was posted to 26 Company, Royal Engineers, and sent to France in September 1939, where he was posted under French command on the Maginot line. With the retreat to Dunkirk in 1940, he was given the task of repairing damaged quayside installations in readiness for rescue ships. At one point, having threatened with his pistol some panicking soldiers who were destroying their weapons, Hamilton-Baillie was clubbed with a rifle by one of them and, later that same day, wounded by shrapnel. His division eventually surrendered to the Germans under Rommel and, after various attempts to escape, he was sent to a camp at Titmonning, deep in Bavaria. One night in spring 1941, he cut through the perimeter wire, climbed down a cliff, and set off towards Switzerland before being recaptured a few days later, having misread a small-scale map.

Hamilton-Baillie was next sent to a particularly well-protected officers' camp at Warburg in Hesse, where he joined an escape committee. He was a central figure in one of the boldest and most successful 'over-the-wire' escapes of the war, the 'Warburg wire job'. Using timber from the huts to make five scaling-ladders with extension ramps, the idea was to rush the extensive wire entanglements and fences after the camp lights had been fused. The lights were successfully fused and three men made it back to England, although Hamilton-Baillie himself was captured by an elderly armed forester while taking a daytime nap on his journey.

Hamilton-Baillie was then transferred to Eichstätt in Bavaria. He got to work immediately, designing and constructing a tunnel under the trapdoor in a lavatory floor and equipping it with props, lighting and an air-supply. He was constantly at the work face, digging his way slowly towards the perimeter wire. The night of escape went according to plan and 63 men, including Hamilton-Baillie, escaped in ones and twos, hoping to reach neutral territory. None succeeded, however, and Hamilton-Baillie was sent to Colditz. From Colditz, he made further escape attempts, on one occasion wearing a burglar's black catsuit and long hair. He was apprehended by Germans shouting *Das Theatermädel!* ('the theatre girl') – he had been the leading lady in the prisoners' production of Noel Coward's *Blithe Spirit*, and used to grow his hair long and shave his legs, rub them in brown shoe polish, and draw a line down the back of his legs in pencil to simulate the appearance of silk stockings.

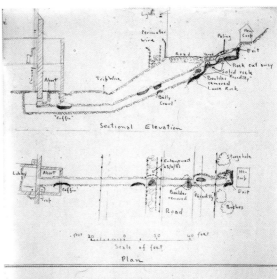

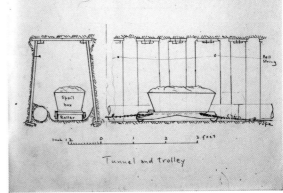

This allowed him special 'bath privileges' in the German guards' washroom, since the prisoners' showers were unable to get the polish off his legs. He was later awarded an MC for his efforts. In 1945 Hamilton-Baillie was released; he went up to Sidney in 1947 where he took a prize-winning first in mechanical sciences before continuing a career in the Royal Engineers. He died in 2003.

Fifty years after leaving Colditz, when he was visiting the Colditz museum in what was by then a mental asylum – and where a hand-made sewing machine of his was on display – Hamilton-Baillie amazed the curator in front of the locked guardroom by producing the keys for it, which he had stolen while a prisoner.

The Prisoner: Ian Horobin

All this time our twenty-five men had stood fast, but the officer next to me, Ian Horobin, though still on his feet, was dead to this world, a condition that did all honour to him. He, like the rest of us, was living out each last second with those two humble, nameless victims, and living them through with neither hope, nor pity, nor expectation for himself. But at the first bayonet-stab he winced, as though he himself had received the blow, and swayed on his feet. —Laurens van der Post, *Venture to the Interior*, 1961

While in Colditz, Jock Hamilton-Baillie kept a notebook in which he recorded details of the famous Eichstaett Tunnel Escape. It contains drawings of security arrangements at Oflag VIIB in November 1942, notes on the stars, mathematical equations and escape details. This drawing, made just after the end of the war, is based on the notebook and is accompanied by a typescript about the tunnelling and the escape of 65 prisoners.

On the Beaches

Coventry-born Fred Shotton went up to Sidney in 1924 and studied geology. During the Second World War he was Britain's most important military geologist, his hydrological studies of the desert proving critical in the success of the British advance after El Alamein in 1942. Shotton was then put in charge of the studies of the D-Day landing beaches and the cross-country mobility possible in the advance to the Rhine. He was awarded the MBE in 1945 and elected a Fellow of the Royal Society in 1956. After the war, as a professor at Birmingham, Shotton became one of the major figures in British Quaternary geology. He died in 1990.

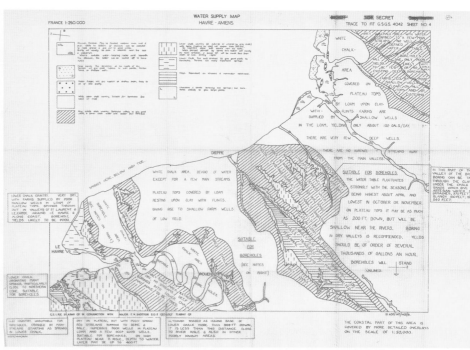

Fred Shotton's water supply map, compiled in connection with the Allied invasion of northwest Europe. Lapworth Museum of Geology, University of Birmingham

Sir Ian Macdonald Horobin, photograph by Bassano, 1959. National Portrait Gallery, London

Ian Horobin was probably Sidney's only wartime prisoner later to be jailed in Britain for a criminal offence, and certainly the only one for the kind of offence he committed. The son of the principal of Homerton College, Cambridge, he entered Sidney from Highgate School after service in the RNVR and the RAF during the First World War. After taking a degree in economics in 1921, he became warden of the Mansfield House University Settlement in 1923. This had been founded in 1889, and was intended to give students of Mansfield College, Oxford first-hand experience of living and working with working-class people. The settlement provided eastenders, who might otherwise have spent all their time and money in the pub, with opportunities for leisure, recreation and self-improvement. Rejuvenated by the energetic Horobin, Mansfield House ran 'The Wave' lodging house, intended to provide cheap and clean accommodation for working men. The settlement also provided a wide range of welfare services, including a 'Sick Benefit Society', a 'coal club', and a 'Poor Man's Lawyer', one of the first examples of free legal advice.

In 1931, Horobin entered parliament as National MP for Southwark Central, and during the 1930s published three very highly regarded volumes of poetry. At the outbreak of war he rejoined the RAF as a squadron leader in Burma before being captured and sent to the high-security Soekaboemi prison in Java, where 6,000 men were crowded into a space originally designed by the Dutch for 300 murderers. Horobin, with a wealth of appropriate experience, volunteered as hygiene and sanitation officer, and for the next three and a half years, acting also as unofficial padre and camp clown, helped to keep the men's morale high in appalling conditions of squalor and brutality. He himself was beaten and tortured for refusing to reveal details of escape routes for key prisoners.

Horobin's close officer colleague in the camp was the Afrikaner writer Laurens van der Post, one of the beneficiaries of Horobin's resistance to torture, whose experiences were made into the film *Merry Christmas Mr Lawrence* in 1983, starring David Bowie and Tom Conti. Horobin impressed van der Post from the start, his sermons getting through to most men, his stoic wit sustaining many faint hearts and his poetic talent making him a fascinating friend. Above all he had saved van der Post's life. Horobin was appointed 'prime minister' of the camp and organised a political and education system for it, with lavatory paper used for all writing and minutes. He continued to write poetry, vividly evoking the horrors of the camp, its cruelties, filth and insects:

'Next, whining trumpeters of Night
Envenomed, denghi-laden spite,
    Toad's eye and charnel worm befall thee!
Blood-thirsty, almond stinking bug
Slow, fat, immortal, hungry thug,
    Warlock and dream - o' - dread beset thee!
Cockroach and louse, intrusive ant
Convoying, collumned emigrant,
    Planet and falling star bewray thee!
You and your man-ape counterparts, Farewell!
Shuffle and grunt yourselves, thrice damned, to hell.'
('Malediction', c1943)

After the war Horobin returned to Mansfield House and became Conservative MP for Oldham in 1951. He was knighted in 1955 and made parliamentary secretary to the Minister of Power, 1958–9. In 1962, having been gazetted a life peer, he pleaded guilty to committing indecent offences with boys at Mansfield House and was sentenced to four years' imprisonment. After his release in 1964 he moved to Tangier, considering himself a 'dead man' in Britain, and died there in 1976. In his response to his admirer John Betjeman's request for information for an introduction to his 1973 *Collected Poems*, Horobin wrote: 'All I ask is that you don't fluff anything or be apologetic. I broke the law with my eyes open all my life till I went to prison. I broke it while I was in prison. And I broke it immediately I came out of prison, and have not the slightest intention of ever paying attention to it.'

CHAPTER 10

'Sidney Yet is Young'
1945–2009

There is something to be said for a place which retains the academic privacy and quietude which the renowned beauty spots are apt to lose. Under the creeper-clad tower, the gates open on to a busy street, but few visitors give more than a glance into the courts. Those who penetrate the unimposing façade are rewarded by the discovery of the most beautiful modern chapel in the university, and old gardens of great loveliness, and evidence of an historic past in portraits in the hall.

—C W Scott-Giles, *Sidney Sussex College: A Short History*, 1951

THE 1939–1945 WAR memorial in the antechapel records that 70 students were killed during the Second World War. The 1945 and 1946 College *Annuals* contain obituaries of these men and also record changes within the College. Weekes retired as master in the summer of 1945 and was succeeded by Tommy Knox-Shaw, who had been at Sidney since 1905. William Philip Sidney VC was the new visitor, succeeding his father Algernon, Lord de L'Isle and Dudley, who had died at the age of 90. Reginald Hackforth was elected vice-master and B T D Smith continued as tutor for a further year, before retiring to the house in Wiltshire that he later left to the College. Hackforth's eminence as a classical scholar was recognised that year by his election as a fellow of the British Academy, a Sidney first, the College having produced many fellows of the Royal Society but none of its sister institution. The great survivors of Sidney's Victorian revival, the mathematicians H C Robson and R H D Mayall, had recently died. James Passant was now working at the Foreign Office as director of research and librarian; Gordon Welchman had moved on to work for the John Lewis Partnership.

In 1945 Alexander McCance was appointed a university professor and David Thomson and John Agar were elected to fellowships, the latter through the support of ICI. Science and industry were to become increasingly important in the development of Cambridge during the post-war years. In 1946, the fellowship was further strengthened by the elections of two Sidney men, the classicist Arthur Beattie and the historian R C 'Otto' Smail; from Imperial College, London, came the chemist

OPPOSITE: *The Mong Building, 2009. Designed by Peter Barton and Bob Bowman and built using fossil-rich Portland stone*

The Sidney Fellowship, 1950

Standing, left to right: N C Hunt, D H Smith, R C Smail, J W A Thornely, D Thomson,
O M B Bulman, R A McCance, J N Agar, A J Beattie, K F Smith.

Sitting, left to right: E A G Robinson, H L H H Green, A H Davenport, G A Weekes,
T Knox-Shaw (Master), R Hackforth, B T D Smith, J A Ratcliffe, K H Angus

Harry Eméleus who held a personal chair in the university. All had served during the
war, Eméleus working with the British contingent on the atomic bomb at Oak Ridge,
Tennessee. Sidney's fellowship, however, was still very small: in 1946 it numbered
the master, 15 fellows and five honorary fellows.

As was the case after the Great War, there were now boys fresh from school living
and working alongside war veterans. The *Annual* reported: 'The ages of men in residence now range from 17 to 30…These changes naturally raise many problems for all
administrative officers of the College and university; the greatest being the complexities of release and selection of entrants and the severe pressure on accommodation.'
The problem of 'release' concerned the requirements of the new national conscrip-
tion scheme, and the accommodation squeeze meant that sets of rooms designed to
house one undergraduate in some comfort now had to be shared between two. With
180 men in residence the problems also extended to catering, the kitchen manager
Harry Littlechild describing the 'peculiar difficulties' of new 'feeding arrangements'
due to shortages and rationing. The 'two hall' system was revived to help deal with
the problem in the evenings.

Alan Holt Lancashire, son of a gown manufacturer, came to Sidney straight from Leicester City Boys' School in 1945 to read mechanical sciences at the age of 18. He felt very young: 'There were boys like me straight from day school, and the men. The men – just back from fighting the war – killing people! – the difference in maturity was immeasurable (an even bigger intake of men took place in 1946). For example, in 1945 five of us started to read mechanical sciences…; one had been a submarine commander, one an airman who had flown pathfinder Mosquitos and had been a prisoner of war, and three grammar school boys.' He remembers the privations of 'austerity Sidney' after the war: 'Life was hard. Most things were rationed: food, clothing, bread and coal. Others were unobtainable, I seem to remember that it was not until my second year that a very occasional bottle of sherry was available for purchase from Arthur at the College buttery; it was so valuable that many of us took it home to be sold at a considerable profit.' Alan went to the 'British Restaurant' set up in the Pitt Club to eat, before the Hall opened again after Christmas. He recalls the winter of 1946–7, one of the coldest on record: 'For about six weeks Sidney Street was covered by compacted snow nearly a foot deep and the temperature recorded at the weather station by Great St Mary's never rose above freezing. Coal was rationed to one hundredweight per week for a set; enough to last with care for only three or four days. I had a set on 'G' staircase where all the water pipes on the staircase froze so water had to be fetched through the snow from the wash basins in 'Whitechapel' (the name given to the washroom off the passageway from Chapel Court to Garden Court). But more importantly, one had to plough across the Court first thing in the morning to spend a penny, wash and shave. I well remember one cold morning when I awoke to find ice on the sheet where my breath had frozen. Study became a secondary matter to keeping warm, so that I developed a routine to eke out the coal; at least one trip to the cinema each week, play squash, visit the bath-house as frequently as possible, visit friends who had a centrally heated or electrically heated room – I always listened to 'ITMA' ['It's That Man Again', a popular radio comedy programme] in B6, a friend's room which was heated by a built-in electric fire. The electricity supply on G was such that anything more than about 250 watts blew the fuses…When the snow did eventually melt the flood water reached from Cambridge to Ely.' Alan's daughter Sarah was one of the first 25 women to enter Sidney in 1976, when accommodation was a little more comfortable.

In 1948 Sidney had a record 203 students in residence, though it was now the smallest college in Cambridge, necessitating a greater proportion of undergraduates living in digs than ever before. Nevertheless, and perhaps because of these numbers, the sports clubs and social, arts and intellectual societies reformed themselves quickly. In 1946,

1953 staff outing to Great Yarmouth, including bedders, and kitchen, maintenance, gardening and office staff

the general secretary of the Amalgamated Clubs, J F Q Switzer, later a fellow, mas-
terminded an Earl Haig's Day ('Poppy Day') collection that was the highest in the
university's history. The College also maintained its good Tripos record in spite of
the adverse conditions, with around 20 per cent of firsts gained each year in the
immediate post-war period.

'The Inferno': Dorothy L Sayers at Sidney, 1947

'I shall travel to Cambridge direct from Witham without doubling back on London…
Of course if by that time we find ourselves already in the Lowest Circle, wholly covered
in ice, or with only the head emerging, or if the trains have stopped for lack of coal, or
if the loosing of the waters has swept the permanent way into the Ouse, or anything of
that sort, we shall be sunk – but we will hope for the best.' —Dorothy L Sayers to Wilfrid
Scott-Giles, 11 February 1947

In 1936 Dorothy L Sayers had been contacted by the Confraternitas Historica stal-
wart Wilfrid Scott-Giles about the family history of her fictional hero Lord Peter
Wimsey. As a result she gave a talk on the subject to the 'Confrat' in 1937. She also
wrote an essay during the 1930s claiming that Sherlock Holmes had been at Sidney.
In 1946, while working on her translation for Penguin of Dante's *Divina Commedia*
(published in 1949), she met Scott-Giles again and discovered that he was a keen
reader of the great Italian writer. He worked closely with her, giving historical and
editorial advice and drawing remarkable sectional diagrams of the geography of hell,
from the circles of Incontinence and Violence to the Great Barrier and Malebolge,
and from the Well of the Giants to, suitably for the time, the Ice. Sayers greatly
admired his drawings, which were included in the Penguin translation, for being
'bold and clear, with enough pictorial quality to keep it interesting…'. Scott-Giles
included all manner of extra details, such as pubs and public conveniences for the
damned inhabitants of Dis.

In February 1947, at the invitation of the *Princeps* T P Blackburn and Scott-Giles,
Sayers gave a lecture on Dante to the Confraternitas Historica, taking as her subject
'The City of Dis'. It was the winter Alan Lancashire and most other undergraduates
were freezing in their beds, as well as pondering wider post-war realities, and Sayers's
robust questioning about the contemporary significance of Dante would have been
highly relevant to her audience. She arrived at the Blue Boar on Trinity Street on
a freezing evening and then walked to Sidney with Scott-Giles,where she was met
by the tutor David Thomson in his Garden Court rooms with their gilded walls and
black ceiling. Also present were the new master, Knox-Shaw, the Sidney history
fellow, Otto Smail, the *Princeps* and the brilliant young historian Norman Hunt,
later the constitutional scholar, minister of state and broadcaster Lord Crowther-
Hunt. Hunt was one of the 'men' Alan Lancashire had described, a Royal Artillery
veteran, and took the minutes of the meeting that evening.

Following a lavish, ration-defying dinner, Sayers delivered her talk in the Senior
Combination Room in front of an open fire to an audience of about 60 men in

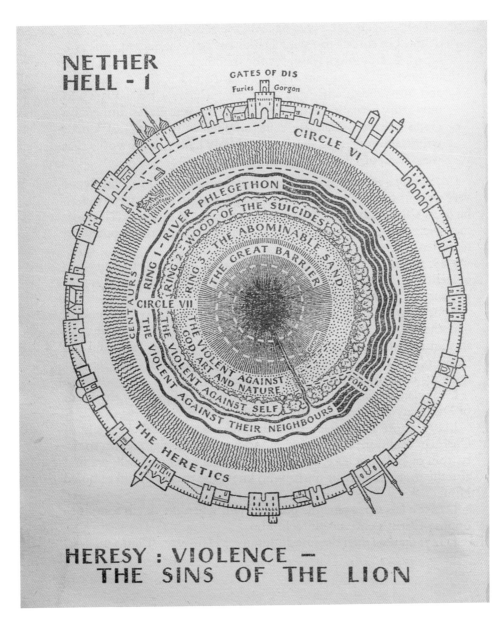

C W Scott-Giles,
*illustration commissioned
by Penguin for the 1949
translation of* The Inferno
*by Dorothy L Sayers. The
London Library*

dinner jackets, aided by Scott-Giles's drawings, which were prominently displayed. She stressed that the literal meaning of Dante was far less important than that 'the real environment within which all the events take place is the human soul'. It was a 'journey of self-knowledge' into the 'black heart' of each human and the 'possibilities of depravity'. She pointed out contemporary parallels, from the evils of totalitarianism to the blandishments of capitalist advertising 'by which people are flattered and frightened into a greedy hankering after goods they do not really need'. Usurers, blasphemers, gluttons, counsellors of fraud, flatterers and sodomites were all made starkly real for her young audience. They were sitting at the Vestibule of Hell, she said, and she challenged them to wonder if they were like those who 'never come to any decision…They shrink from responsibility, lest it should blind them; they condemn nothing, for fear of being thought narrow.' Sayers then led her audience into Hell through the various circles of Lust and Violence to the ninth circle, the last and lowest, the frozen surface of the river Cocytus divided into four variations of treachery. 'Here, in the heart of cold, in the place that knows neither obligation nor community nor coherence nor exchange, treachery devours treachery forever.' The lecture was a call to public moral responsibility, was rapturously received and led to over an hour's discussion. One history student present was Colin Jordan, a school-master's son who had entered Sidney from Warwick School in 1946. A contributor to *Pheon*, Jordan formed a Nationalist Club at Cambridge and became founder of the British National Party and the National Socialist Movement. He became one of Britain's most extreme and notorious Nazi agitators.

'Remarkable Distinction for its Size': Sidney under Knox-Shaw, 1945–57

Pages from The Bull and Porcupine, *1959, with artwork by Timothy Robinson (1956)*

'Cambridge men have as much to learn from Camberwellians as vice versa. It is well to remember that one day the social boot may be on the other foot.'—From an article in the Sidney Boys' Club, Cambridge House, Camberwell, where many Sidney students had contributed to the mission of the poor since the 1890s, *Bull and Porcupine*, 1, 1952

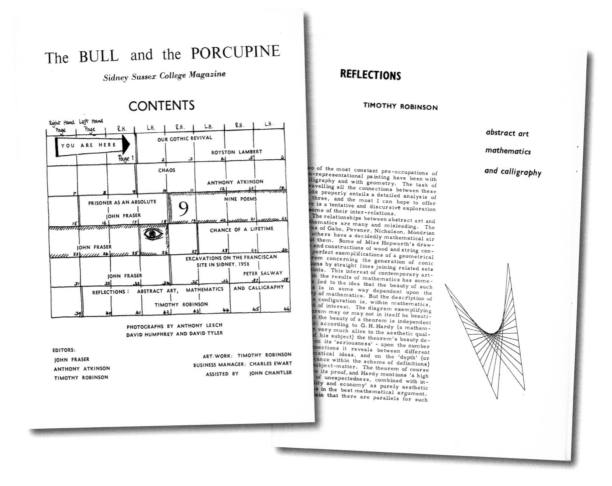

In 1957, when Knox-Shaw retired and David Thomson was elected master, there were 20 fellows, three research fellows, and six honorary fellows. There were 80 undergraduates, including the future Sidney professor of international relations, James Mayall, and the future England cricketer Roger Prideaux. The schools Sidney drew on had changed little since 1914 – minor and middling public schools, with grammar schools beginning to dominate. Results continued to hold up well, with Sidney second in the Tripos in 1955.

In 1952 the ailing *Pheon* was succeeded, after a gap of a few years, by *The Bull and Porcupine*, which in the first few years was edited by the future headmaster of Westminster and educational controversialist, John Rae. It carried poems, stories, images and articles on a wide range of topics, including new Cambridge architecture and Sidney's own buildings. Royston Lambert, a future fellow, historical and cultural theorist and head of Dartington Hall, wrote a piece on 'Our Gothic Revival' and Anthony Atkinson one titled 'Chaos', which left the reader in no doubt as to the authors' opinions about Sidney's built heritage. The archaeologist Peter Salway went further back, and wrote about his important excavations of the Franciscan friary in Cloister Court in 1956, which unearthed the stained-glass fragments later re-set into the windows in the Chapel and Old Library. The magazine registered a new attitude among students, more independent and less deferential. An anonymous article, entitled 'November 1983', imagined a Peoples' Planning Committee dismissing Sidney's appeal against demolition to make way for 'Highway 5': 'Two days and the College bell will ring no more.'

Sidney did no substantial building work during Knox-Shaw's mastership to augment the 'chaos', but improved the existing fabric as necessary. The chapel was refaced with stone in 1955 and a clock placed above the porch, just beneath the bell. In 1951 Wilfrid Scott-Giles wrote Sidney's second history, the 'little blue book' familar to many Sidney students over the years. He was able to describe Sidney as a 'society of remarkable distinction for its size. In 1951 the governing body of 16 includes five University Professors and two Readers, a Nobel Prizeman, and Fellows of the Royal Society [5] and British Academy [1]...' Knox-Shaw encouraged his historians, classicists and scientists, though seems not to have been much tempted by English literature, philosophy or modern languages. In the High Churchman R P Casey, elected fellow in theology in 1950, Sidney had a remarkable recruit, both for

Excavations in Cloister Court, 1958, photograph from The Bull and Porcupine, *1959*

The Chapel at night, 30
October 1954, photograph
by R N H McMillan
(1952)

his scholarship in Russian and Coptic Christianity and in Gnosticism, and for his
undisguised homosexuality. He was a brilliant man, but notoriously left a priceless
Armenian manuscript on a plane in Germany in 1952. The *Bull and Porcupine* carried a limerick about him in 1955:

'There once was a Dean of a College
Who was full of extraordinary knowledge,
If you said "Sir, you're dry,"
He'd say "That I deny,
But the fact I'm High I acknowledge".'

Perhaps the most important development in the fellowship was the appointment in 1948 of John Thornely as Sidney's first law fellow. A Trinity Hall undergraduate who had trained cadets at an officer cadet training unit alongside Otto Smail during the war, Thornely galvanised law studies at Sidney, inheriting John, later Lord, Mackenzie-Stuart as a final year student and recruiting from then on students who went on to the highest office, and achievement, in the legal profession, such as Sir Derek Bradbeer and Sir William Gage.

'Rather an Odd Way': Knox-Shaw's Students

It is difficult after so many years to remember what motivates undergraduate behaviour, but some few of us Porcupines decided to move Len's bed from his rooms in his absence and relocate it upon the roof above the Porter's Lodge. It was a warm and pleasant night for sleeping under the stars so we moved his bedding and his pyjamas with the bed and left a note to let him know of the changes to his dormitory arrangements. In the morning Len was observed to be asleep in his bed on top of the lodge. He had flown his pyjamas from the flagpole; a signal, presumably, that he was 'in residence'. In due course the master noticed this phenomenon and despatched Janssen [sic] with a courteous request that the

Rehearsal of The Knight of the Burning Pestle *in Cloister Court, 1948*

Post-War Drama

Geoffrey Darby (1948), a post-war classics undergraduate, remembers 'austerity' Cambridge as a place full of energy and fun, in spite of rationing, watery beer and early front gate closure. A school friend of Kenneth Tynan and a keen thespian, in 1950 he produced the Jacobean play *The Knight of the Burning Pestle* (1607) by Francis Beaumont in the Hall. Through an aggressive publicity campaign, Darby filled the Hall for each of the three performance nights. In 1951 he produced *Hamlet* at the ADC Theatre, advised by Tynan and Alec Guinness, with the future director Sir Peter Hall as the Player King and the cartoonist 'Marc' Boxer as Polonius. The play enjoyed packed audiences for the week it was on.

'flag' should be struck from the pole and that Len should now rise and resume his normal activities. Janssen duly delivered the message and prepared to descend the stairway. Then he paused and, turning to Len, said with a deadpan expression, 'I'm afraid your shoes haven't been cleaned this morning, Mr Brunt.' —Geoff Darby (1948) on the head porter Walter I'Anson and Len Brunt (1947)

Sidney's undergraduate and graduate students under Knox-Shaw, as we have seen, were drawn from the usual schools and backgrounds, and maintained the College's reputation as a 'working college'. Derek Beales and Hugh Tinker, the historians; Bernard Pagel, the astro-physicist; Peter Gay, the crystallographer; Sir Philip Randle, the biochemist; Norman Greenwood, the chemist; Roger Carter, the mathematician; David Crompton, the zoologist; Alan MacDiarmid, the Nobel Prize-winning

The Boat House

Sidney's boat house was designed by David Roberts, later the designer of Cromwell Court, and erected in 1959 (left above). Shared with Corpus originally and now also with Girton and Wolfson, it is a listed modernist building of considerable architectural merit (left below).

The Cambridge 'Bumps' began in 1827 and a Sidney boat first appeared on the Cam in 1837 and then again in 1841. In 1848 it was third and in the 1860s and 1870s was a very successful boat in the first division. Subsequently it has mainly been a second division boat. A major revival in fortunes occurred between 1905 and 1913 when the boat was sixth. A women's boat was first put out in 1978 and since then has moved between the first and second divisions. Below: the 1913 1st Lent boat, after its fourth bump. Photograph by Stearn & Sons

chemist; Sir Ravinder Maini, the rheumatologist; Richard Wright, the archaeologist; R G Abrahams, the anthropologist; Nigel Calder, the science writer; David West, the classicist; Sir Christopher Curwen, head of MI6 in the 1980s; Air Commodore Henry Probert, the military historian – these men represented some of the great academic and 'establishment' successes Sidney was still expected to produce, rising to the top as professors at universities and senior figures in Whitehall and the armed services.

With hindsight, some undergraduates from those years felt that, friendly and supportive as it was, Sidney was slightly dull at the time, perhaps reflecting the Cold War period in general. Certainly the Wyatville stucco was looking very drab by then, and in 1954 Nikolaus Pevsner gave his fatal opinion that Sidney was the least attractive of the old Oxbridge colleges. When the bursar, E H K Dibden, a veteran of naval radar work in the war, painted much of the College grey, this did not improve things. It is also true that there were no future *Beyond the Fringe* or *Monty Python* stars. Indeed, the actor and playwright Alan Bennett recalls applying to Sidney in 1951 and, because it seemed less glamorous and had not offered him an award, went instead to Exeter College, Oxford, which took him as a scholar. A grammar school 'history boy' from Leeds, he thought Sidney's architecture 'Gothick' rather than 'Gothic', and that this architectural failing, along with its socially lower status students, made it less of a catch for him in his 'self-serving frame of mind'. He was also in love with a fellow applicant to Oxford and determined to go where he went. Bennett remembers the 'geniality of everyone and their kindness' during the interview. He also noted the behaviour of the public school intake in hall. 'Seated at long

ABOVE LEFT: *Dick Heckstall-Smith, c1954, with a jazz band at Sidney*

ABOVE RIGHT: *David Owen at the wheel of a car c1957, with Brian Christopher seated, and Hugh Guinness standing*

Blundell Court from the garden. Opened in 1969, the building was refurbished and had a new floor added, the 'Gledhill Skyline', in 2005

refectory tables, the walls hung with armorial scutcheons and the mellow portraits of Tudor and Stuart grandees, neat, timorous and genteel we grammar school boys were the interlopers; these slobs, as they seemed to me to be, the party in possession.' There weren't that many of them, in fact.

Yet if Sidney missed out on Alan Bennett, or he missed out on Sidney, there were to be many important figures beyond the lawyers, scientists, doctors, teachers, civil servants and university academics. We have noted the maverick political figure Colin Jordan and the England cricketer Roger Prideaux already. The great tenor singer Wilfred Brown and the jazz musician Dick Heckstall-Smith in music; the Somerset cricketer, and later headmaster of Radley, Dennis Silk, and the newspaper columnist Colin Malam in sport; David, later Lord, Owen, along with Ian, later Lord, Lang who went up in 1959 to read history, the first Sidney political peers since the 17th century; David Robert, later Lord, Stevens, the Fleet Street magnate; such students suggest that Sidney retained the good mix it had always enjoyed.

Although Knox-Shaw had no great academic achievement behind him, he had a nose for talent and enjoyed the freedom to choose students as he pleased. David Owen, who went up to study medicine in 1956, the year of Suez, recalls with affection his first encounter with 'Knox', 'a small, bouncy, bespectacled man. His first act was to punch me in the solar plexus, which was rather an odd way to start. Commenting that my solar plexus muscles were good, he proceeded to show us round the College. Without formal interview or meeting any other dons he told me that if I got my first MB in physics, chemistry and biology by the summer of 1956, I would come to Sidney that autumn.' Owen's memoirs paint a fascinating picture of the hedonistic member of The Lunaticks battling with the earnest moralist and budding politician. Ian Lang's memoirs of joining Footlights during perhaps its greatest period and eventually deciding to become a politician instead of a comedian like his friend John Cleese, tells another kind of social and political tale.

'Hederatus': Nightclimbing in the 1960s

> This wall was about nine feet long and the crux was a pendulum swing, feet on the top of the mantelpiece, hands as far out on the picture rail as possible, onto a Yale lock on the door, during which it was essential for the feet to be kept clear of the wall, so as to avoid unnecessary damage. All climbing equipment was banished, only stockinged feet were allowed to tarnish the wall of the room which is purported (by Brian anyway) to have housed in its time, Oliver Cromwell, Canon Collins and Colin Jordan – a most curious Trinity! We idled the time away failing and succeeding on 'Euclid's Stretch', until the hall bell sounded unexpectedly, and we were forced to drag our sweaty bodies to dinner.
> —'Hederatus', *Cambridge Nightclimbing*, 1970

In 1963, Mike McConville (aka 'Hederatus' – meaning 'climbing ivy') arrived at Sidney from Cowbridge Grammar School, South Wales, to read geography. Mike and his Sidney friends Brian Rollin, who was reading classics, Nick Raynsford, later a member of the most recent Labour government, the short-lived David Ainger, and a future professor of medicine, Edwin Gale, soon became Cambridge's most notorious nightclimbers. They were part of a tradition that goes back at least to the exploits of Trinity's Geoffrey Winthrop Young, whose 1898 guide to climbing Trinity's buildings parodied the heroic accounts of Sidney's J F Hardy and others in the 1860s. The geologist W G Fearnsides (1897) had been an early practitioner: a Wesleyan, he had shown his dislike of Sidney's High Church culture by taking the clapper out of the College bell and dropping it down a chimney in the Master's Lodge.

'Hederatus' remembers being quickly bored by life at Cambridge, which he described as 'artificial and stultifying', and his account has the full flavour of the brewing student discontent of the 1960s. His exploits were fuelled by vast quantities of beer, cigarettes and curry. Among an extraordinary number of nocturnal conquests around Cambridge's many challenging buildings, he and his friends made the most famous attempt ever on King's College Chapel. King's had taken advice from the authors of the well-known book by 'Whipplesnaith' on nightclimbing of 1937 about how to prevent further attempts, and had blocked the approach to the Chapel. The students thus had to try another route. The first section was the most dangerous, requiring 80 feet of vertical climbing. The last section was the spires, where they unfurled a banner proclaiming 'Peace in Vietnam' and climbed down undetected. 'We had to maintain our anonymity. We had our degrees to think about,' Nick Raynsford later recalled.

'There is, of course, one easy way up the Senate House. This is to climb the south face of Caius, and then get on to the building by way of the Senate House Leap.'
From Cambridge Nightclimbing, by 'Hederatus', 1970

Edwin Gale, now a professor at Bristol and diabetes expert, went with McConville and the others on a climb a few weeks later. 'We did the Bridge of Sighs and Trinity's Wren library,' he remembered. 'Then we went up Clare College. I was so full of adrenaline I was careless'. He fell, breaking his leg and forcing the others to get help: this led to their apprehension by the police and proctors.

'That was the beginning of the tragedies,' remembered Nick Raynsford, who was suspended by Sidney for a year. Soon afterwards one of the four, David Ainger, died climbing in the Dolomites. Brian Rollin was expelled after being caught on the roof of the Senate House with McConville in October 1965. He died in a car crash a few months later. Mike McConville himself had to restart his degree at another university and became a professor in Hong Kong, specialising in the history and sociology of law. McConville remembers with some sympathy how difficult it seemed for the master and fellows to punish him and Rollin; but they did so, in November 1965.

'Our judges sat solemnly round a long polished table. All were in academic robes, all looked stern. I recognised a few of them immediately, but the majority were new faces to me. We sat down in very comfortable chairs, and were then asked by the master if we had anything to say. Brian said something about us both having better Tripos results than half the college, but no one was quite sure if that was really

Poster for Michael Winner's film I'll Never Forget What's 'isname, *1967, scenes from which were shot in Sidney*

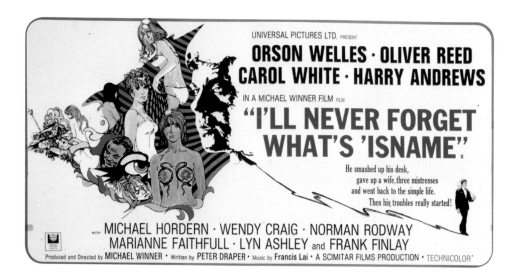

relevant. After all, that was not the point at issue. The decision that we were to be sent down was delivered in a fine, solemn tone, with the merry afterthought that we had to leave college by 6 p.m. the next day.'

Something was in the air in the 1960s and like all colleges, Sidney breathed it in. When the College council voted to allow the director Michael Winner to film part of his 1967 'swinging London' film *I'll Never Forget What's 'isname*, starring Oliver Reed, Marianne Faithfull and Orson Welles, in the Old Library, they probably didn't know it was to be famous mainly because it was the first film to include the f-word. In fact the Old Library was used as a backdrop to a public school scene where Reed, playing the quintessential dissatisfied modern man, an advertising executive called Michael Quint, returns for a reunion only to find the bullies of Alan Bennett's imagination have regrouped. Inevitably they beat him up.

John Conway (fellow 1964–70) with a sculpture 'Music of the Sphere', by George W Hart, 1997

'Only Gentlemen Prefer Blondes': David Thomson and John Linnett

Third-year undergraduate, finding himself opposite 18-year-old Miranda Bethell at Hall in October 1976: 'I thought we ordered 25 blondes?'
Miss Bethell: 'I thought only *gentlemen* preferred blondes.'

When the distinguished chemist John Linnett succeeded David Thomson in 1970, there were 38 fellows and 84 freshmen. The fellowship had nearly doubled since Thomson had been elected in 1957, but the number of undergraduates had barely increased. It was a period of enormous social and educational change, somewhat like the one in which Sidney was founded. The intervening 13 years had seen the huge expansion of higher education in Britain, a process that had started with the 1944 Education Act. In 1900 there were 20,000 university students; in 1980 there were 250,000. In 1900 a third of the students had been at Oxbridge; in 1980 the figure was eight per cent. Teachers and pupils might see as many advantages in applying to

Sussex as to Sidney Sussex. Not only were there now many other universities and new comprehensive schools, which had seen the extinction of so many of Thomson's beloved grammar schools, but Sidney was now considering taking women. This marked a dramatic change in the College's character.

On 23 January 1974 the College voted to become the fourth male college in Cambridge to admit women. After much discussion, it was a near-unanimous decision. However, at the announcement of the vote at College council, one senior fellow, the great botanist Edred Corner, who had come to Sidney in the 1920s, got up, left his keys on the table and only returned to his alma mater many years later. In fact, the first female fellow, the social anthropologist Lynne Brydon, had already been elected, at 2.20 p.m. on 18 June 1975. She was succeded in the following decade by women fellows such as the linguist Vivien Law, the literary scholar Janet Todd, and the chemist Maria Vargas.

While the fellowship in 1976 was still the same size as in recent years, that year the 102 freshmen who came into residence included 25 women. Sidney could no longer have survived with its old residential accommodation. In 1969 Lord De Lisle had opened Blundell Court in front of 700 alumni, and Sidney had its first major new building since South Court was built over 30 years earlier. The gutting of the early-17th-century Clerke range in 1970 to provide modern amenities attractive to conference delegates was another sign of the times. Under today's conservation regulations it would not have been allowed.

The expansion of the fellowship since 1957 had brought in talent from both traditional Sidney disciplines and newer ones: Tim Blanning and Tony Badger in history; John Conway, the inventor of surreal numbers and 'The Game of Life', in

Freshers photograph, 1976, showing the first 25 women undergraduates, including Alison Brown, 2nd row, 6th from right and Alison Barrett, 3rd row, 3rd from right

Alison Barrett became the object of national concern in April 1983 when she and 11 others were kidnapped by the Tigre People's Liberation Front while working for the Save the Children Fund in Ethiopia. The TPLF described their prisoners as 'guests' to whom they wanted to show the local conditions. The Princess Royal appealed for their release, which took place in June

mathematics; Ken Carpenter in nutrition; David Crompton and John Birks in biology; John Billingsley and Keith Glover in engineering; Paul Scott in astro-physics; Alan Hughes in economics; J D Evans in classics; Christopher Parish in medicine; Harry Whittington in geology. These were elections to be expected at Sidney and a continuance of traditions that went back many years. In the geographer and chronicler of Sherlock Holmes's time at Sidney, Dick Chorley, the literary scholar Pat Rogers, the linguists Tom Wyatt, Peter Collier and Barry Nisbet, the lawyers Geoffrey Marston and (briefly) the Watergate prosecutor Archibald Cox, Sidney ventured into previously uncharted or only recently developed subject areas. This considerably broadened its appeal, both intellectually and in terms of student intake. Virtually all these fellows went on to professorships at Cambridge or elsewhere, many in the new universities.

Sidney's students continued to supply universities with academics, courts with lawyers, schools with teachers, and Whitehall with civil servants. In its traditional subjects it maintained the highest standards, though by now religious studies had

The Sidney Fellowship, 1970

The master and fellows on the admission of Professor J W Linnett as master, 26 September 1970

First row: J W A Thornely, R C Smail, Sir Hugh Park, Rt Revd K Riches, Sir Ben Lockspeiser, J F Q Switzer, Viscount De L'Isle, J W Linnett (Master), T Knox-Shaw, A H Davenport, H L H H Green, O M B Bulman, Sir Frederick Brundrett, J A Ratcliffe, W T Stearn

Second row: W G Rathmell, J A Kiernan, T C W Blanning, J Billingsley, D E D Beales, D S Green, D W T Crompton, R J Chorley, R C Andrew, H P Hutchison, J N Agar, E J H Corner, C Parish, T S Wyatt, R W Stoddart

Third row: J Brewer, J D G Evans, Revd J K Riches, G D James, P C Clemmow, J M Stewart, J A C H Reddick, T R Langley

been eclipsed by the scientific and secular culture of the times. The victory in ITV's *University Challenge* in 1970 put the College on the map in the media world for perhaps the first time in its history.

The geologist Derek Briggs, who worked with Sidney's Professor Harry Whittington on the great Burgess Shale project in the 1970s, was the latest in a long line of Sidney geologists stretching back through Oliver Bulman and Whitehead Watts to Frederick Kendall. James, later Lord, Drummond Young, has followed in the footsteps of Lord Mackenzie Stuart in the great legal achievements nurtured by John Thornely since the 1950s. Peter Riddell, the *Times* political writer, has emulated the success of his forebears Frank Owen and Michael Curtis.

Director John Madden, actors Ben Affleck and Gwyneth Paltrow, and screenwriter Tom Stoppard at the premiere of their film Shakespeare in Love, *1998*

By the 1970s, however, new horizons continued to expand. Nick Raynsford, John Patten and Andrew Puddephatt, a founder of Charter 88, represent the full spectrum of political positions, as Sidney continued the trend set in train in the 1950s by David Owen and Ian Lang. The soldier and Balkans peace-keeper John Drewienkiewicz has combined two traditional Sidney cultures. The modernist composers James Wood and Huw Spratling extended Sidney's musical profile, and Stephen Pimlott brought together music and acting in his remarkable career as a director of drama and opera at the highest level on the British stage. The internationally acclaimed film and TV directors John Madden and John Amiel both entered Sidney in 1966, one from Clifton School and the other from William Ellis School, London, underlining the changing mixture of the undergraduate population. Sidney's literary achievements had been somewhat in abeyance since the 18th century, but the careers of the science-fiction writer Stephen Baxter and the novelist Rupert Thomson have marked a distinguished return to that tradition. More recently they have been followed by the critical successes of the playwright Diane Samuels, the poet Nick Laird and the novelist Matt Thorne.

'Sidney Yet is Young': Donald Northcote, Gabriel Horn and Sandra Dawson, 1976–2009

The biochemist Donald Northcote succeeded Jack Linnett as master in 1976, the second in a sequence of three distinguished scientists to head the College. Having left school to become a laboratory assistant, Northcote had taken an evening degree at the University of London, before becoming a leading authority on cell differentiation as a fellow at St John's. Northcote welcomed the initial 25 women undergraduates in his first year, and during his mastership the proportion of female to male students quickly became equal. By the time he retired in 1992, there were nearly 50

Cromwell Court, King Street, designed by David Roberts and opened on 18 March 1983

fellows and the annual intake of undergraduates stood at just over 100, a figure maintained today. Under Northcote, supported by the shrewd and energetic bursar Roger Andrew, Sidney undertook a major building project that considerably increased the capacity to house students in College accommodation: Cromwell Court, one of the last works of the Cambridge architect David Roberts, which opened in 1983 a few hundred yards down King Street and provided an extra 46 rooms and two sets for fellows.

Northcote's students more than did their bit; the Tripos results in the late 1970s were particularly impressive, and in 1979 the *University Challenge* team gave Sidney a remarkable second championship. That team reunited in 2002 to become the contest's all-time 'champions of champions', led by a current shadow minister, David Lidington. By the 1970s and 1980s, Sidney was also producing its first major TV and radio personalities, two of whom brought traditional Sidney strengths in mathematics and history and politics to a mass audience – Carol Vorderman of *Countdown* and the political commentator Andrew Rawnsley. Among Northcote's students there was a trend, perhaps typical of the time, to nurture major figures in business – the

The Sidney Fellowship, 1984

First row: R C Andrew, H B Whittington, D S Green, T S Wyatt, J W A Thornely, R C Smail, Sir Austin Robinson, D H Northcote (Master), R A McCance, H J Emeléus, P C Clemmow, J F Q Switzer, D W T Crompton, T C W Blanning, C Parish.

Second row: R I Woods, G Henderson, M D Vargas, H B Nisbet, P H W Hawkins, J M Todd, M J Woodfield, J R Vince, G Marston, S G O'Cathasaigh, G W Sedgley, P J Collier, D J L Bennett, P G McHugh.

Third row: S P Salt, P J F Henderson, J P Russell, R L Conn, A Hughes, M S Kumar, R R Horgan, G D James, W Jones, A L Greer.

Sidney Sussex, University Challenge winners, 1979. The winning team members were: John Gilmore, John Adams, David Lidington and Nicholas Graham

The Royal Visit, 1996

HM Queen Elizabeth II and HRH Prince Philip, Duke of Edinburgh, visited Sidney on 8 March 1996, the year of the quatercentenary, the first ever visit by a reigning British monarch. The master and Mrs Horn are seen in Hall Court with the royal visitors, who were given various gifts, including a piece of Caithness glass inset with fragments of Franciscan glass excavated in Cloister Court in 1958 and crowned with a glass porcupine. The company took lunch in Hall, the Queen sitting close to the portrait of Oliver Cromwell. The master was able to assure Her Majesty during lunch that, in spite of the presence of the Lord Protector's portrait in the Hall, the royal visitors had no cause for anxiety as Sidney was a very loyal college.

The first British royal visit had been in 1861 when Albert Edward, Prince of Wales (later King Edward VII) was a guest at a fund-raising concert in the Hall at which Mendelssohn's *Elijah* was performed. King Christian VII of Denmark visited in 1768, and the College has also had visits from Prince Albert Victor (1884), King Peter II of Yugoslavia (1943), Princess Alexandra (1961) and Princess Margaret (1994).

lawyers Daniel Levy, head of ENIC and chairman of Tottenham Hotspur FC, and the Cobra beer magnate Lord Bilimoria are high-profile examples. Even Sidney's engineering student, Alison Brown, one of the pioneering 1976 intake, did not remain in academia, moving on to found the internationally successful NAVSYS Corporation in the USA. Along with law, engineering has become one of Sidney's many great post-war success stories, beginning with Donald Green's arrival in 1966 and continuing through the elections of Keith Glover and Ann Dowling as fellows in the 1970s to the present day.

Sidney's unique atmosphere has survived the expansion in numbers and buildings in ways some other colleges have not managed. In 1980 the College featured in a BBC series of 12 programmes, *The Roots of England*, which looked at various communities in England. The Sidney programme focused on the work and lives of the 90 or so College staff, such as the kitchen manager Harry Littlechild, who had recently written some fascinating memoirs of his career at Sidney since the 1920s, and bedmakers Joyce Waterfall and Vera Taylor. The bedders talked fondly about their students, even the newly arrived women, whom they at first thought would be trouble. Mrs Waterfall admitted she was wrong: 'They're really smashing'. Vera Taylor spoke of Sidney as 'like a family'. Harry Littlechild, the fellows' butler Ernie Green, and the second chef Michael Daynes regularly played darts against the fellows.

When Donald Northcote retired in 1992, Sidney elected its first Jewish master, the neurobiologist Gabriel Horn, a fellow at King's, who soon further increased the number of professorial fellows in the College, including the Nobel prize-winning pioneer of molecular bioenergetics Sir John Walker. By the time Horn retired in 1999, the

The pinnacles on the Chapel belfry were restored in 1993. The heads were based on fellows and members of staff. The central head here is of Ted Barrett, senior maintenance engineer, who worked at Sidney from 1950 to 1993

Matthew Foulds, captain of the Cambridge rugby team that beat Oxford 16–12 in December 1999 after going 15–0 down, hoisting the Bowring Bowl at Twickenham. Matthew came to Sidney from New Zealand in 1997 to study law and is a fairly rare example of a Sidneian attaining the very highest honours in university sport

fellowship stood at over 60 and there were also an unparalleled 19 honorary fellows, including Archbishop Desmond Tutu, continuing Sidney's South African traditions.

Through the generosity of Hong Kong businessman and honorary fellow Man-Wai William Mong, Sidney was able to extend its performing and social facilities in 1999. The Mong Building was opened by the Duke of Edinburgh, who had come to the College in 1996, Sidney's quartercentenary year, with the Queen. Sidney had also revived its appointment of fellow-commoners, allowing it to acknowledge the many different kinds of contributions its members made to the College. The Mong Building was the last of Roger Andrew's many important projects; he died a few months later. Since his arrival in 1968, the bursar had overseen work on virtually all the College buildings, old and new, including the expansion of the library in Garden Court and the erection of the bridge over Sussex Street that allowed direct access from the main site to the newly renovated rooms in Sussex House.

In 1999, Sandra Dawson, the director of Judge Business School, was elected master, the first female head of one of the original all-male colleges in Cambridge. During her mastership, Sidney's undergraduate population has changed more in character than in size, the College being among those in Cambridge with the highest state school intake. Sidney's research student population, which had grown significantly since the 1960s, has continued to expand along with the fellowship, which now numbers nearly 70. From fundraising, in particular through the expansion of the

The Sidney Choir with David Skinner, Director of Music, standing in their new stalls, 2009

highly successful 1596 Foundation, to the further beautification of the gardens and the development of award-winning chefs, Sidney's 25th master has made a major impact. Two major achievements, however, demand special mention here and give a small indication why she is now Dame Sandra Dawson and was inducted into the International Women's Hall of Fame in the USA in 2006. The first was the complete renovation of Blundell Court, and the addition to it of a new floor, which has transformed Sidney's expectations for standards of accommodation, with undergraduates now enjoying luxurious en-suite rooms. This was made possible by the College's fundraising and in particular the generosity of Mrs Kyoko Gledhill in memory of her husband David Gledhill. The second was the appointment of Sidney's first director of

Three Sidney masters in the Audit Room in the Lodge, summer 2009, left to right: Sir Gabriel Horn (1992–99), Dame Sandra Dawson (1999–2009), and Andrew Wallace-Hadrill, elected master in 2009

The electropop band Hot Chip released their debut album in 2004 and are one of Britain's most successful bands of recent years. Sidney's Al Doyle, guitarist, and percussionist Felix Martin, make up two of the five-strong group who have now made three albums. Al and Felix also make film music and work as DJs all over the world.

Hot Chip, left to right: Al Doyle (1998), Jo Goddard, Alexis Taylor, Owen Clarke, Felix Martin (1999)

The Sidney Fellowship, 2008

music. Following the achievements of the current vice-master Christopher Page, for-merly director of the hugely successful Gothic Voices medieval musical group in the 1980s and 1990s, David Skinner, the first incumbent of the post, has rapidly trans-formed Sidney's choir into one of the finest in Cambridge. The choir has recorded a number of highly regarded CDs of Renaissance music. This new direction has been possible through the initiative and support of the late bursar Charles Larkum and the generosity of a Sidney alumnus, the businessman John Osborn. Dame Sandra's suc-cessor, the classicist Andrew Wallace-Hadrill, formerly director of the British School in Rome and director of the Herculaneum Project, has not only four centuries of history and achievement to build on, but also a preceding decade of remarkable development. Sidney has a promising future ahead of it. As the 1900 'Song of Sidney Sussex' has it:

'Sidney yet is young:
We're growing, and we *mean to grow*, for Centuries to come!'

The master and fellows, 2008. A list of the current fellowship appears on page 382

Masters of Sidney Sussex College

James Montagu 1596–1608
Francis Aldrich 1608–09
Samuel Ward 1610–43
Richard Minshull 1643–86
Joshua Basset 1686–88
James Johnson 1688–1704
Bardsey Fisher 1704–23
Joseph Craven 1723–28
John Frankland 1728–30

John Adams 1730–46
Francis Sawyer Parris 1746–60
William Elliston 1760–1807
Francis John Hyde Wollaston 1807–08*
Edward Pearson 1808–11
John Davie 1811–13
William Chafy 1813–43
Robert Phelps 1843–90
Charles Smith 1890–1916

George Arthur Weekes 1918–45
Thomas Knox-Shaw 1945–57
David Thomson 1957–70
John Wilfrid Linnett 1970–75
Donald Northcote 1976–92
Gabriel Horn 1992–99
Sandra Dawson 1999–2009
Andrew Wallace-Hadrill 2009–
Election declared void

The Sidney Sussex College Fellowship 2009

Fellows

With year of election

1952 Dr Phillip Clemmow
1955 Professor Derek Beales
1957 Mr Jeffery Switzer
1962 Dr Paul Scott
1965 Professor Tim Blanning
1966 Mr Donald Green
1966 Professor Harry Whittington
1968 Mr Christopher Parish
1972 Dr Roderick Woods
1973 Dr Peter Collier
1973 Professor Alan Hughes
1976 Professor Keith Glover
1979 Professor Dame Ann Dowling
1980 Professor William Jones
1982 Professor Barry Nisbet
1982 Professor Ronald Horgan
1984 Dr Paul McHugh
1984 Professor A Lindsay Greer
1985 Dr Christopher Page
1990 Professor Timothy M Cox
1990 Dr Claire Preston
1992 Professor Sir Gabriel Horn
1992 Dr Antony Jackson
1992 Dr John Longley
1994 Dr Helen Castor
1994 Dr Michael Pollitt
1995 Professor Alan Dashwood
1995 Professor Sir Tom Blundell
1997 Dr Abir Al-Tabbaa
1997 Professor Sir John Walker
1998 Professor James Mayall
1999 Professor Dame Sandra Dawson
1999 Dr Andrew Flewitt
1998 Dr Ian Baxendale
2000 Dr Christopher Doran
2000 Mr Massimo Beber
2001 Mrs Natasha Franklin
2002 Dr Janice Stargardt
2002 Professor Richard Penty

2002 Dr Nikolai Ssorin-Chaikov
2002 Mr Colin Britton
2003 Dr Jillaine Seymour
2003 Dr Frances Hall
2004 Professor Christopher Hill
2004 Dr Mette Eilstrup-Sangiovanni
2005 Dr Rebecca Kilner
2005 Rev. Dr Peter Waddell
2005 Mr Clive Wilmer
2005 Dr Colin Roberts
2005 Dr Paul Flynn
2006 Dr Emma Gilby
2006 Dr Robert Busch
2007 Dr Michelle Oyen
2007 Professor Rosamond McKitterick
2007 Dr Brian Billups
2007 Dr Tae Kyun Kim
2007 Dr Richard Flower
2007 Dr Iain Black
2007 Dr Marko Cvitas
2007 Dr Bernard Fulda
2007 Dr David Skinner
2007 Dr Kirsten Dickers
2007 Dr Julius Ross
2008 Mr Nick Allen
2008 Dr Myles Lavan
2008 Dr Erika Eisner
2008 Dr Clare Blaukopf
2008 Dr Scott Chapman
2008 Mr Michael Ramage
2008 Professor Michael Lamb
2008 Professor Martin Kilduff
2008 Dr Eugenio Biagini
2008 Dr Tomislav Friscic
2009 Dr David Beckingham
2009 Mr David Doupé
2009 Dr Paul White

Honorary Fellows

With year of election

1968 Lord (Asa) Briggs

1977 Lord (David) Owen
1977 Lord (Jack) Lewis
1981 Sir Michael Stoker
1981 Sir Terence Beckett
1991 Sir Patrick Neville Garland
1991 Lord (David) Stevens
1994 Professor Charles Thurstan Shaw
1994 Mr David Gwilym Morris Roberts
1995 Dr Ramon Barton Jenkins
1996 Dr William Man-Wei Mong
1996 Professor Arthur Kwok Cheung Li
1999 The Most Reverend Archbishop
       Desmond Mpilo Tutu
2000 Mr John Philip Madden
2003 Professor Alan MacDiarmid
2003 Baroness (Barbara) Young
2003 Professor Anthony John Badger
2004 Sir Ravinder Nath Maini
2005 Dr Alison Brown
2005 Lord Justice (William) Gage
2005 Mr Peter John Robert Riddell
2007 Lord (Karan) Bilimoria
2007 Major General John Drewienkiewicz
2008 Professor Herman Waldmann

Fellow-Commoners

With year of election

1977 Mr Christopher Greek Stoneman
1993 Dr Stewart Reid Lang
1999 Ms Priscilla Barrett
2000 Dr Graham John Davies
2000 Dr Hagen Schulze
2001 Mr Joseph C Fox
2003 Dr Richard Chisnall
2003 Mrs Kyoko Gledhill
2004 Dr Michael Purshouse
2006 Mr David Purchase
2008 Mr Henry Dawson
2009 Mr John Osborn
2009 Dr George Reid

Acknowledgements

My first thanks go to Dame Sandra Dawson and the fellows of Sidney Sussex for agreeing to support so wholeheartedly the writing of this history. That support, financial, material and intellectual, has been the foundation upon which this ambitious publication has been developed and written over the last few years.

The book could not have been achieved without the extraordinary assistance of Sidney's archivist, Nicholas Rogers. There are so many ways in which this is true: his patient assistance in retrieving material from the Muniment Room; his endless efforts to follow up half-clues to help the research; his great historical and scholarly knowledge in general, and in particular about Sidney, as is evident in his many learned articles for the *Annual* over the years; his fastidious reading of drafts and proofs; his great enthusiasm for all matters concerning Sidney; and his good humour and friendship during the time I have spent at Sidney and while writing the book.

Among the fellows I should like to thank in particular Derek Beales and Claire Preston for their careful, critical and always helpful reading of my various drafts. Derek Beales was the editor, with Barry Nesbit, of the superb 1996 collection of essays on Sidney's history and his vast historical knowledge and personal experience of the College over more than 50 years have proved enormously helpful. Claire Preston also undertook a more microscopic reading of the all-important first proof. Without that the book would have been a far poorer effort.

The vice-master Christopher Page supported the writing in many invaluable ways throughout the project with his knowledge, wisdom and humour, and the bursar, Nick Allen, has been the most supportive member imaginable of that breed whose job it is to say 'no'. His predecessor, the late Charles Larkum, such a generous Sidney benefactor, took a deep interest in College history and in the development of this book.

For other input, intellectual, historical and imaginative, from fellows, I am especially grateful to Richard Flower, Lindsay Greer, Sir Gabriel Horn, James Mayall, Paul McHugh, Rosamund McKitterick, David Skinner, Janice Stargardt, Peter Waddell and Clive Wilmer. The Director of Studies for English, Edward Wilson-Lee, gave me much useful advice.

I am also grateful to the former research fellow and curator of Sidney's paintings, Jon Conlin, for his pioneering work on aspects of Sidney's visual heritage, in particular that of the 18th century. Christopher Parish's researches into Sidney's history over the years have provided me with immensely useful material. I should also mention those no longer with us who, from the first history of the College written by the fellow G M Edwards in 1899, have made the history of Sidney a special interest and made my work so much easier: R H D Mayall, Wilfred Scott-Giles and T S Wyatt.

Many members of the Sidney staff have helped in various ways: Kay Fieldhouse, the master's personal assistant; in all matters concerning accommodation, Karolyn Duke, Suzanne Flack and Marianne Oyler; Solly Cham and all the Hall staff; for the delicious and award-winning meals in the Hall, the head chef Stephen Mather and his team; Pat Gates and Simon Bayes in IT; Sam White and his ever-helpful team of porters; Trevor Rees, Stuart Cross and the gardeners; Keith Willox the manciple; Keith Halls and David Soley in maintenance. I am especially grateful to Wendy Hedley and Zoe Swenson-Wright in the Development Office: their enthusiasm and knowledge of Sidney have been of huge assistance throughout. Zoe knew Sidney members would support this book, and they have done so generously.

Sidney alumni who have helped me greatly in myriad ways include Dudley Ankerson, Michael Duffett, John Dugard (and his family), John Herivel, Phil Judkins, Alan Lancashire, Peter Lipscomb, Tim Newell Price, Chris Parker, Alan Samson, Andrew Sanders and Stewart Trotter.

The greatest thanks among Sidney alumni, however, must go to my editor Sally Simmons of the Cambridge Editorial Partnership, who produced the book. She has patiently dealt with the outrageous developments I demanded, such as increasing the book by a third, and adding endless further illustrations and extra bits of text. She has read the many drafts with enormous skill while working closely with the designer, photographers, printers and all those who have contributed to the book. As one of the legendary 1976 intake of women I hope these words and the reproduction of her year's matriculation photograph make my debt to her clear. In addition I should like to thank Sally's colleague Rosalind Horton, who also made tremendous efforts towards the completion of this project.

One important figure in College life is often overlooked: the Visitor. Philip Sidney, Viscount De L'Isle, and his wife Isobel, Viscountess De L'Isle, give Sidney enormous support in many areas. I would like to thank them for their marvellous hospitality at Penshurst and their great interest in, and support for, the book, throughout my research and writing.

Beyond Sidney I should like to thank the photographer Martyn Chillmaid, who, with the assistance of his wife Colette, transformed the book with his vision, technical expertise and enthusiasm. On Martyn's behalf, I would like to thank Donald Insall and Associates for allowing him to climb all over their desks to obtain the photograph of the Tower on page 252. I must also acknowledge the valuable support of Elizabeth Bradshaw, Edward Cheese and Melvin Jefferson of the Cambridge Colleges Conservation Consortium for their help with conservation and photography.

I am also grateful to Anne Dunan-Page, John Morrill and Sarah Ponting for their advice and knowledge of all matters 17th-century. In respect of the same century I should like to thank Nigel Clark for finding me a Harington farthing. The Duke of Buccleuch and Queensbury KBE, Cecil Woolf and David Wright also gave invaluable help.

The book would have looked very different without the exceptional efforts of the picture researcher, Gill Metcalfe. She found things that seemed lost for ever and indeed helped to change the book as it was being written. A unique contribution.

The book's designer, Paul Barrett, has my sincere thanks for his creative imagination and also his patience and flexibility as the book evolved. By a very satisfactory coincidence, Paul's father worked at Sidney for 43 years, retiring as head of maintenance in 1993.

On a more personal note I would like to thank, for their support, patience and interest, my daughter Olivia, my partner Jo Banham, my mother Mary Humphreys, and my parents-in-law Daniel and Pam Waley. Daniel, a Kingsman, had many useful memories of Sidney fellows and students from the 1930s onwards and much good historical advice to offer. Finally, Pam and Daniel's daughter, my late wife and Olivia's mother, Cat, would have enjoyed this book tremendously.

Richard Humphreys, October 2009

Copyright material

We are grateful to the following for permission to reproduce copyright material:

Sidney Sussex College for extracts from *Acta Collegii* (January 1681, 2 November 1775, and 1728) and from *Pheon*: 1922 James Passant as 'Clio', in 'A Masque of Vice and Virtue', *Pheon* IX, ii, 1932; Thomas Wrott (MA Borstal), 'An Architectural Tour of Sidney Sussex', *Pheon* 1924; 'A Sidney Alphabet' *Pheon* 1929; quotation *Pheon* 1932; article on the Sidney Boys' Club, Cambridge House, Camberwell, *Bull and Porcupine*, I, 1952; and limerick about R P Casey, *The Bull and Porcupine*, 1955 copyright © Sidney Sussex College; and The Society of Authors for an extract from *You Never Can Tell* by George Bernard Shaw copyright © 1897, reproduced with permission from The Society of Authors, on behalf of the Bernard Shaw Estate.

In some instances we have been unable to trace the owners of copyright material and we would appreciate any information that would enable us to do so.

Illustrations

A note from the picture researcher

The range and number of people I have encountered and who have helped me in researching the illustrations for this book are extraordinary. I am grateful to all of them for making this such a wonderful project with which to have been involved. Of those with whom I have worked more closely my thanks go to Jacqueline Boyle for her ever-cheerful and efficient support throughout, and to Charlotte Rogers for her excellent photography. Others who have very generously helped are Steven Archer, Frank Bowles, Les Goodey, Helen Hills, Naomi van Loo, Don Manning, Colin Mills, Matthew Morgan and Joanna Snelling.

I would like to give special thanks to the following for all their enthusiasm, interest and help: Viscount and Viscountess Campden, the children of Brigadier Jock Hamilton-Baillie, John Herivel, Leslie Illing, Mary Illing, Mr and Mrs D J Metcalfe and Andrew Metcalfe, John Moxon-Hill, Richard Simmons, Dr and Mrs D H Tew, and Lady Williams.

Above all, however, my thanks are to Richard Humphreys, who made it possible for me have this fabulous work to do.

Gill Metcalfe

Unless otherwise indicated, all images reproduced are the property of Sidney Sussex College. The author and Sidney Sussex College wish to thank the following for kindly giving permission to reproduce the illustrations on the following pages:

Ackland Art Museum, University of California at Chapel Hill. The William A Whitaker Art Foundation Fund 131; Copyright 2008 © The Estate of W Ross Ashby. Reproduced with kind permission of Jill Ashby, Sally Bannister, and Ruth Pettit 337; BFI 372; Blundell's School Archive 41; The Bridgeman Art Library 13, 185; © The British Library Board 262; © The Trustees of the British Museum 52, 109, 158; Annabel Brown 4; The Trustees of the 9th Duke of Buccleuch's Chattels Fund 108 (bottom); Reproduced by kind permission of the Syndics of Cambridge University Library. MS Add. 9597/18/8 121, and RCS.A. 528 p2.1 273; Corbis © Museum of the City of New York/Corbis 230; By permission of the President and Fellows of Corpus Christi College, Oxford. LE.12.30(7) George Cokayn's Sermon to Parliament, 1648, 113; Crown Copyright – Used with the permission of the Director GCHQ 351 (top); © Devonshire Collection, Chatsworth. Reproduced by permission of the Chatsworth Settlement Trustees 85; Alan Duncan, www.aerialphotographerkent.com 3; By kind permission of the Master and Fellows of Emmanuel College, Cambridge 27; By kind permission of Exton Estate 11; © English Heritage Photo Library 107; Copyright the Francis Frith Collection 252; John Frost Newspapers 340; Reproduced

by kind permission of Gillman & Soame www.gsarchive.co.uk 381; Copyright Guardian News and Media Ltd 2004/Roger Bamber 338 (bottom); Reproduced courtesy of the Geological Society, London/NHMPL 285 (right); Getty Images/Hulton Archive 189 (left), 196/Topical Press Agency 330, 347/Time & Life Pictures/Marion Curtis 375; Father Michael Gill, Rector of Cranford 101; © Hugh J Griffiths 162; George W Hart 372; By kind permission of Ben Hamilton-Baillie 355; © and by kind permission of Patricia Haggar 107 (bottom); By kind permission of John Herivel and his daughter 352; Christian Him's JAZZ INDEX 369 (top right); By permission of Bob Hesk, churchwarden, St Wilfrid's church, South Kilverton, Thirsk 262 (top); Rev. Christopher Hopkins at Peasmarsh Church 191; By kind permission Tom Hughes 353; © David Islip 205; Courtesy of ITV 377 (top & centre); © Rev. I Jorysz Parish Church of St Peter, South Weald 231 (left); Courtesy Lapworth Museum of Geology, University of Birmingham 356 (top); Reproduced by kind permission of the Board of Lees Court 123; Lighthouse for Education 292 (bottom); © Ian Lipscomb 260; City of London, London Metropolitan Archives 5 (top); Courtesy Los Alamos Historical Photos Museum Archive 348 (left); Los Alamos National Laboratory 348 (bottom right); The Warden and Fellows of New College, Oxford 173; Daily News Pix, New York/Copyright 2000 Daily News LP/Peterson 341; © National Portrait Gallery, London 89, 92 (left), 105, 106, 111, 142, 155, 207, 320, 356 (bottom), © Julia Hedgecoe 379 (top); Courtesy of Lord Owen 369 (top right); © Purbeck Radar Museum Trust 346; Rex Features/Daily Mail 342/ NBCUPHOTOBANK 380 (bottom); © The Royal Collection 2009, Her Majesty Queen Elizabeth II 84; © Photo SCALA, Florence, 55; Scott Polar Research Institute, University of Cambridge 287; Science Photo Library/NASA 282 (left)/C T R Wilson 282 (right); By courtesy of the Trustees of Sir John Soane's Museum 145; Reproduced courtesy of the Sydney Town Hall Collection, City of Sydney 275; The University of Sydney, Australia/Rhonda Myers 263; Topfoto/Granger Collection 108 (top), 300; V&A Images 30; The Original Vanity Fair Print Company 274, 277, 278; By kind permission of Gordon Welchman's children 351 (bottom); The Wellcome Library, London/Wellcome Images 131, 212; © Dean and Chapter of Westminster 9; © Palace of Westminster Collection 112; Courtesy of the Wisbech and Fenland Museum 304; Reproduced by kind permission of the Dean and Chapter of York 49.

Every effort has been made to trace the owners of copyright material. Where we have been unable to do so, we would welcome information that will enable us to correct any omissions in future editions of this title.

For commissioned photography, the author and Sidney Sussex College wish to thank:

Annabel Brown 5 (bottom); Martyn f. Chillmaid title page, 2, 15 (bottom), 16, 20, 30, 33, 36, 37 (left & right), 40, 42, 46, 58, 60, 75, 77, 80, 81, 90, 102 (top & bottom), 114, 132, 141, 148, 166, 176, 179, 180, 181,182, 183 (top left), 189 (right), 155, 204, 239, 250, 251, 252, 256, 271 (top & bottom), 296–7, 306, 307 (top & bottom), 308, 309, 313, 358-9, 360, 368 (bottom), 370, 378 (bottom right); Richard Hill 262 (top); Chris Hopkins 191, 194, 254; Melvin Jefferson 15 (top), 35, 65, 152, 209, 214 (right), 221, 226, 228, 229, 235, 240, 247, 248, 249, 261, 264, 267, 279, 281, 291 (bottom), 311, 312, 315, 326 (top), 327, 332, 377 (bottom); Antonio Jimenez 49; Colin Mills 59, 70, 93, 172, 285 (left), 262; Matthew Morgan 186, 337; Charlotte Rogers 8, 14, 22, 23, 24, 28–9, 31, 38, 39, 44, 48, 56, 60, 62, 67, 68, 71, 82, 86, 94, 100, 102, 129, 135, 138, 146, 153, 164, 170, 174, 179, 183 (bottom), 192, 193, 195, 209, 211(left), 214 (left), 215, 216, 217, 218, 223, 231 (right), 233, 238, 242, 268, 269, 274, 277, 278, 280, 288, 290, 291 (top), 292 (top) 293, 295, 305, 314, 318, 321, 324 (bottom), 326 (bottom), 328, 331, 332 (top), 334, 336, 338 (top), 343, 347 (top), 360, 361, 364, 365, 366, 371, 373, 374, 376 and 378; Richard Simmons 95, 187, 355.

Index